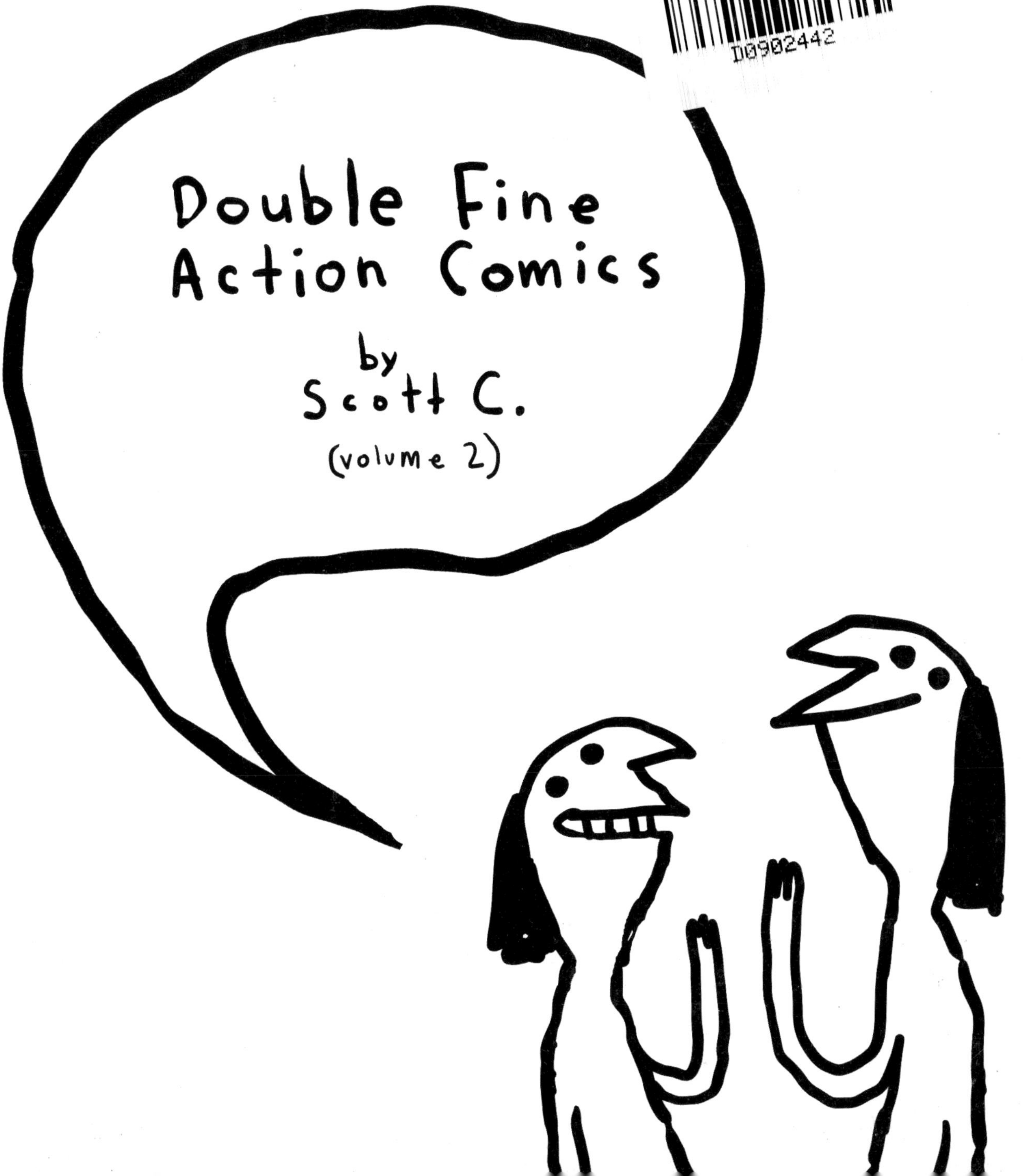
Double Fine Action Comics
by Scott C.
(volume 2)

Double Fine Action Comics, Volume 2

This volume collects comic strips #301 - #600 from the Double Fine Action Comics,
originally published online from March, 2006 through September, 2008.

Designed by Scott C. with Keith Wood

Edited by George Rohac and Keith Wood

Published by Oni Press, Inc.

Joe Nozemack, publisher
James Lucas Jones, editor in chief
Keith Wood, art director
George Rohac, director of business development
Tom Shimmin, director of sales and marketing
Jill Beaton, editor
Charlie Chu, editor
Troy Look, digital prepress lead
Jason Storey, graphic designer
Robin Herrera, administrative assistant

ONI PRESS, INC.
1305 SE Martin Luther King Jr. Blvd.
Suite A
Portland, OR 97214
U.S.A.

onipress.com
doublefine.com
pyramidcar.com

Become our fan on Facebook: facebook.com/onipress
Follow us on Twitter: @onipress
onipress.tumblr.com

First edition: April 2013
ISBN 978-1-62010-086-8
Library of Congress Control Number: 2013931987

10 9 8 7 6 5 4 3 2 1
PRINTED IN U.S.A.

Vol. 2
DOUBLE FINE
ACTION COMICS

by: Scott C.

foreword by: Erik Wolpaw

Foreword by Erik Wolpaw

Nowadays when I think of Scott, I'm reminded of something someone once said to me in the Denzel Washington movie *Remember the Titans*: "We'll get old, we'll get fat. And there ain't gonna be all this black-white between us."

Much like how the football players in the Denzel Washington movie *Remember the Titans* went through hell playing football in the segregated South, Scott and I went through a couple of tumultuous years working on the video game *Psychonauts*. Because we're both white guys, I don't actually remember a lot of racial tension between us, but I think the part of that quote you should really be focusing on is that we're both older and fatter now. There's also a kind of wistfulness to it — the idea that Scott and I might be reunited someday. Maybe to make another game.

If we ever did do that, we'd probably have to hire some people to help us. And it's entirely possible at least one of them would be black. So I suppose there could still be some black-white between us, especially if the black guy we hire turns out to be some kind of lunatic.

"I think we made a real mistake with this hire," I'd say.

"Ha ha! What do you mean, bro?" Scott would say.

"Scott," I'd say, "Terry literally has me in a headlock right now."

"Ha ha! Terry! Oh man, that dude," Scott would say.

The point of this racially charged psychodrama that I ripped from today's headlines and also a little from the Denzel Washington movie *Remember the Titans* is that most creative people are miserable humans. I certainly am, and if you need proof look no

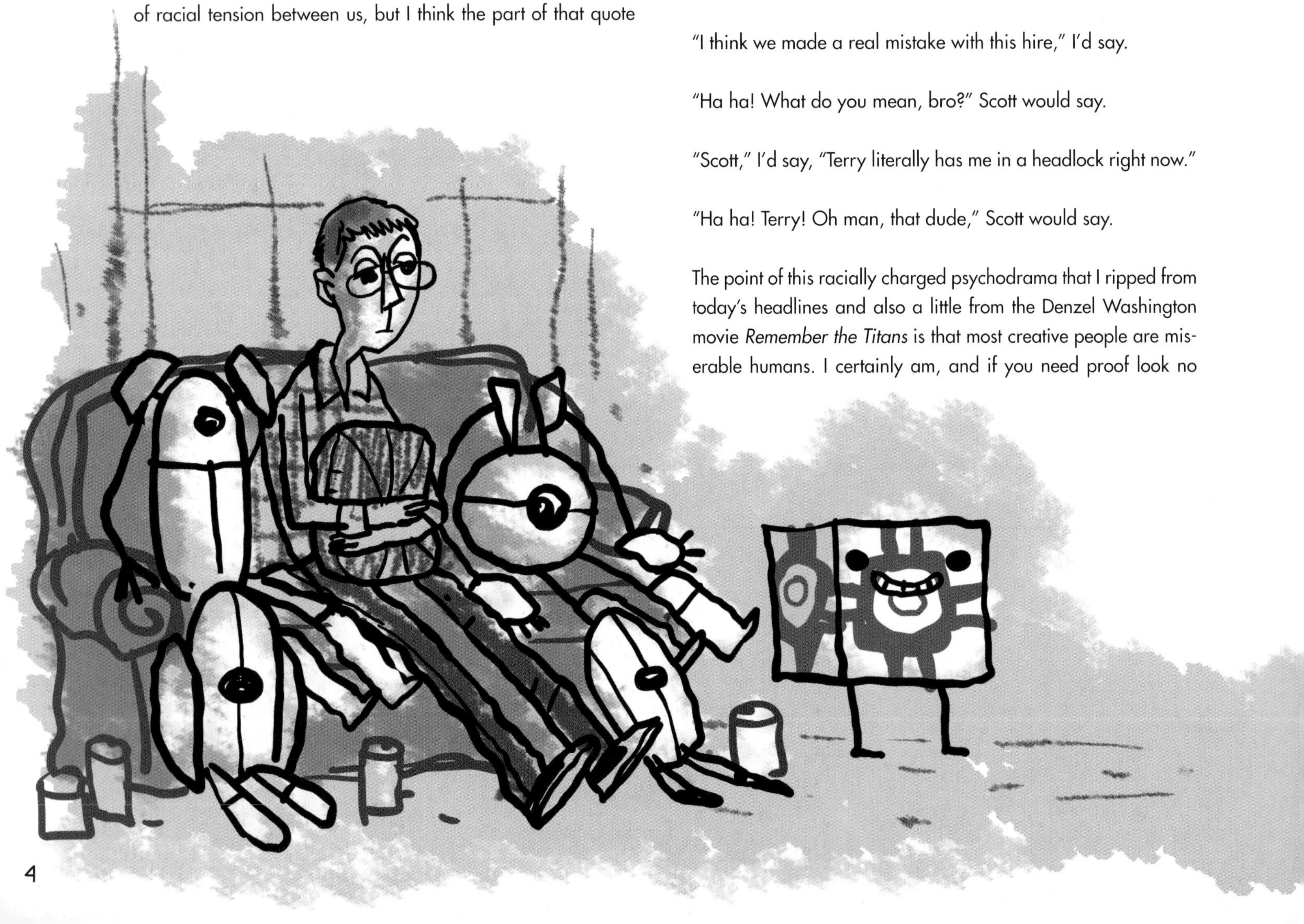

further than the first sentence of this very paragraph where I actually deployed the phrase "creative people." I suppose I could use the backspace key to go delete it, but that sounds like a lot of work, leading me to point number two: Most creative people are also lazy.

Scott, however, is neither. He's a hardworking, nice man. The confident, reassuring good humor, enthusiasm and decentness that come through in his work aren't an act. That's Scott. He's so genuinely pleasant that for the first six months we worked together, I seriously thought he was always f***ing with me, and it made me furious.

Most days, I was the first person to arrive at Double Fine. Scott was the second. I'd spend the morning nurturing a stomachache and silently cataloging all the ways in which I'm a creative fraud, which gave me something to do while I put off starting any actual work. Scott, on the other hand, would dive right into writing and drawing these comics, which had nothing to do with the project we were working on.

Think about that: Scott wrote and drew this entire collection as a little warmup to a full day of work on something else. They're basically drawing and writing exercises. And now he's somehow convinced you to give him twenty dollars for them. But because of that mysterious Scott magic, you're probably not even mad about it.

In closing, Scott is in no way ripping you off with this book, certainly not in a technical legal sense. Also, re-reading this intro, I may have given you the impression that Scott is a sweetly imbecilic Forest-Gump-like figure. Not the case, though it would take a bunch of rewriting to correct that impression, so we're going to have to agree to disagree about whether Scott is mildly retarded. Also #2, I haven't actually said anything about the comics themselves, but that's only because I haven't read them. Anyway, I expect this introduction will result in me being asked to write a lot more introductions, so enjoy all the reading you're about to do and I'll see you all in another book!

Erik Wolpaw
Professional Writer

Words From An Ancient Mummy by a Window

The sands tell stories of days past when titans fought titans for the love of gods and goddesses. I am a lover of these tales. I have been since the early days of Ancient Egypt. For I am a Mummy. You may have heard of me before. I've done many book reviews and commentaries on films. I have a smash hit show called *Mummy By The Window* that has many fans. I am a snappy dresser and I make splendid drinks. I know what I am talking about.

How old am I? I do not remember. Scientists have tried to carbon date me for ages, but who can be sure. Suffice to say, I am an old fellow. Ancient Egypt, a place of great legend and mystery. In my early years, I used to read hieroglyphs day in and day out. I could not get enough of them. Every day a new hieroglyph came out, I was first in line to check it out. Later, when they began printing them on scrolls, I enjoyed reading them in my home or on the steps outside Horus' pyramid. Reading is a part of me.

I took a nap for a very long while and when I was awakened by some safari explorers, I discovered that the world was FILLED with hieroglyphs! It took me a while to get past the fact that most had no pictures, but I am cool with evolution. I love the classics like *Moby Dick*, *Robinson Crusoe* and *Harry Potter*, but it is the COMIC GENRE that particularly excites me. I think perhaps because I am nostalgic for my hieroglyphs.

What you hold in your hand is one of the greatest collections of comics I have ever laid eyes upon. There was a previous collection, but that one is just a precursor to the meat of the matter: this collection. If you are a returning reader, welcome back. Your friends are waiting for you inside with some refreshments. If you are new to these comics, let me just tell you that you are in for a real treat. Some of the gang can be a little standoffish at first, but they will warm up to you. Some guys, you don't really want to be friends with anyway, so feel free to be selective. I happen to be very good friends with most of

the guys in these stories. A few of my cousins make prevalent appearances that I am a bit embarrassed about, but what can I do. Cousins are cousins.

I've enjoyed reading these on my ancient stone computer, but I am happy that I now have the option to read them on paper like this and hold them in my arms while I sip a beverage by my window. I look forward to the day when all of these strips adorn the walls of the Great Pyramid. Then I can gaze upon them as they were truly intended to be experienced.

But for now, enjoy this book, my friends. Feel free to watch my videos.

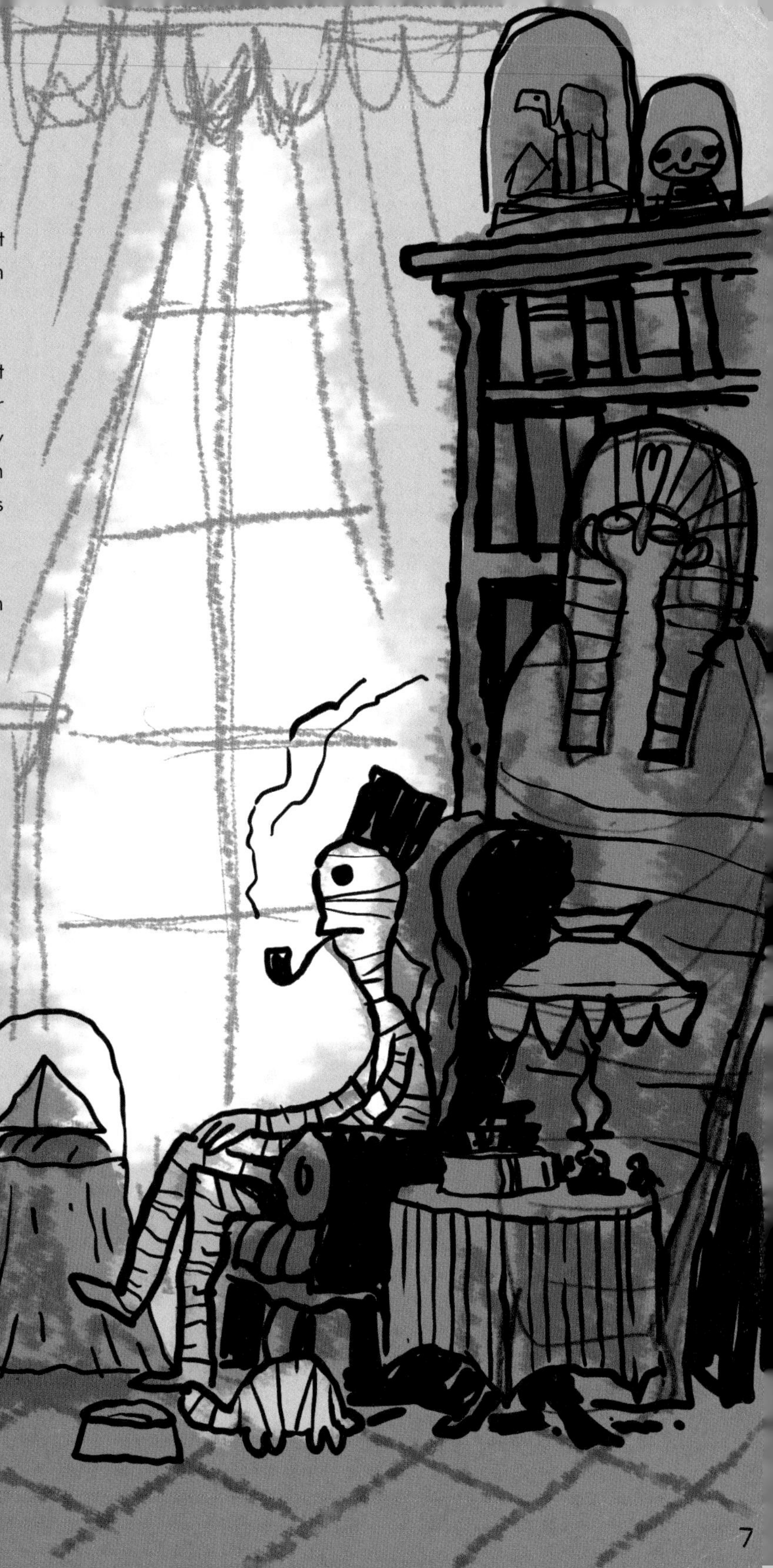

A. Mummy

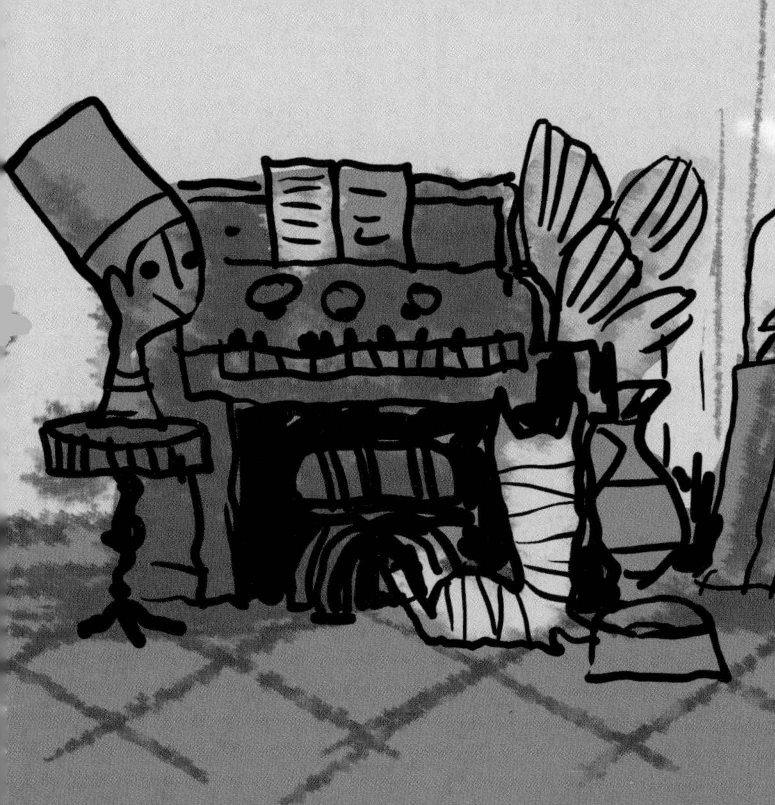

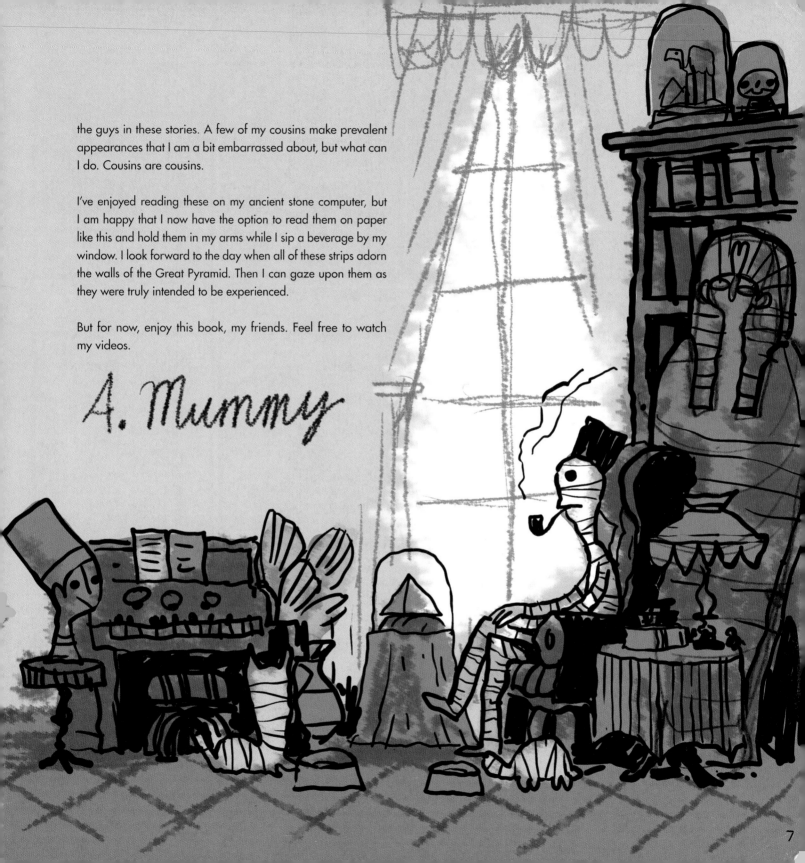

301

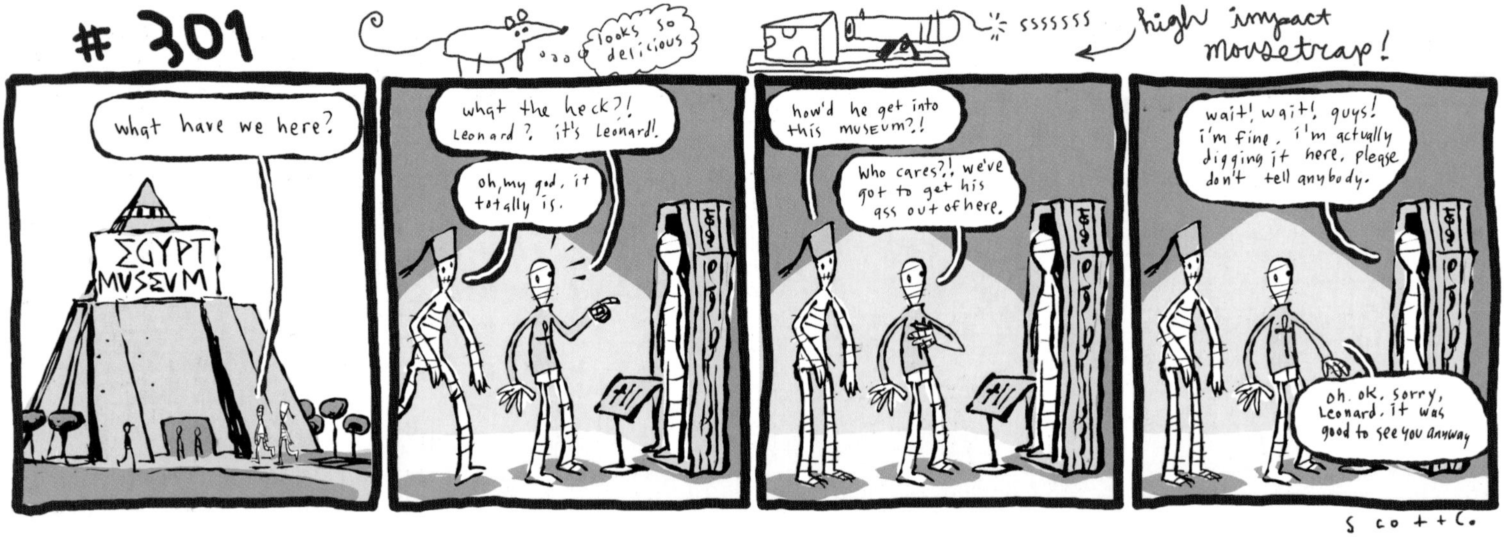

looks so delicious
ssssssss
high impact mousetrap!
what have we here?
EGYPT MUSEUM
what the heck?! Leonard? it's Leonard!
oh, my god, it totally is.
how'd he get into this museum?!
Who cares?! we've got to get his ass out of here.
wait! wait! guys! i'm fine, i'm actually digging it here. please don't tell anybody.
oh. ok. sorry, Leonard. it was good to see you anyway
scott c.

302

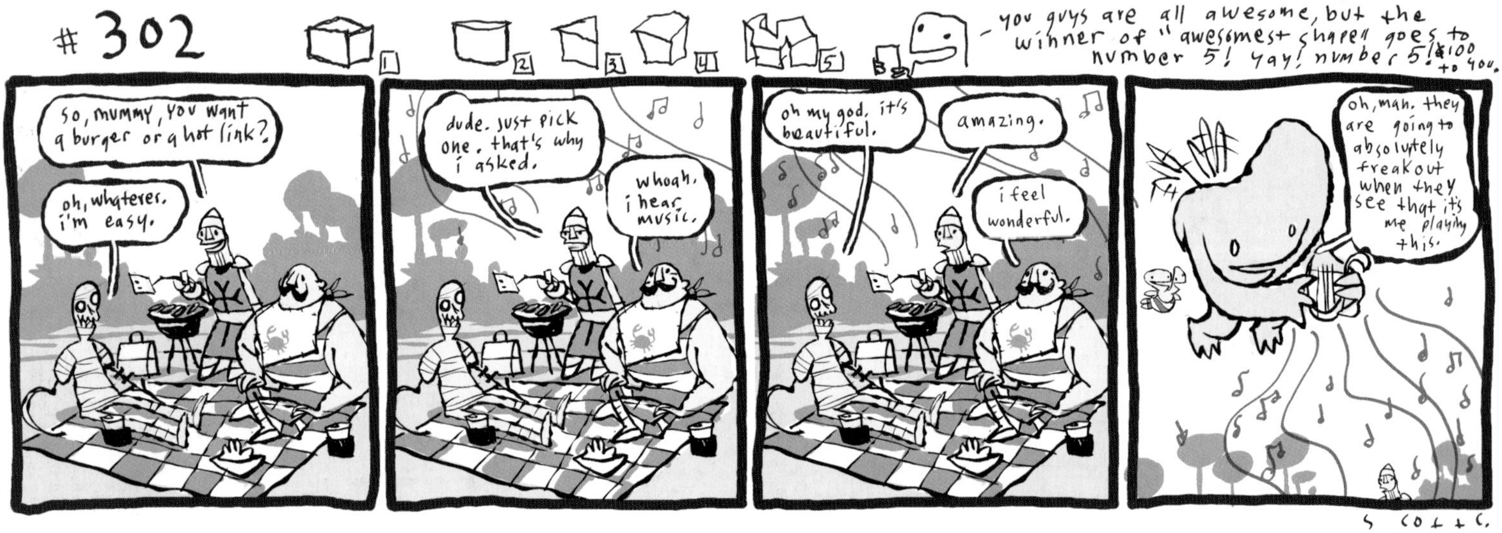

1 2 3 4 5
- you guys are all awesome, but the winner of "awesomest shape" goes to number 5! yay! number 5! $100 to you.
so, mummy, you want a burger or a hot link?
oh, whatever. i'm easy.
dude. just pick one. that's why i asked.
whoah, i hear music.
oh my god, it's beautiful.
amazing.
i feel wonderful.
oh, man. they are going to absolutely freak out when they see that it's me playing this.
scott c.

303

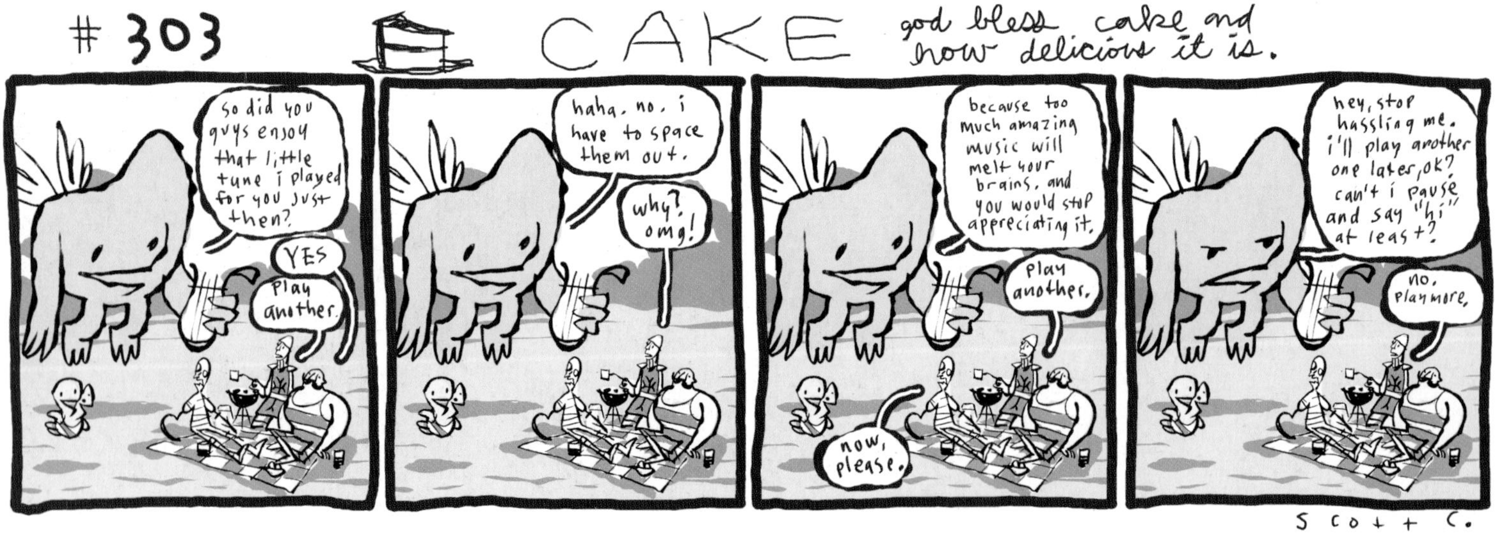

CAKE
god bless cake and how delicious it is.
so did you guys enjoy that little tune i played for you just then?
YES
play another.
haha. no. i have to space them out.
why? omg!
because too much amazing music will melt your brains, and you would stop appreciating it.
play another.
now, please.
hey, stop hassling me. i'll play another one later, ok? can't i pause and say "hi" at least?
no, play more.
scott c.

#304

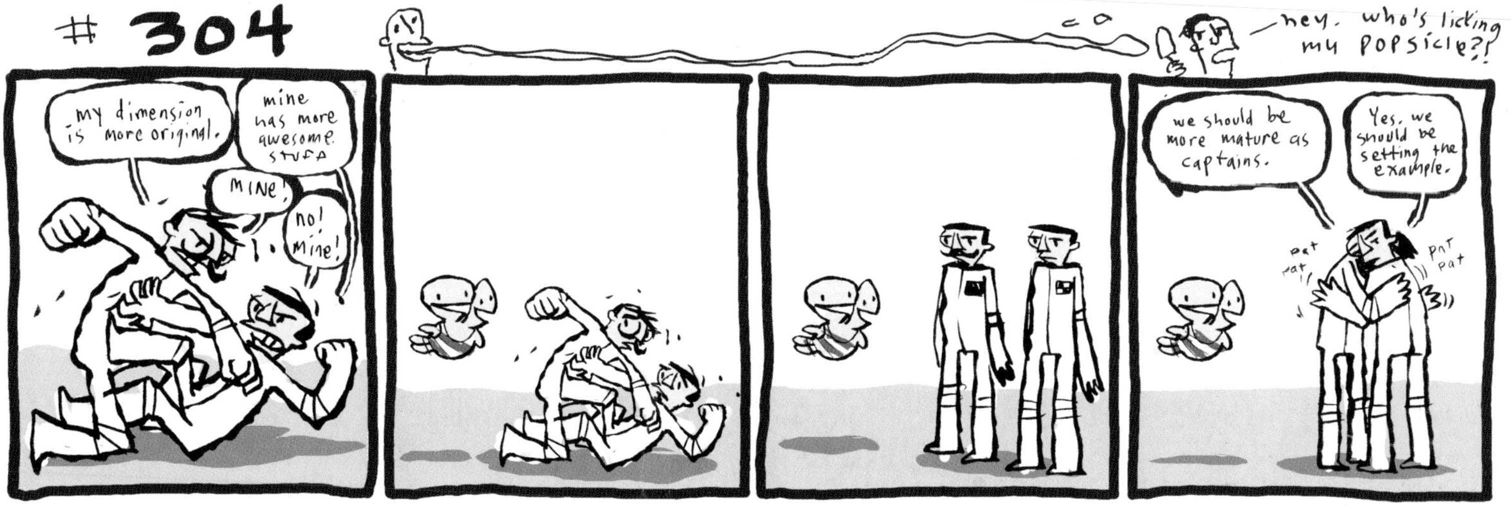
hey. who's licking my popsicle?!
my dimension is more original.
mine has more awesome stuff
MINE!
no! MINE!
we should be more mature as captains.
Yes. we should be setting the example.
pat pat
pat pat
scott c.

#305

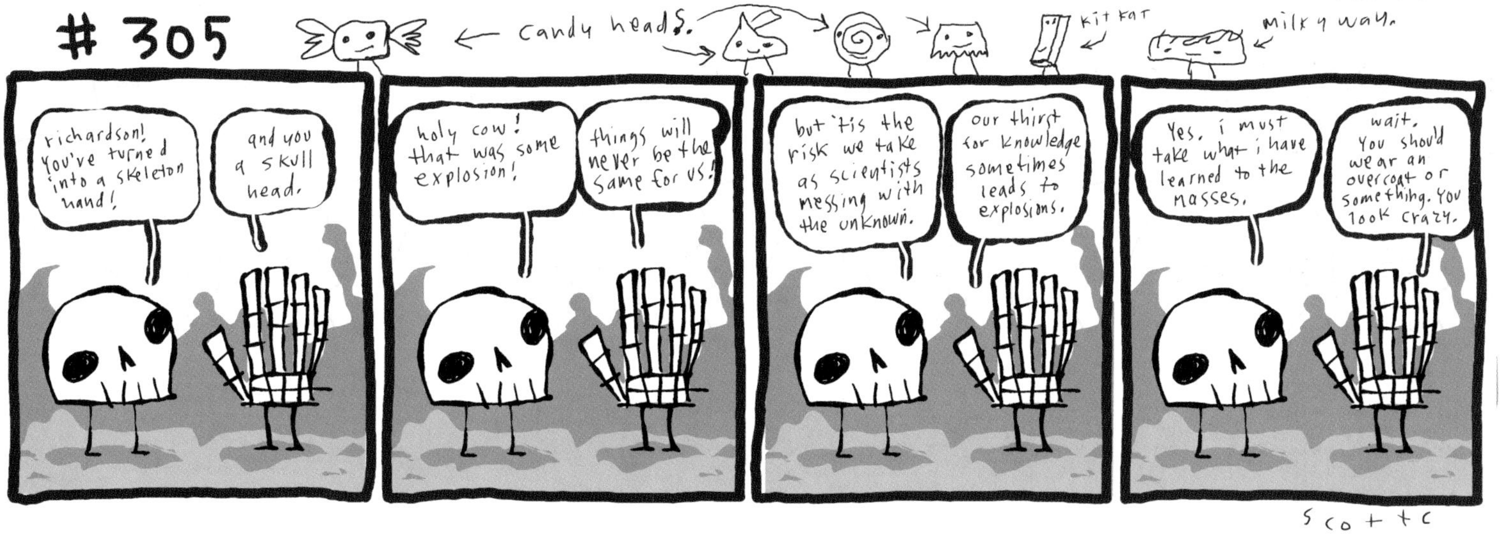
candy heads.
kit kat
milky way.
richardson! You've turned into a skeleton hand!
and you a skull head.
holy cow! that was some explosion!
things will never be the same for us!
but 'tis the risk we take as scientists messing with the unknown.
our thirst for knowledge sometimes leads to explosions.
Yes. i must take what i have learned to the masses.
wait. You should wear an overcoat or something. You look crazy.
scott c

#306

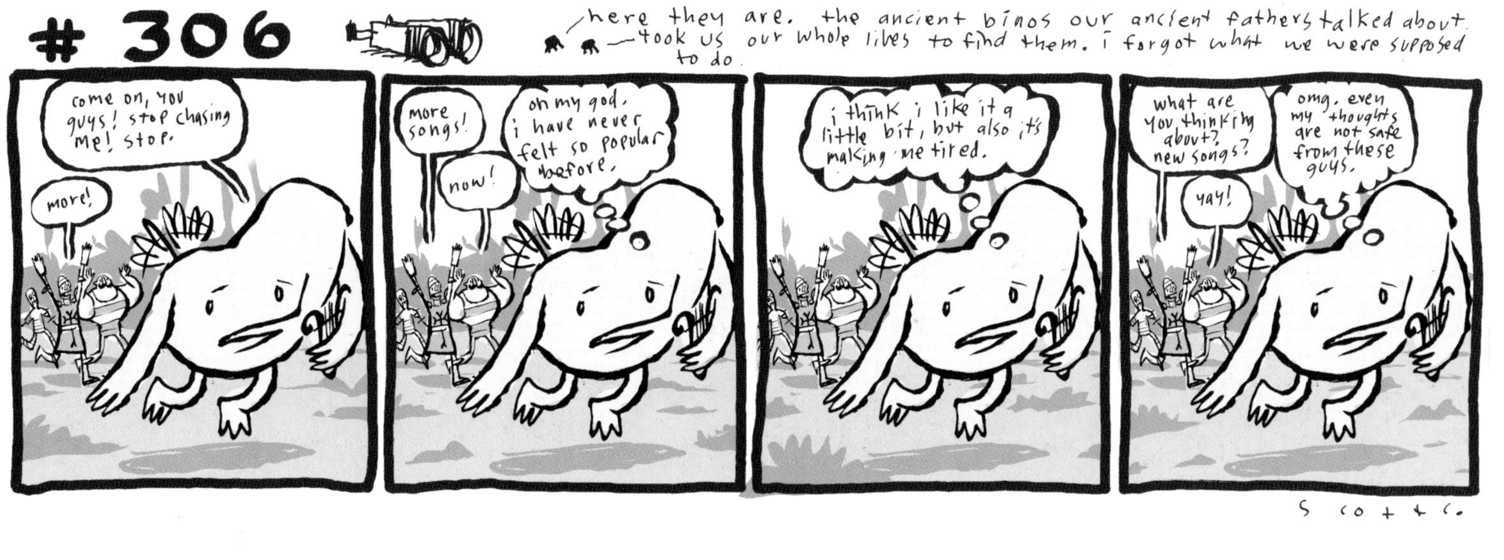
here they are. the ancient binos our ancient fathers talked about.
took us our whole lives to find them. i forgot what we were supposed to do
come on, you guys! stop chasing me! stop.
more!
more songs!
now!
oh my god. i have never felt so popular before.
i think i like it a little bit, but also it's making me tired.
what are you thinking about? new songs?
yay!
omg. even my thoughts are not safe from these guys.
scott c.

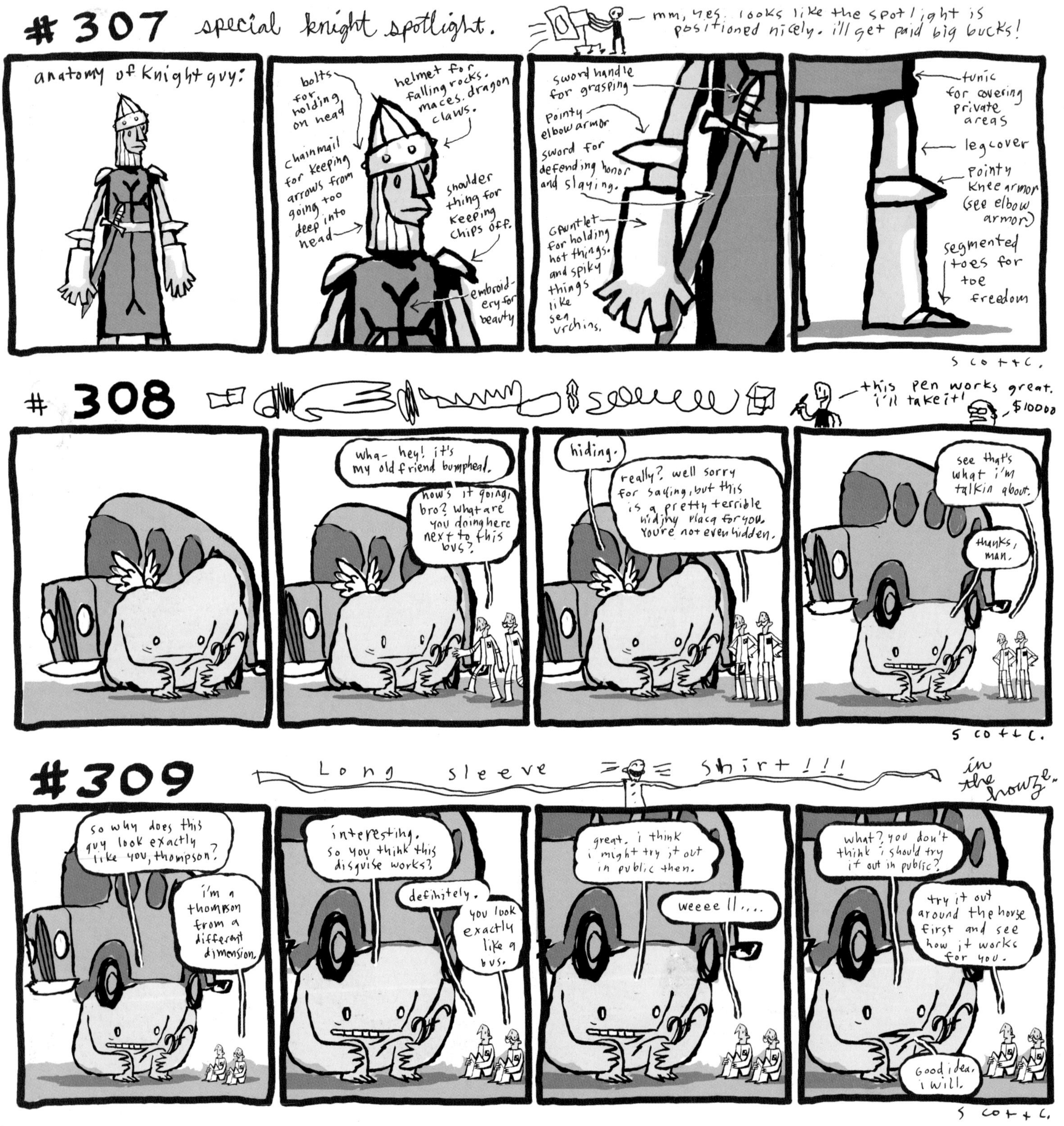
#307 special knight spotlight.
mm, yes. looks like the spotlight is positioned nicely. i'll get paid big bucks!
anatomy of knight guy:
bolts for holding on head
helmet for falling rocks. maces. dragon claws.
chainmail for keeping arrows from going too deep into head
shoulder thing for keeping chips off.
embroidery for beauty
sword handle for grasping
pointy elbow armor
sword for defending honor and slaying.
gauntlet for holding hot things. and spiky things like sea urchins.
tunic for covering private areas
legcover
pointy knee armor (see elbow armor)
segmented toes for toe freedom
scott c.
#308
this pen works great. i'll take it!
$10000
wha- hey! it's my old friend bumphead.
how's it going, bro? what are you doing here next to this bus?
hiding.
really? well sorry for saying, but this is a pretty terrible hiding place for you. you're not even hidden.
see that's what i'm talkin about.
thanks, man.
scott c.
#309
Long sleeve shirt!!!
in the houze.
so why does this guy look exactly like you, thompson?
i'm a thompson from a different dimension.
interesting. so you think this disguise works?
definitely.
you look exactly like a bus.
great. i think i might try it out in public then.
weeee ll....
what? you don't think i should try it out in public?
try it out around the house first and see how it works for you.
good idea. i will.
scott c.

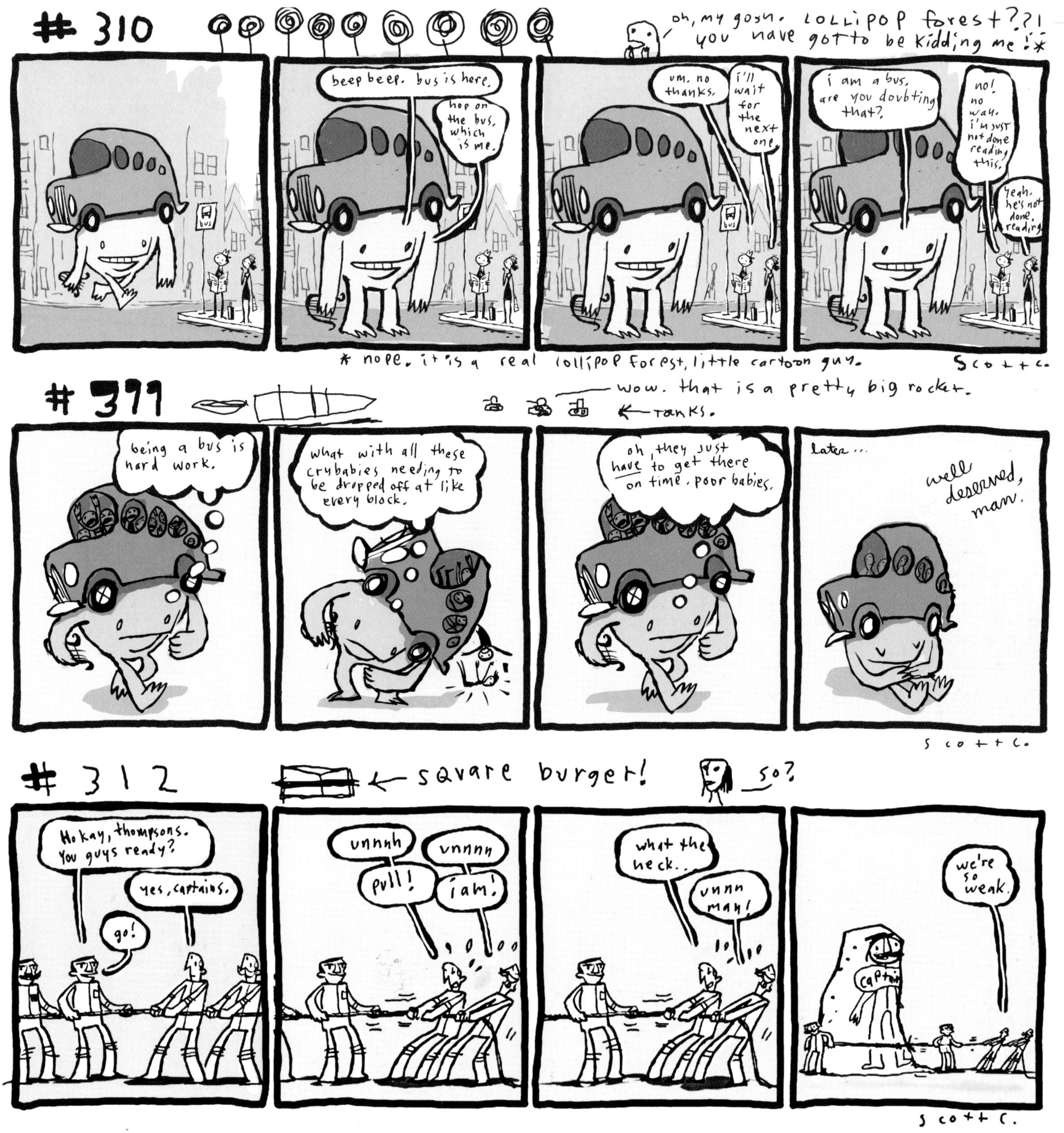
#310
oh, my gosh. lollipop forest??! you have got to be kidding me!*
beep beep. bus is here.
hop on the bus, which is me.
um. no thanks.
i'll wait for the next one.
i am a bus, are you doubting that?
no! no way. i'm just not done reading this.
yeah, he's not done reading.
bus
* nope. it is a real lollipop forest, little cartoon guy.
scott c.
#311
wow. that is a pretty big rocket.
← tanks.
being a bus is hard work.
what with all these crybabies needing to be dropped off at like every block.
oh, they just have to get there on time. poor babies.
later...
well deserved, man.
scott c.
#312
← square burger!
so?
Hokay, thompsons. You guys ready?
yes, captains.
go!
unnnh
unnnn
pull!
i am!
what the heck..
unnn man!
we're so weak.
captain
scott c.

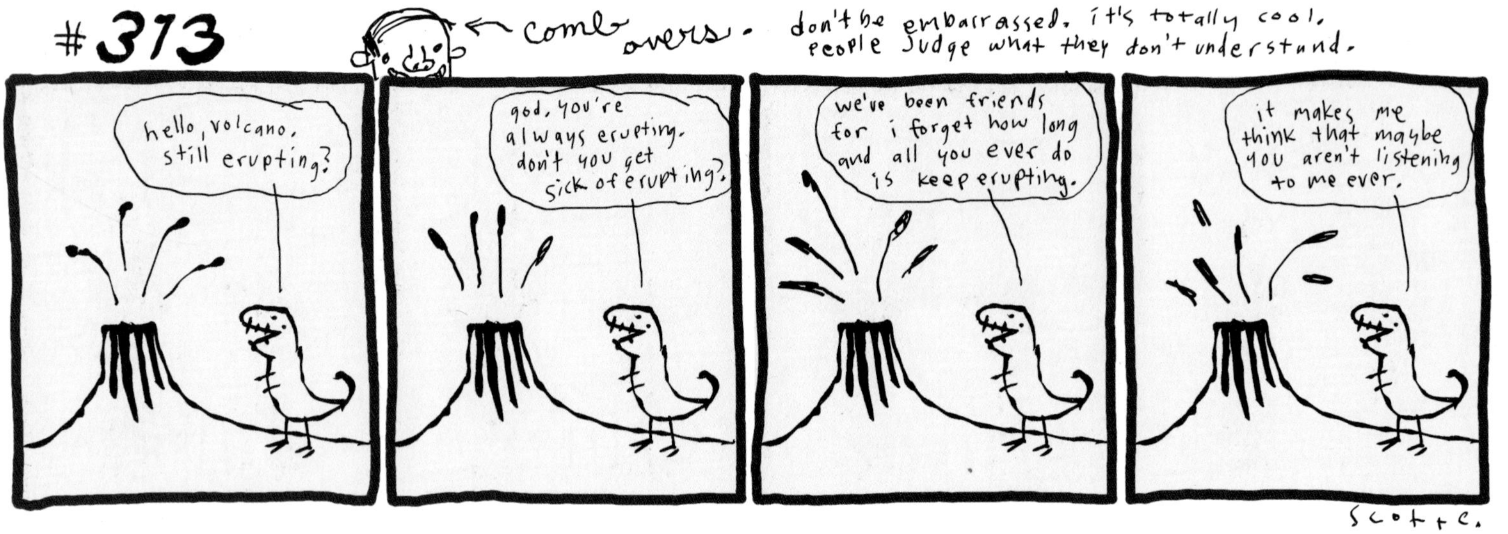
#313
comb overs. don't be embarrassed. it's totally cool. people judge what they don't understand.
hello, volcano, still erupting?
god, you're always erupting. don't you get sick of erupting?
we've been friends for i forget how long and all you ever do is keep erupting.
it makes me think that maybe you aren't listening to me ever.
scott c.

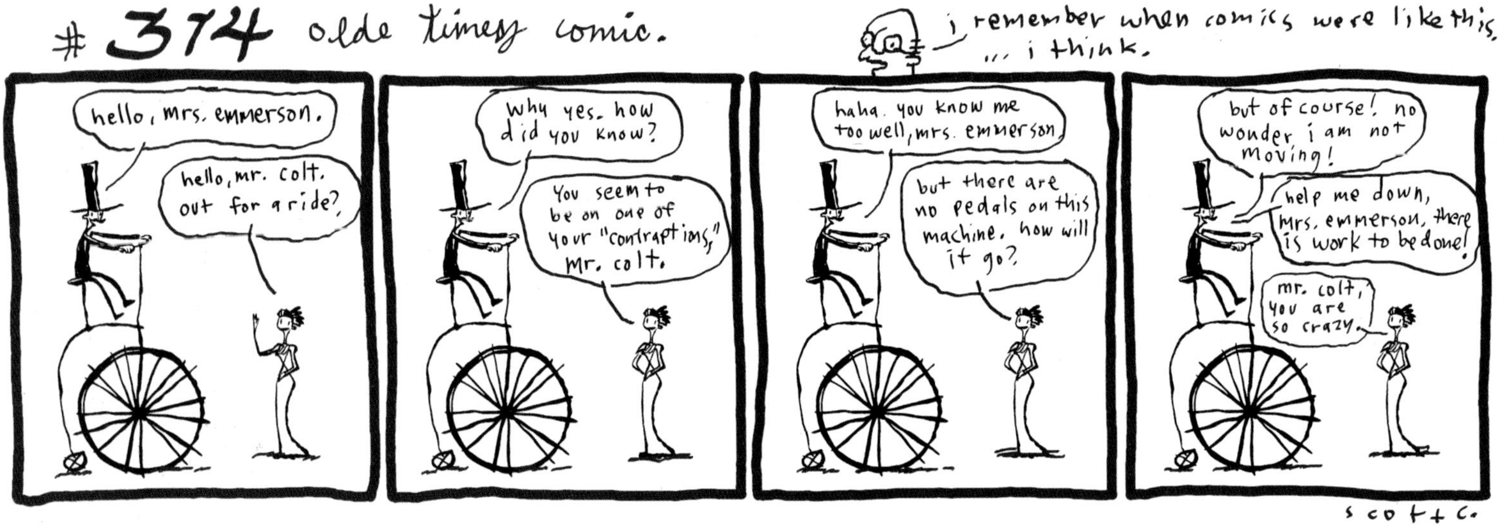
#374 olde timey comic.
i remember when comics were like this, ... i think.
hello, mrs. emmerson.
hello, mr. colt. out for a ride?
why yes. how did you know?
you seem to be on one of your "contraptions," mr. colt.
haha. you know me too well, mrs. emmerson.
but there are no pedals on this machine. how will it go?
but of course! no wonder i am not moving!
help me down, mrs. emmerson, there is work to be done!
mr. colt, you are so crazy.
scott c.

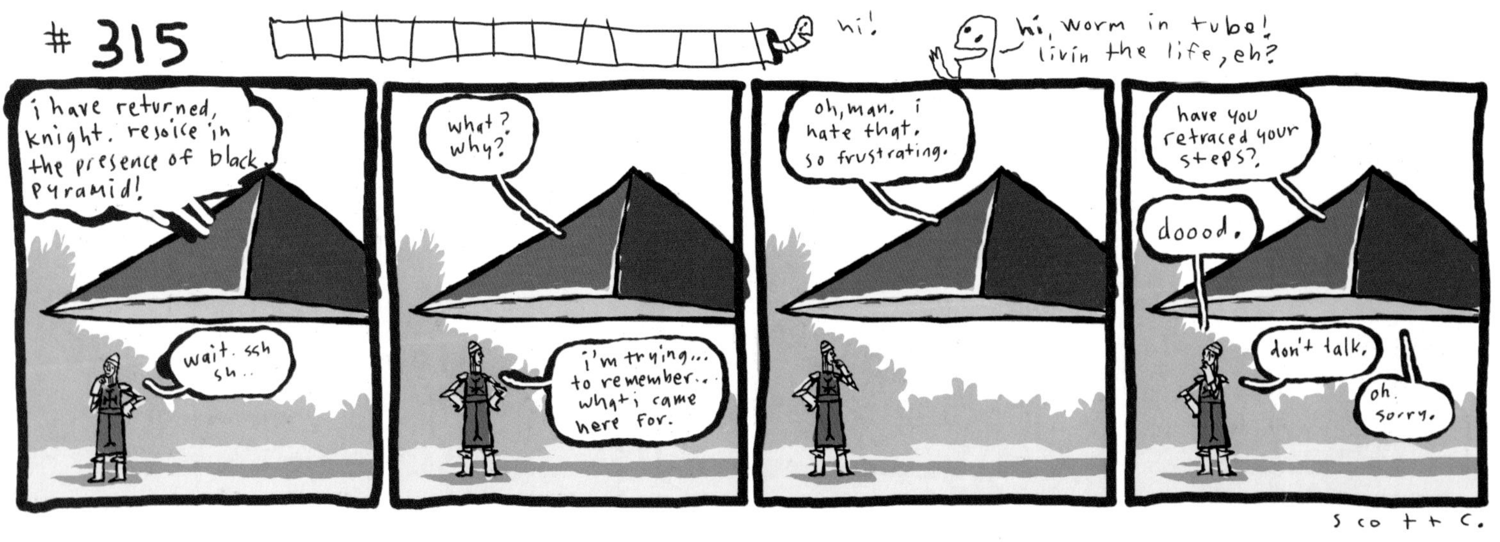
#315
hi!
hi, worm in tube! livin the life, eh?
i have returned, knight. rejoice in the presence of black pyramid!
wait. ssh sh..
what? why?
i'm trying... to remember.. what i came here for.
oh, man. i hate that. so frustrating.
have you retraced your steps?
doood.
don't talk.
oh. sorry.
scott c.

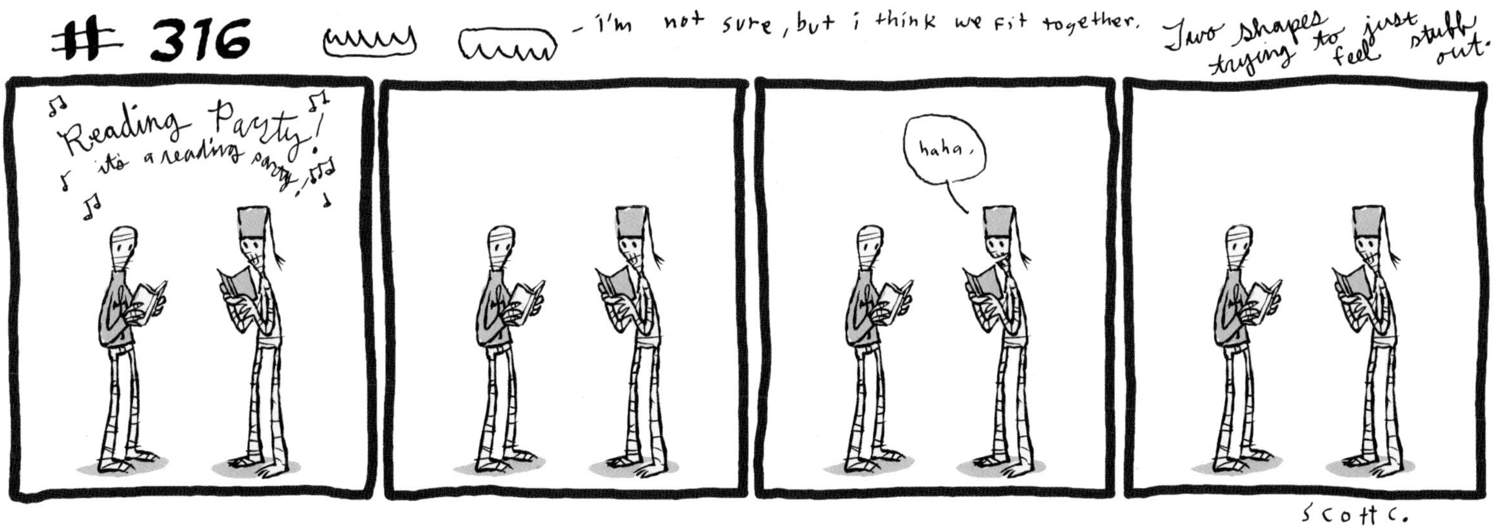
#316
- i'm not sure, but i think we fit together.
Two shapes trying to just feel stuff out.
Reading Party!
it's a reading party!
haha.
scott c.

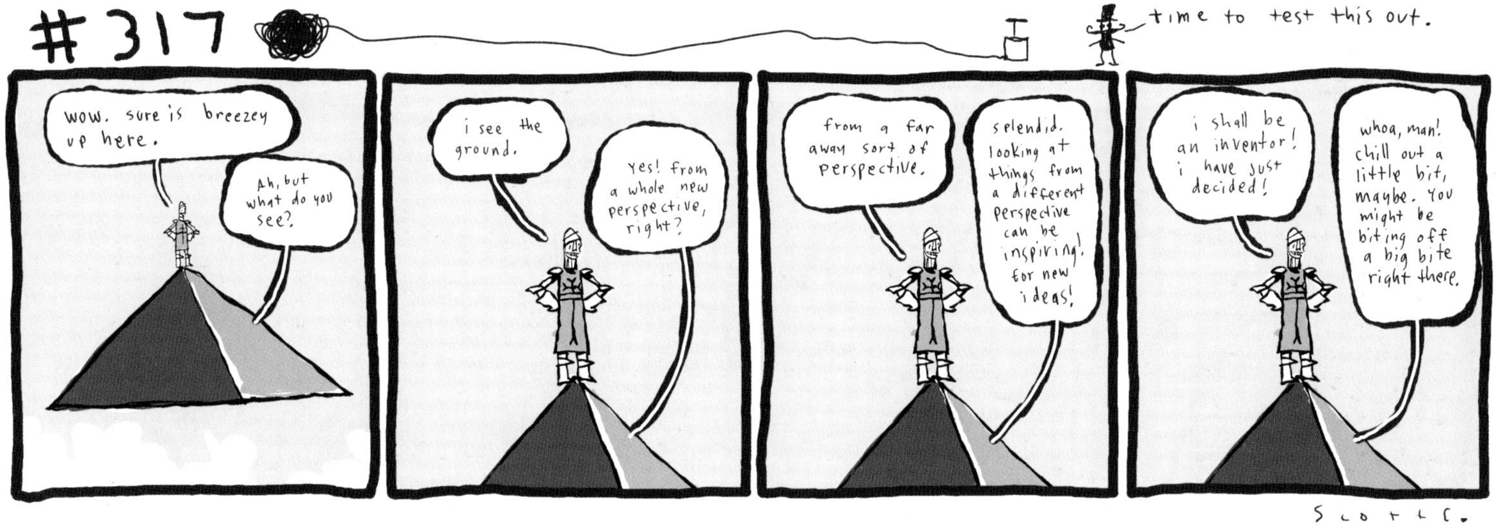
#317
time to test this out.
wow. sure is breezey up here.
Ah, but what do you see?
i see the ground.
Yes! from a whole new perspective, right?
from a far away sort of perspective.
splendid. looking at things from a different perspective can be inspiring! for new ideas!
i shall be an inventor! i have just decided!
whoa, man! chill out a little bit, maybe. You might be biting off a big bite right there.
scott c.

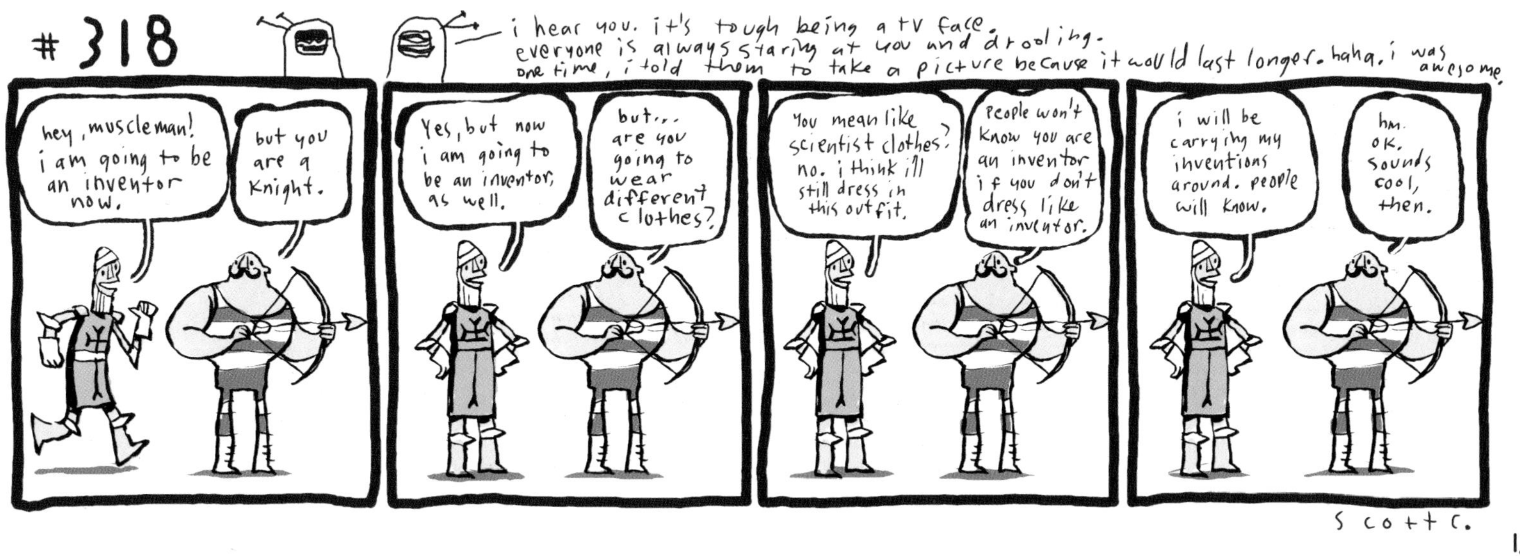
#318
i hear you. it's tough being a tv face. everyone is always staring at you and drooling. one time, i told them to take a picture because it would last longer. haha. i was awesome.
hey, muscleman! i am going to be an inventor now.
but you are a knight.
Yes, but now i am going to be an inventor, as well.
but... are you going to wear different clothes?
You mean like scientist clothes? no. i think i'll still dress in this outfit.
People won't know you are an inventor if you don't dress like an inventor.
i will be carrying my inventions around. people will know.
hm. OK. sounds cool, then.
scott c.

319

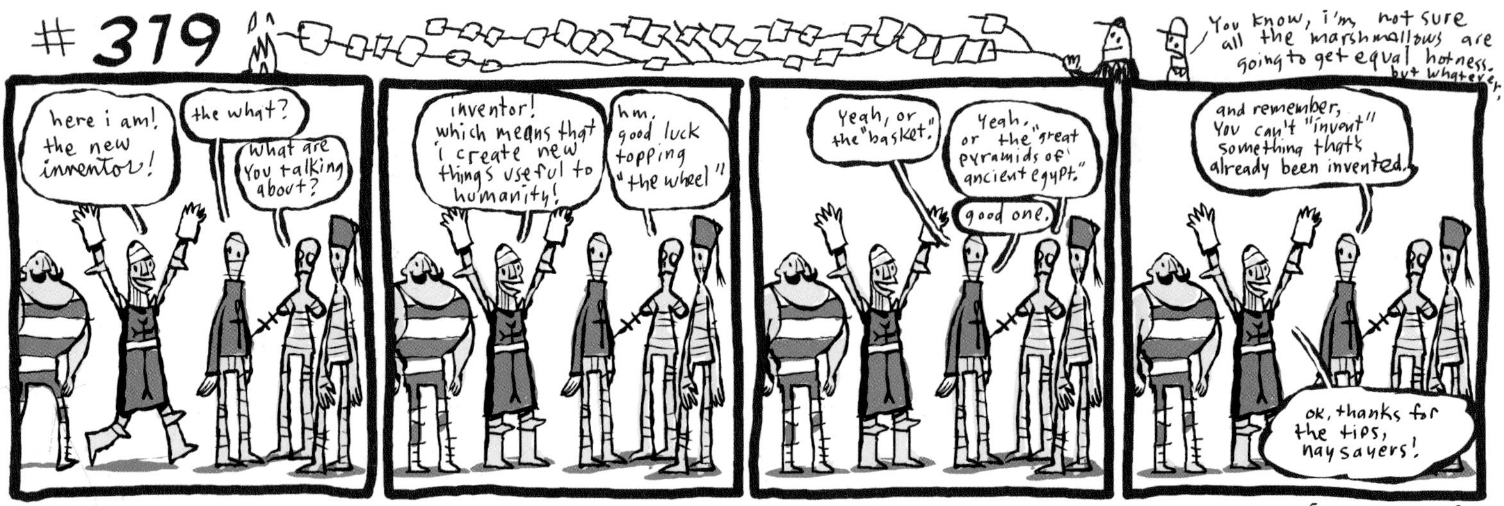
You know, i'm not sure all the marshmallows are going to get equal hotness. but whatever.
here i am! the new inventor!
the what?
what are you talking about?
inventor! which means that i create new things useful to humanity!
hm. good luck topping "the wheel"
yeah, or the "basket."
yeah, or the "great pyramids of ancient egypt."
good one.
and remember, you can't "invent" something that's already been invented.
ok, thanks for the tips, naysayers!

scott c.

320 special new people issue.

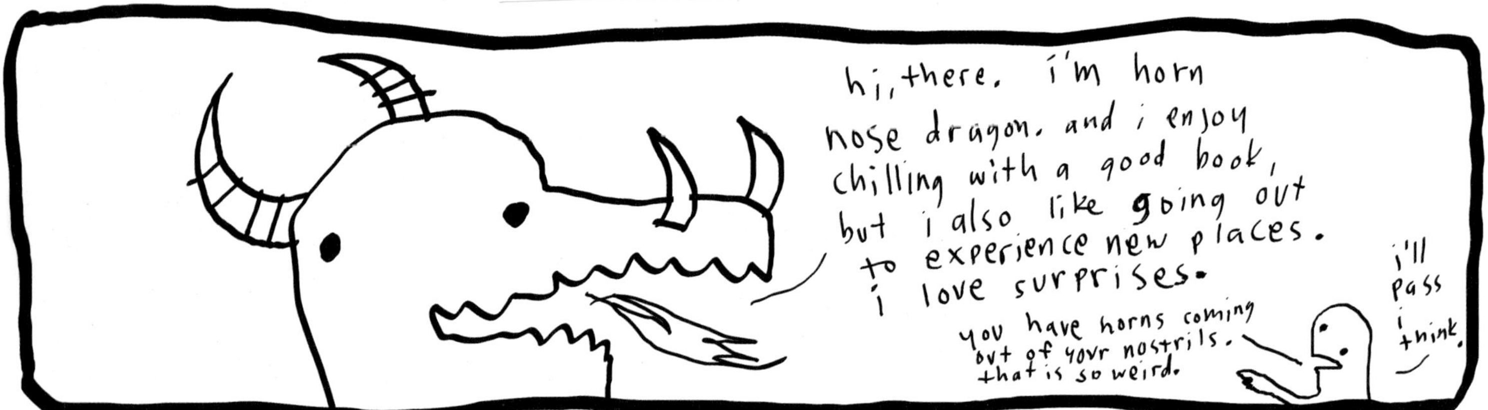
hi, there. i'm horn nose dragon. and i enjoy chilling with a good book, but i also like going out to experience new places. i love surprises.
you have horns coming out of your nostrils. that is so weird.
i'll pass i think.

scott c.

321

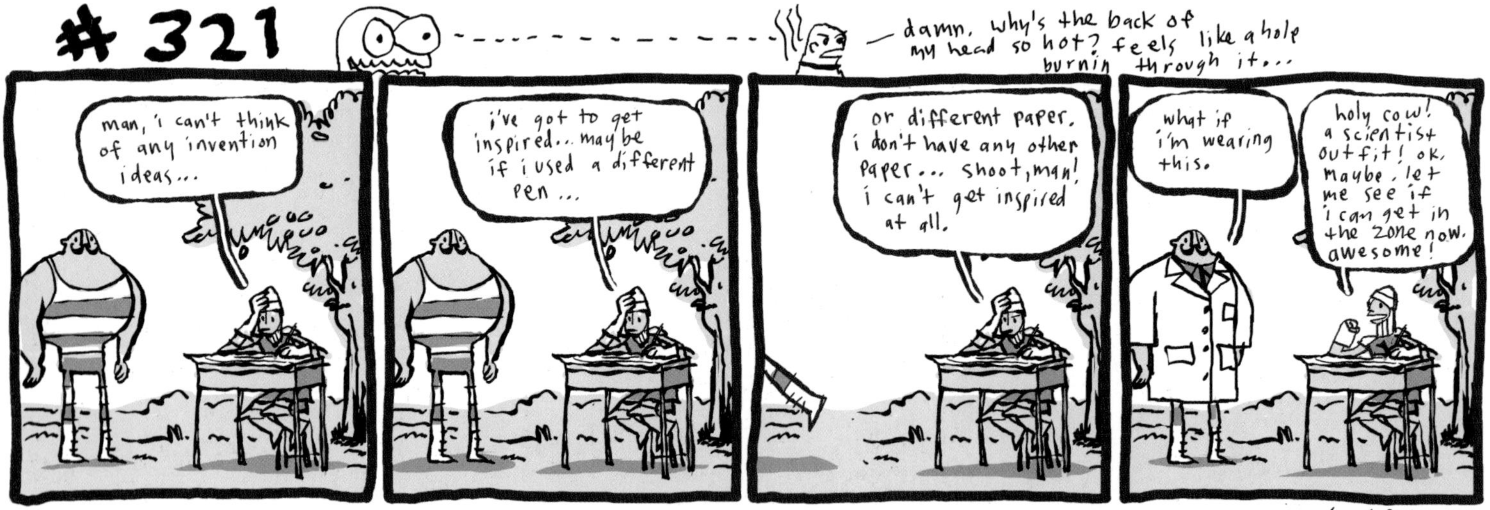
damn. why's the back of my head so hot? feels like a hole burnin through it...
man, i can't think of any invention ideas...
i've got to get inspired... maybe if i used a different pen...
or different paper. i don't have any other paper... shoot, man! i can't get inspired at all.
what if i'm wearing this.
holy cow! a scientist outfit! ok, maybe, let me see if i can get in the zone now. awesome!

scott c.

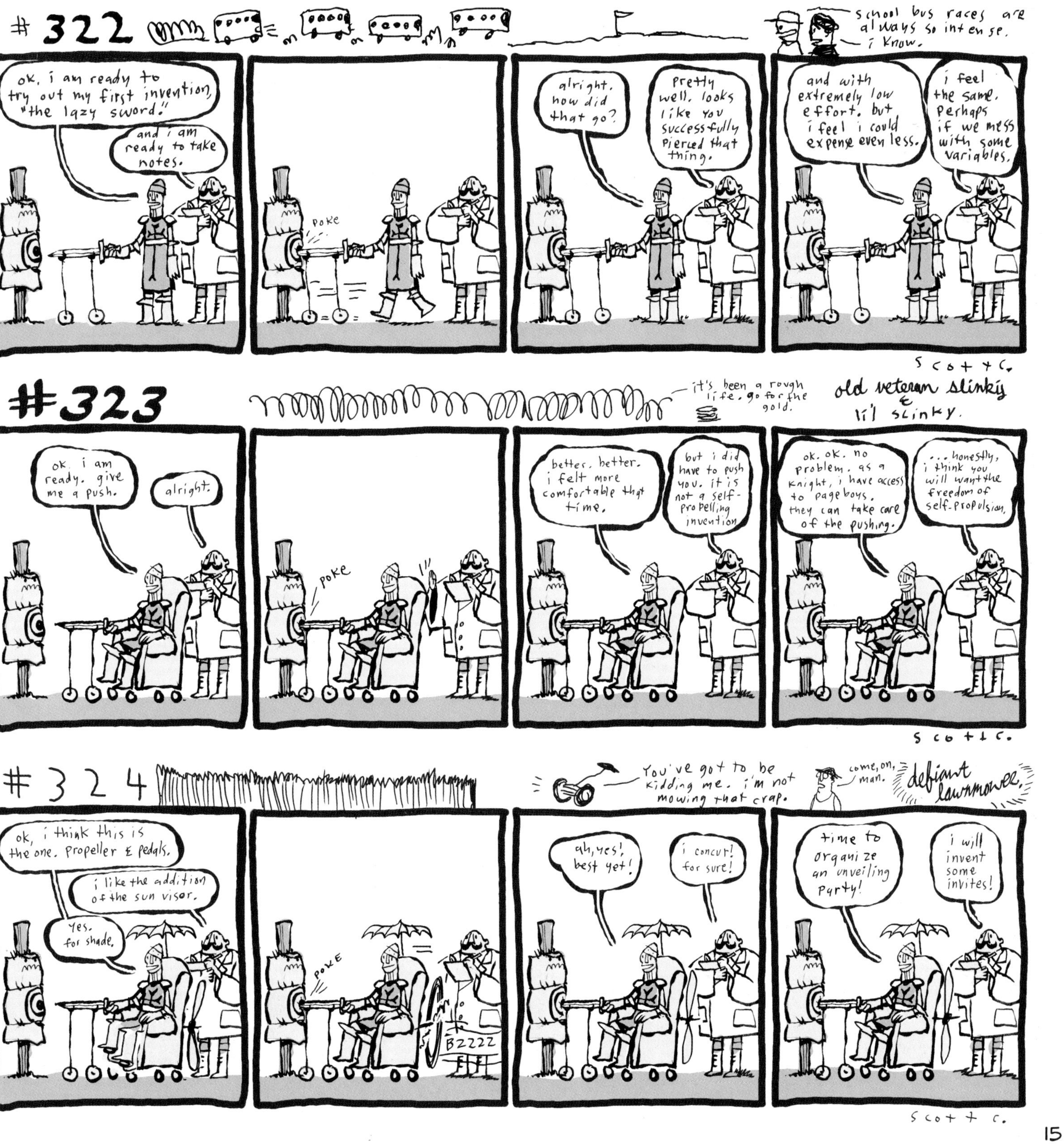
#322
school bus races are always so intense.
i know.
ok, i am ready to try out my first invention, "the lazy sword."
and i am ready to take notes.
POKE
alright. how did that go?
Pretty well. looks like you successfully pierced that thing.
and with extremely low effort. but i feel i could expense even less.
i feel the same. perhaps if we mess with some variables.
scott c.
#323
it's been a rough life. go for the gold.
old veteran slinky & li'l slinky.
ok. i am ready. give me a push.
alright.
poke
better. better. i felt more comfortable that time.
but i did have to push you. it is not a self-propelling invention
ok. ok. no problem. as a knight, i have access to pageboys. they can take care of the pushing.
...honestly, i think you will want the freedom of self-propulsion.
scott c.
#324
You've got to be kidding me. i'm not mowing that crap.
come, on, man.
defiant lawnmower.
ok, i think this is the one. propeller & pedals.
i like the addition of the sun visor.
yes. for shade.
POKE
BZZZZ
ah, yes! best yet!
i concur! for sure!
time to organize an unveiling party!
i will invent some invites!
scott c.

#325

—woe is me. poor flashlight who was dropped by some frightened teen in the woods before being murdered. i guess i'll just wait here until my batteries run out.

teen flashlight.

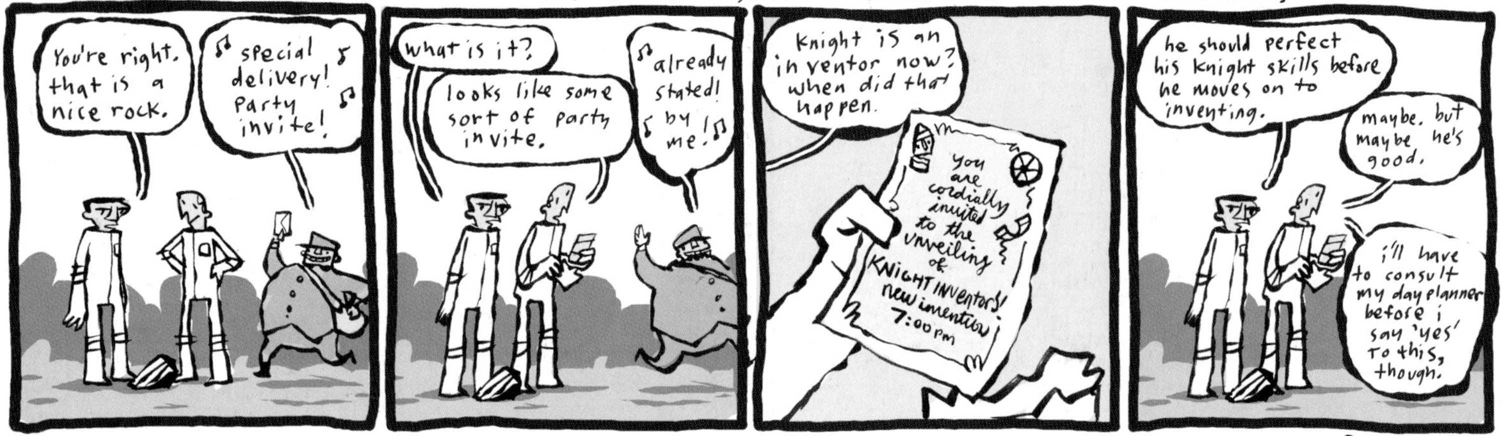

You're right. that is a nice rock.
special delivery! Party invite!
what is it?
looks like some sort of party invite.
already stated! by me!
Knight is an inventor now? when did that happen.
you are cordially invited to the unveiling of KNIGHT INVENTOR'S! new invention 7:00pm
he should perfect his knight skills before he moves on to inventing.
maybe. but maybe he's good.
i'll have to consult my dayplanner before i say 'yes' to this, though.

scott c.

#326

match web spider

—here's my art piece! what? anybody could have done that—

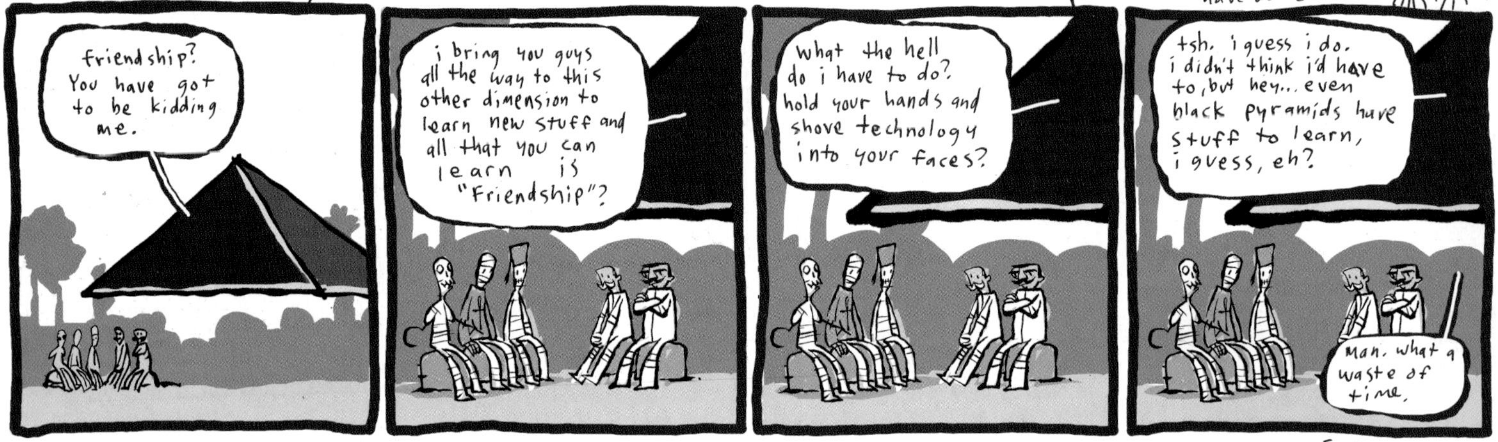

Friendship? You have got to be kidding me.
i bring you guys all the way to this other dimension to learn new stuff and all that you can learn is "Friendship"?
What the hell do i have to do? hold your hands and shove technology into your faces?
tsh. i guess i do. i didn't think i'd have to, but hey... even black pyramids have stuff to learn, i guess, eh?
Man. what a waste of time.

scott c.

#327 the Big Night

a variation to that could be "the big knight" if you want to be hilarious.

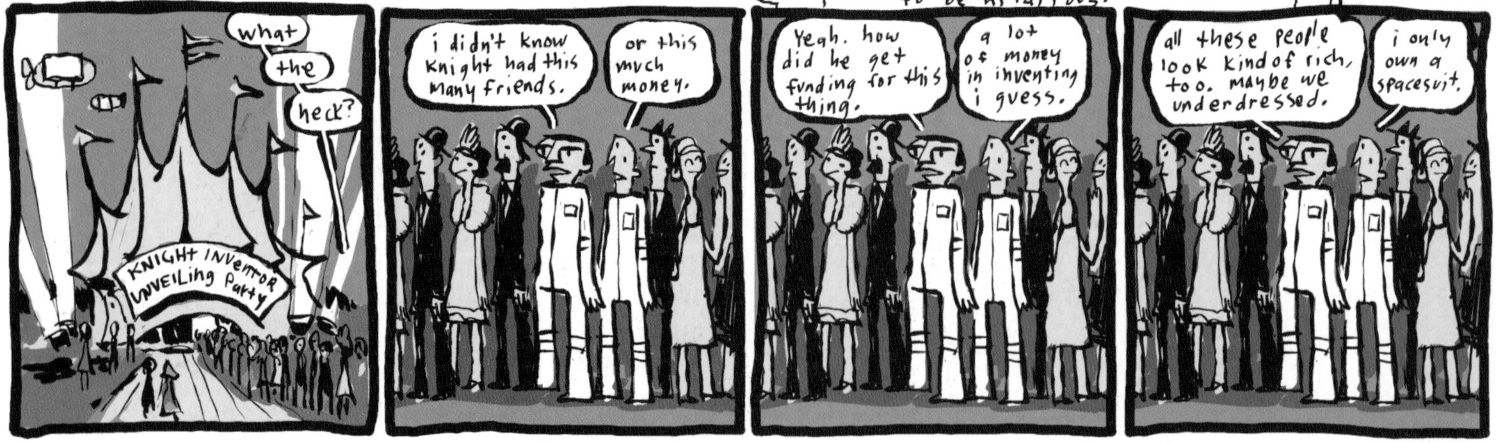

what the heck?
KNIGHT INVENTOR UNVEILING Party
i didn't know Knight had this many friends.
or this much money.
Yeah. how did he get funding for this thing.
a lot of money in inventing i guess.
all these people look kind of rich, too. maybe we underdressed.
i only own a spacesuit.

scott c.

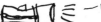

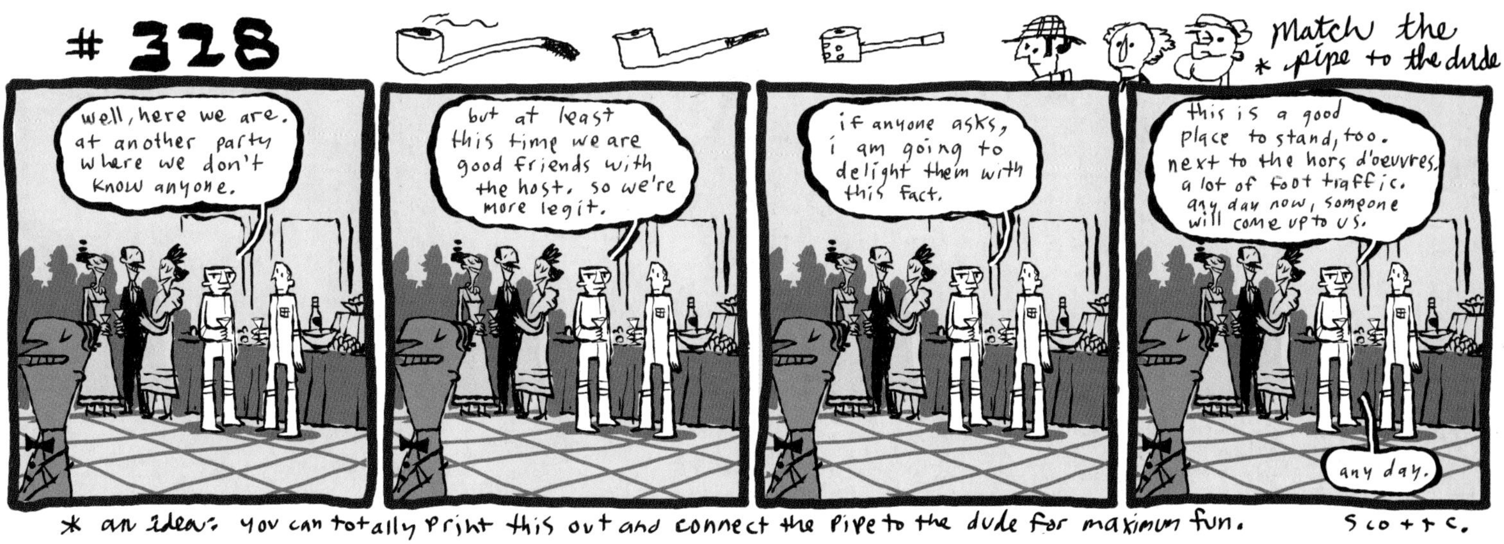
#328
Match the pipe to the dude *
well, here we are. at another party where we don't know anyone.
but at least this time we are good friends with the host. so we're more legit.
if anyone asks, i am going to delight them with this fact.
this is a good place to stand, too. next to the hors d'oeuvres, a lot of foot traffic. any day now, someone will come up to us.
any day.
* an idea: you can totally print this out and connect the pipe to the dude for maximum fun.
scott c.

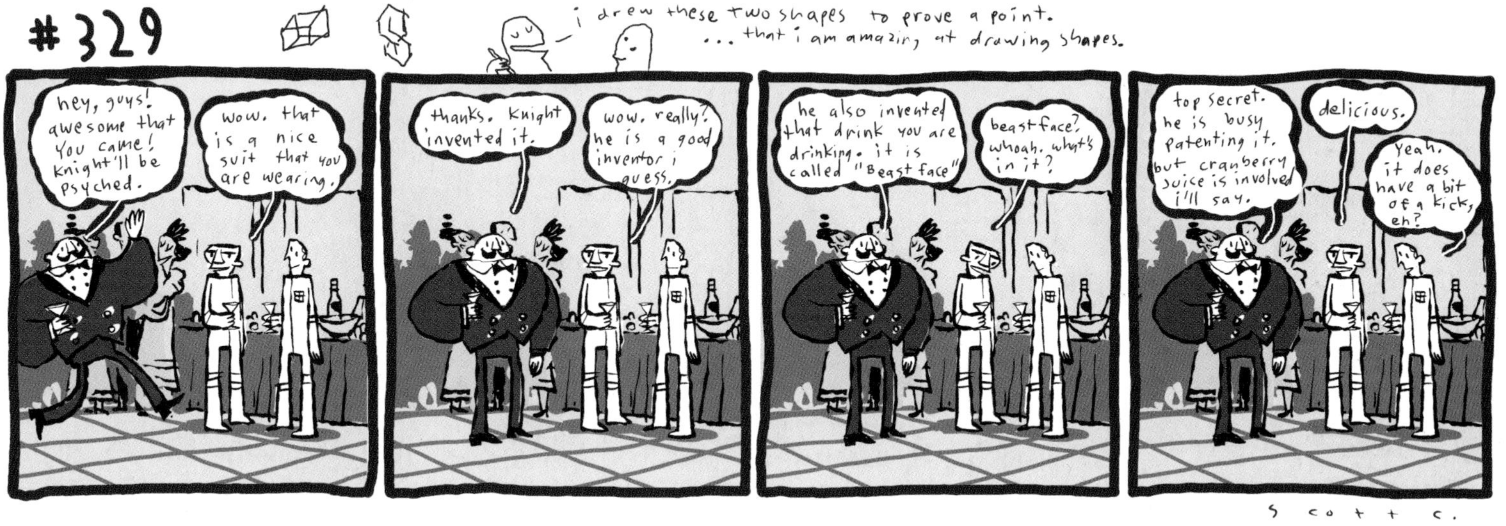
#329
i drew these two shapes to prove a point.
... that i am amazing at drawing shapes.
hey, guys! awesome that you came! knight'll be psyched.
wow. that is a nice suit that you are wearing.
thanks. knight invented it.
wow, really? he is a good inventor i guess.
he also invented that drink you are drinking. it is called "beast face"
beastface? whoah. what's in it?
top secret. he is busy patenting it. but cranberry juice is involved i'll say.
delicious.
yeah. it does have a bit of a kick, eh?
scott c.

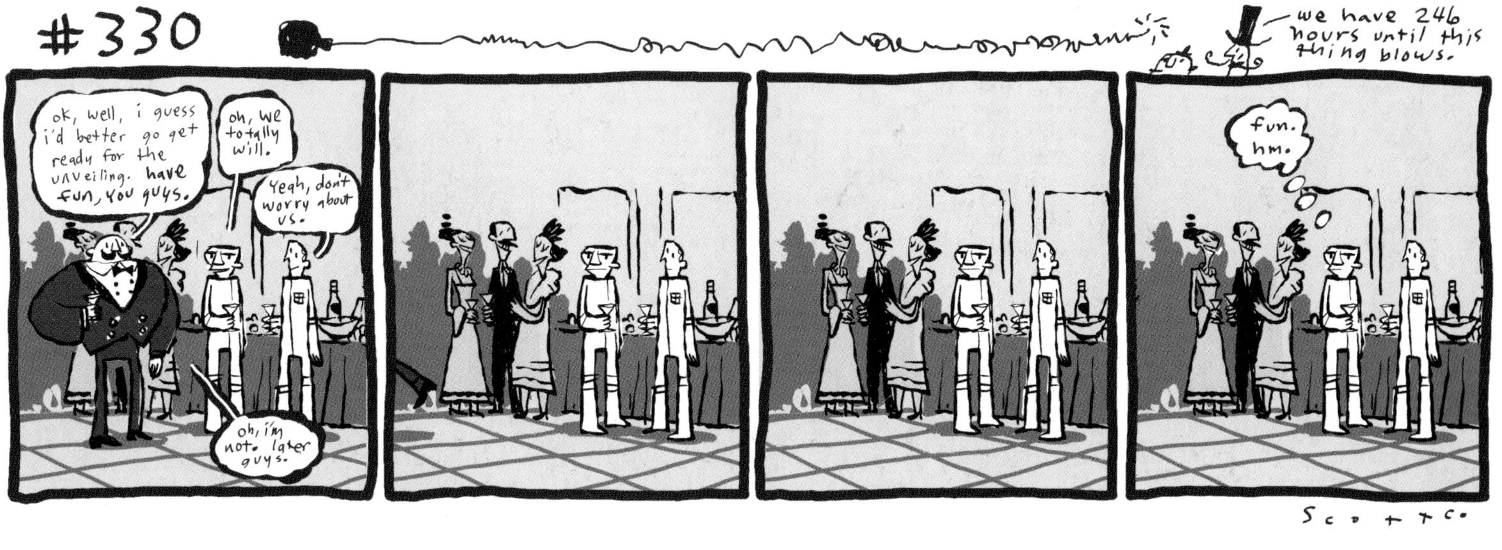
#330
we have 246 hours until this thing blows.
ok, well, i guess i'd better go get ready for the unveiling. have fun, you guys.
oh, we totally will.
yeah, don't worry about us.
oh, i'm not. later guys.
fun. hm.
scott c.

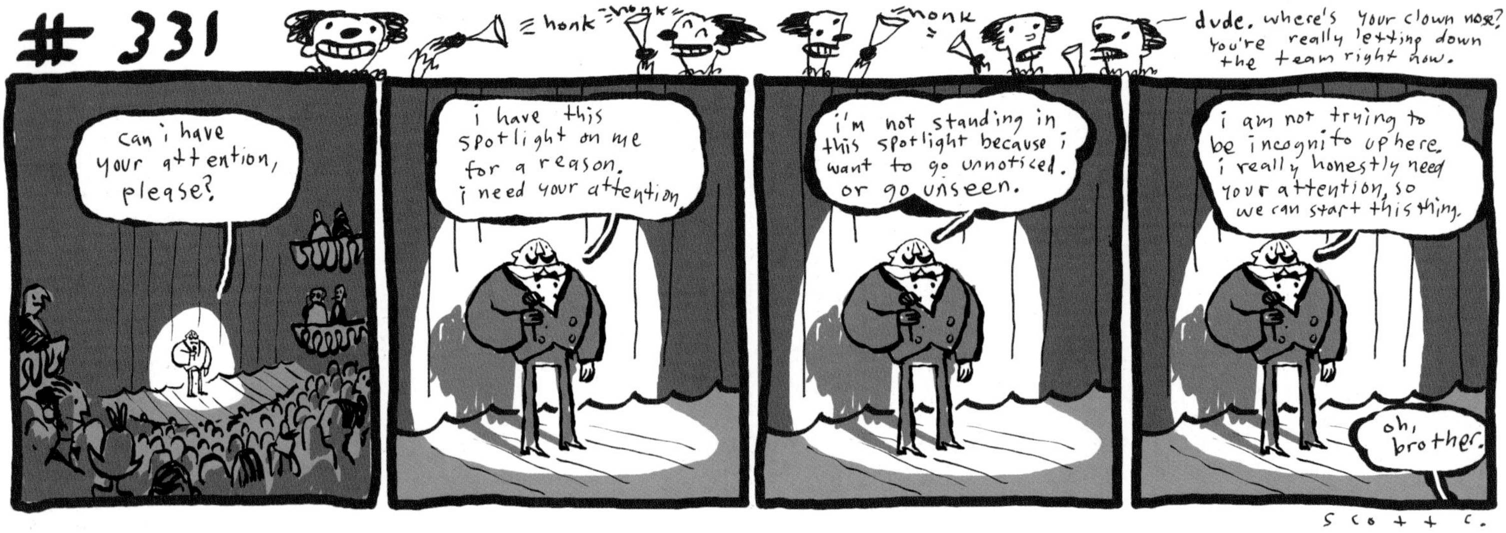
#331
honk
honk
honk
dude. where's your clown nose? you're really letting down the team right now.
can i have your attention, please?
i have this spotlight on me for a reason. i need your attention
i'm not standing in this spotlight because i want to go unnoticed. or go unseen.
i am not trying to be incognito up here. i really honestly need your attention, so we can start this thing.
oh, brother.
scott c.

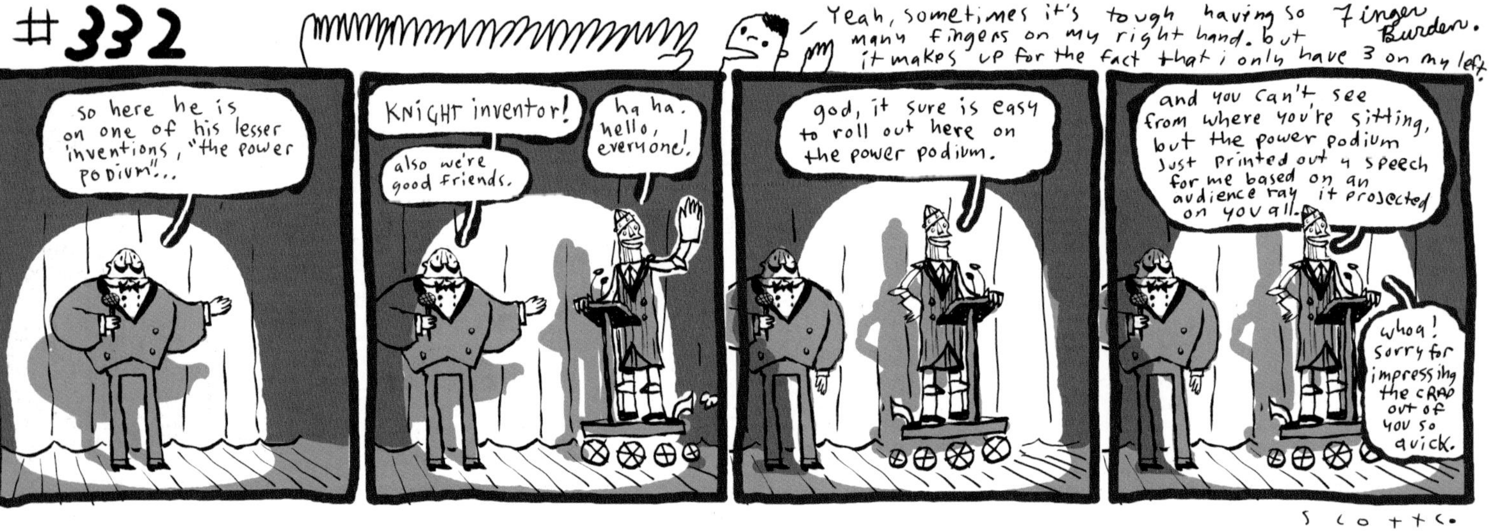
#332
Yeah, sometimes it's tough having so many fingers on my right hand. but it makes up for the fact that i only have 3 on my left.
7 finger Burden.
so here he is on one of his lesser inventions, "the power podium"...
KNIGHT inventor!
also we're good friends.
ha ha. hello, everyone!
god, it sure is easy to roll out here on the power podium.
and you can't see from where you're sitting, but the power podium just printed out a speech for me based on an audience ray it projected on you all.
whoa! sorry for impressing the CRAP out of you so quick.
scott c.

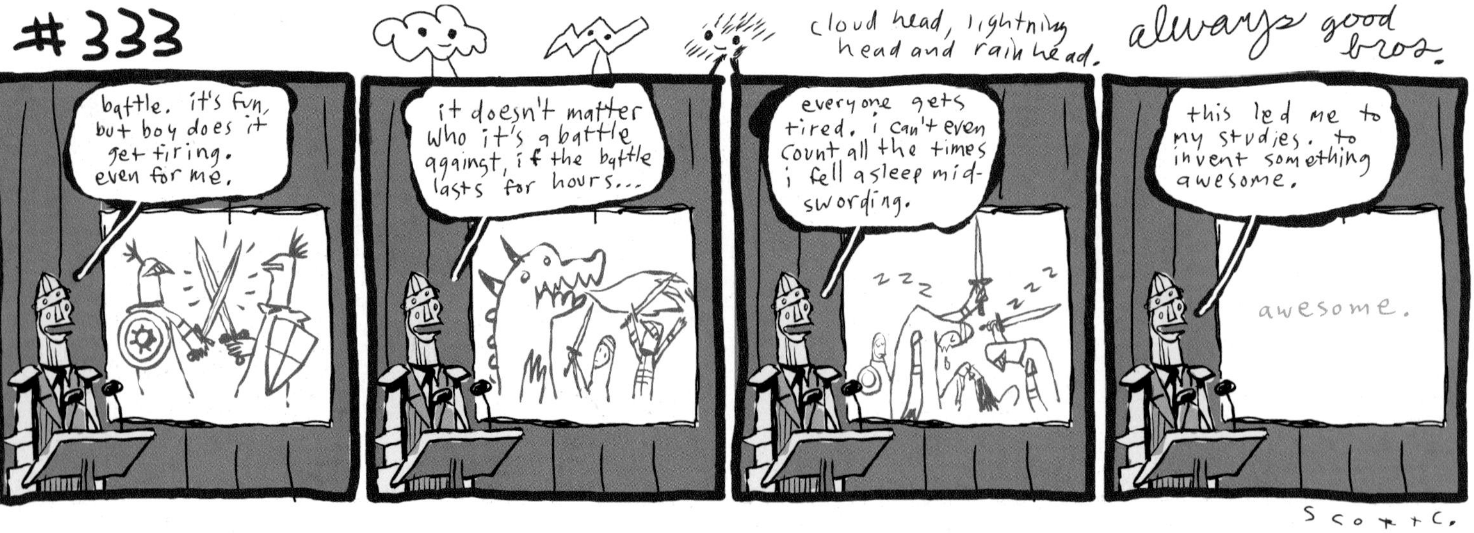
#333
cloud head, lightning head and rain head.
always good bros.
battle. it's fun, but boy does it get tiring. even for me.
it doesn't matter who it's a battle against, if the battle lasts for hours...
everyone gets tired. i can't even count all the times i fell asleep mid-swording.
zzz
zzz
this led me to my studies. to invent something awesome.
awesome.
scott c.

334

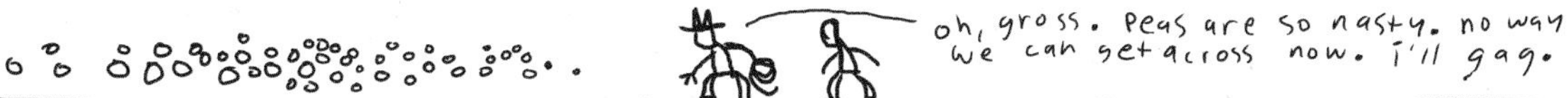
oh, gross. peas are so nasty. no way we can get across now. i'll gag.

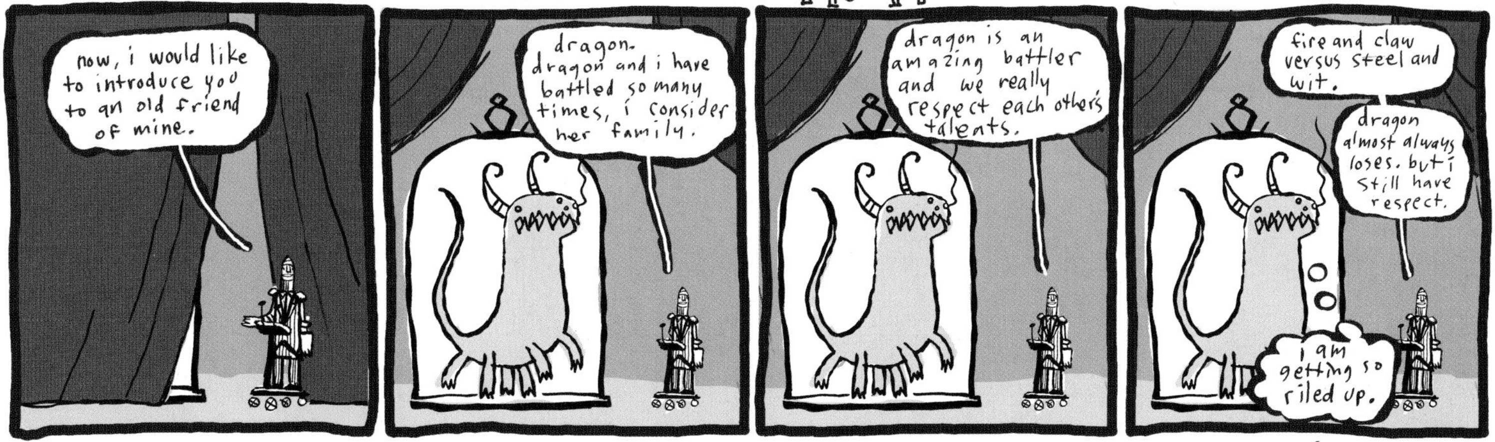
now, i would like to introduce you to an old friend of mine.
dragon. dragon and i have battled so many times, i consider her family.
dragon is an amazing battler and we really respect each other's talents.
fire and claw versus steel and wit.
dragon almost always loses. but i still have respect.
i am getting so riled up.

scott c.

335

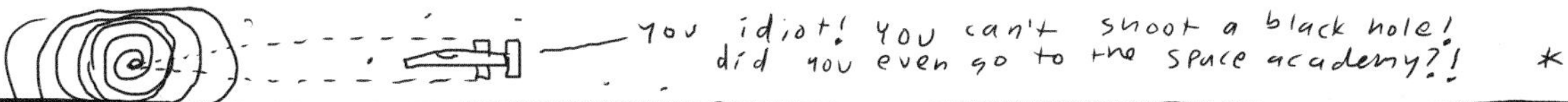
you idiot! you can't shoot a black hole! did you even go to the space academy?! *

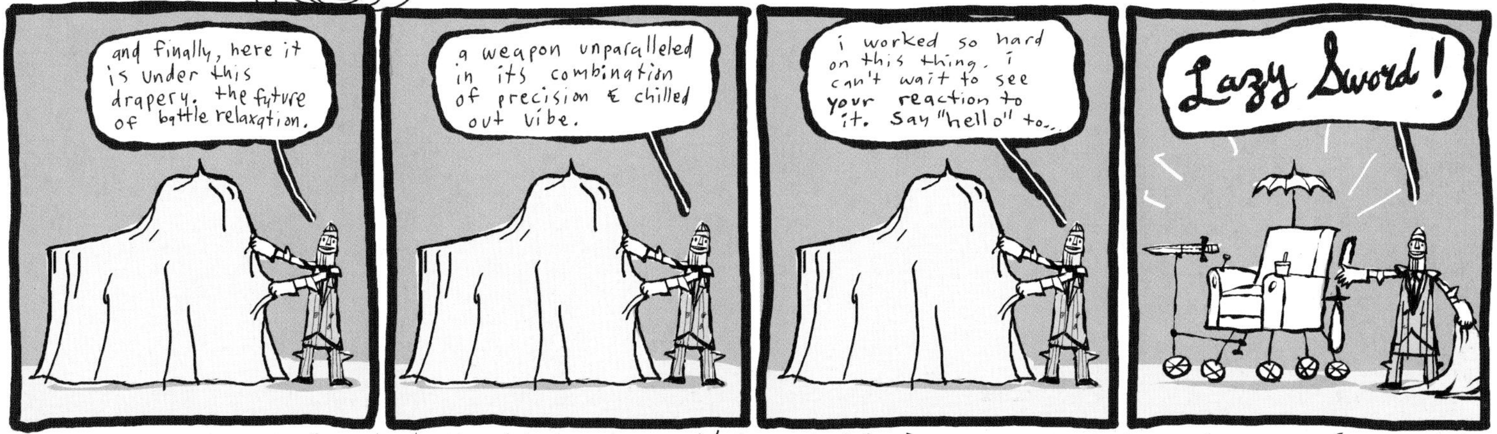
and finally, here it is under this drapery. the future of battle relaxation.
a weapon unparalleled in its combination of precision & chilled out vibe.
i worked so hard on this thing. i can't wait to see your reaction to it. say "hello" to...
Lazy Sword!

* above comic about the black hole would look better if space was black. sorry.

scott c.

336 The Audience Reaction to Lazy Sword

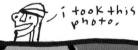

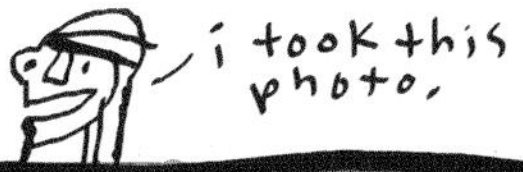
i took this photo.

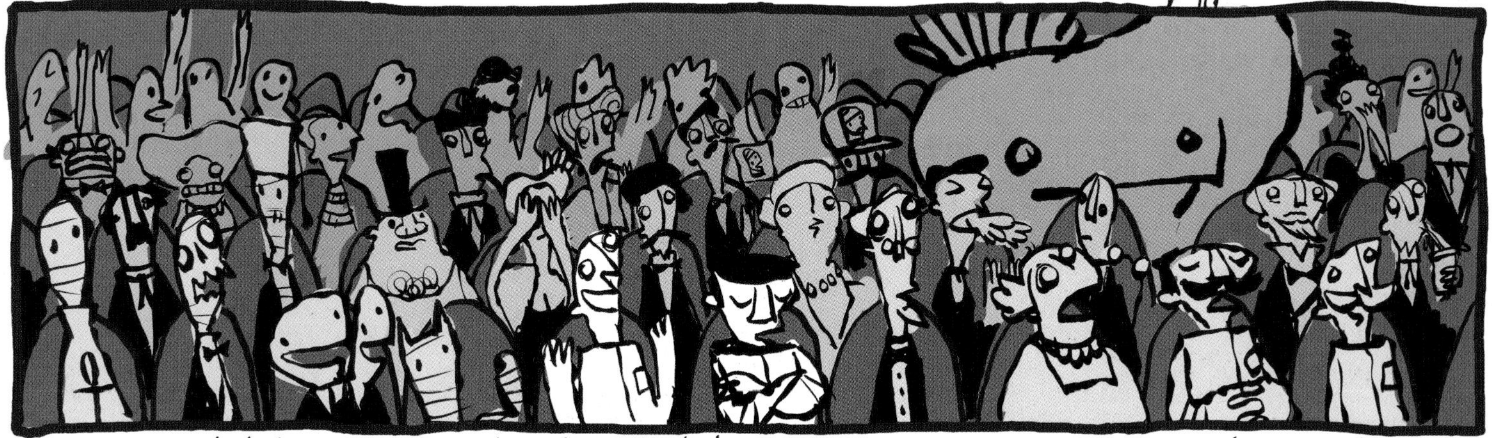

P.S. that last row is a bunch of naked people.

scott c.

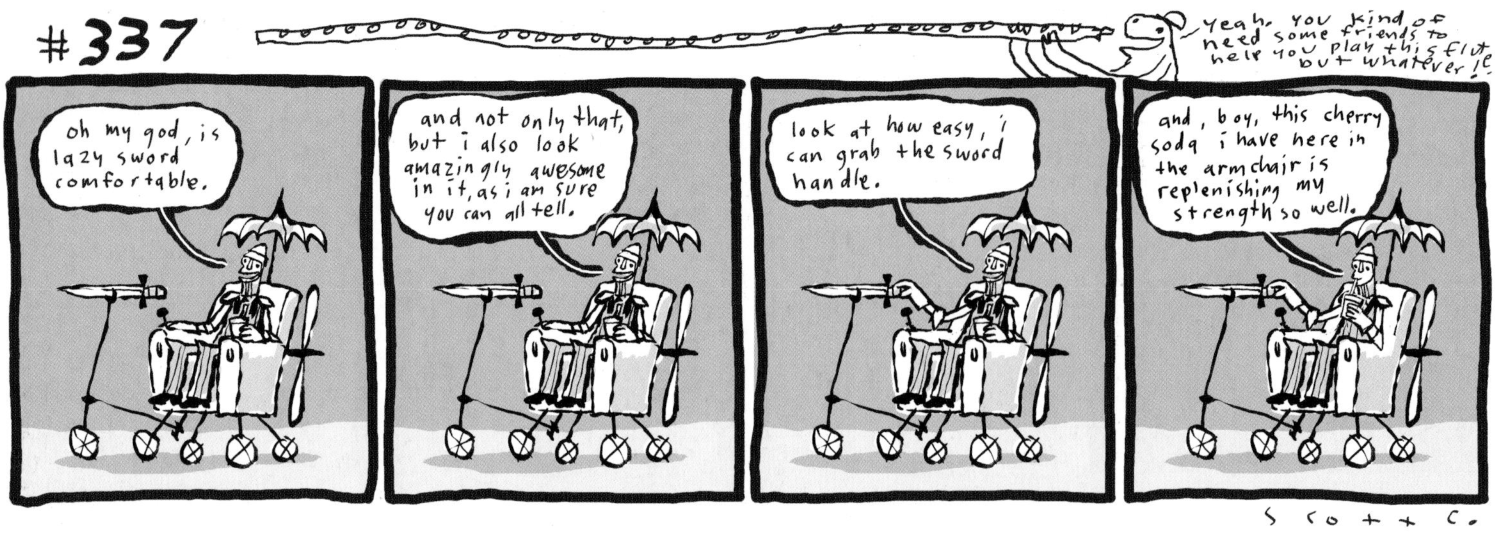
#337
yeah. you kind of need some friends to help you play this flute but whatever!
oh my god, is lazy sword comfortable.
and not only that, but i also look amazingly awesome in it, as i am sure you can all tell.
look at how easy, i can grab the sword handle.
and, boy, this cherry soda i have here in the armchair is replenishing my strength so well.
scott c.

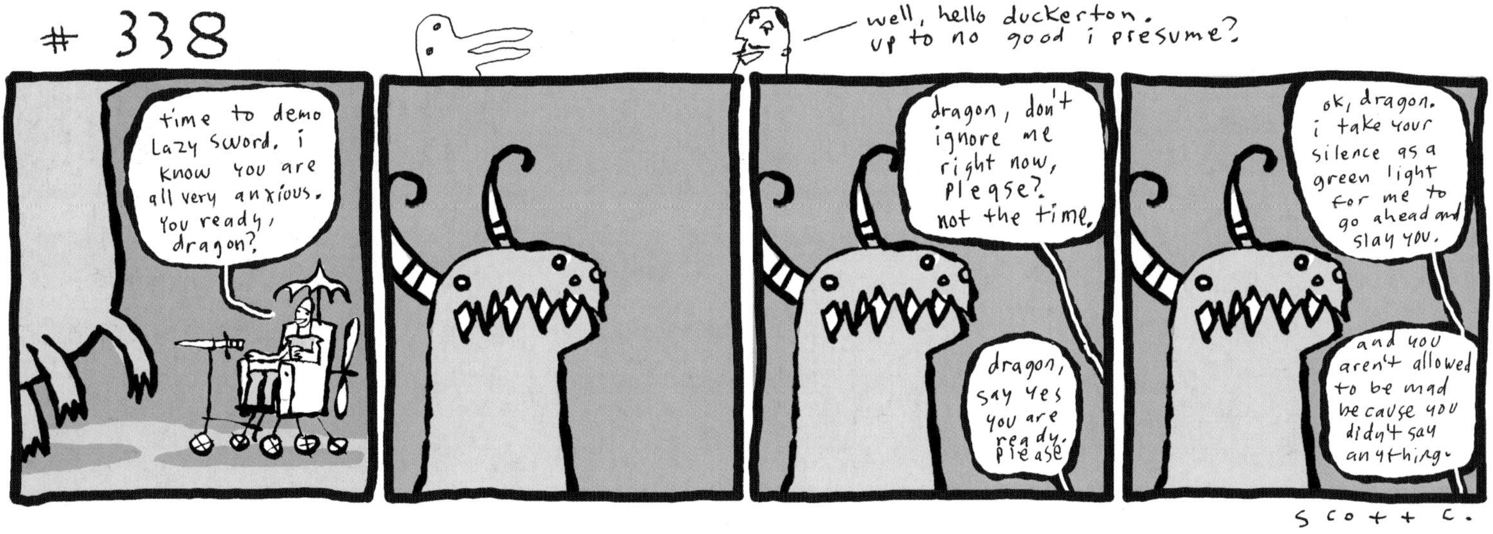
338
well, hello duckerton. up to no good i presume?
time to demo lazy sword. i know you are all very anxious. you ready, dragon?
dragon, don't ignore me right now, please? not the time.
dragon, say yes you are ready. please
ok, dragon. i take your silence as a green light for me to go ahead and slay you.
and you aren't allowed to be mad because you didn't say anything.
scott c.

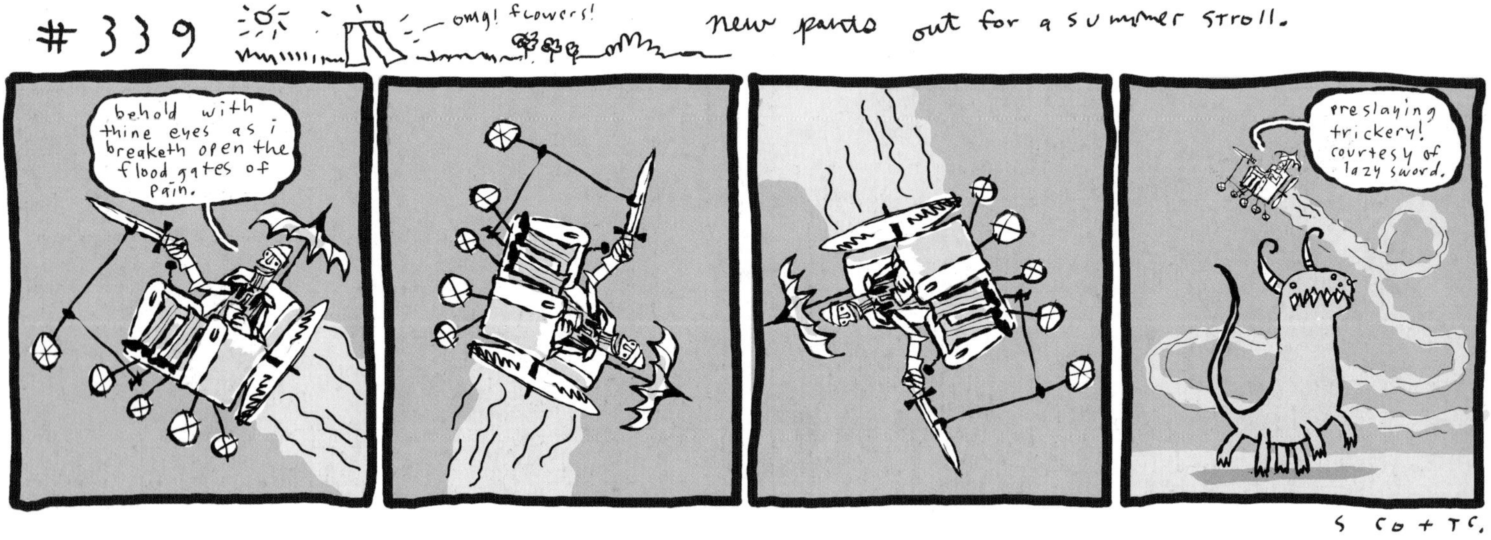
339
omg! flowers!
new pants out for a summer stroll.
behold with thine eyes as i breaketh open the flood gates of pain.
preslaying trickery! courtesy of lazy sword.
scott c.

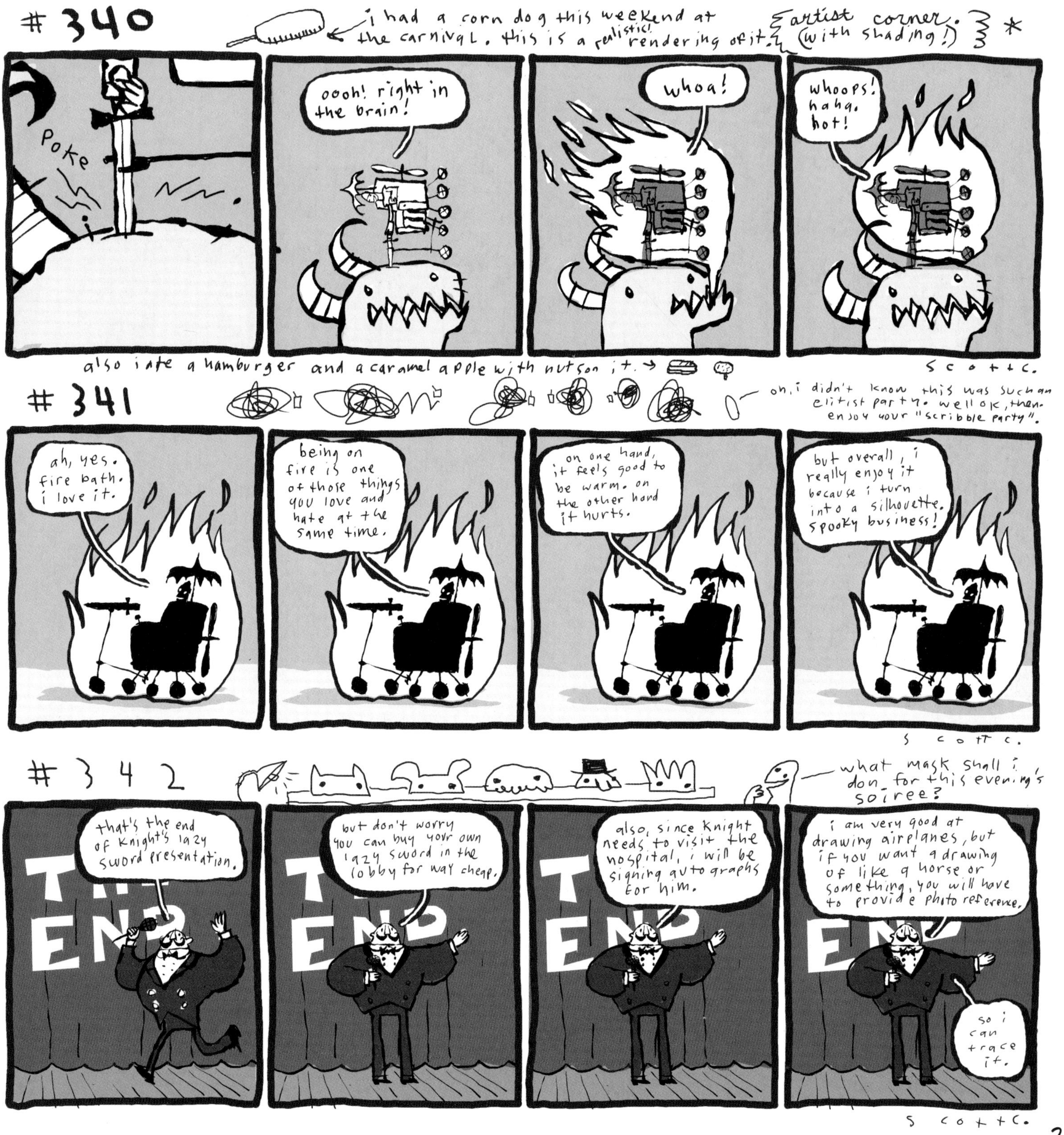
#340
i had a corn dog this weekend at the carnival. this is a realistic! rendering of it.
artist corner. (with shading!) *
Poke
oooh! right in the brain!
whoa!
whoops! haha. hot!
also i ate a hamburger and a caramel apple with nuts on it.
scott c.
#341
oh, i didn't know this was such an elitist party. well ok, then. enjoy your "scribble party".
ah, yes. fire bath. i love it.
being on fire is one of those things you love and hate at the same time.
on one hand, it feels good to be warm. on the other hand it hurts.
but overall, i really enjoy it because i turn into a silhouette. spooky business!
scott c.
#342
what mask shall i don for this evening's soiree?
that's the end of knight's lazy sword presentation.
but don't worry you can buy your own lazy sword in the lobby for way cheap.
also, since knight needs to visit the hospital, i will be signing autographs for him.
i am very good at drawing airplanes, but if you want a drawing of like a horse or something, you will have to provide photo reference.
so i can trace it.
scott c.

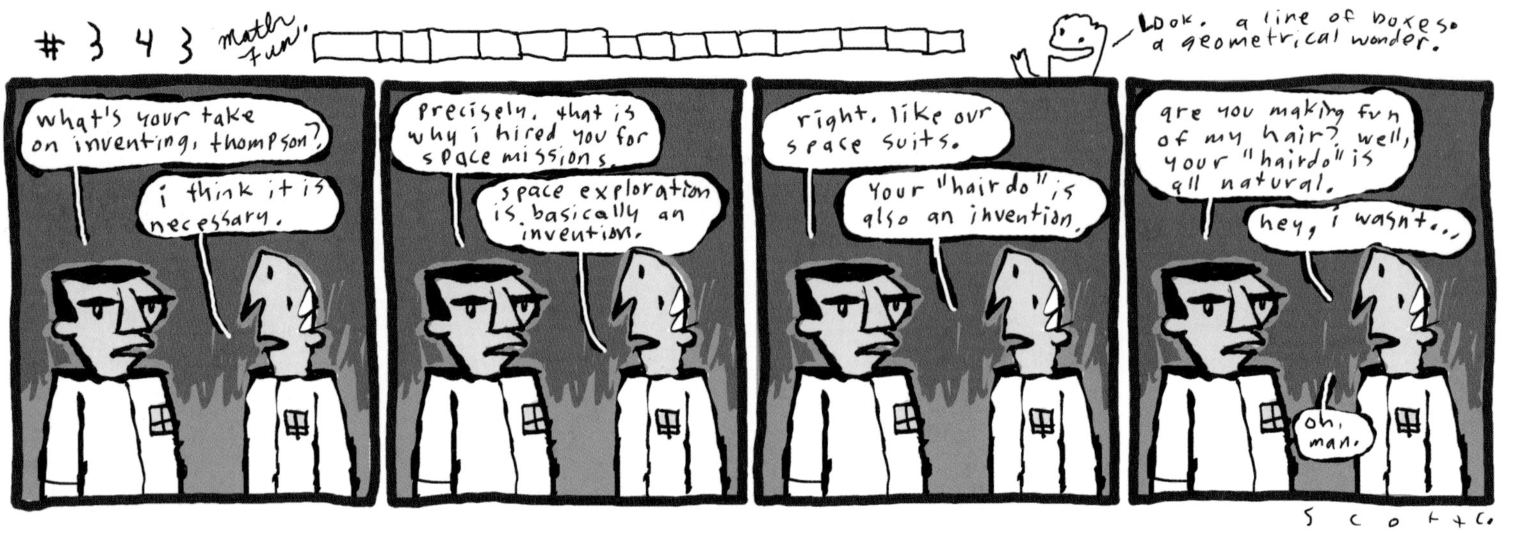
#343 math fun.
Look. a line of boxes. a geometrical wonder.
what's your take on inventing, thompson?
i think it is necessary.
Precisely. that is why i hired you for space missions.
space exploration is basically an invention.
right. like our space suits.
your "hairdo" is also an invention.
are you making fun of my hair? well, your "hairdo" is all natural.
hey, i wasn't...
oh, man.
scott c.

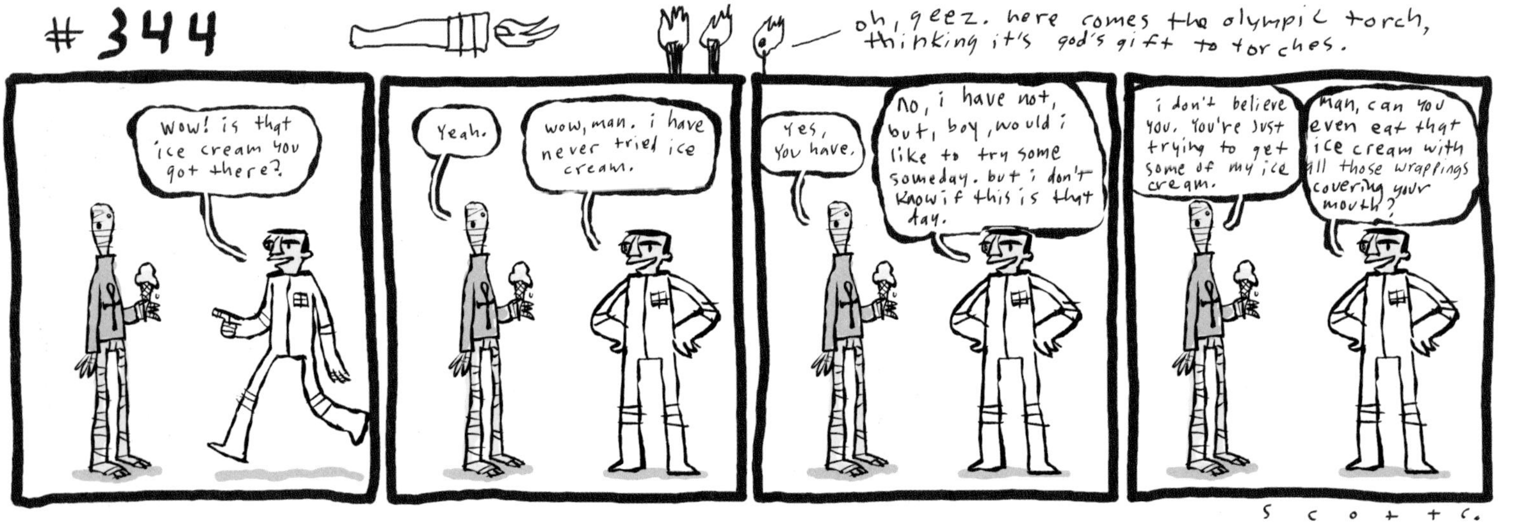
#344
oh, geez. here comes the olympic torch, thinking it's god's gift to torches.
wow! is that ice cream you got there?
Yeah.
wow, man. i have never tried ice cream.
yes, you have.
No, i have not, but, boy, would i like to try some someday. but i don't know if this is that day.
i don't believe you. you're just trying to get some of my ice cream.
man, can you even eat that ice cream with all those wrappings covering your mouth?
scott c.

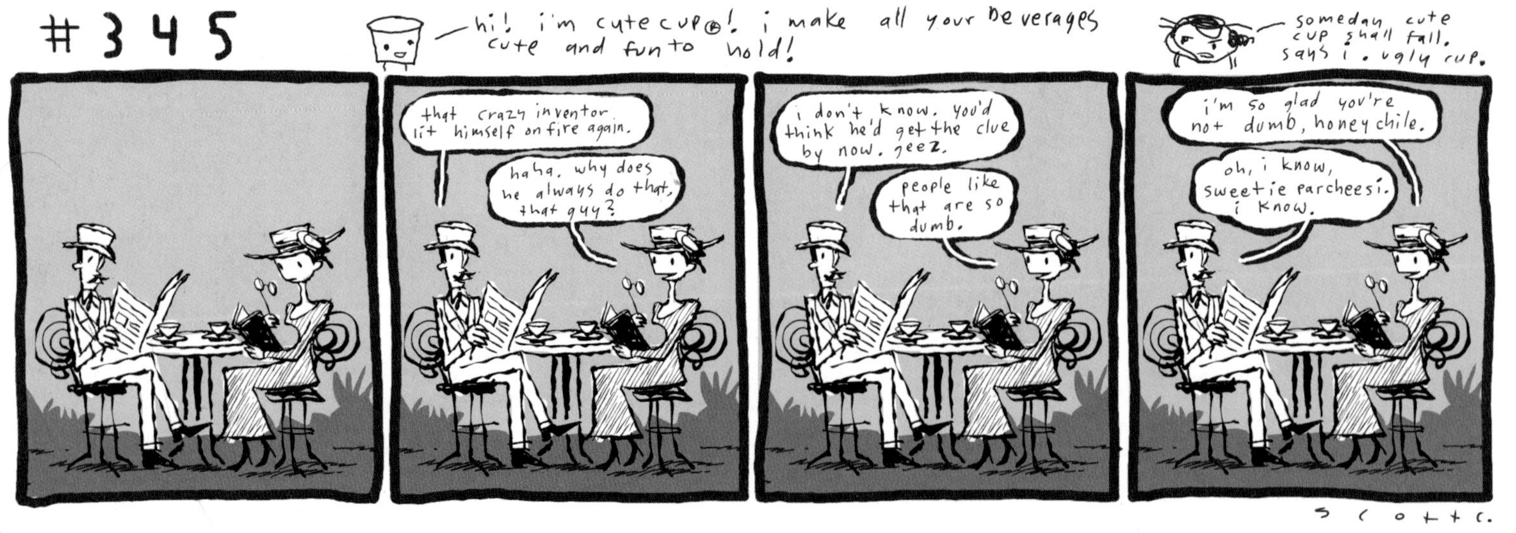
#345
hi! i'm cutecup®! i make all your beverages cute and fun to hold!
someday cute cup shall fall. says i. ugly cup.
that crazy inventor lit himself on fire again.
haha. why does he always do that, that guy?
i don't know. you'd think he'd get the clue by now. geez.
people like that are so dumb.
i'm so glad you're not dumb, honey chile.
oh, i know, sweetie parcheesi. i know.
scott c.

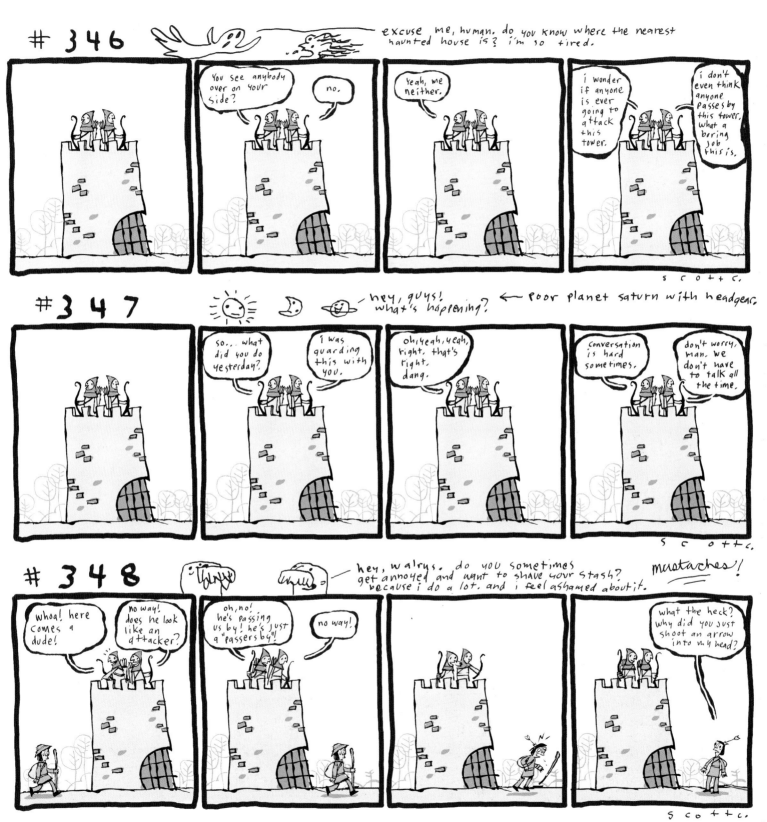

346

excuse me, human. do you know where the nearest haunted house is? i'm so tired.

you see anybody over on your side?

no.

yeah, me neither.

i wonder if anyone is ever going to attack this tower.

i don't even think anyone passes by this tower. what a boring job this is.

scott c.

347

hey, guys! what's happening? ← poor planet saturn with headgear.

so... what did you do yesterday?

i was guarding this with you.

oh, yeah, yeah, right. that's right. dang.

conversation is hard sometimes.

don't worry, man. we don't have to talk all the time.

scott c.

348

hey, walrus. do you sometimes get annoyed and want to shave your stash? because i do a lot. and i feel ashamed about it.

mustaches!

whoa! here comes a dude!

no way! does he look like an attacker?

oh, no! he's passing us by! he's just a "passers by"!

no way!

what the heck? why did you just shoot an arrow into my head?

scott c.

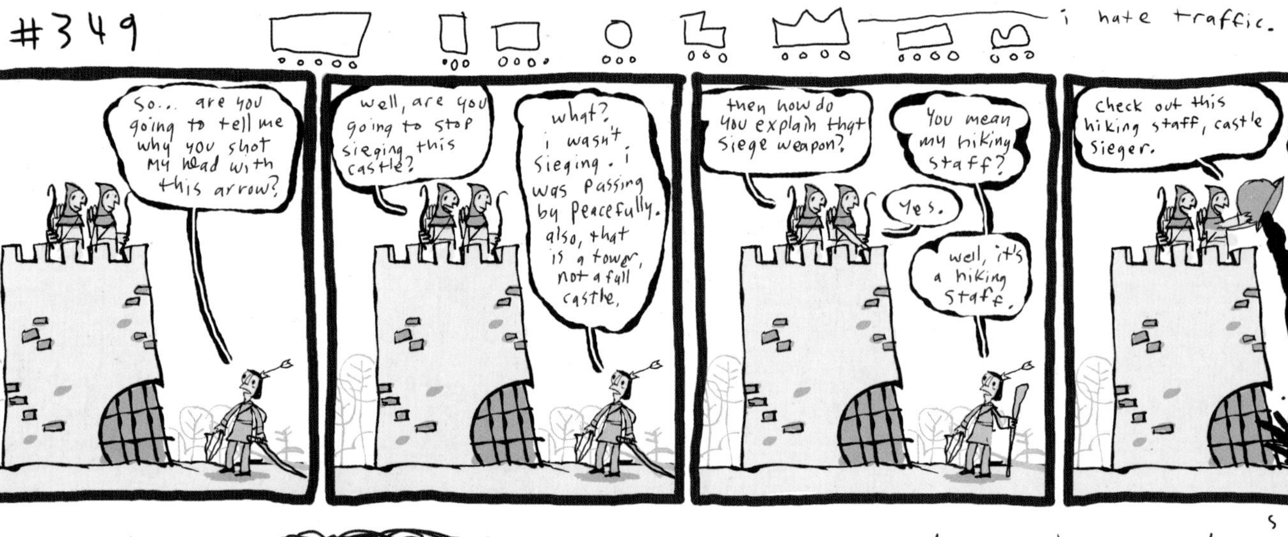
#349
i hate traffic.
So... are you going to tell me why you shot my head with this arrow?
well, are you going to stop sieging this castle?
what? i wasn't sieging. i was passing by peacefully. also, that is a tower, not a full castle.
then how do you explain that siege weapon?
You mean my hiking staff?
Yes.
well, it's a hiking staff.
Check out this hiking staff, castle sieger.
ooow! hot oil! holy crap! that is some hot stuff! ow!
scott c.

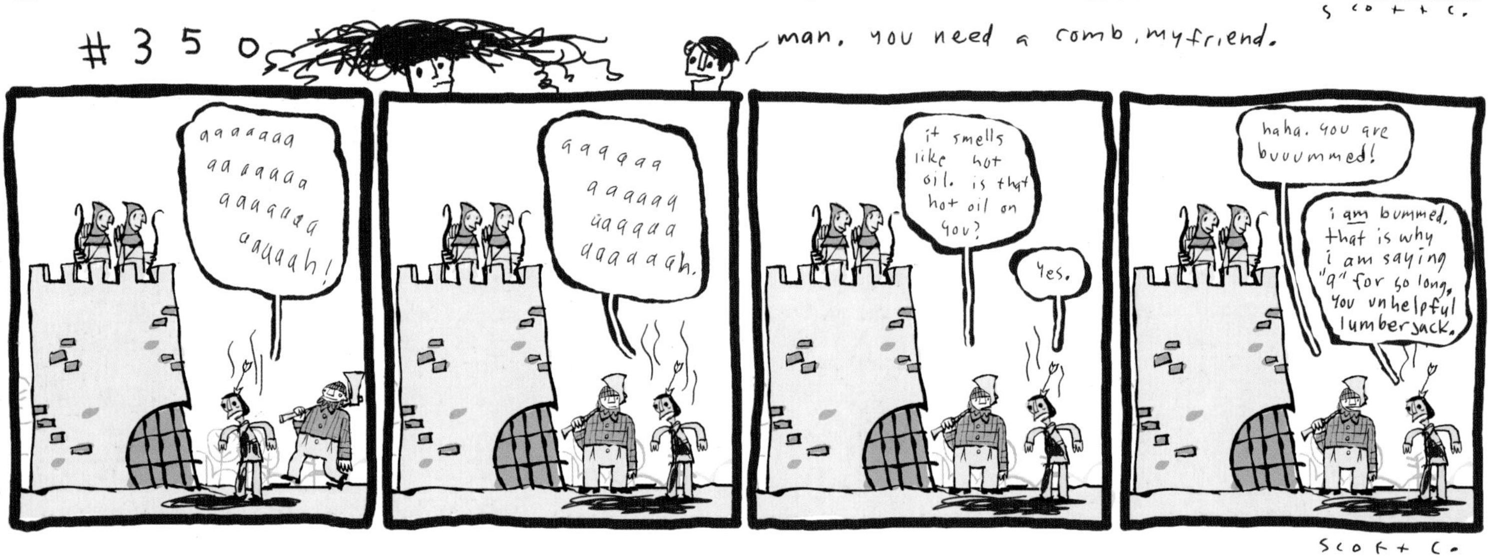
#350
man. you need a comb, myfriend.
aaaaaaa aaaaaa aaaaaaa aaaah!
aaaaaa aaaaaa aaaaaa aaaaaah.
it smells like hot oil. is that hot oil on you?
Yes.
haha. you are buuummed!
i am bummed. that is why i am saying "a" for so long, you unhelpful lumberjack.
scott c.

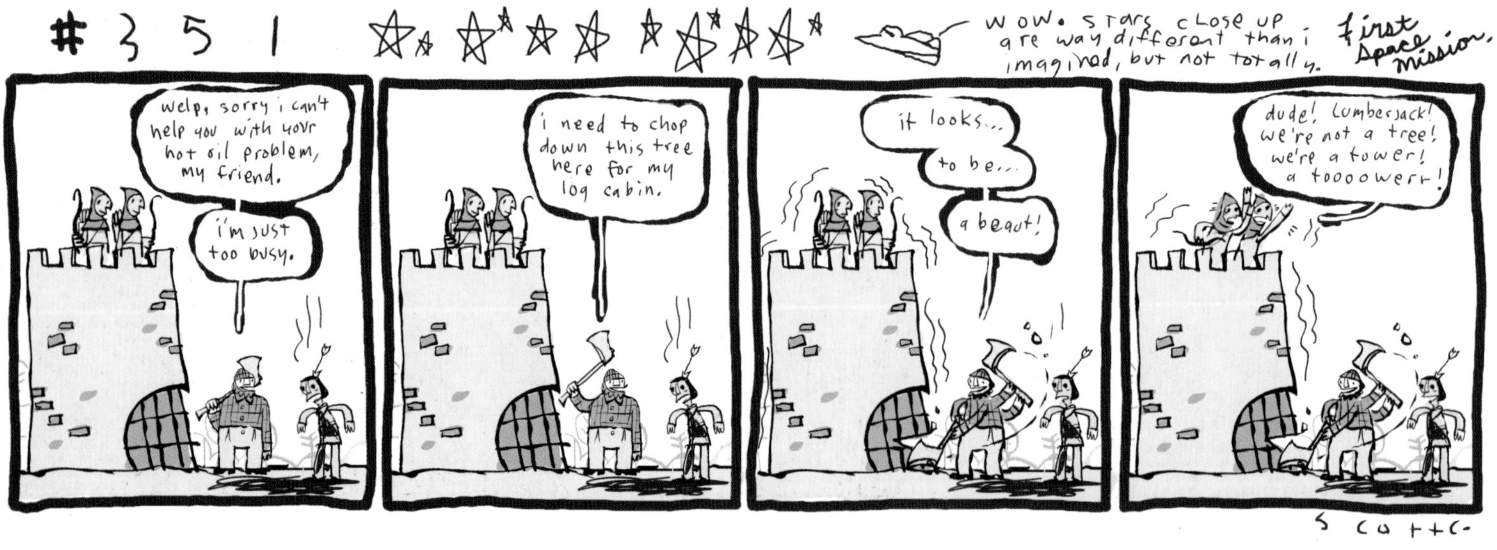
#351
wow. stars close up are way different than i imagined, but not totally.
First Space Mission.
welp, sorry i can't help you with your hot oil problem, my friend.
i'm just too busy.
i need to chop down this tree here for my log cabin.
it looks...
to be...
a beaut!
dude! lumberjack! we're not a tree! we're a tower! a toooowerr!
scott c.

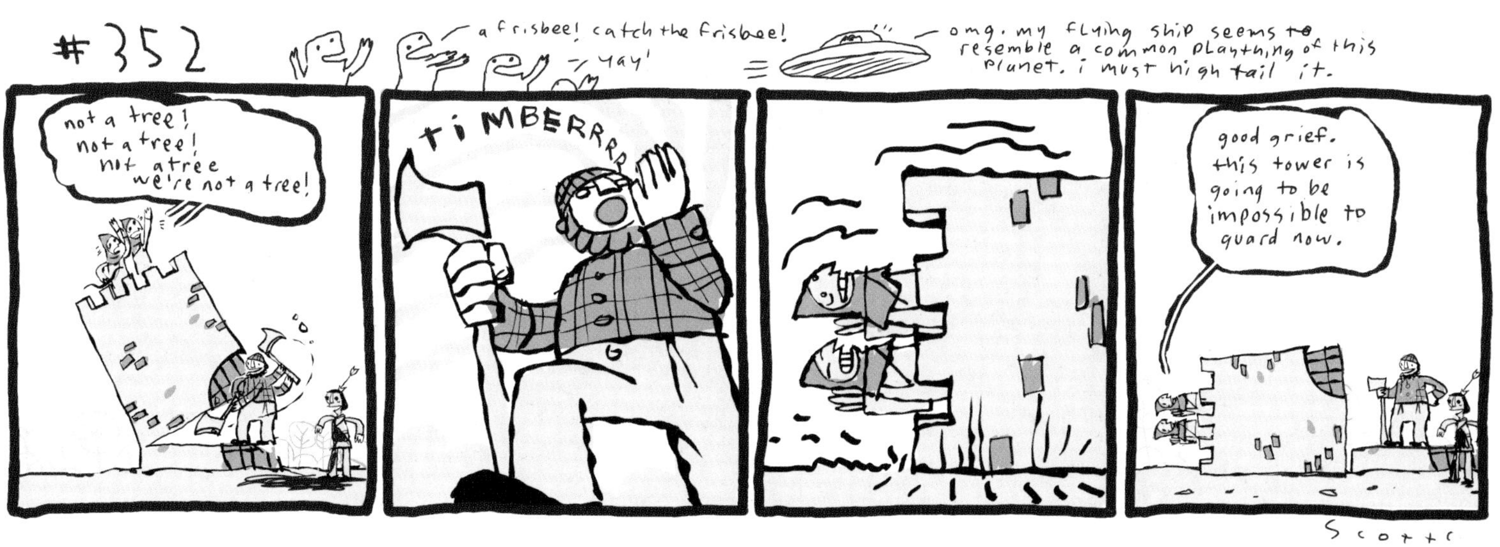
#352
a frisbee! catch the frisbee!
yay!
omg. my flying ship seems to resemble a common plaything of this planet. i must high tail it.
not a tree! not a tree! not a tree we're not a tree!
TIMBERRRR
good grief. this tower is going to be impossible to guard now.
scott c

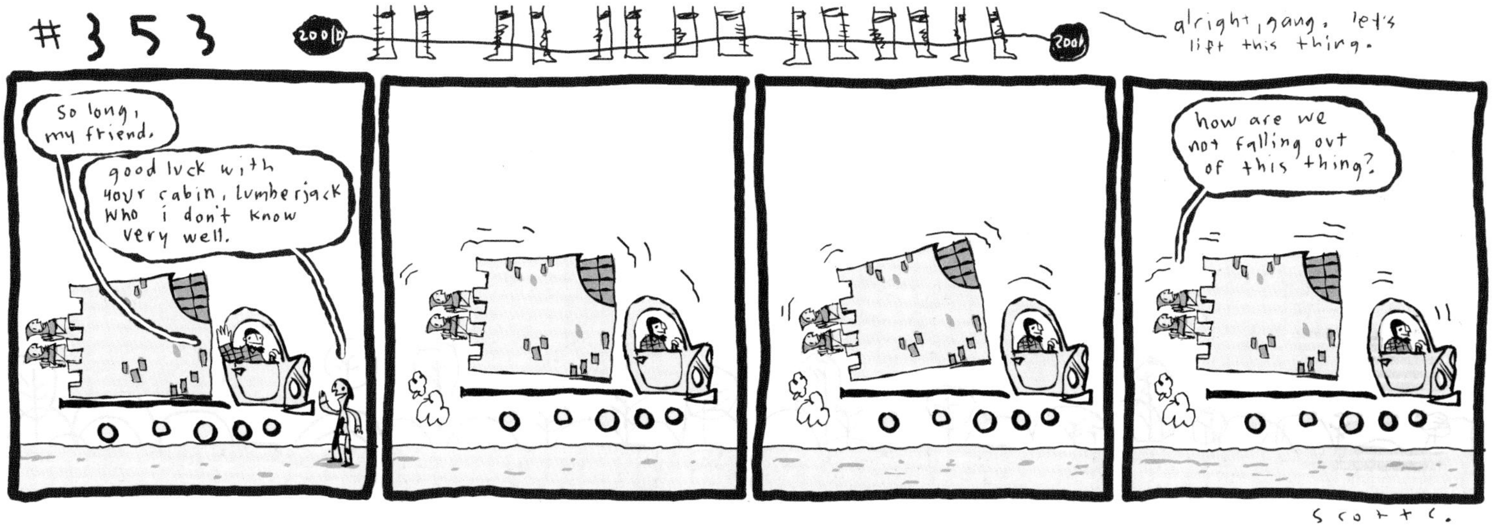
#353
2001
2001
alright, gang. let's lift this thing.
so long, my friend.
good luck with your cabin, lumberjack who i don't know very well.
how are we not falling out of this thing?
scott c.

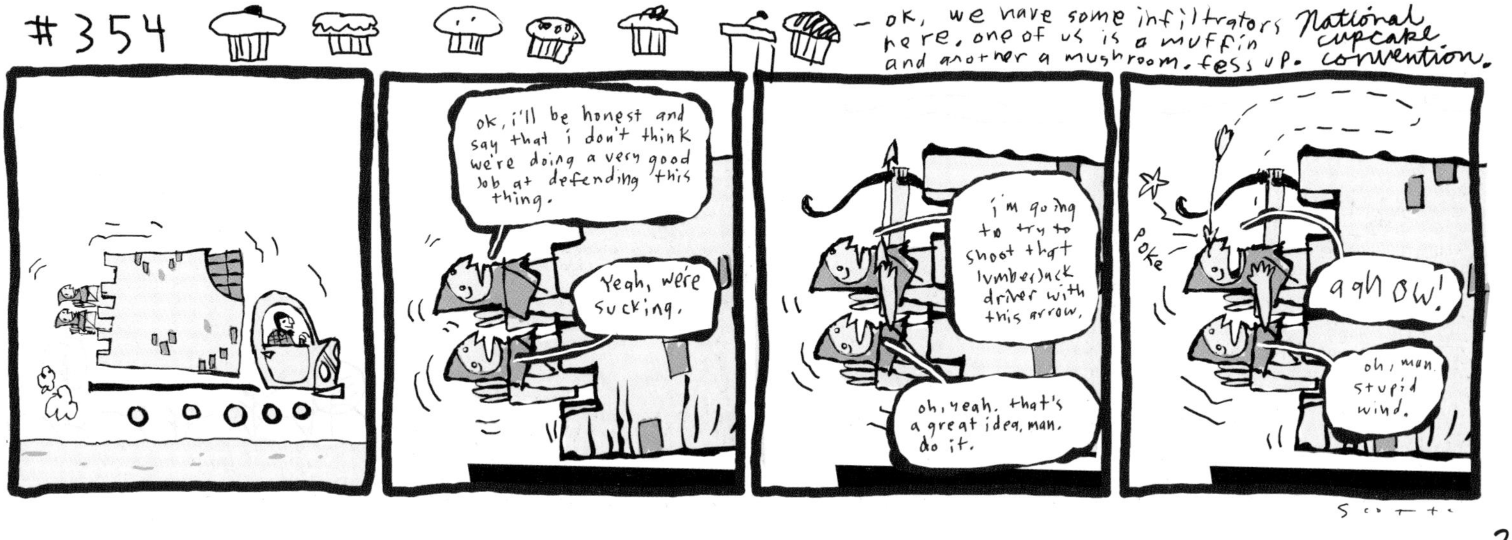
#354
ok, we have some infiltrators here. one of us is a muffin and another a mushroom. fess up.
National cupcake convention.
ok, i'll be honest and say that i don't think we're doing a very good job at defending this thing.
yeah, we're sucking.
i'm going to try to shoot that lumberjack driver with this arrow.
oh, yeah. that's a great idea, man. do it.
poke
aah ow!
oh, man. stupid wind.
scott c

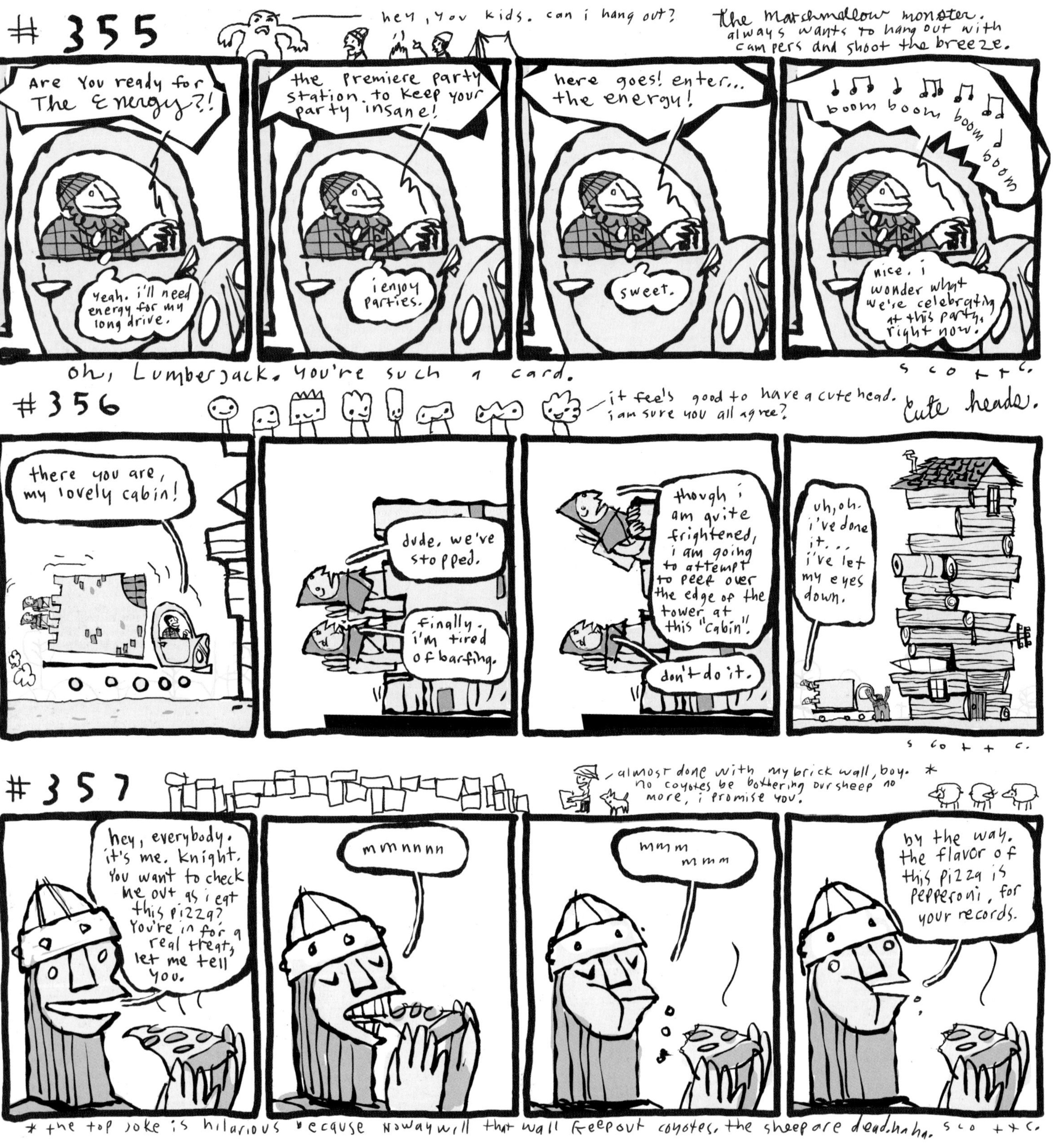

#355
hey, you kids. can i hang out?
The marshmallow monster. always wants to hang out with campers and shoot the breeze.
Are you ready for The Energy?!
yeah. i'll need energy for my long drive.
the premiere party station. to keep your party insane!
i enjoy parties.
here goes! enter... the energy!
sweet.
boom boom boom boom
nice. i wonder what we're celebrating at this party right now.
oh, Lumberjack. you're such a card.
scott c.
#356
it feels good to have a cute head. i am sure you all agree?
cute heads.
there you are, my lovely cabin!
dude, we've stopped.
finally. i'm tired of barfing.
though i am quite frightened, i am going to attempt to peer over the edge of the tower at this "cabin".
don't do it.
uh, oh. i've done it... i've let my eyes down.
scott c.
#357
almost done with my brick wall, boy. * no coyotes be bothering our sheep no more, i promise you.
hey, everybody. it's me. knight. you want to check me out as i eat this pizza? you're in for a real treat, let me tell you.
mmmnnnn
mmm mmm
by the way. the flavor of this pizza is pepperoni, for your records.
* the top joke is hilarious because no way will that wall keep out coyotes. the sheep are dead. ha ha.
scott c.

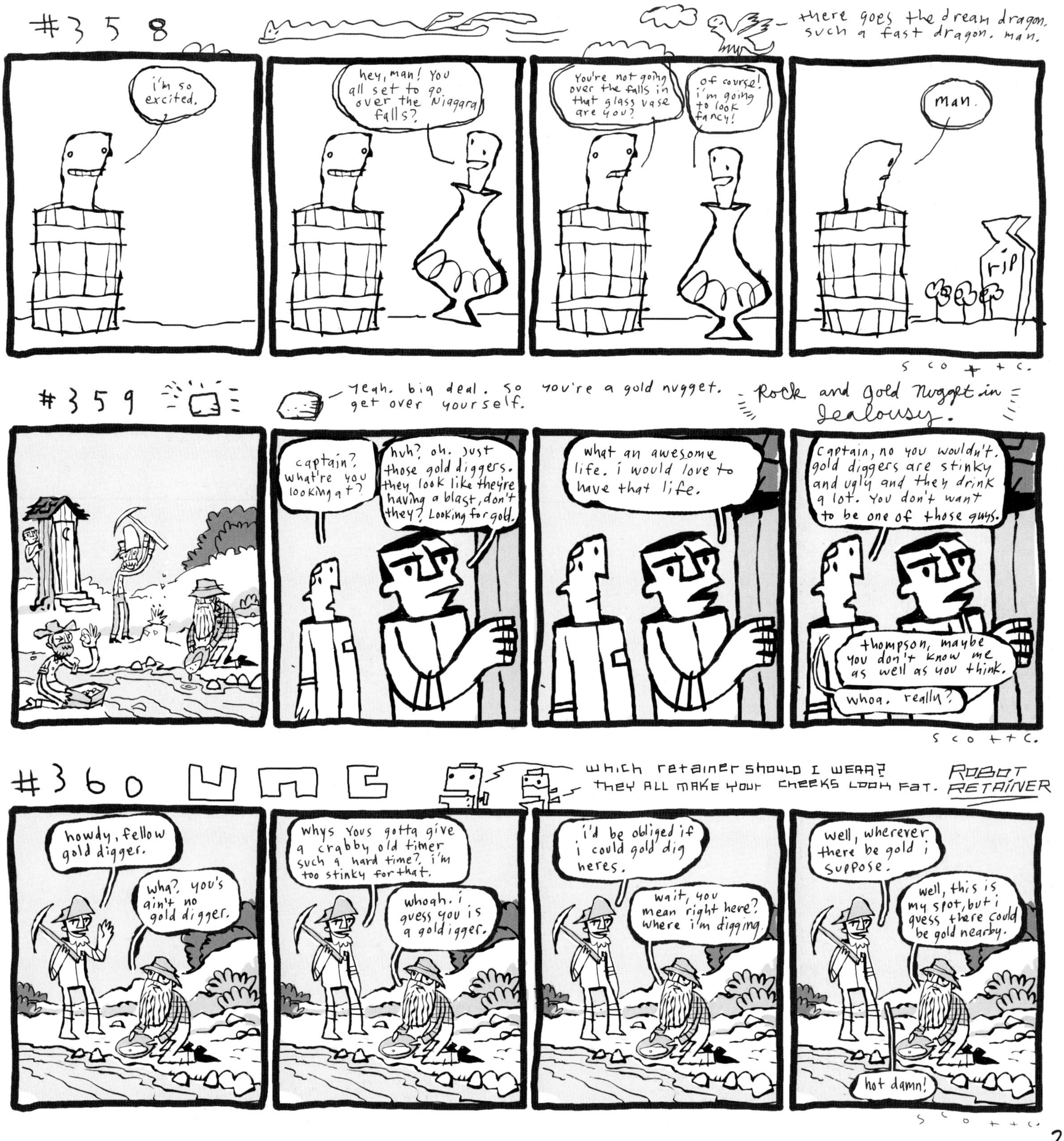
#358
there goes the dream dragon. such a fast dragon, man.
i'm so excited.
hey, man! You all set to go over the Niagara falls?
You're not going over the falls in that glass vase are you?
of course! i'm going to look fancy!
man.
rip
scott c.
#359
yeah. big deal. so you're a gold nugget. get over yourself.
Rock and Gold Nugget in Jealousy.
captain? what're you looking at?
huh? oh. just those gold diggers. they look like they're having a blast, don't they? Looking for gold.
what an awesome life. i would love to have that life.
captain, no you wouldn't. gold diggers are stinky and ugly and they drink a lot. You don't want to be one of those guys.
thompson, maybe you don't know me as well as you think.
whoa. really?
scott c.
#360
WHICH RETAINER SHOULD I WEAR? THEY ALL MAKE YOUR CHEEKS LOOK FAT.
ROBOT RETAINER
howdy, fellow gold digger.
wha? you's ain't no gold digger.
whys yous gotta give a crabby old timer such a hard time? i'm too stinky for that.
whoah. i guess you is a goldigger.
i'd be obliged if i could gold dig heres.
wait, you mean right here? where i'm digging.
well, wherever there be gold i suppose.
well, this is my spot, but i guess there could be gold nearby.
hot damn!
scott c.

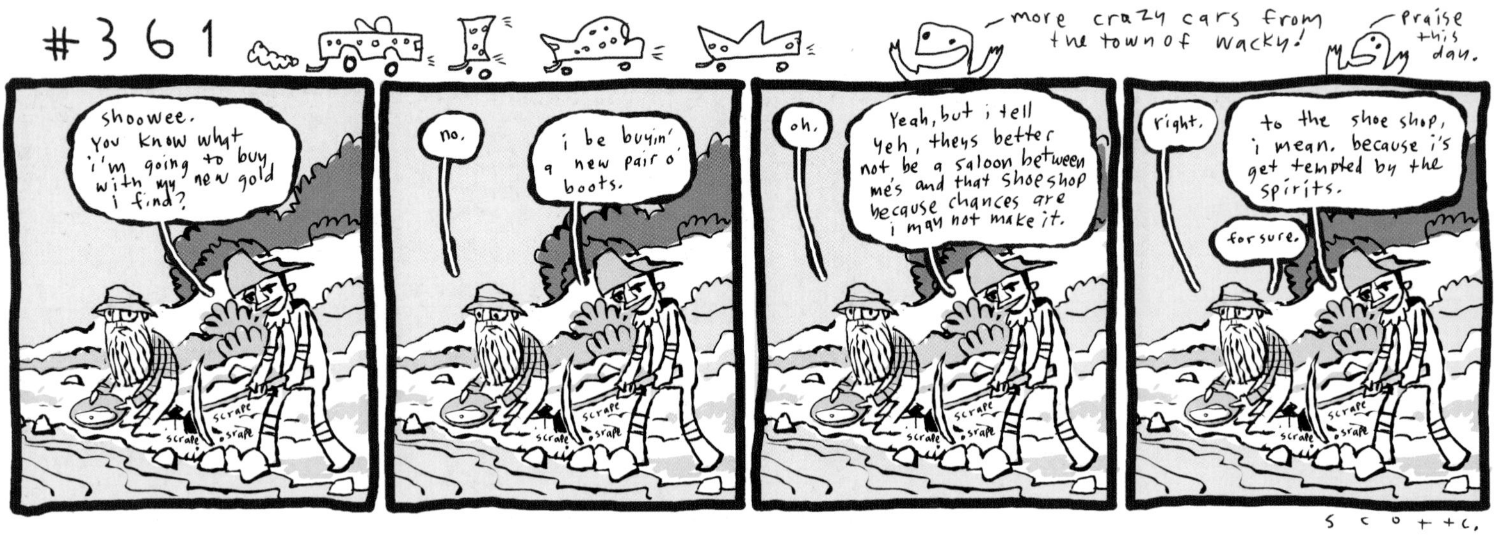
#361
more crazy cars from the town of wacky!
Praise this day.
shoowee. You know what i'm going to buy with my new gold i find?
no.
i be buyin' a new pair o' boots.
scrape scrape scrape
oh.
Yeah, but i tell yeh, theys better not be a saloon between me's and that shoeshop because chances are i may not make it.
right.
to the shoe shop, i mean. because i's get tempted by the spirits.
for sure.
scott c.

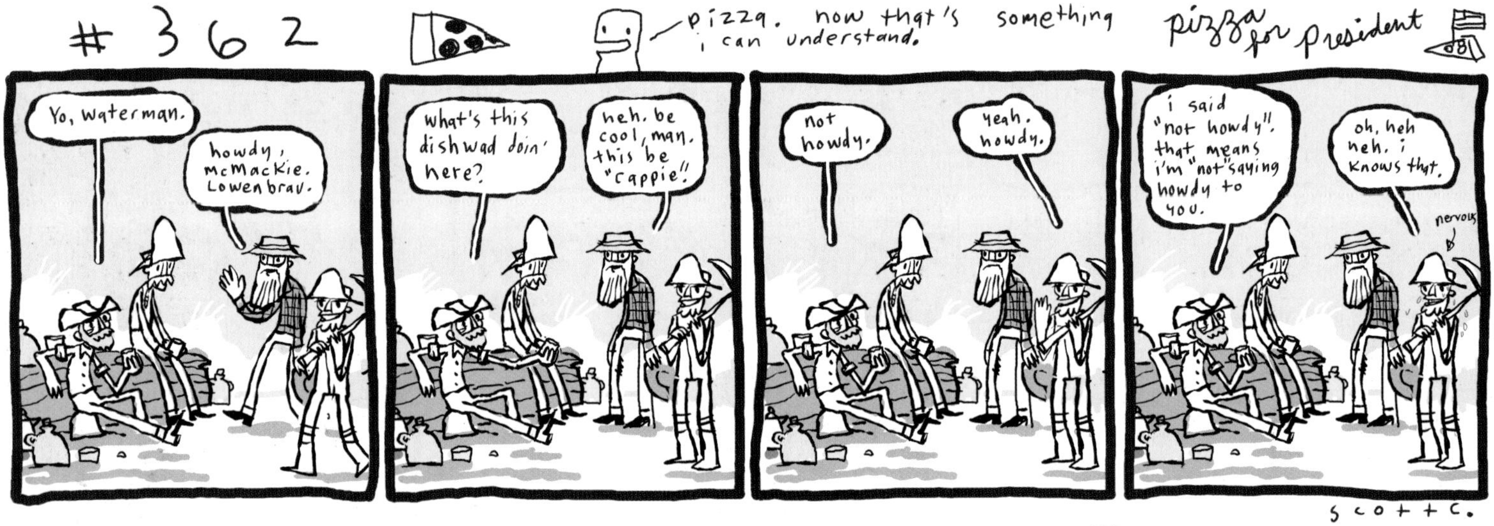
#362
pizza. now that's something i can understand.
pizza for president
Yo, waterman.
howdy, McMackie. Lowenbrau.
what's this dishwad doin' here?
heh. be cool, man. this be "cappie".
not howdy.
yeah. howdy.
i said "not howdy". that means i'm "not" saying howdy to you.
oh, heh heh. i knows that.
nervous
scott c.

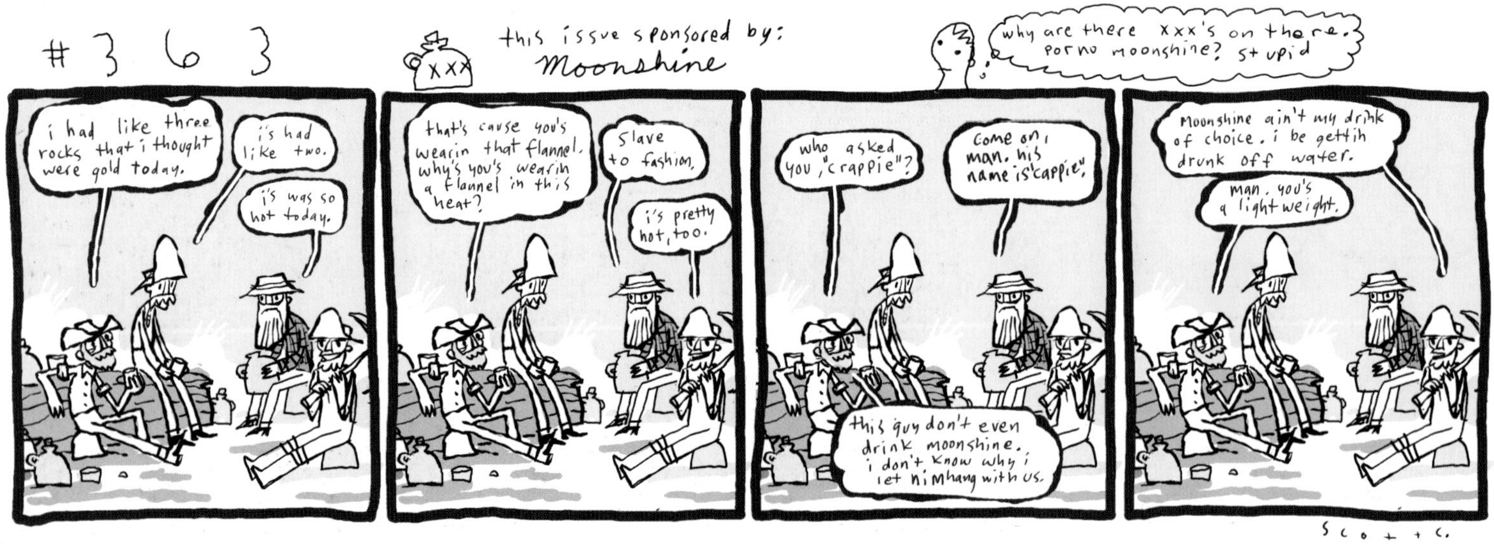
#363
this issue sponsored by: Moonshine
XXX
why are there XXX's on there. porno moonshine? stupid
i had like three rocks that i thought were gold today.
i's had like two.
i's was so hot today.
that's cause you's wearin that flannel. why's you's wearin a flannel in this heat?
Slave to fashion.
i's pretty hot, too.
who asked you, "crappie"?
Come on, man. his name is "cappie".
this guy don't even drink moonshine. i don't know why i let him hang with us.
Moonshine ain't my drink of choice. i be gettin drunk off water.
man. you's a lightweight.
scott c.

#364

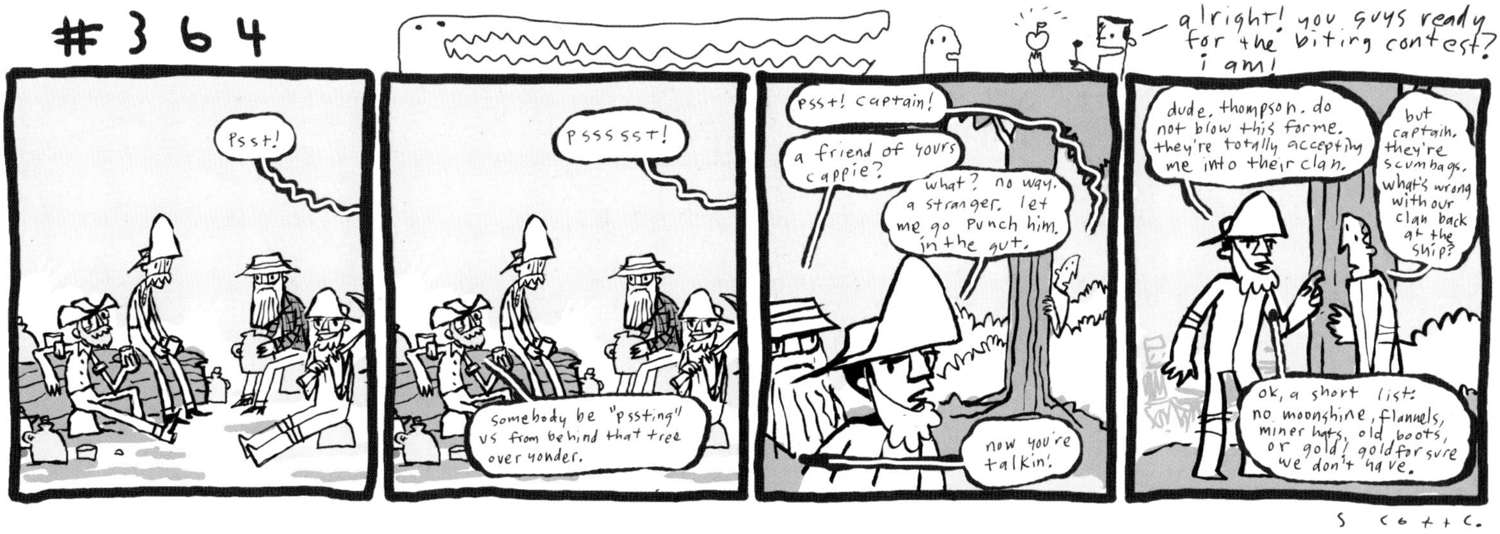

- alright! you guys ready for the biting contest?
i am!
psst!
pssssst!
somebody be "pssting" us from behind that tree over yonder.
psst! captain!
a friend of yours cappie?
what? no way. a stranger. let me go punch him in the gut.
now you're talkin'.
dude, thompson. do not blow this for me. they're totally accepting me into their clan.
but captain, they're scumbags. what's wrong with our clan back at the ship?
ok, a short list: no moonshine, flannels, miner hats, old boots, or gold! gold for sure we don't have.
scott c.

#365

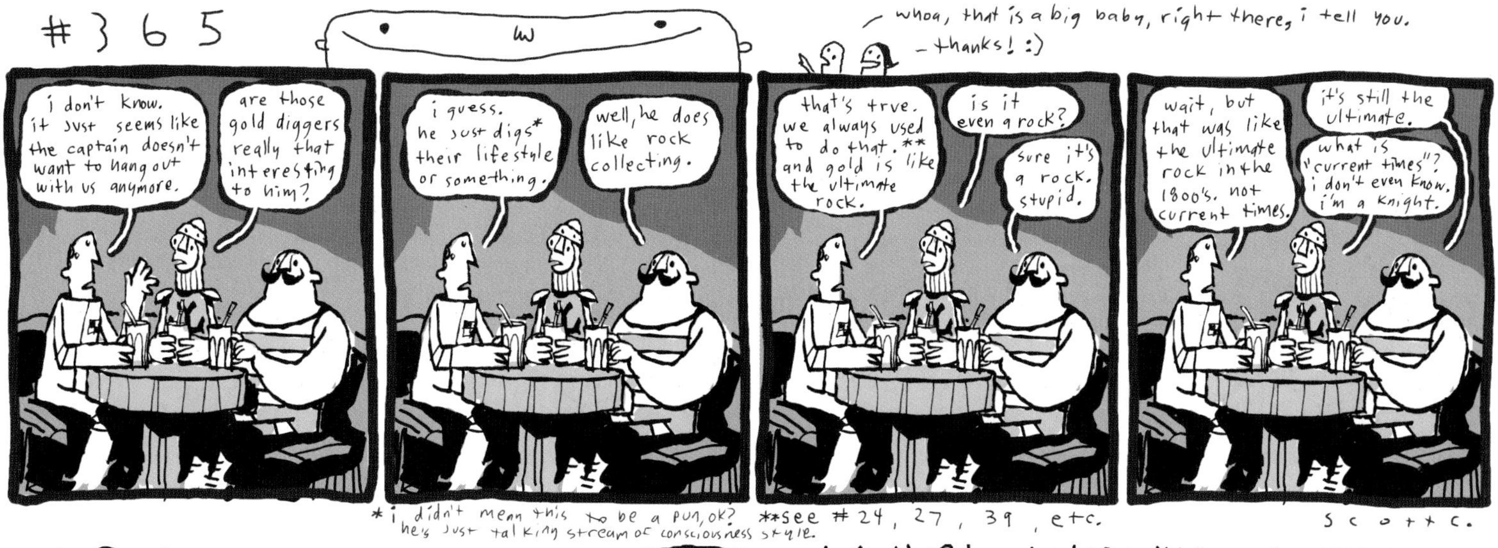

- whoa, that is a big baby, right there, i tell you.
- thanks! :)
i don't know. it just seems like the captain doesn't want to hang out with us anymore.
are those gold diggers really that interesting to him?
i guess. he just digs* their lifestyle or something.
well, he does like rock collecting.
that's true. we always used to do that.** and gold is like the ultimate rock.
is it even a rock?
sure it's a rock, stupid.
wait, but that was like the ultimate rock in the 1800's, not current times.
it's still the ultimate.
what is "current times"? i don't even know. i'm a knight.
*i didn't mean this to be a pun, ok? he's just talking stream of consciousness style.
**see #24, 27, 39, etc.
scott c.

#366

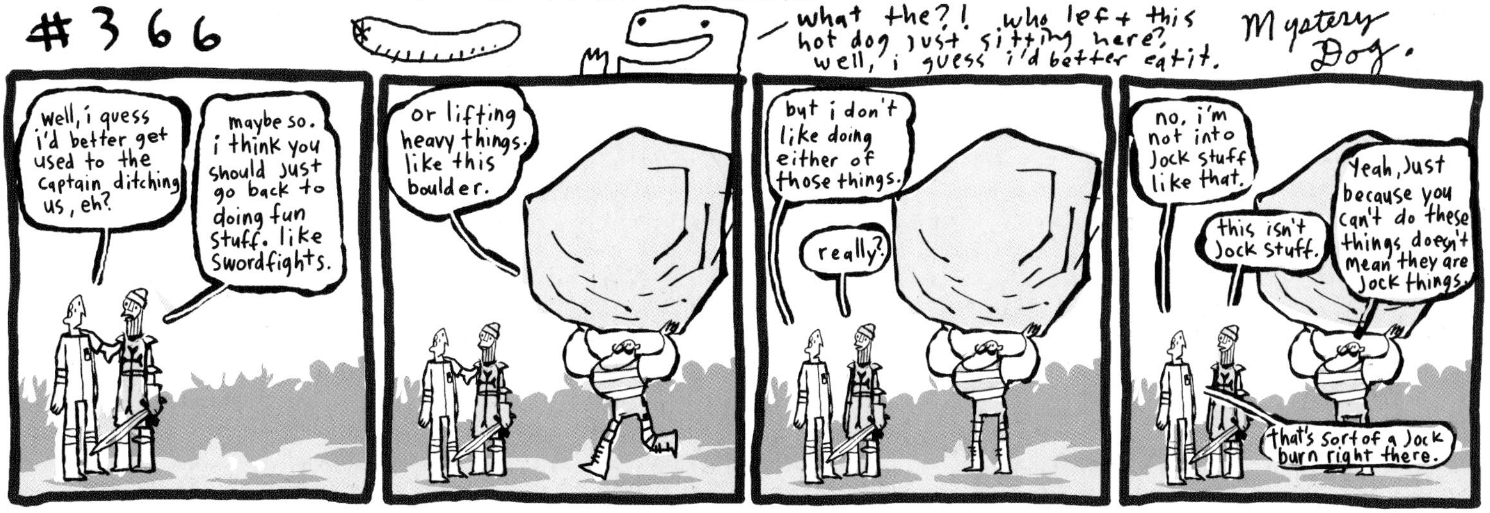

- what the?! who left this hot dog just sitting here? well, i guess i'd better eat it.
Mystery Dog.
well, i guess i'd better get used to the captain ditching us, eh?
maybe so. i think you should just go back to doing fun stuff. like swordfights.
or lifting heavy things. like this boulder.
but i don't like doing either of those things.
really?
no, i'm not into jock stuff like that.
this isn't jock stuff.
yeah, just because you can't do these things doesn't mean they are jock things.
that's sort of a jock burn right there.

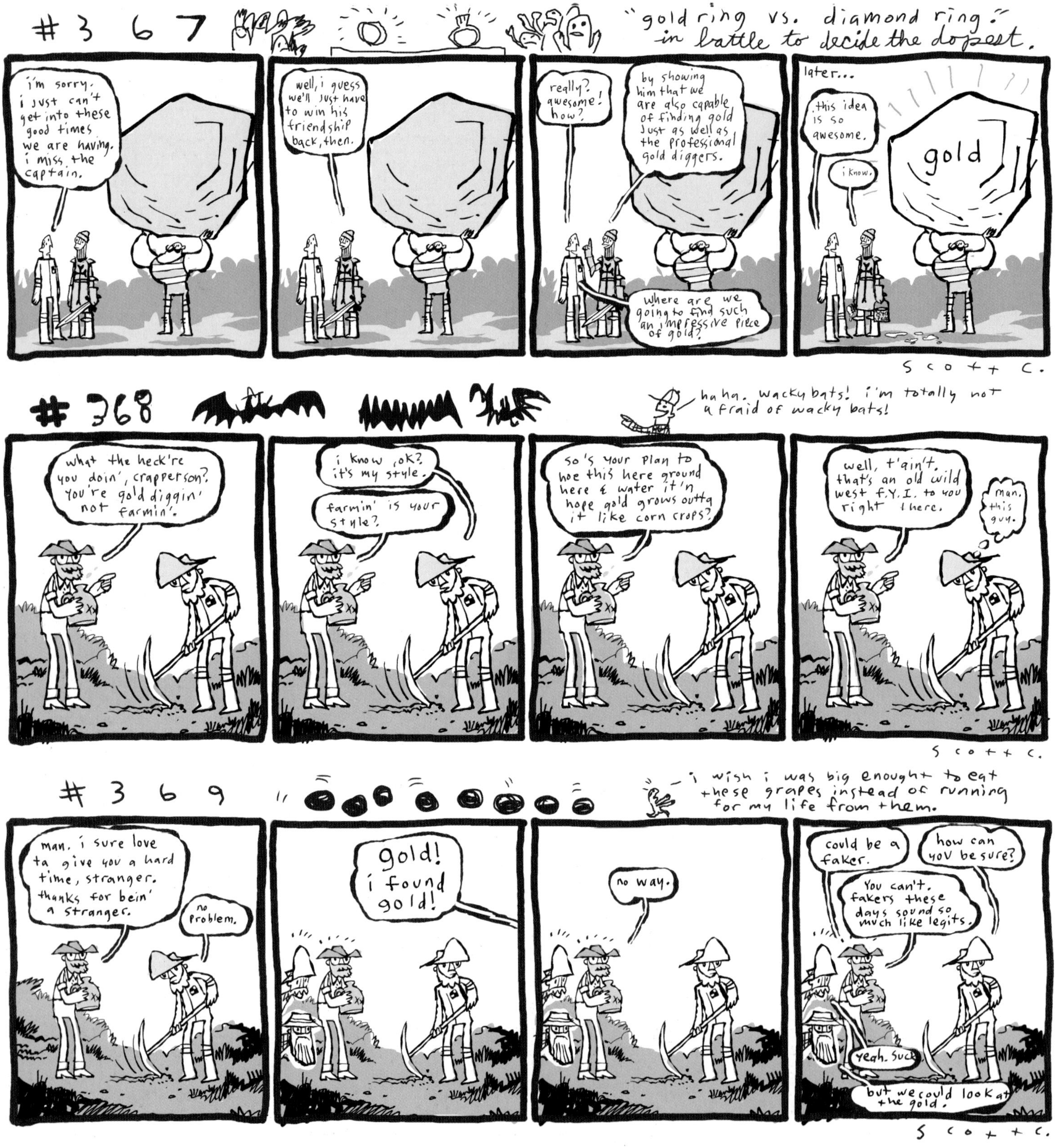
#367
"gold ring vs. diamond ring:" in battle to decide the dopest.
i'm sorry. i just can't get into these good times we are having. i miss the captain.
well, i guess we'll just have to win his friendship back, then.
really? awesome! how?
by showing him that we are also capable of finding gold just as well as the professional gold diggers.
where are we going to find such an impressive piece of gold?
later...
this idea is so awesome.
i know.
gold
scott c.
#368
haha. wacky bats! i'm totally not afraid of wacky bats!
what the heck're you doin', crapperson? you're gold diggin' not farmin'.
i know, ok? it's my style.
farmin' is your style?
so's your plan to hoe this here ground here & water it'n hope gold grows outta it like corn crops?
well, t'ain't. that's an old wild west f.y.i. to you right there.
man, this guy.
scott c.
#369
i wish i was big enought to eat these grapes instead of running for my life from them.
man, i sure love ta give you a hard time, stranger. thanks for bein' a stranger.
no problem.
gold! i found gold!
no way.
could be a faker.
how can you be sure?
you can't. fakers these days sound so much like legits.
yeah. suck.
but we could look at the gold.
scott c.

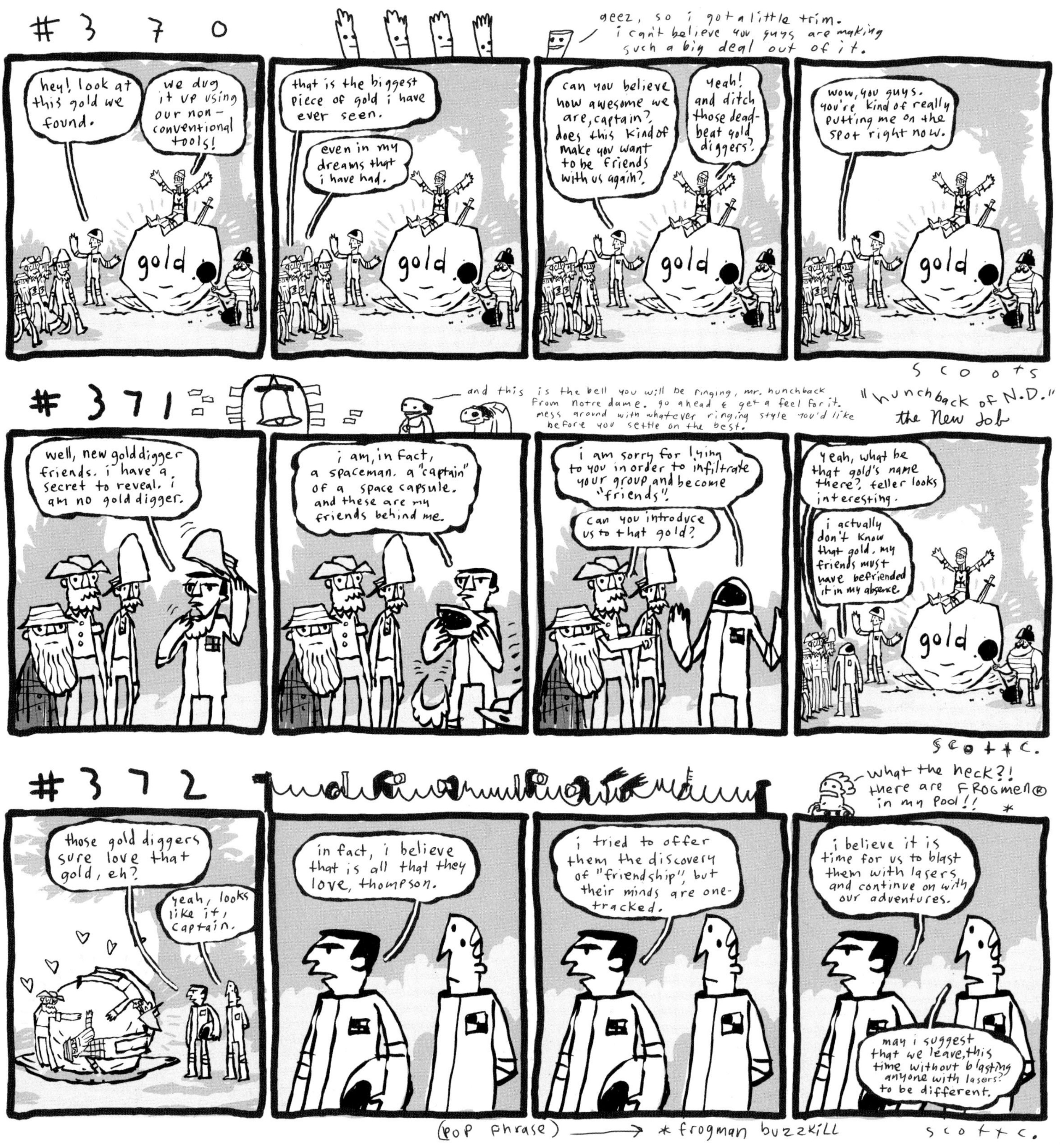
#370
geez, so i got a little trim. i can't believe you guys are making such a big deal out of it.
hey! look at this gold we found.
we dug it up using our non-conventional tools!
gold
that is the biggest piece of gold i have ever seen.
even in my dreams that i have had.
can you believe how awesome we are, captain? does this kind of make you want to be friends with us again?
yeah! and ditch those dead-beat gold diggers?
wow, you guys. you're kind of really putting me on the spot right now.
scoots
#371
and this is the bell you will be ringing, mr. hunchback from notre dame. go ahead & get a feel for it. mess around with whatever ringing style you'd like before you settle on the best.
"hunchback of N.D." the New Job
well, new gold digger friends. i have a secret to reveal. i am no gold digger.
i am, in fact, a spaceman. a "captain" of a space capsule. and these are my friends behind me.
i am sorry for lying to you in order to infiltrate your group and become "friends".
can you introduce us to that gold?
yeah, what be that gold's name there? feller looks interesting.
i actually don't know that gold. my friends must have befriended it in my absence.
scott c.
#372
what the heck?! there are FROGMEN® in my pool!! *
those gold diggers sure love that gold, eh?
yeah, looks like it, captain.
in fact, i believe that is all that they love, thompson.
i tried to offer them the discovery of "friendship", but their minds are one-tracked.
i believe it is time for us to blast them with lasers, and continue on with our adventures.
may i suggest that we leave, this time without blasting anyone with lasers? to be different.
(pop phrase) ⟶ * frogman buzzkill
scott c.

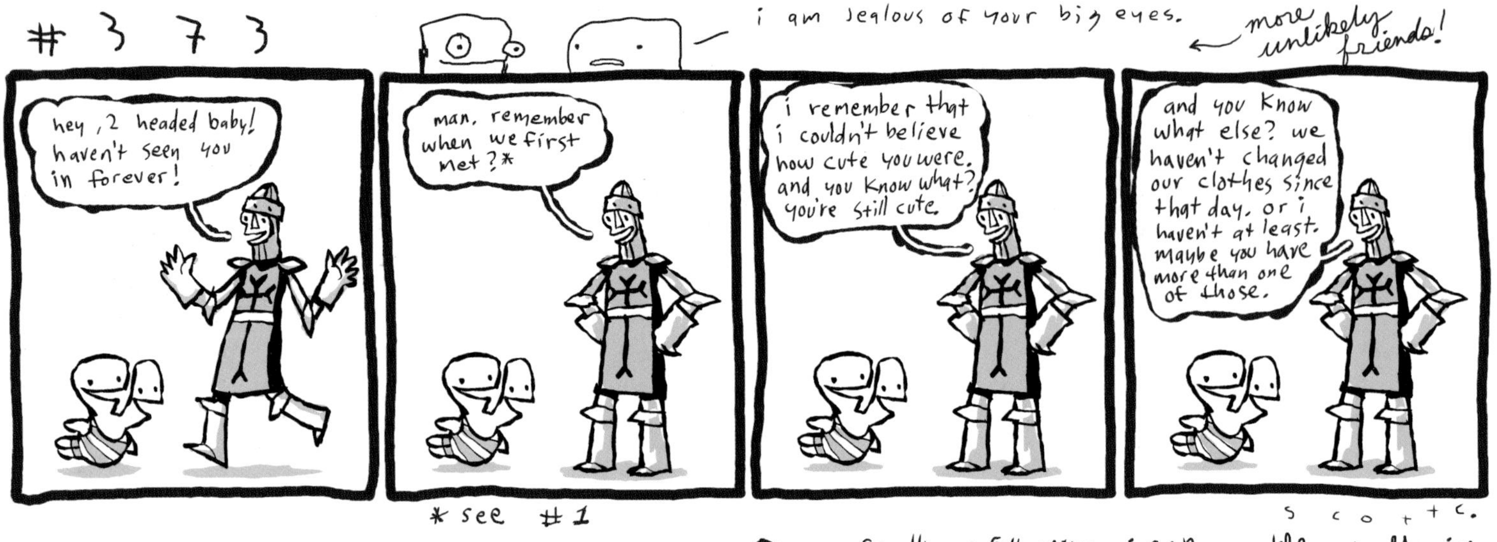
#373
i am jealous of your big eyes.
← more unlikely friends!
hey, 2 headed baby! haven't seen you in forever!
man, remember when we first met?*
i remember that i couldn't believe how cute you were. and you know what? you're still cute.
and you know what else? we haven't changed our clothes since that day. or i haven't at least. maybe you have more than one of those.
* see #1
scott c.

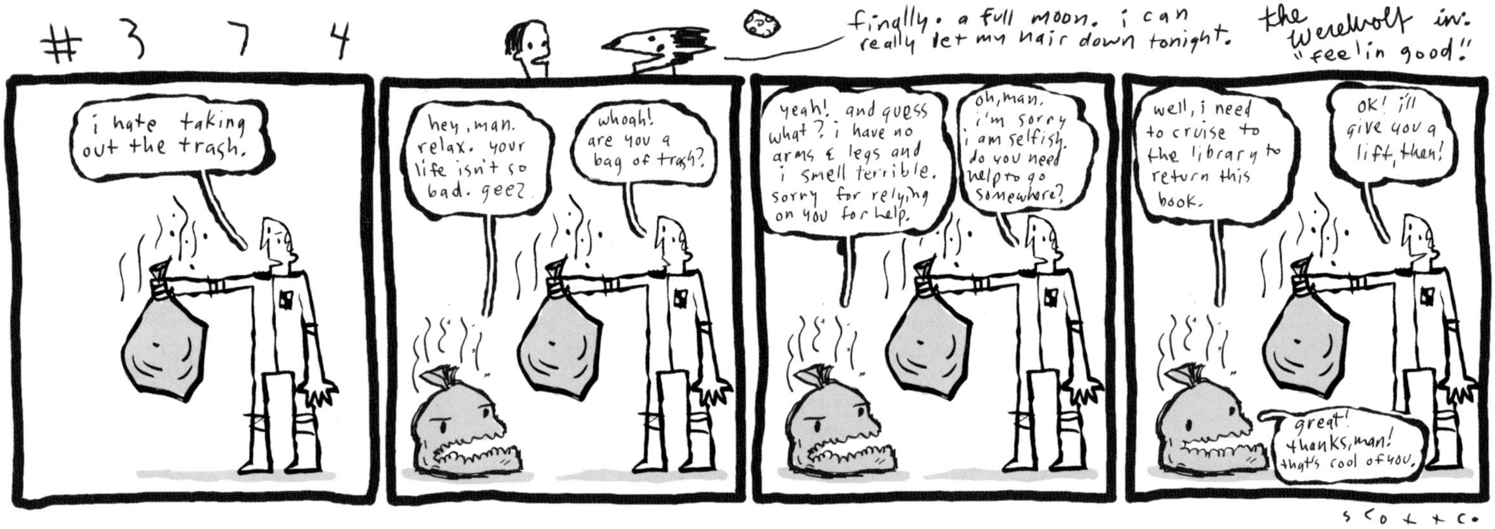
#374
finally. a full moon. i can really let my hair down tonight.
the werewolf in: "feel'in good!"
i hate taking out the trash.
hey, man. relax. your life isn't so bad. geez
whoah! are you a bag of trash?
yeah! and guess what? i have no arms & legs and i smell terrible. sorry for relying on you for help.
oh, man. i'm sorry i am selfish. do you need help to go somewhere?
well, i need to cruise to the library to return this book.
OK! i'll give you a lift, then!
great! thanks, man! that's cool of you.
scott c.

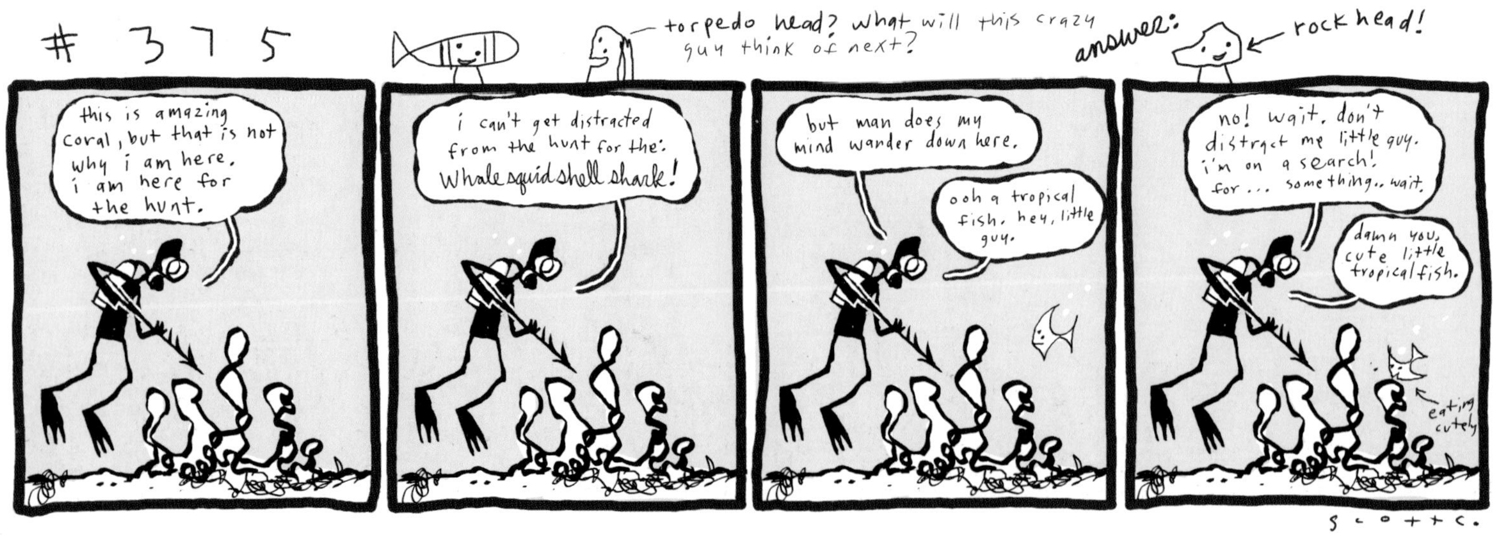
#375
torpedo head? what will this crazy guy think of next?
answer: rock head!
this is amazing coral, but that is not why i am here. i am here for the hunt.
i can't get distracted from the hunt for the: Whalesquidshellshark!
but man does my mind wander down here.
ooh a tropical fish. hey, little guy.
no! wait. don't distract me little guy. i'm on a search! for... something.. wait.
damn you, cute little tropical fish.
eating cutely
scott c.

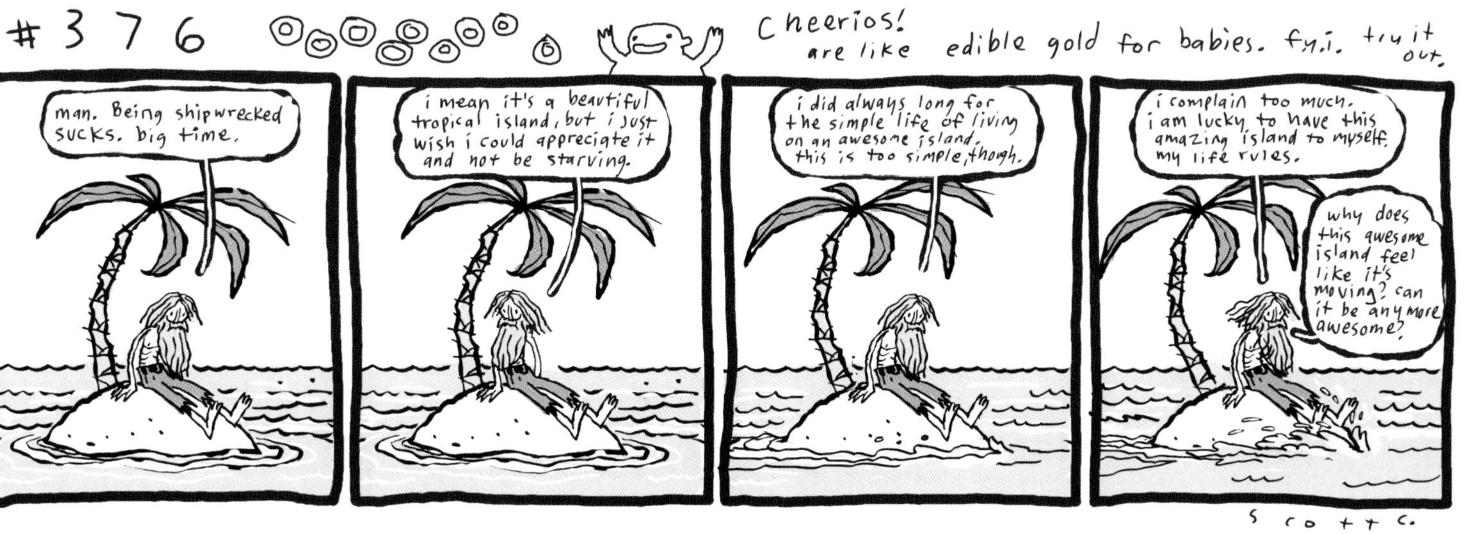
#376
Cheerios! are like edible gold for babies. f.y.i. try it out.
man. Being shipwrecked sucks. big time.
i mean it's a beautiful tropical island, but i just wish i could appreciate it and not be starving.
i did always long for the simple life of living on an awesome island. this is too simple, though.
i complain too much. i am lucky to have this amazing island to myself. my life rules.
why does this awesome island feel like it's moving? can it be any more awesome?
scott c.

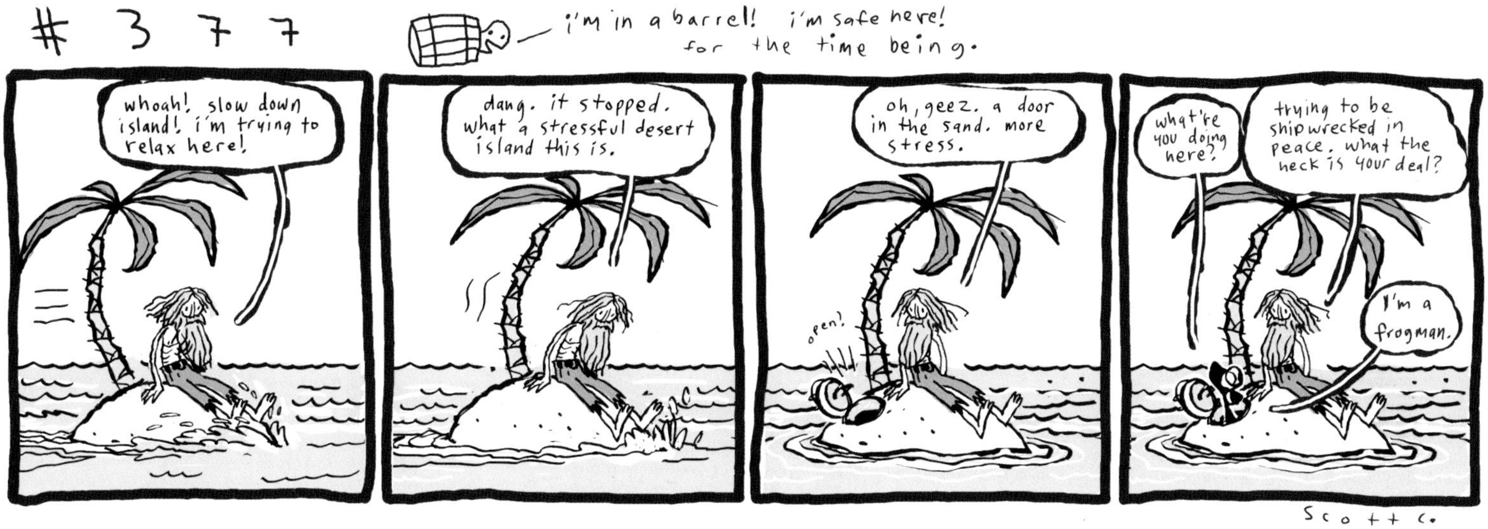
#377
i'm in a barrel! i'm safe here! for the time being.
whoah! slow down island! i'm trying to relax here!
dang. it stopped. what a stressful desert island this is.
oh, geez. a door in the sand. more stress.
open!
what're you doing here?
trying to be shipwrecked in peace. what the heck is your deal?
i'm a frogman.
scott c.

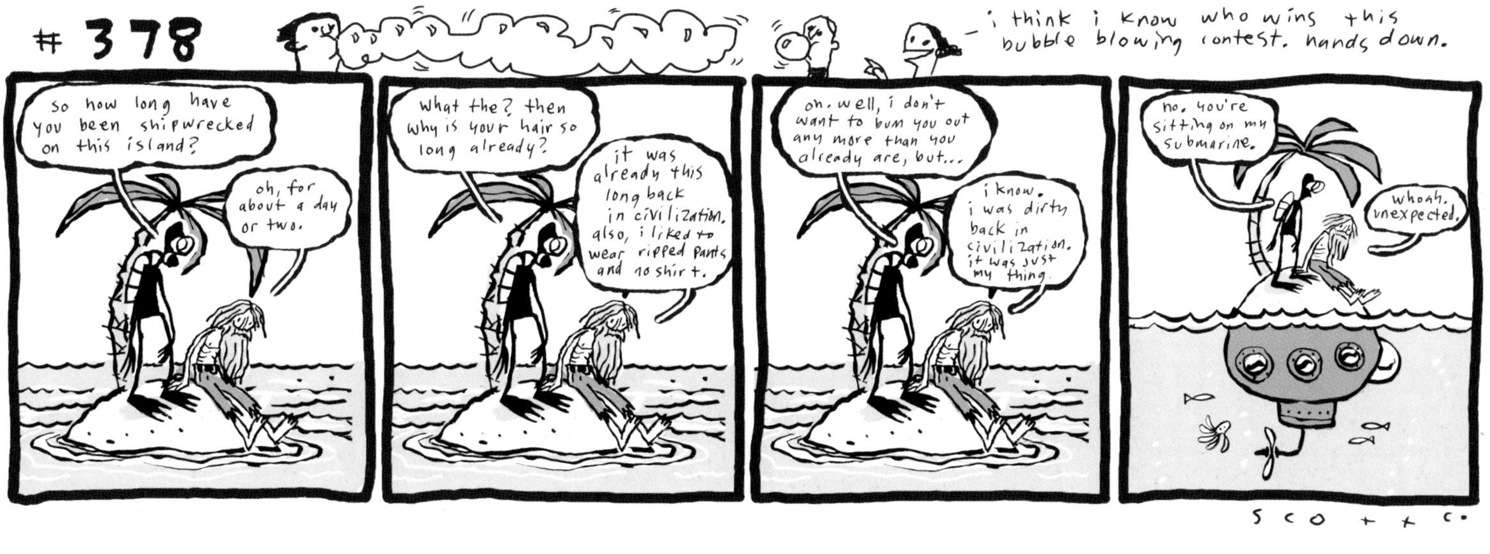
#378
i think i know who wins this bubble blowing contest. hands down.
so how long have you been shipwrecked on this island?
oh, for about a day or two.
what the? then why is your hair so long already?
it was already this long back in civilization. also, i liked to wear ripped pants and no shirt.
oh. well, i don't want to bum you out any more than you already are, but...
i know. i was dirty back in civilization. it was just my thing.
no. you're sitting on my submarine.
whoah. unexpected.
scott c.

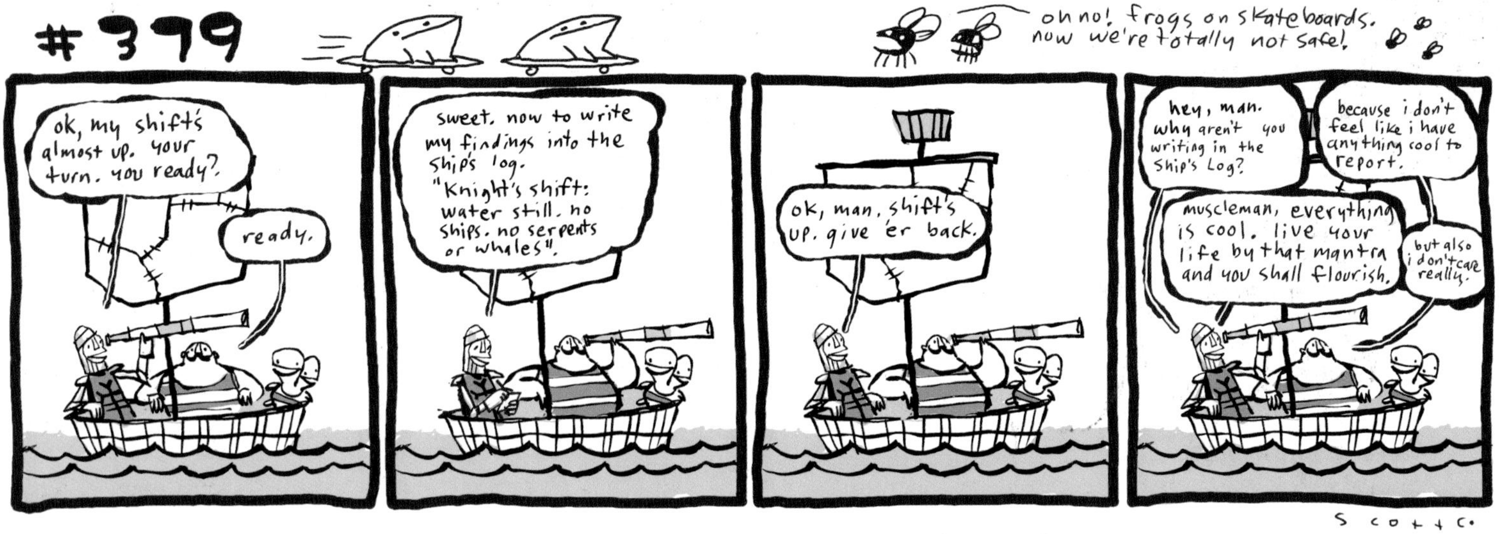
#379
oh no! frogs on skateboards. now we're totally not safe!
ok, my shift's almost up. your turn. you ready?
ready.
sweet. now to write my findings into the ship's log. "Knight's shift: water still. no ships. no serpents or whales".
ok, man, shift's up. give 'er back.
hey, man. why aren't you writing in the Ship's Log?
because i don't feel like i have anything cool to report.
muscleman, everything is cool. live your life by that mantra and you shall flourish.
but also i don't care really.
scott c.

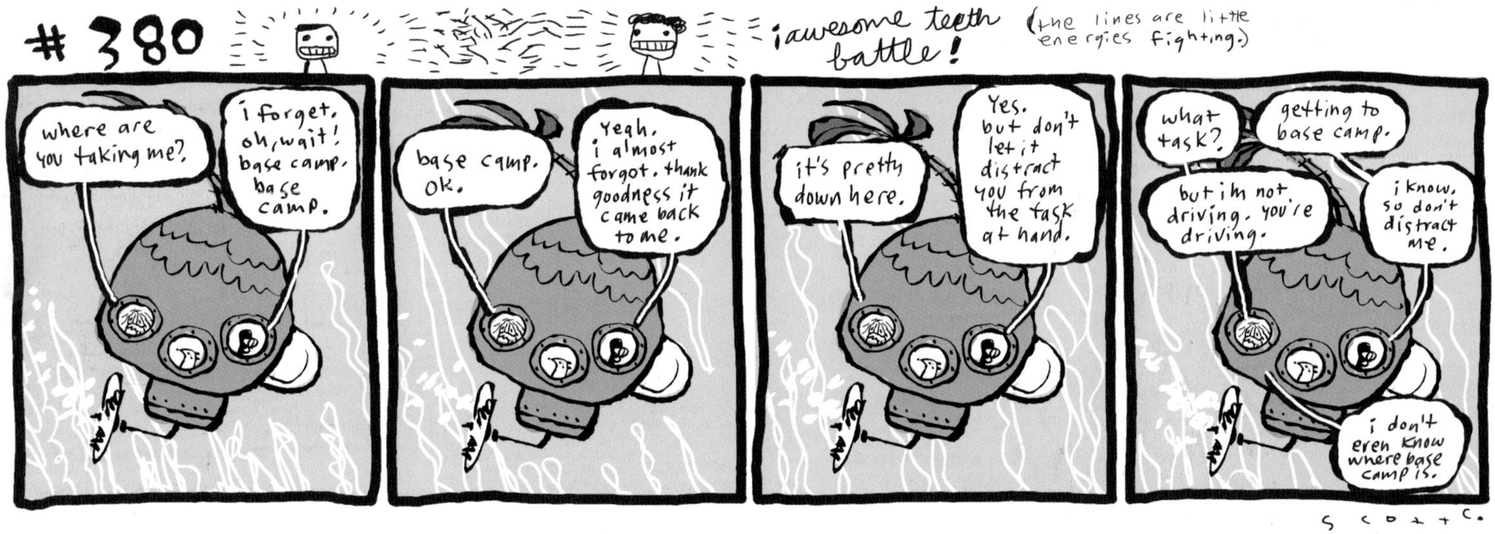
#380
¡awesome teeth battle!
(the lines are little energies fighting.)
where are you taking me?
i forget. oh, wait! base camp. base camp.
base camp. ok.
Yeah. i almost forgot. thank goodness it came back to me.
it's pretty down here.
Yes. but don't let it distract you from the task at hand.
what task?
getting to base camp.
but i'm not driving. you're driving.
i know. so don't distract me.
i don't even know where base camp is.
scott c.

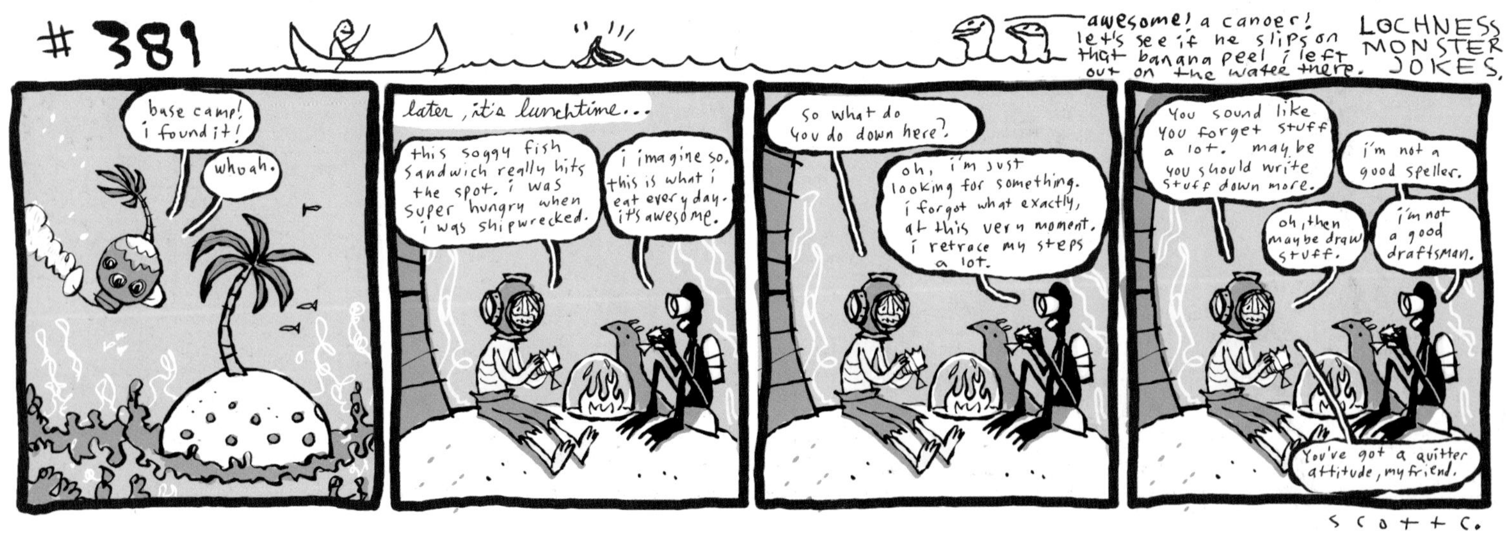
#381
awesome! a canoer! let's see if he slips on that banana peel i left out on the water there.
LOCHNESS MONSTER JOKES.
base camp! i found it!
whoah.
later, it's lunchtime...
this soggy fish sandwich really hits the spot. i was super hungry when i was shipwrecked.
i imagine so. this is what i eat every day. it's awesome.
so what do you do down here?
oh, i'm just looking for something. i forgot what exactly, at this very moment. i retrace my steps a lot.
You sound like you forget stuff a lot. maybe you should write stuff down more.
i'm not a good speller.
oh, then maybe draw stuff.
i'm not a good draftsman.
You've got a quitter attitude, my friend.
scott c.

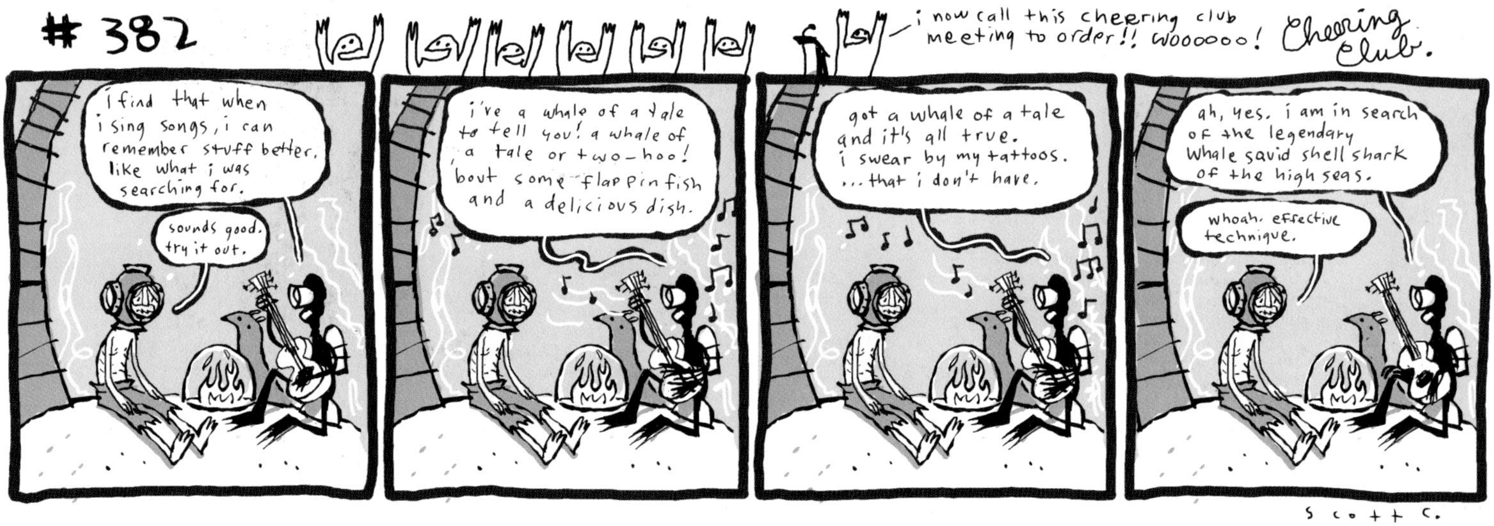
#382
i now call this cheering club meeting to order!! wooooooo!
Cheering Club.
i find that when i sing songs, i can remember stuff better. like what i was searching for.
sounds good. try it out.
i've a whale of a tale to tell you! a whale of a tale or two-hoo! bout some flappin fish and a delicious dish.
got a whale of a tale and it's all true. i swear by my tattoos. ...that i don't have.
ah, yes. i am in search of the legendary whale squid shell shark of the high seas.
whoah. effective technique.
scott c.

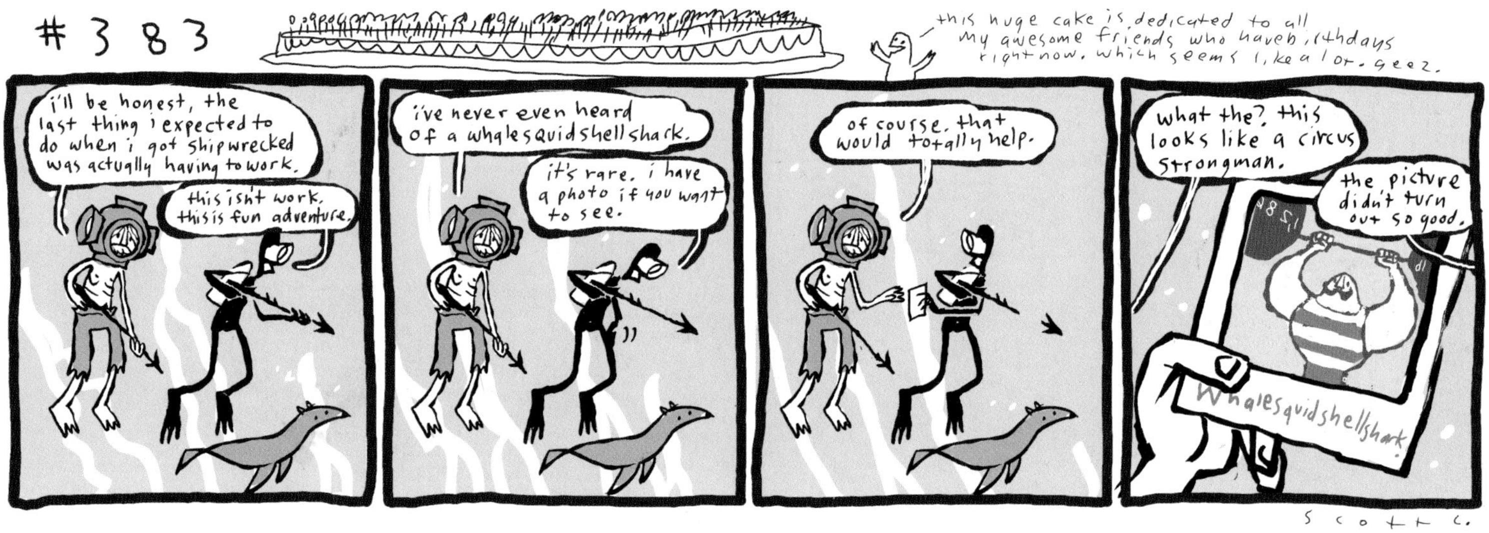
#383
this huge cake is dedicated to all my awesome friends who have birthdays right now. which seems like a lot. geez.
i'll be honest, the last thing i expected to do when i got shipwrecked was actually having to work.
this isn't work. this is fun adventure.
i've never even heard of a whalesquidshellshark.
it's rare. i have a photo if you want to see.
of course. that would totally help.
what the? this looks like a circus strongman.
the picture didn't turn out so good.
Whalesquidshellshark
scott c.

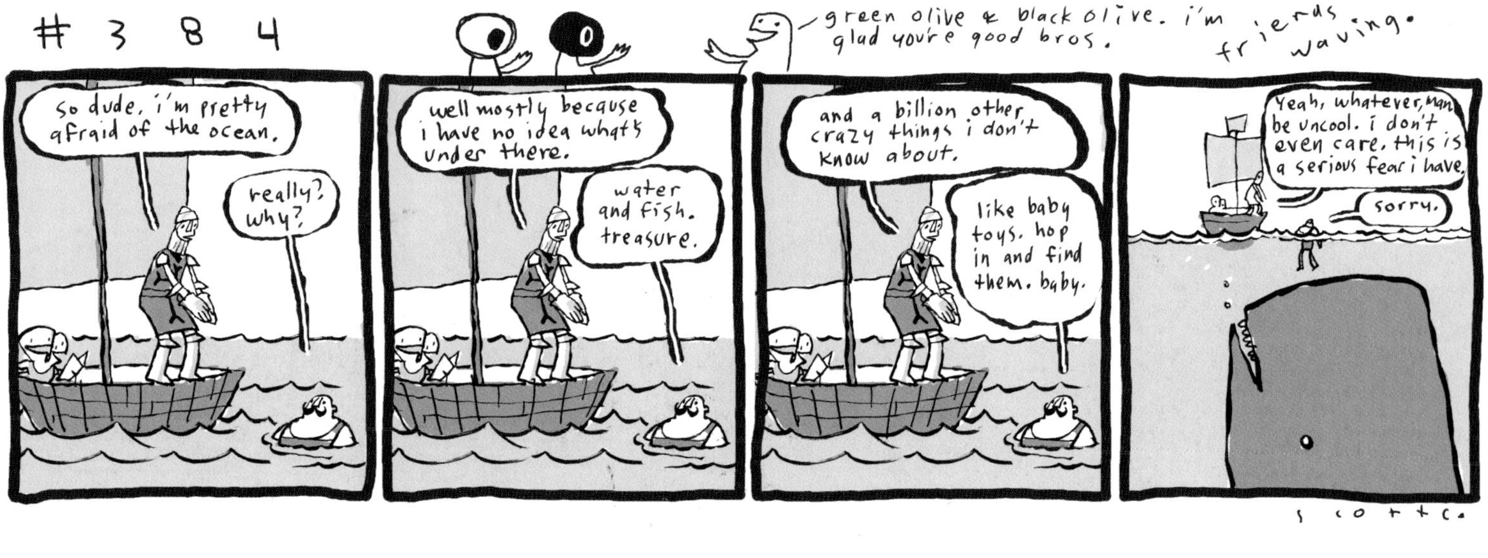
#384
green olive & black olive. i'm glad you're good bros.
friends waving.
so dude, i'm pretty afraid of the ocean.
really? why?
well mostly because i have no idea what's under there.
water and fish. treasure.
and a billion other crazy things i don't know about.
like baby toys. hop in and find them. baby.
Yeah, whatever, man be uncool. i don't even care. this is a serious fear i have.
sorry.
scott c.

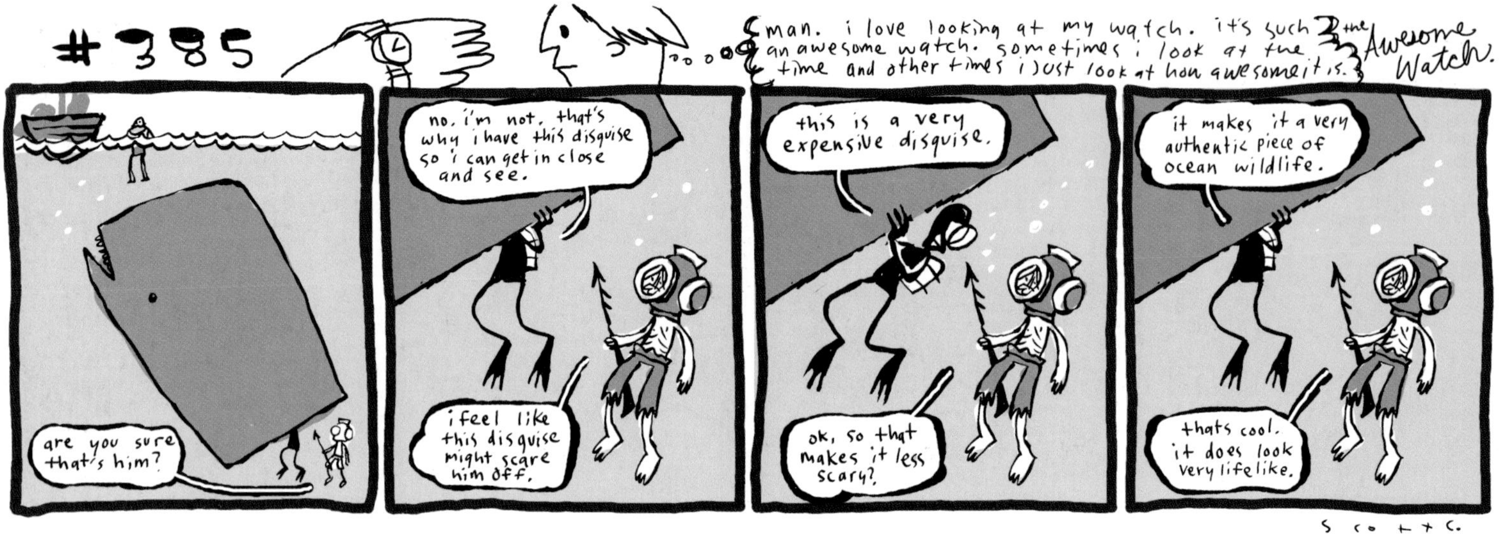
#385
man. i love looking at my watch. it's such an awesome watch. sometimes i look at the time and other times i just look at how awesome it is.
the Awesome Watch.
are you sure that's him?
no. i'm not. that's why i have this disguise so i can get in close and see.
i feel like this disguise might scare him off.
this is a very expensive disguise.
ok, so that makes it less scary?
it makes it a very authentic piece of ocean wildlife.
thats cool. it does look very lifelike.
scott c.

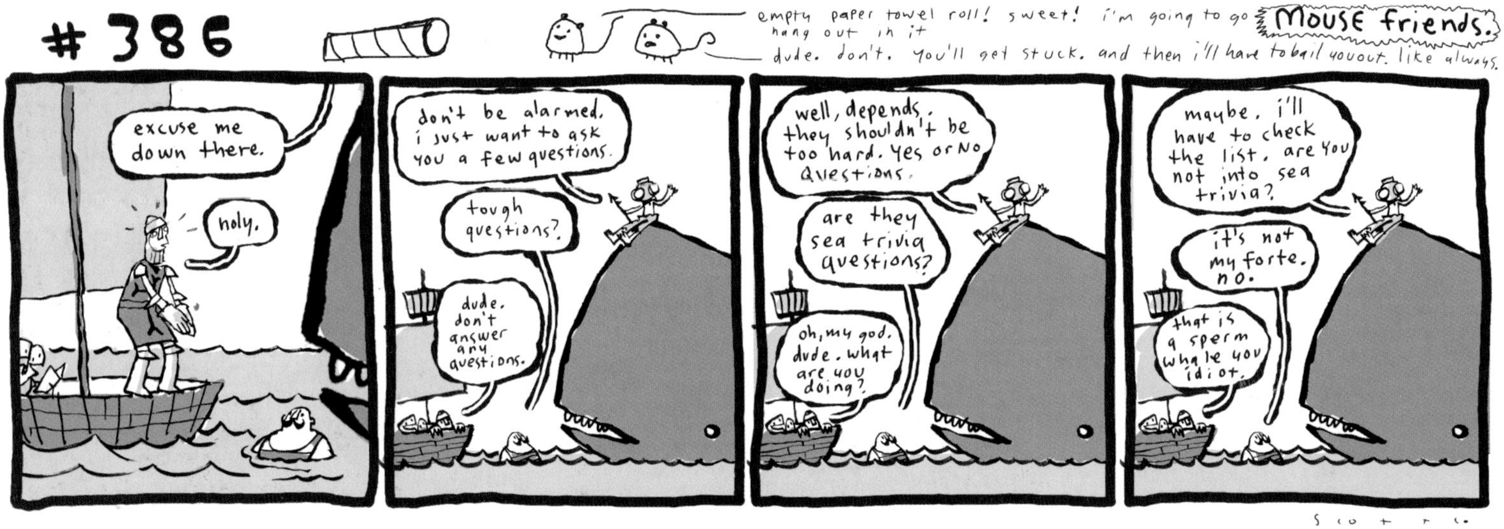
#386
empty paper towel roll! sweet! i'm going to go hang out in it
dude. don't. you'll get stuck. and then i'll have to bail you out. like always.
MOUSE friends.
excuse me down there.
holy.
don't be alarmed. i just want to ask you a few questions.
tough questions?
dude. don't answer any questions.
well, depends. they shouldn't be too hard. yes or no questions.
are they sea trivia questions?
oh, my god. dude. what are you doing?
maybe. i'll have to check the list. are you not into sea trivia?
it's not my forte. no.
that is a sperm whale you idiot.
scott c.

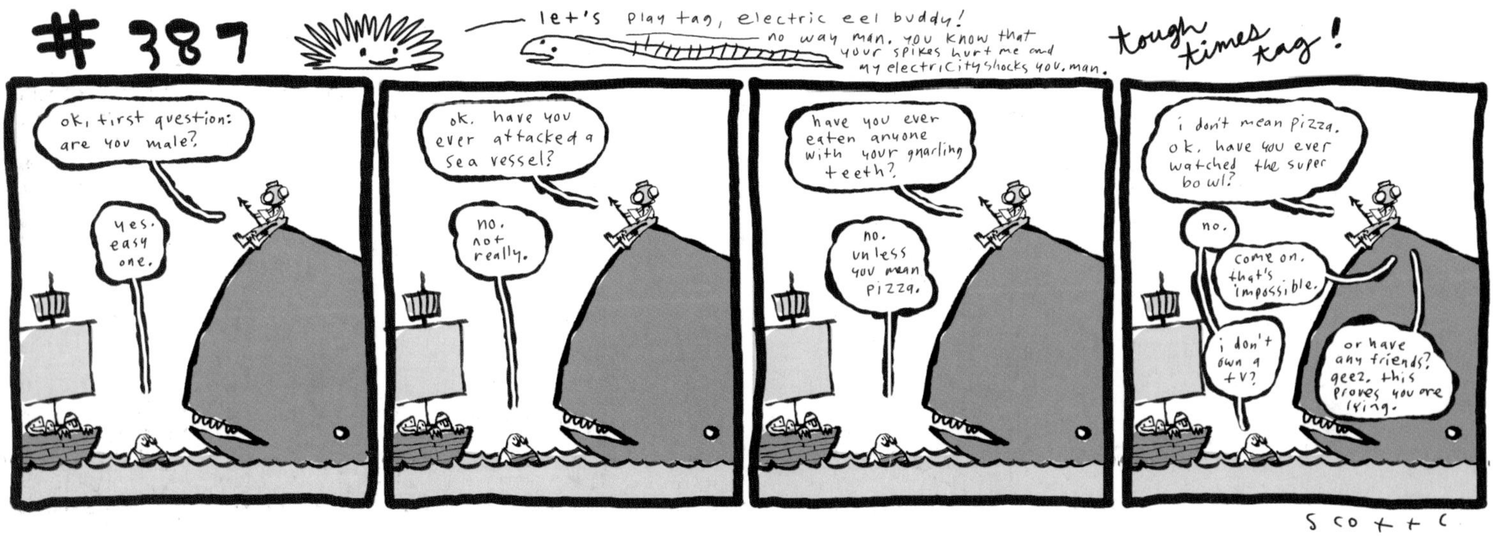
#387
let's play tag, electric eel buddy!
no way man. you know that your spikes hurt me and my electricity shocks you, man.
tough times tag!
ok, first question: are you male?
yes. easy one.
ok. have you ever attacked a sea vessel?
no. not really.
have you ever eaten anyone with your gnarling teeth?
no. unless you mean pizza.
i don't mean pizza. ok. have you ever watched the super bowl?
no.
come on. that's impossible.
i don't own a tv?
or have any friends? geez. this proves you are lying.
scott c

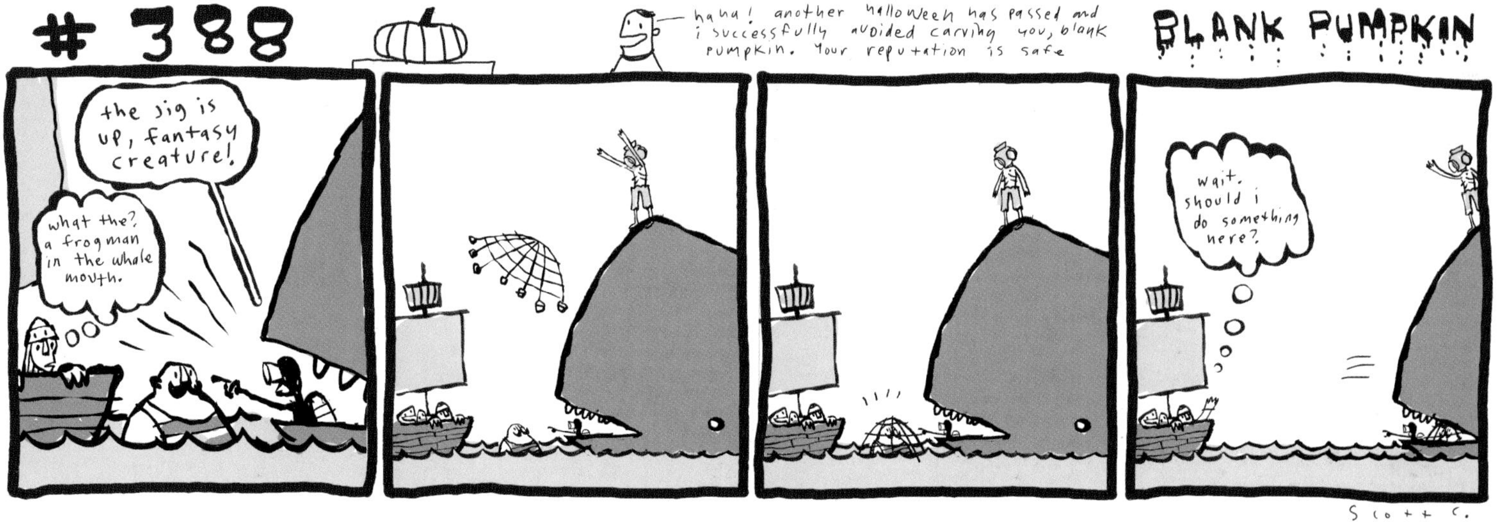
#388
haha! another halloween has passed and i successfully avoided carving you, blank pumpkin. your reputation is safe
BLANK PUMPKIN
the jig is up, fantasy creature!
what the?, a frogman in the whale mouth.
wait. should i do something here?.
scott c.

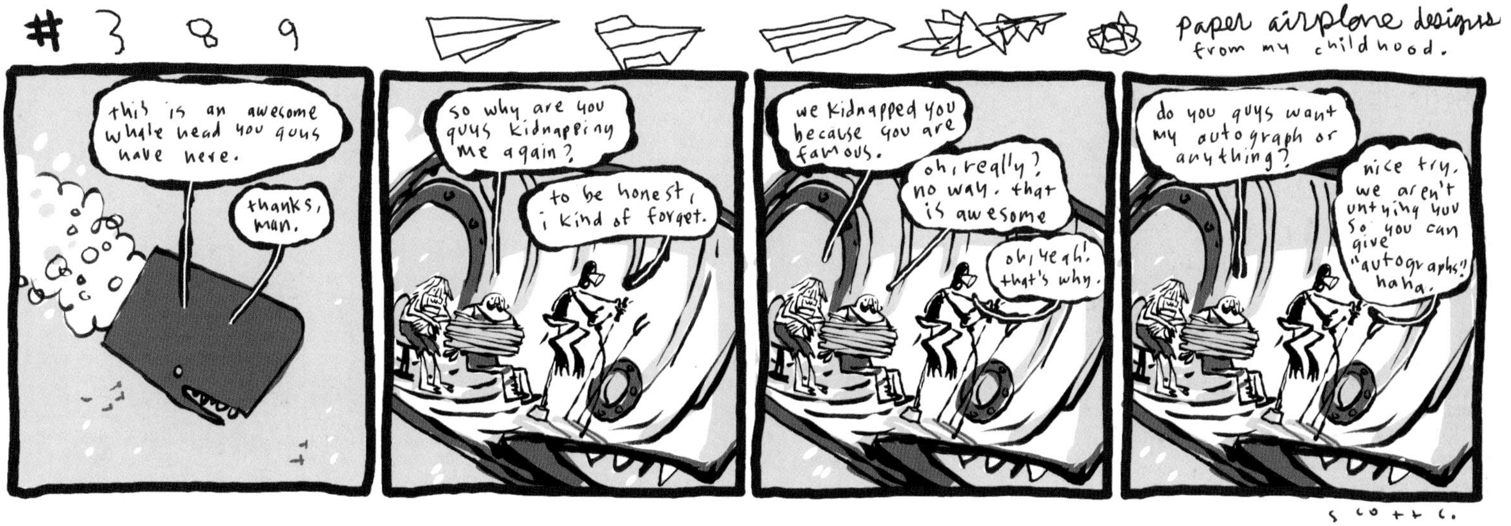
#389
paper airplane designs from my childhood.
this is an awesome whale head you guys have here.
thanks, man.
so why are you guys kidnapping me again?
to be honest, i kind of forget.
we kidnapped you because you are famous.
oh, really? no way. that is awesome
oh, yeah! that's why.
do you guys want my autograph or anything?
nice try. we aren't untying you so you can give "autographs!" haha.
scott c.

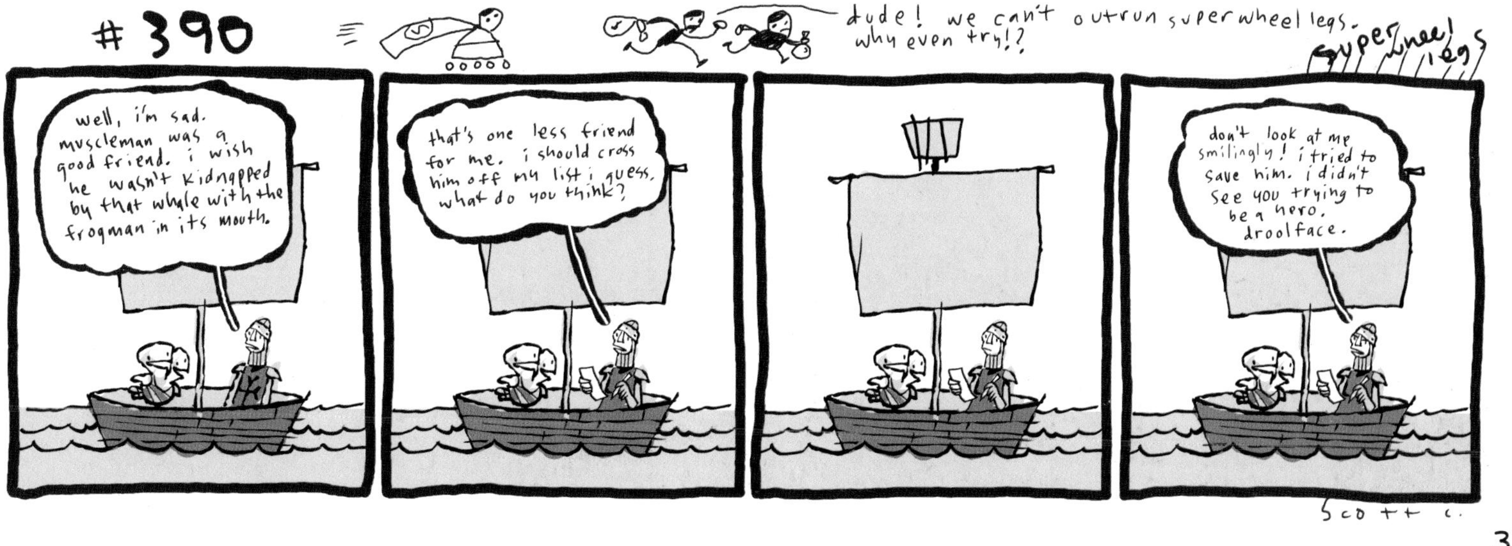
#390
dude! we can't outrun superwheel legs. why even try!?
super wheel legs
well, i'm sad. muscleman was a good friend. i wish he wasn't kidnapped by that whale with the frogman in its mouth.
that's one less friend for me. i should cross him off my list i guess, what do you think?
don't look at me smilingly! i tried to save him. i didn't see you trying to be a hero, droolface.
scott c.

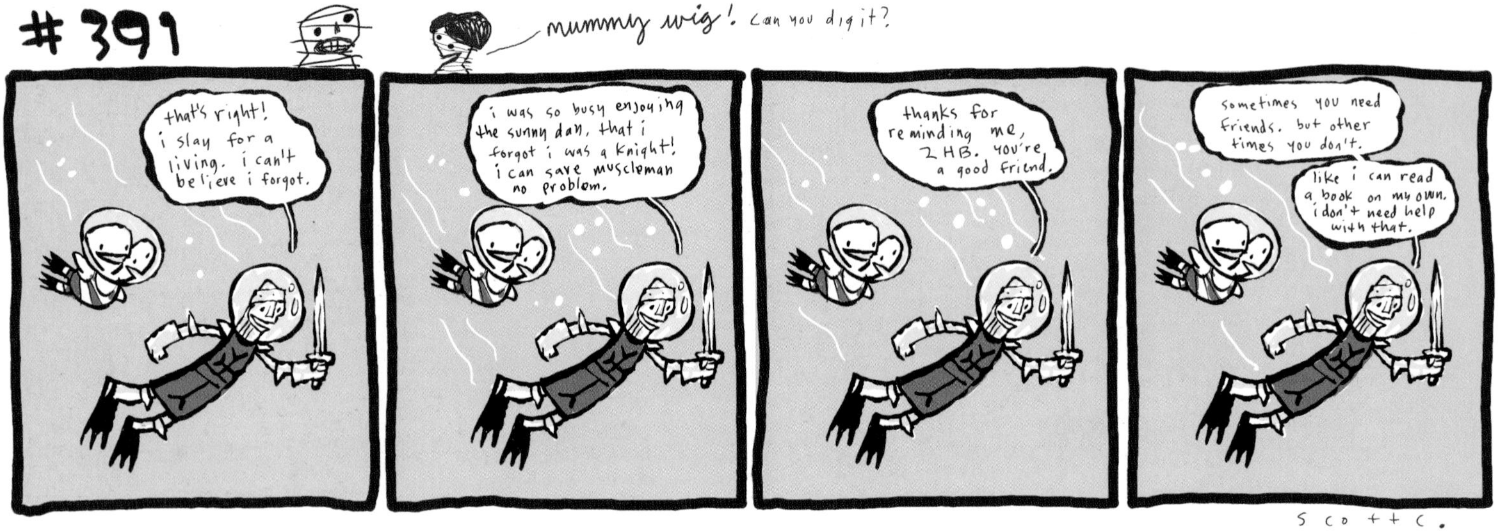
#391
mummy wig! can you dig it?
that's right! i slay for a living. i can't believe i forgot.
i was so busy enjoying the sunny day, that i forgot i was a knight! i can save muscleman no problem.
thanks for reminding me, 2HB. you're a good friend.
sometimes you need friends. but other times you don't.
like i can read a book on my own. i don't need help with that.
scott c.

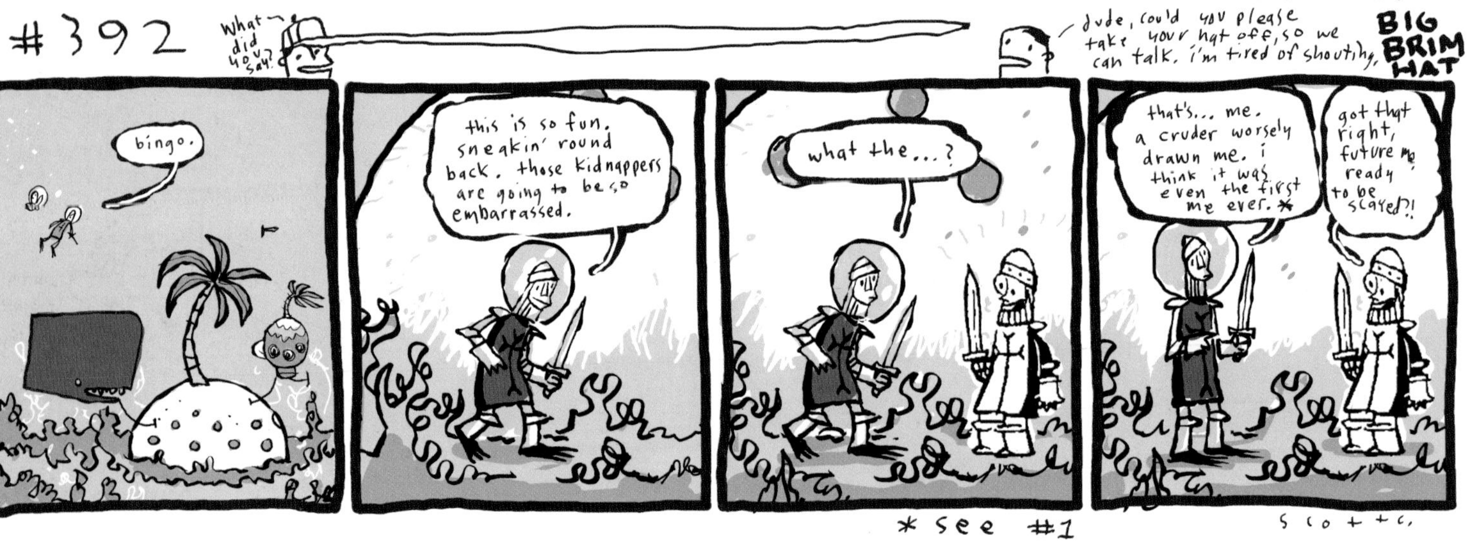
#392
what did you say?
dude, could you please take your hat off, so we can talk. i'm tired of shouting.
BIG BRIM HAT
bingo.
this is so fun. sneakin' round back. those kidnappers are going to be so embarrassed.
what the...?
that's... me. a cruder worsely drawn me. i think it was even the first me ever. *
got that right, future me. ready to be scared?!
* see #1
scott c.

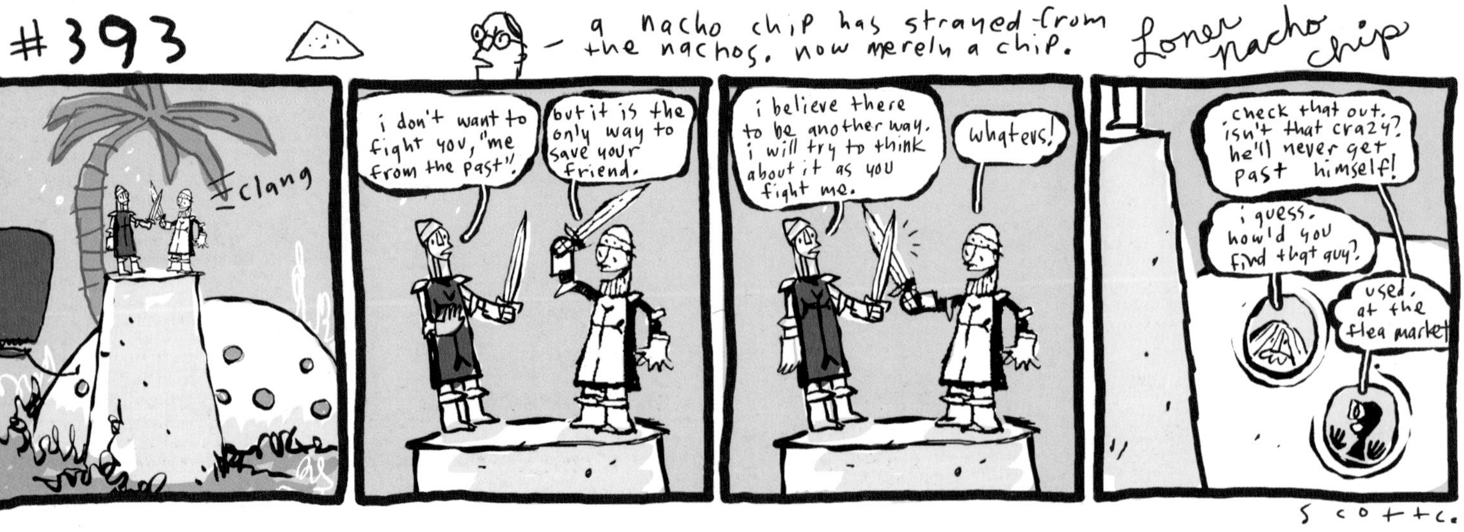
#393
a nacho chip has strayed from the nachos. now merely a chip.
Loner nacho chip
clang
i don't want to fight you, "me from the past"!
but it is the only way to save your friend.
i believe there to be another way. i will try to think about it as you fight me.
whatevs!
check that out. isn't that crazy? he'll never get past himself!
i guess. how'd you find that guy?
used, at the flea market
scott c.

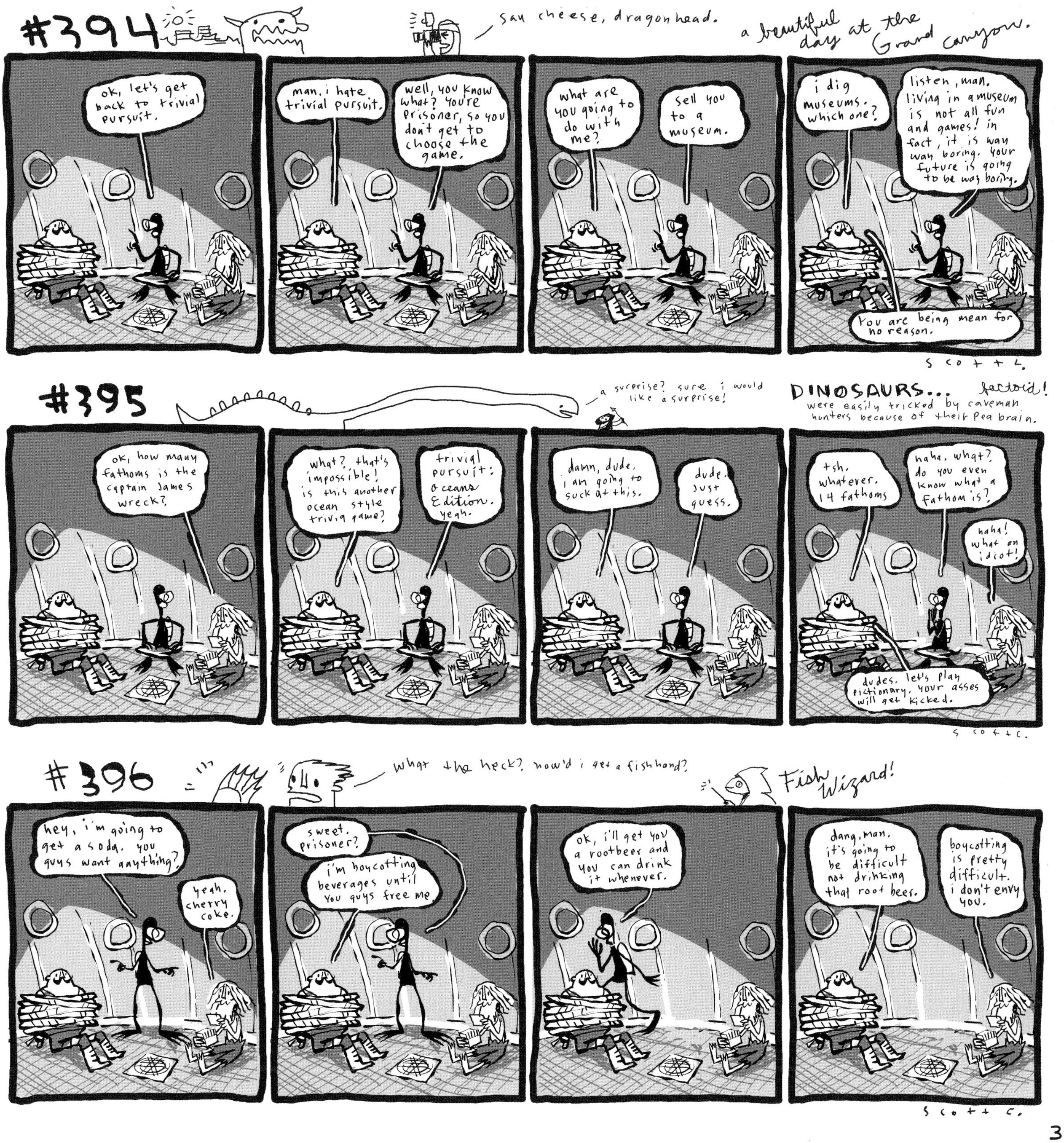
#394
say cheese, dragonhead.
a beautiful day at the Grand Canyon.
ok, let's get back to trivial pursuit.
man, i hate trivial pursuit.
well, you know what? you're prisoner, so you don't get to choose the game.
what are you going to do with me?
sell you to a museum.
i dig museums. which one?
listen, man. living in a museum is not all fun and games! in fact, it is way way boring. your future is going to be way boring.
you are being mean for no reason.
scott c.
#395
a surprise? sure i would like a surprise!
DINOSAURS... factoid!
were easily tricked by caveman hunters because of their pea brain.
ok, how many fathoms is the captain james wreck?
what? that's impossible! is this another ocean style trivia game?
trivial pursuit: oceans edition. yeah.
damn, dude, i am going to suck at this.
dude, just guess.
tsh. whatever. 14 fathoms
haha. what? do you even know what a fathom is?
haha! what an idiot!
dudes, let's play pictionary. your asses will get kicked.
scott c.
#396
what the heck? how'd i get a fishhand?
Fish Wizard!
hey, i'm going to get a soda. you guys want anything?
yeah. cherry coke.
sweet. prisoner?
i'm boycotting beverages until you guys free me.
ok, i'll get you a rootbeer and you can drink it whenever.
dang, man. it's going to be difficult not drinking that root beer.
boycotting is pretty difficult. i don't envy you.
scott c.

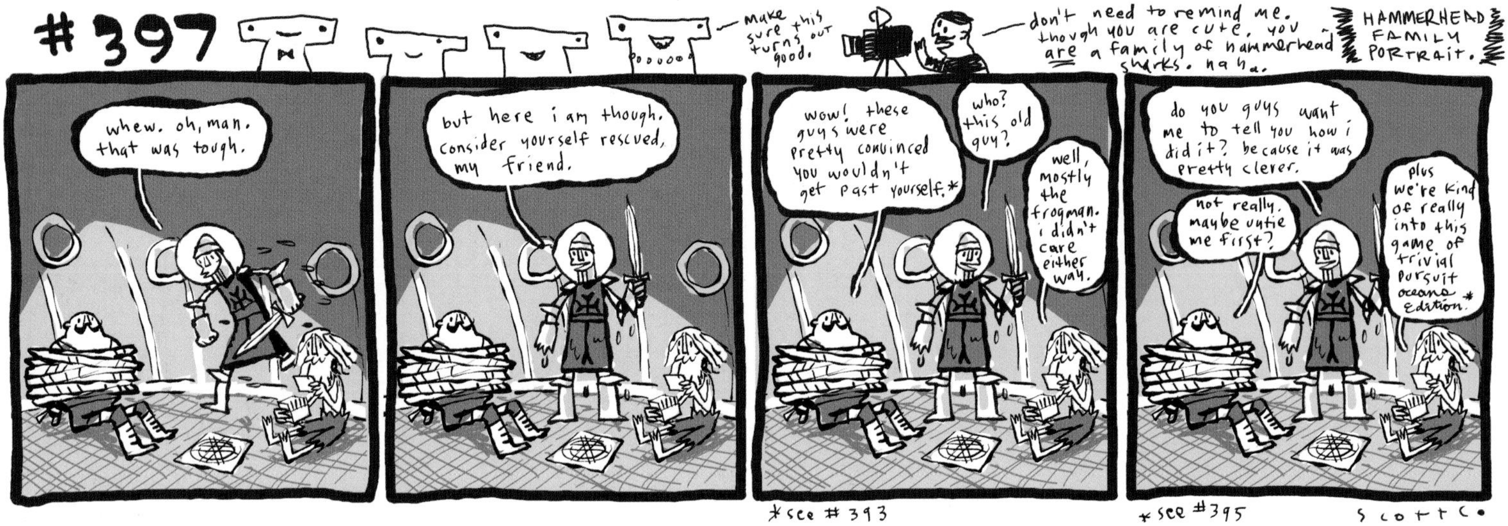
#397
make this sure this turns out good.
don't need to remind me. though you are cute. you are a family of hammerhead sharks. ha ha.
HAMMERHEAD FAMILY PORTRAIT.
whew. oh, man. that was tough.
but here i am though. consider yourself rescued, my friend.
wow! these guys were pretty convinced you wouldn't get past yourself.*
who? this old guy?
well, mostly the frogman. i didn't care either way.
do you guys want me to tell you how i did it? because it was pretty clever.
not really. maybe untie me first?
plus we're kind of really into this game of trivial pursuit oceans edition.*
*see #393
*see #395
scott c.

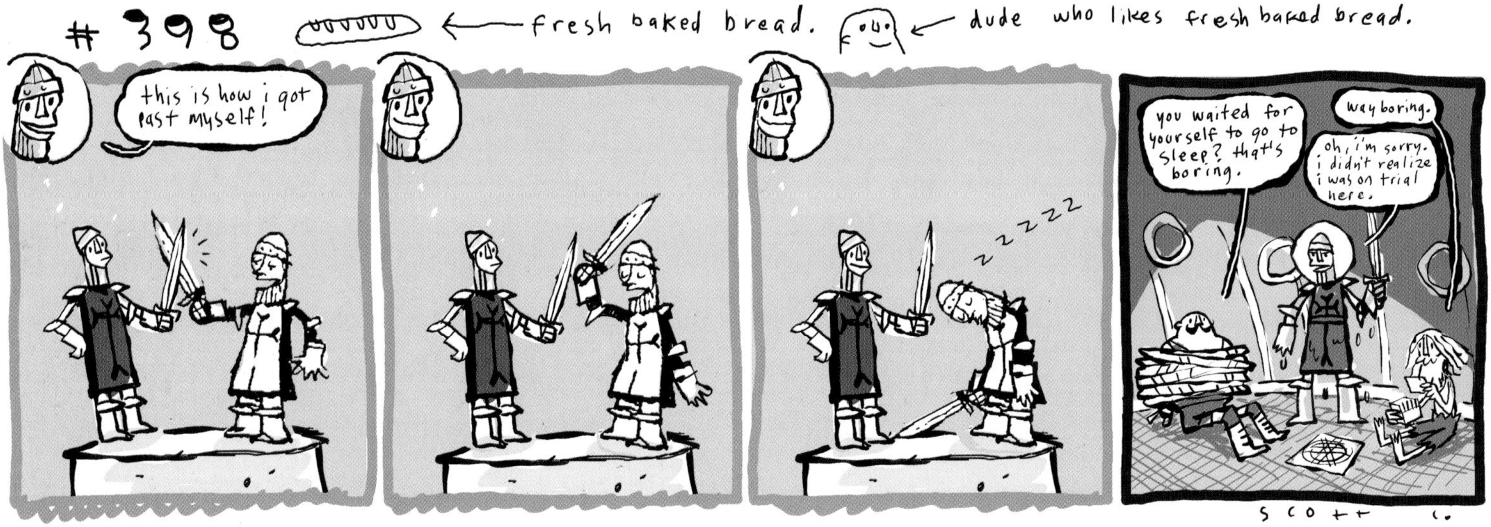
#398
fresh baked bread.
dude who likes fresh baked bread.
this is how i got past myself!
zzzzz
you waited for yourself to go to sleep? that's boring.
way boring.
oh, i'm sorry. i didn't realize i was on trial here.
scott c.

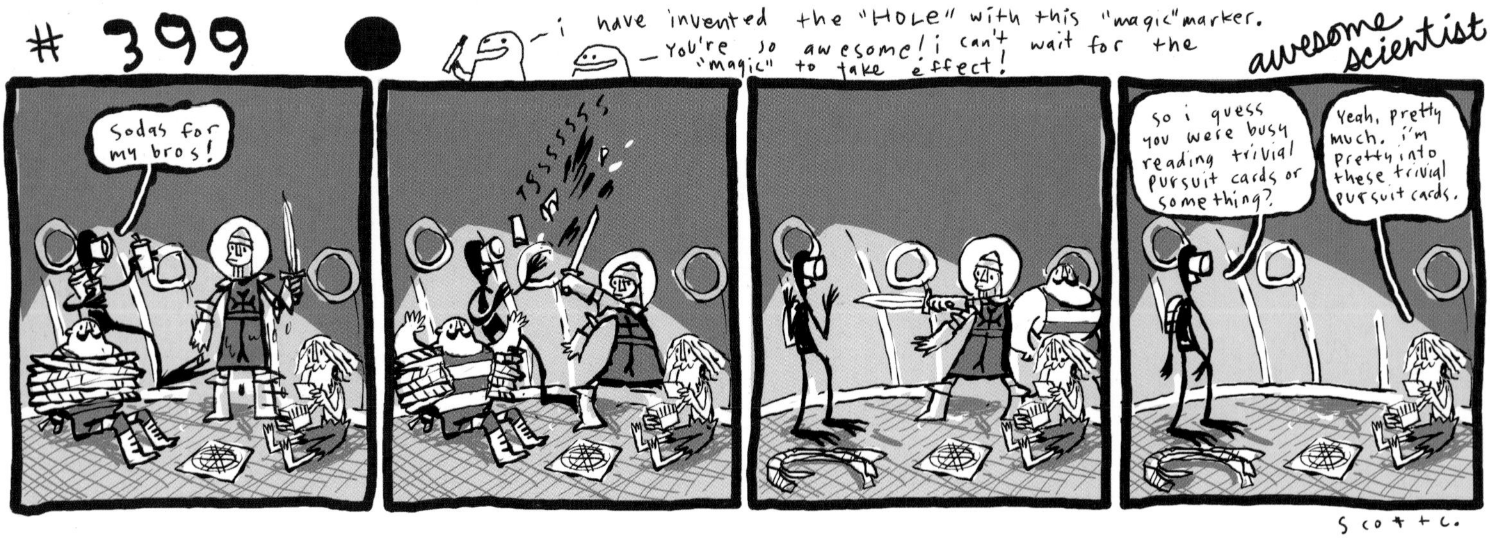
#399
i have invented the "HOLE" with this "magic" marker.
You're so awesome! i can't wait for the "magic" to take effect!
awesome scientist
sodas for my bros!
TSSSSSSS
so i guess you were busy reading trivial pursuit cards or something?
Yeah, pretty much. i'm pretty into these trivial pursuit cards.
scott c.

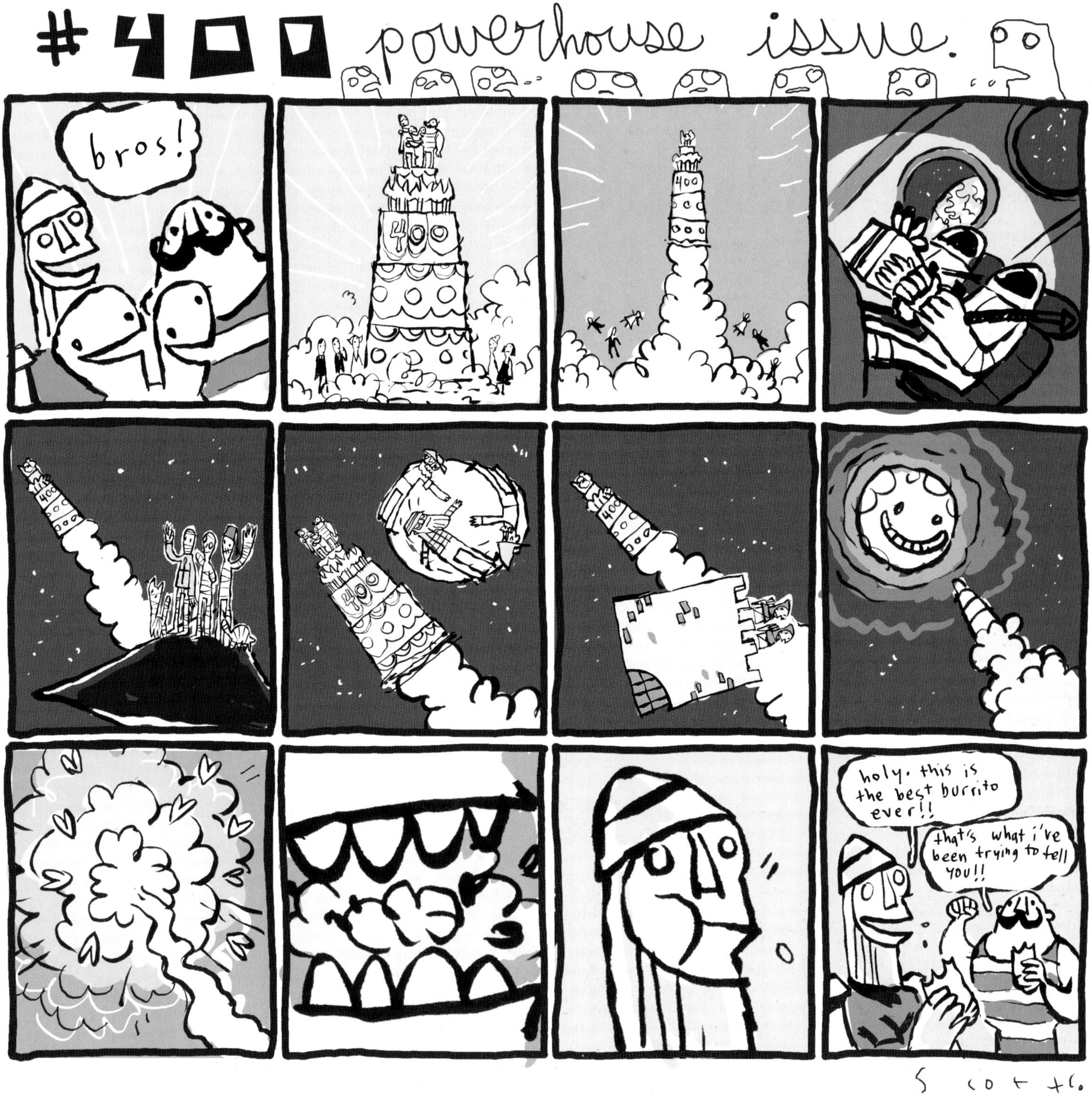
#400 powerhouse issue.
bros!
400
400
400
holy. this is the best burrito ever!!
that's what i've been trying to tell you!!
Scott C.

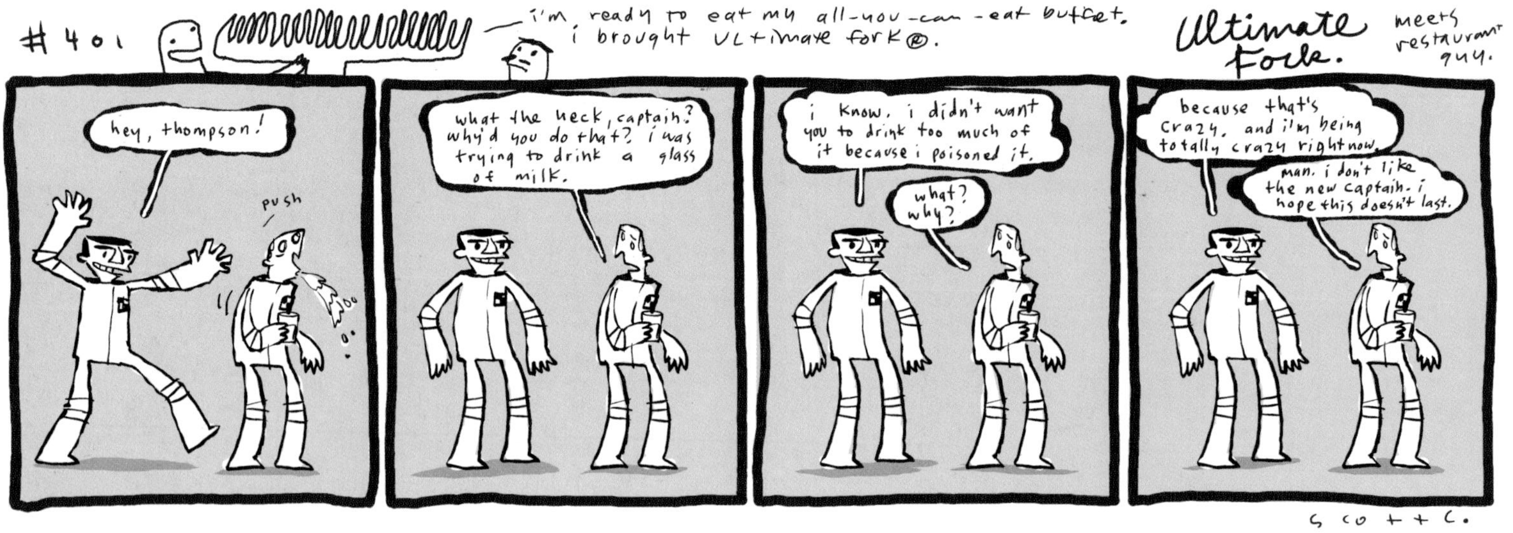
#401
i'm ready to eat my all-you-can-eat buffet. i brought ultimate fork®.
Ultimate Fork.
meets restaurant guy.
hey, thompson!
push
what the heck, captain? why'd you do that? i was trying to drink a glass of milk.
i know. i didn't want you to drink too much of it because i poisoned it.
what? why?
because that's crazy. and i'm being totally crazy right now.
man. i don't like the new captain. i hope this doesn't last.
scott c.

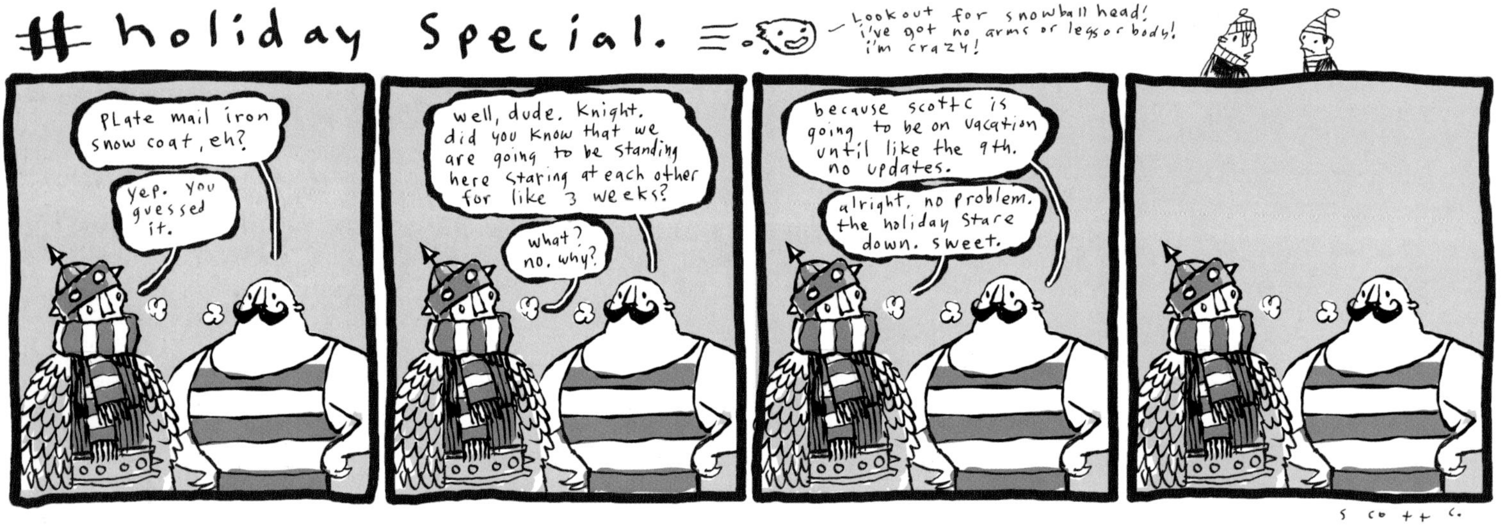
holiday Special.
Look out for snowball head! i've got no arms or legs or body! i'm crazy!
Plate mail iron snow coat, eh?
yep. you guessed it.
well, dude. knight. did you know that we are going to be standing here staring at each other for like 3 weeks?
what? no. why?
because scott c is going to be on vacation until like the 9th. no updates.
alright. no problem. the holiday stare down. sweet.
scott c.

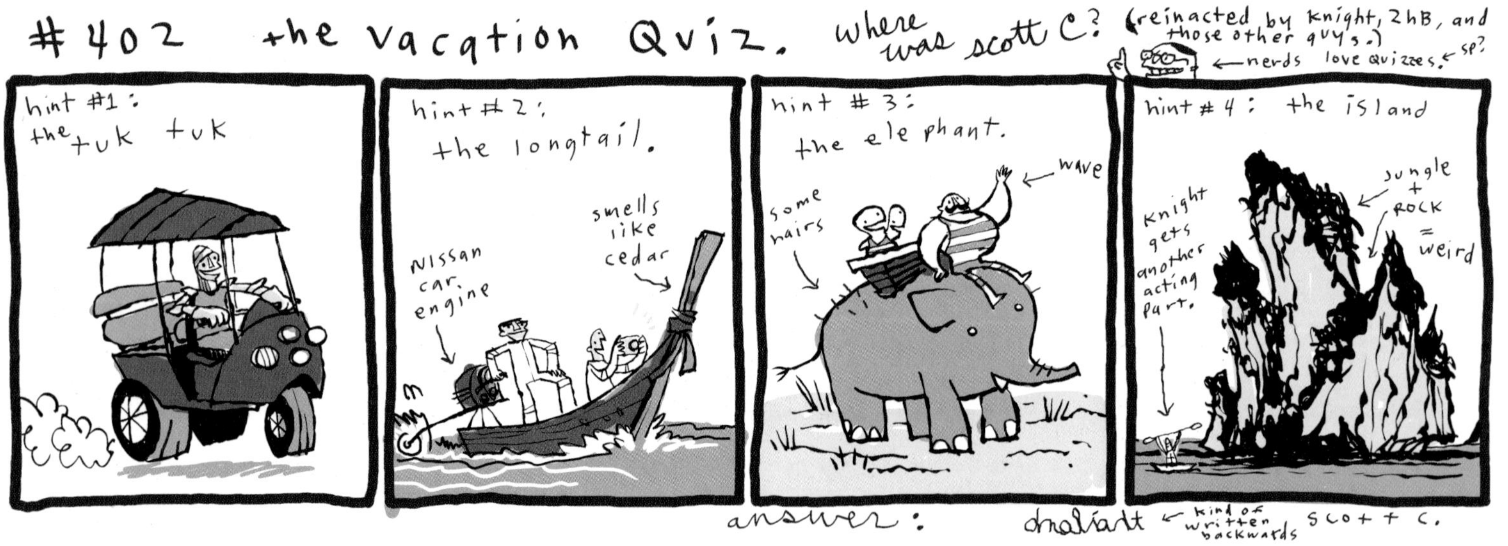
#402 the vacation Quiz.
where was scott c?
(reinacted by knight, 2hB, and those other guy's.)
← nerds love quizzes. ← sp?
hint #1: the tuk tuk
hint #2: the longtail.
smells like cedar
nissan car engine
hint #3: the elephant.
wave
some hairs
hint #4: the island
jungle + rock = weird
knight gets another acting part.
answer: dnaliaht ← kind of written backwards
scott c.

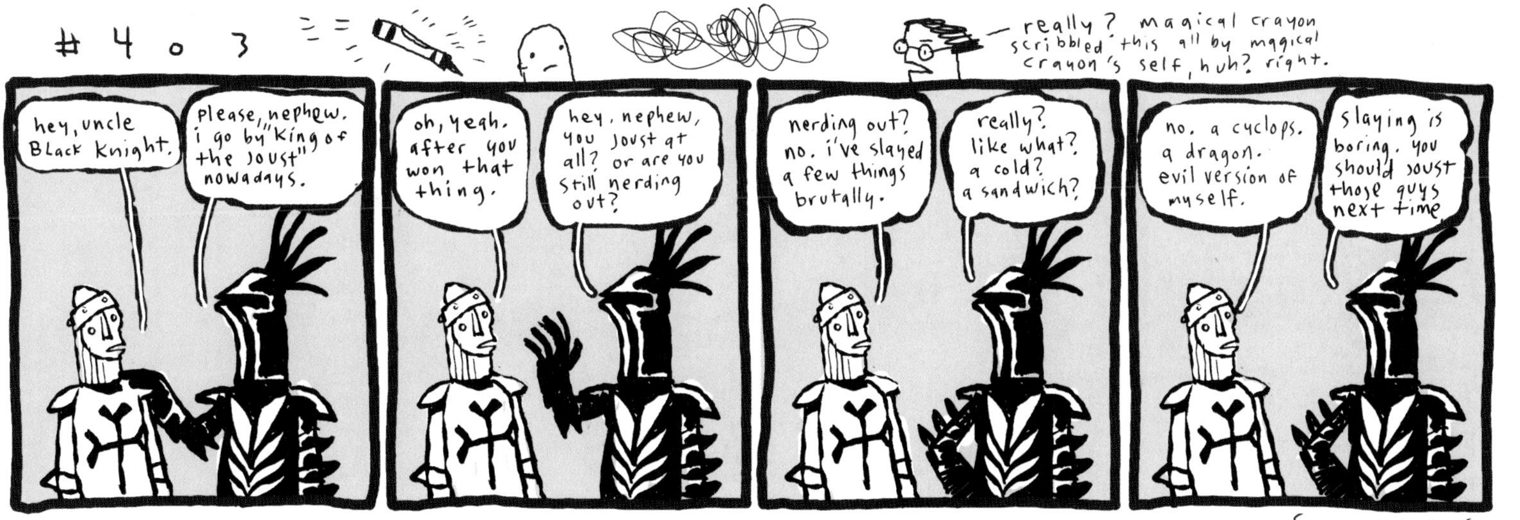
#403
really? magical crayon scribbled this all by magical crayon's self, huh? right.
hey, uncle Black Knight.
please, nephew. i go by "King of the Joust" nowadays.
oh, yeah. after you won that thing.
hey, nephew, you joust at all? or are you still nerding out?
nerding out? no. i've slayed a few things brutally.
really? like what? a cold? a sandwich?
no. a cyclops. a dragon. evil version of myself.
Slaying is boring. You should joust those guys next time.
scott c.

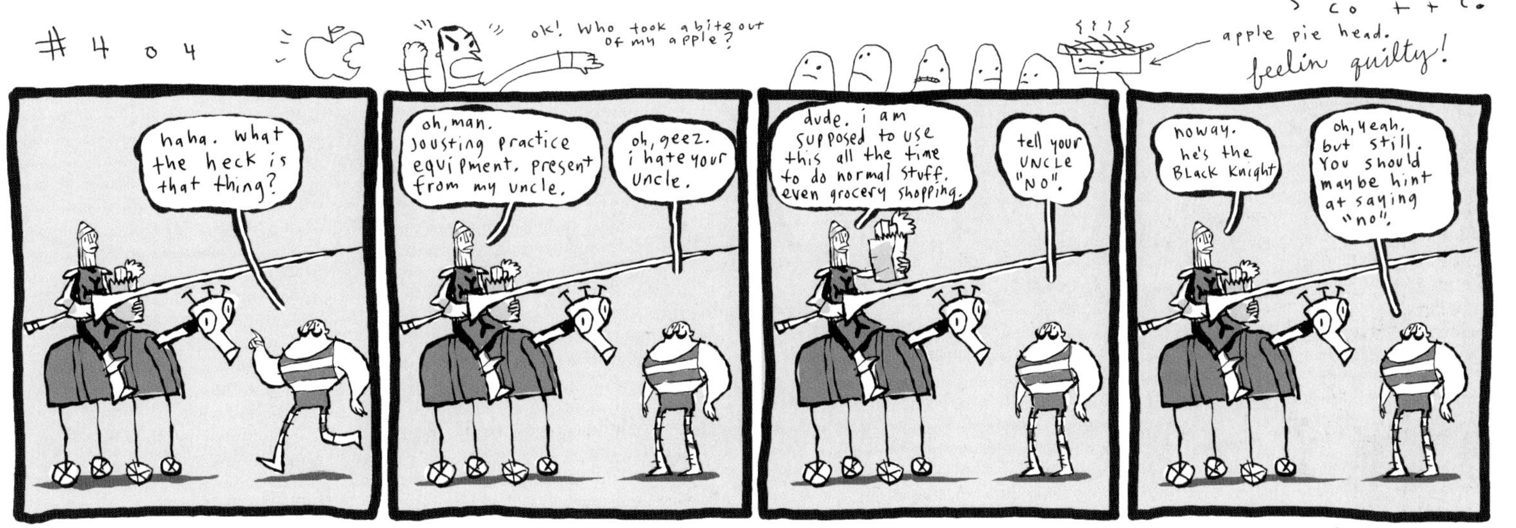
#404
ok! Who took a bite out of my apple?
apple pie head. feelin guilty!
haha. what the heck is that thing?
oh, man. Jousting practice equipment. present from my uncle.
oh, geez. i hate your uncle.
dude. i am supposed to use this all the time to do normal stuff. even grocery shopping.
tell your UNCLE "NO".
no way. he's the Black Knight.
oh, yeah. but still. You should maybe hint at saying "no".
scott c.

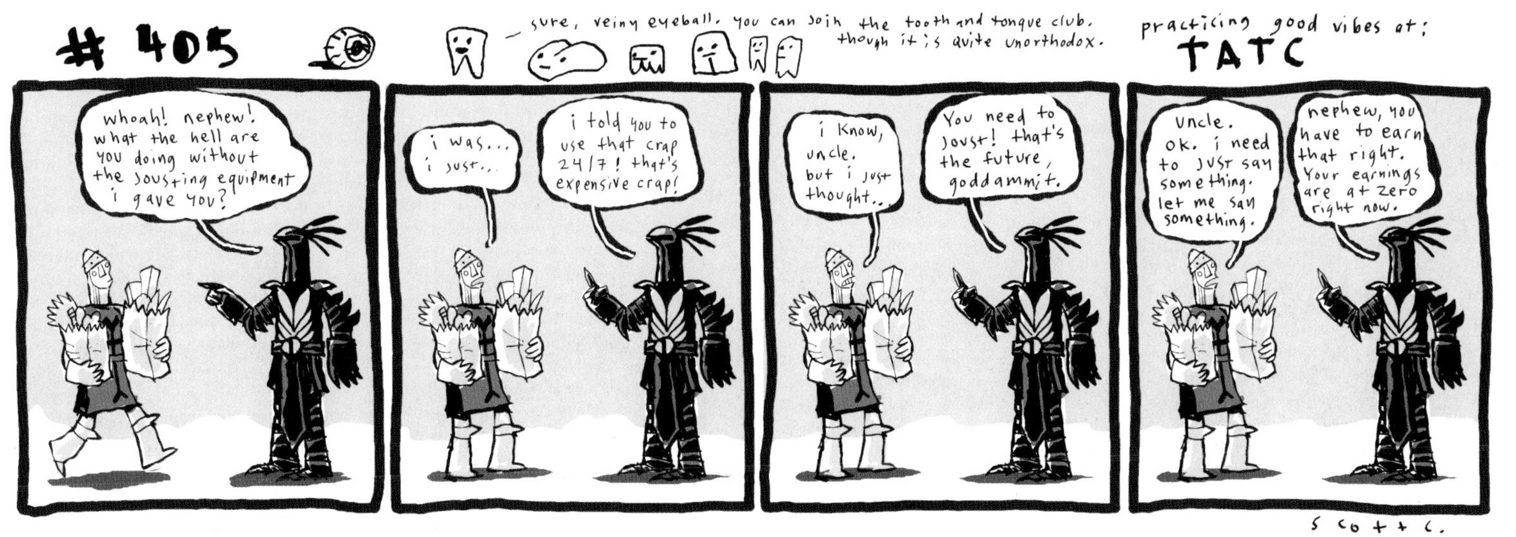
#405
sure, veiny eyeball. you can join the tooth and tongue club. though it is quite unorthodox.
practicing good vibes at: TATC
Whoah! nephew! what the hell are you doing without the jousting equipment i gave you?
i was... i just...
i told you to use that crap 24/7! that's expensive crap!
i know, uncle. but i just thought...
You need to joust! that's the future, goddammit.
Uncle. ok. i need to just say something. let me say something.
nephew, you have to earn that right. Your earnings are at zero right now.
scott c.

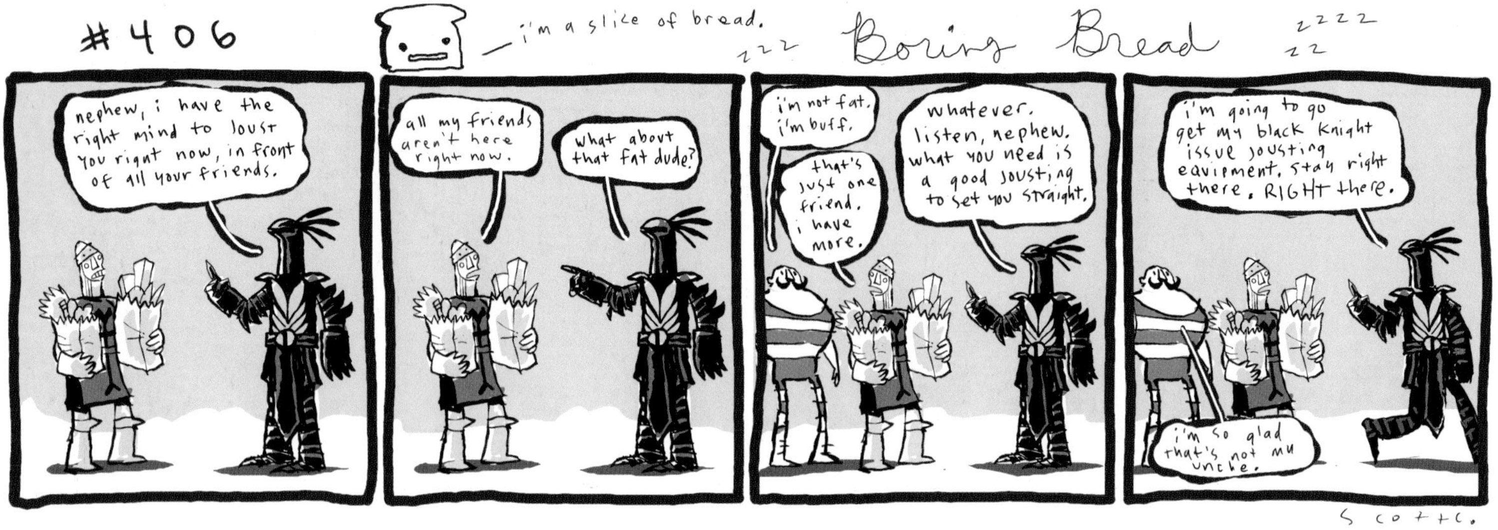
#406
i'm a slice of bread.
zzz
Boring Bread
zzzz zz
nephew, i have the right mind to joust you right now, in front of all your friends.
all my friends aren't here right now.
what about that fat dude?
i'm not fat. i'm buff.
that's just one friend. i have more.
whatever. listen, nephew. what you need is a good jousting to set you straight.
i'm going to go get my black knight issue jousting equipment. stay right there. RIGHT there.
i'm so glad that's not my uncle.
scott c.

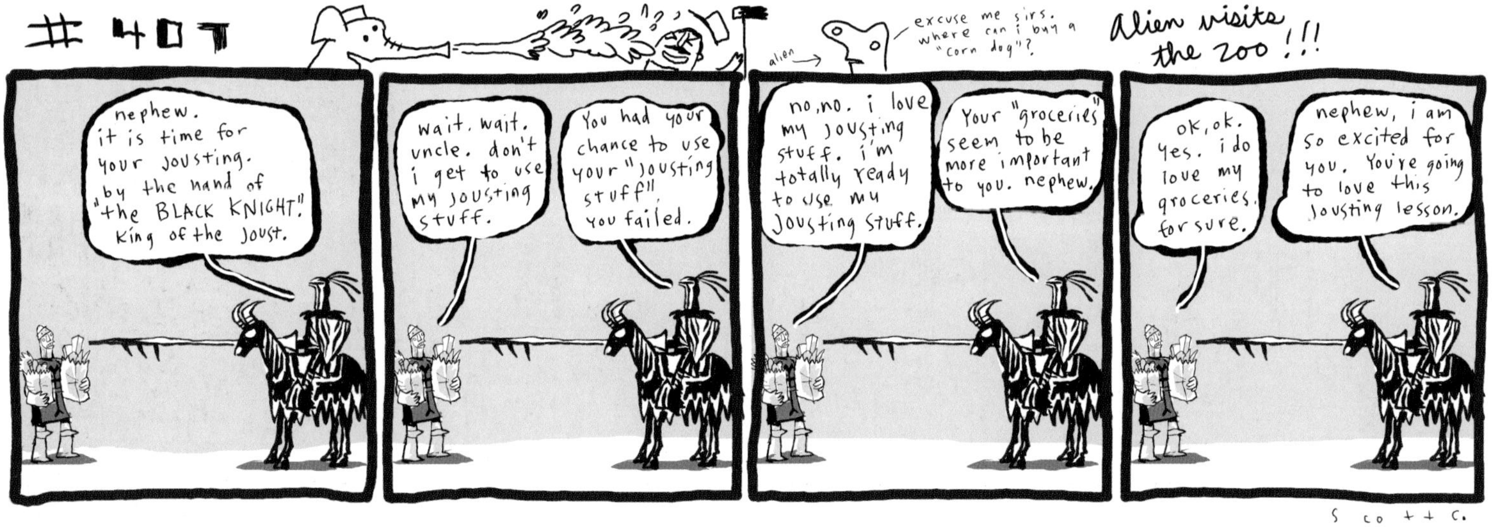
#407
alien
excuse me sirs. where can i buy a "corn dog"?
Alien visits the zoo!!!
nephew. it is time for your jousting. by the hand of "the BLACK KNIGHT." King of the joust.
wait. wait. uncle. don't i get to use my jousting stuff.
You had your chance to use your "jousting stuff." you failed.
no, no. i love my jousting stuff. i'm totally ready to use my jousting stuff.
Your "groceries" seem to be more important to you. nephew.
ok, ok. yes. i do love my groceries. for sure.
nephew, i am so excited for you. you're going to love this jousting lesson.
scott c.

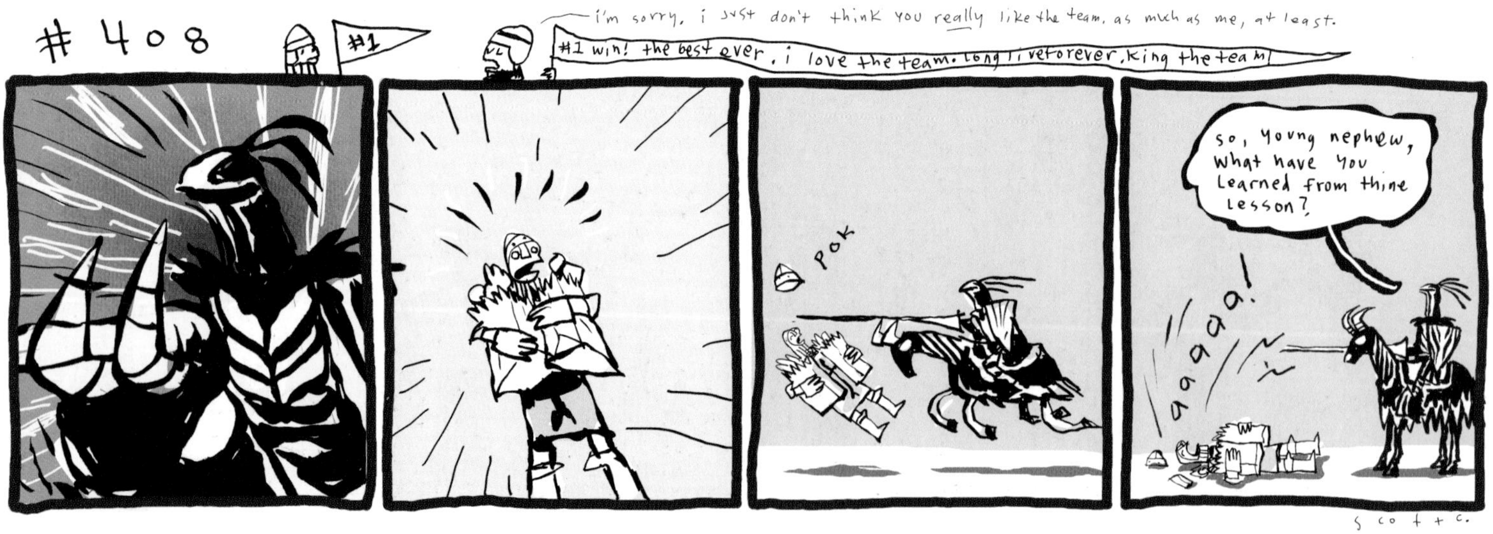
#408
#1
i'm sorry, i just don't think you really like the team. as much as me, at least.
#1 win! the best ever. i love the team. long live forever, king the team
pok
so, young nephew, what have you learned from thine lesson?
aaaaa!
scott c.

409

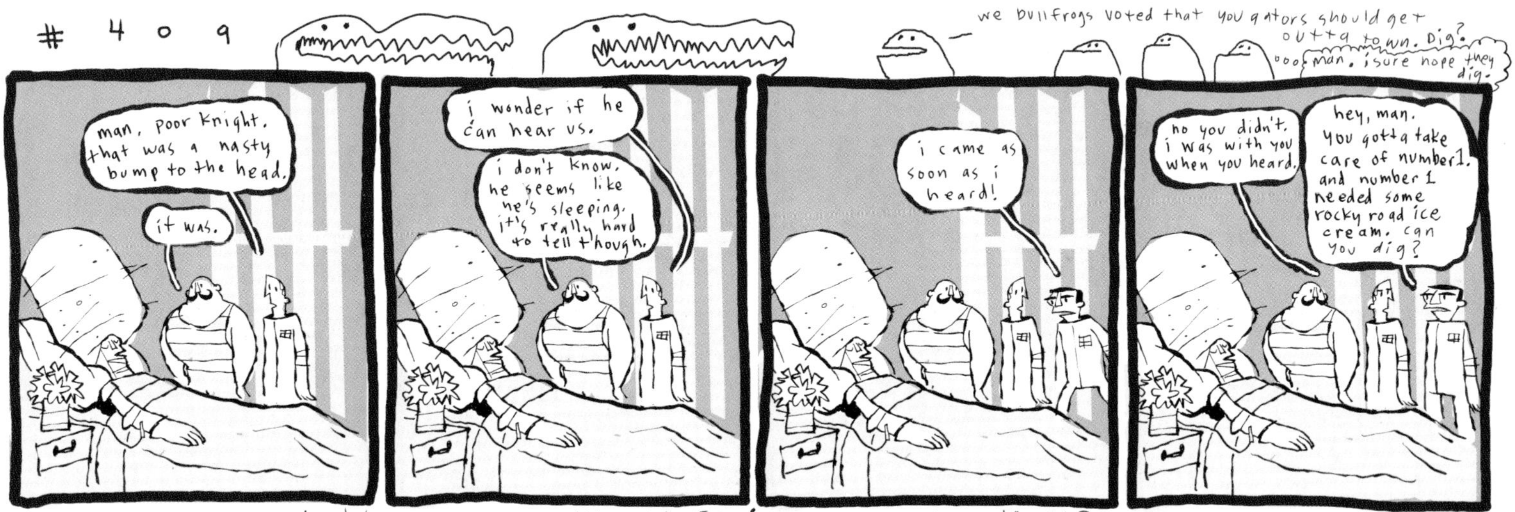
we bullfrogs voted that you gators should get outta town. Dig?
man. i sure hope they dig.
man, poor knight. that was a nasty bump to the head.
it was.
i wonder if he can hear us.
i don't know, he seems like he's sleeping. it's really hard to tell though.
i came as soon as i heard!
no you didn't. i was with you when you heard.
hey, man. you gotta take care of number 1. and number 1 needed some rocky road ice cream. can you dig?

double joke party starring: "can you dig it?"

scott c.

410

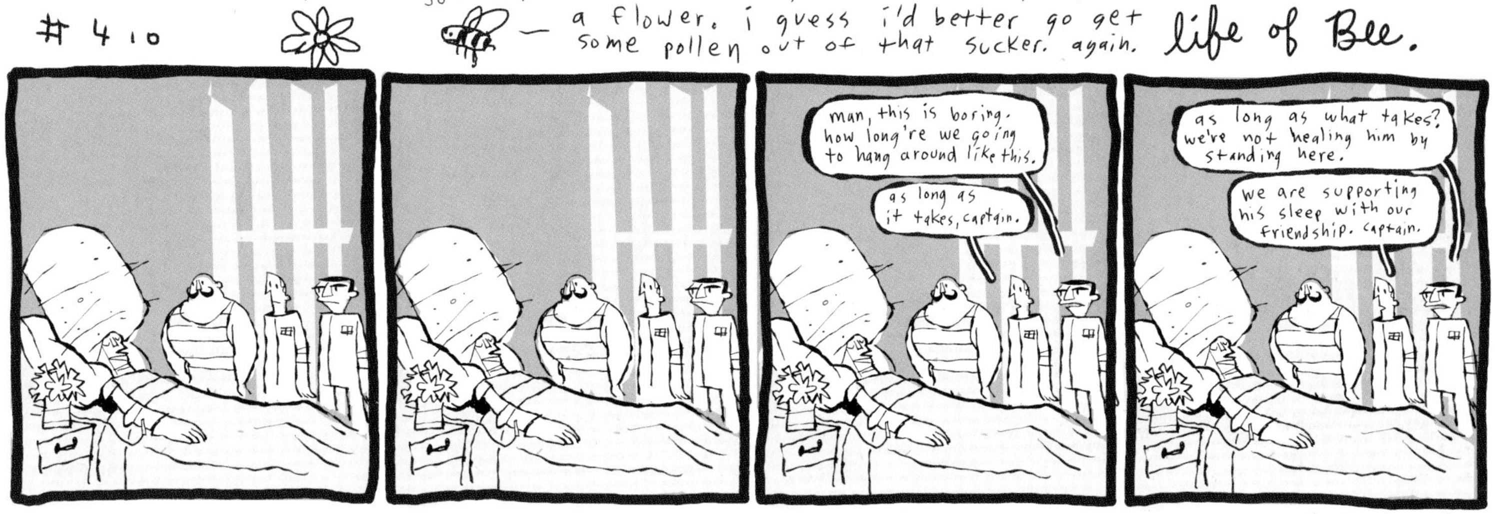
a flower. i guess i'd better go get some pollen out of that sucker. again.
life of Bee.
man, this is boring. how long're we going to hang around like this.
as long as it takes, captain.
as long as what takes? we're not healing him by standing here.
we are supporting his sleep with our friendship. captain.

scott c.

411

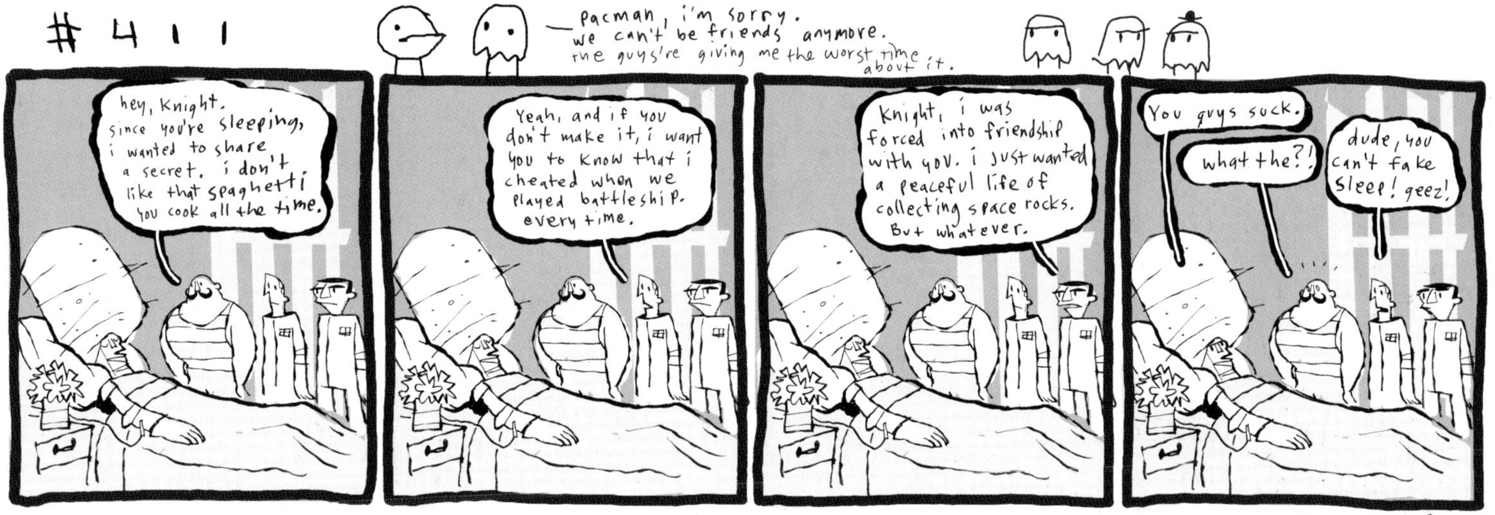
pacman, i'm sorry. we can't be friends anymore. the guys're giving me the worst time about it.
hey, Knight. since you're sleeping, i wanted to share a secret. i don't like that spaghetti you cook all the time.
Yeah, and if you don't make it, i want you to know that i cheated when we played battleship. every time.
Knight, i was forced into friendship with you. i just wanted a peaceful life of collecting space rocks. But whatever.
You guys suck.
what the?!
dude, you can't fake sleep! geez!

scott c.

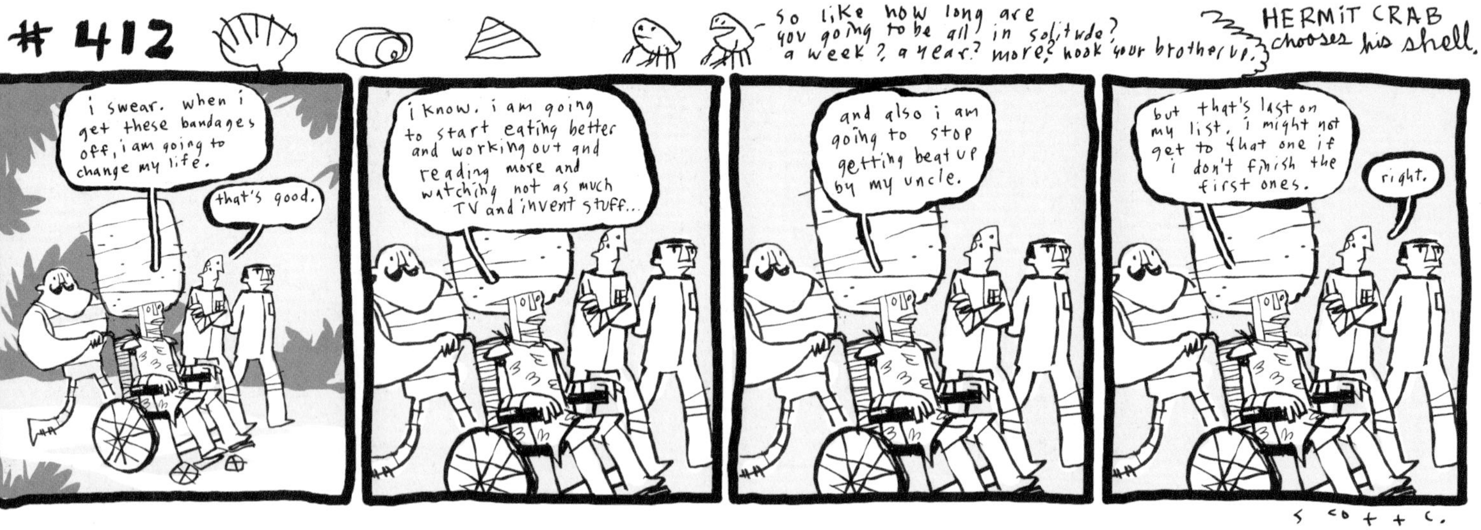
#412
so like how long are you going to be all in solitude? a week? a year? more? hook your brother up.
HERMIT CRAB chooses his shell.
i swear. when i get these bandages off, i am going to change my life.
that's good.
i know. i am going to start eating better and working out and reading more and watching not as much TV and invent stuff...
and also i am going to stop getting beat up by my uncle.
but that's last on my list. i might not get to that one if i don't finish the first ones.
right.
scott c.

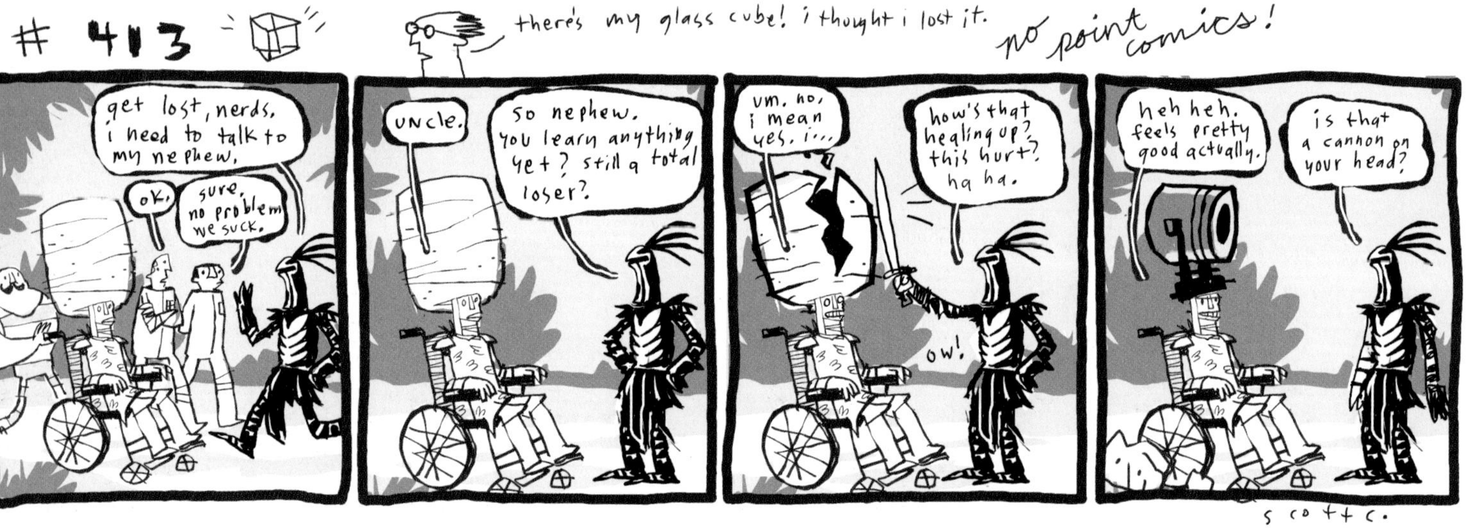
#413
there's my glass cube! i thought i lost it.
no point comics!
get lost, nerds. i need to talk to my nephew.
ok.
sure, no problem we suck.
uncle.
so nephew. you learn anything yet? still a total loser?
um. no, i mean yes. i...
how's that healing up? this hurt? ha ha.
ow!
heh heh. feels pretty good actually.
is that a cannon on your head?
scott c.

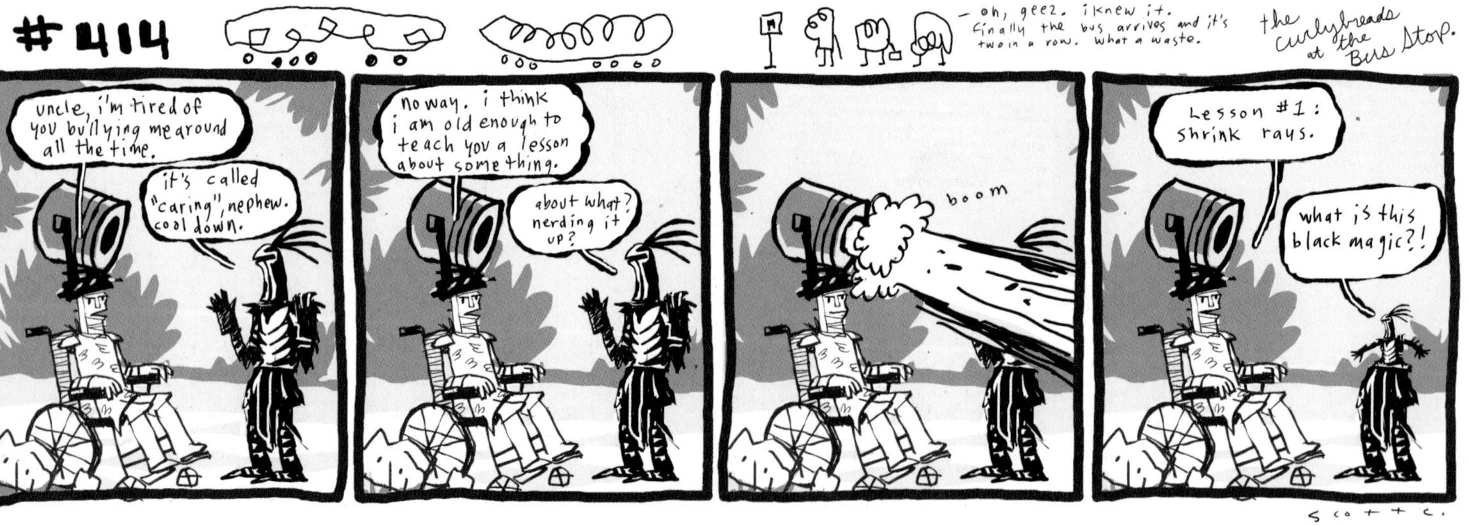
#414
oh, geez. i knew it. finally the bus arrives and it's two in a row. what a waste.
the curlyheads at the Bus Stop.
uncle, i'm tired of you bullying me around all the time.
it's called "caring", nephew. cool down.
no way. i think i am old enough to teach you a lesson about something.
about what? nerding it up?
boom
Lesson #1: shrink rays.
what is this black magic?!
scott c.

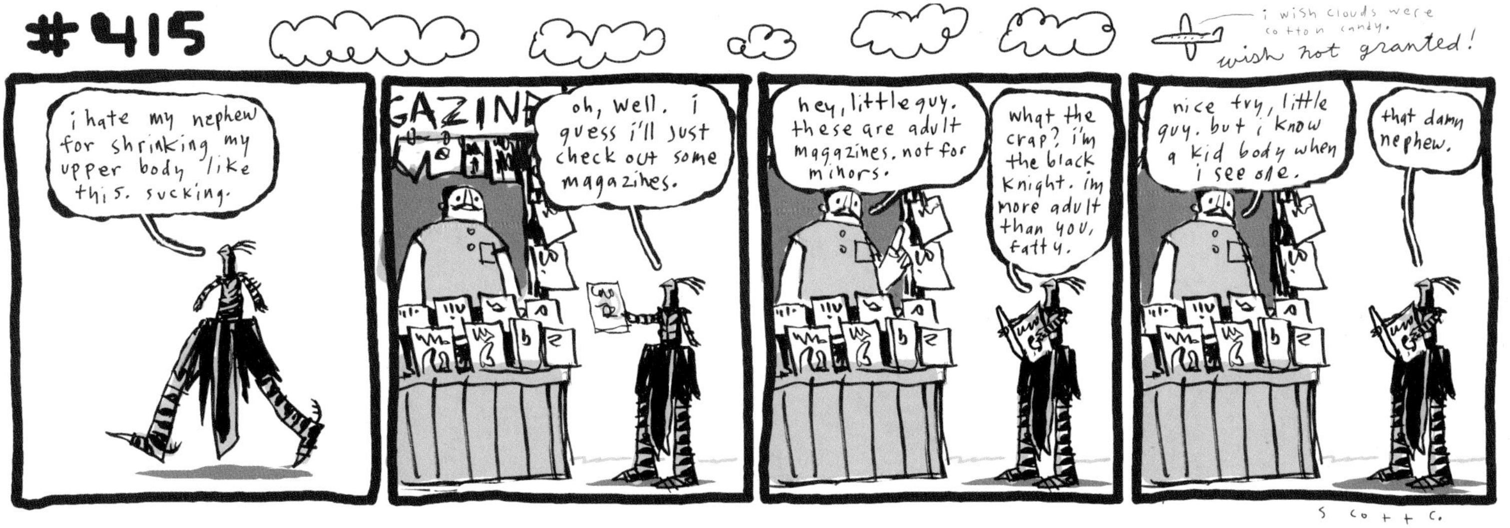
#415
i wish clouds were cotton candy.
wish not granted!
i hate my nephew for shrinking my upper body like this. sucking.
GAZINE
oh, well. i guess i'll just check out some magazines.
hey, little guy. these are adult magazines. not for minors.
what the crap? i'm the black knight. im more adult than you, fatty.
nice try, little guy. but i know a kid body when i see one.
that damn nephew.
scott c.

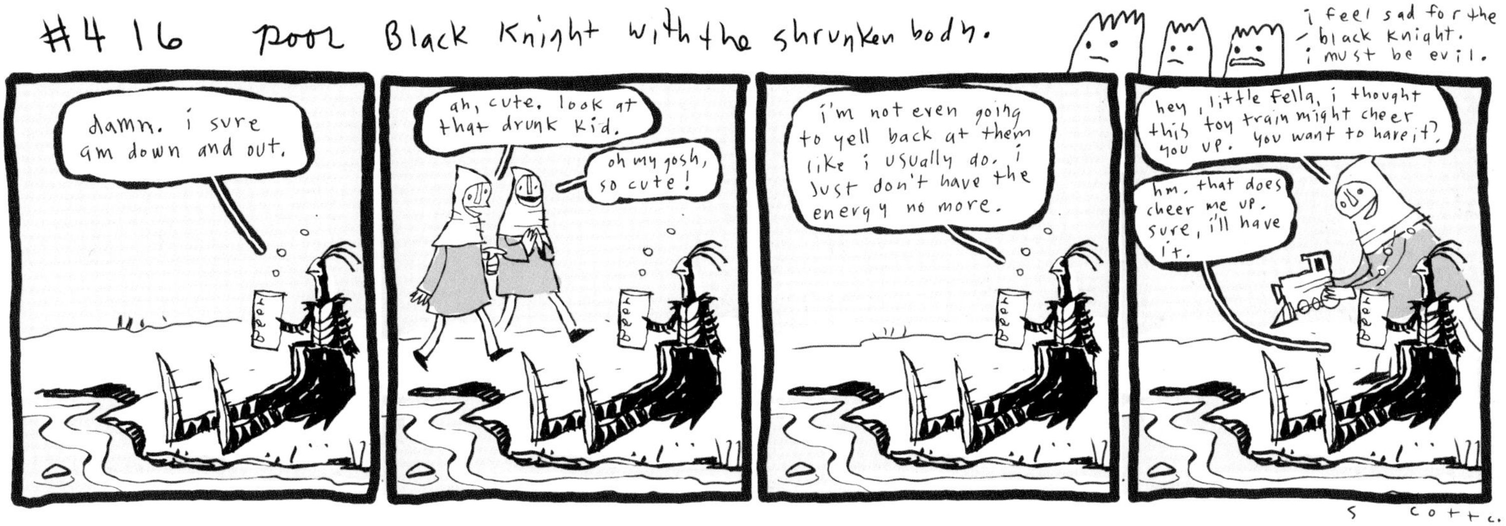
#416 poor Black Knight with the shrunken body.
i feel sad for the black knight. i must be evil.
damn. i sure am down and out.
beer
ah, cute. look at that drunk kid.
oh my gosh, so cute!
i'm not even going to yell back at them like i usually do. i just don't have the energy no more.
hey, little fella, i thought this toy train might cheer you up. you want to have it?
hm. that does cheer me up. sure, i'll have it.
scott c.

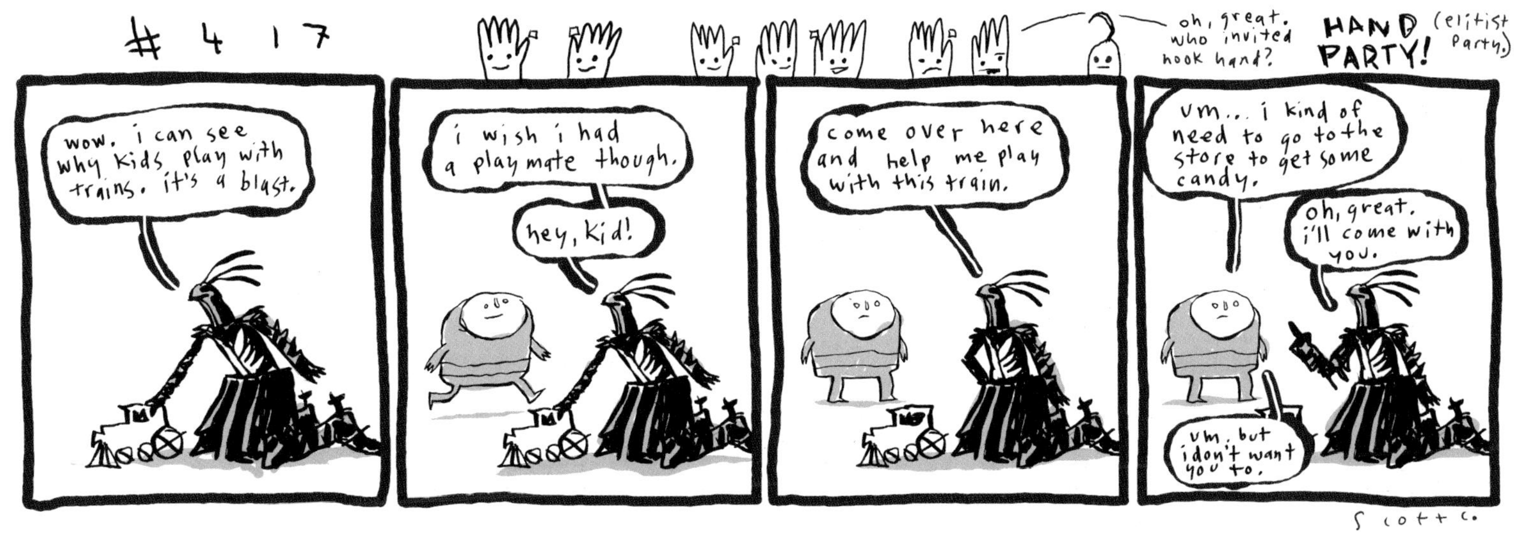
#417
oh, great. who invited hook hand?
HAND PARTY!
(elitist Party)
wow. i can see why kids play with trains. it's a blast.
i wish i had a playmate though.
hey, kid!
come over here and help me play with this train.
um... i kind of need to go to the store to get some candy.
oh, great. i'll come with you.
um, but i don't want you to.
scott c.

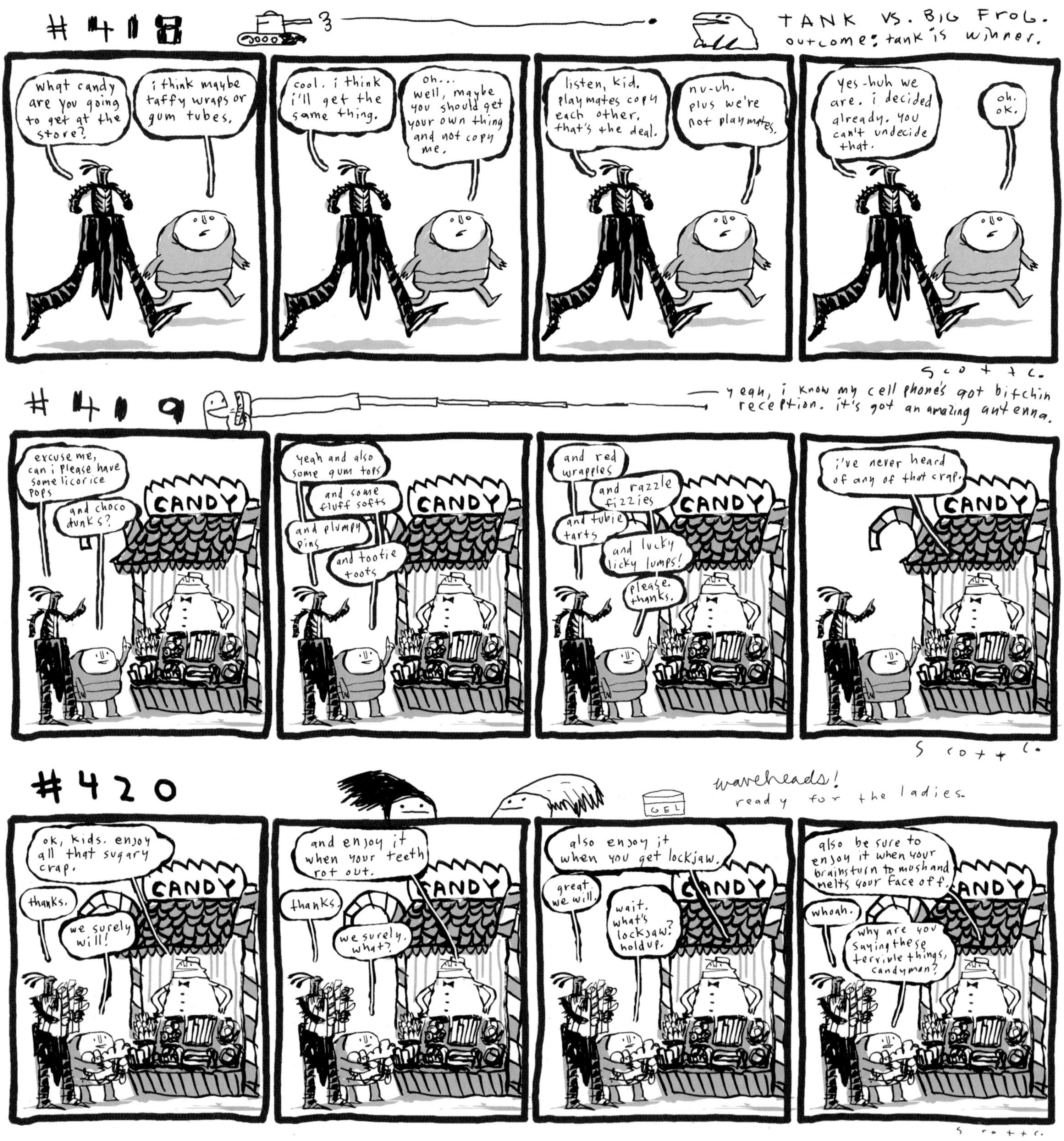
#418
TANK VS. BIG FROG.
outcome: tank is winner.
what candy are you going to get at the store?
i think maybe taffy wraps or gum tubes.
cool. i think i'll get the same thing.
oh... well, maybe you should get your own thing and not copy me.
listen, kid. playmates copy each other. that's the deal.
nu-uh. plus we're not playmates.
yes-huh we are. i decided already. you can't undecide that.
oh. ok.
scott c.
#419
yeah, i know my cell phone's got bitchin reception. it's got an amazing antenna.
excuse me, can i please have some licorice pops
and choco dunks?
CANDY
yeah and also some gum tops
and some fluff softs
and plumpy pins
and tootie toots
and red wrapples
and razzle fizzies
and tubie tarts
and lucky licky lumps!
please. thanks.
i've never heard of any of that crap.
scott c.
#420
waveheads! ready for the ladies.
GEL
ok, kids. enjoy all that sugary crap.
thanks.
we surely will!
and enjoy it when your teeth rot out.
thanks.
we surely, what?
also enjoy it when you get lockjaw.
great. we will.
wait. what's lockjaw? hold up.
also be sure to enjoy it when your brains turn to mush and melts your face off.
whoah.
why are you saying these terrible things, candyman?
scott c.

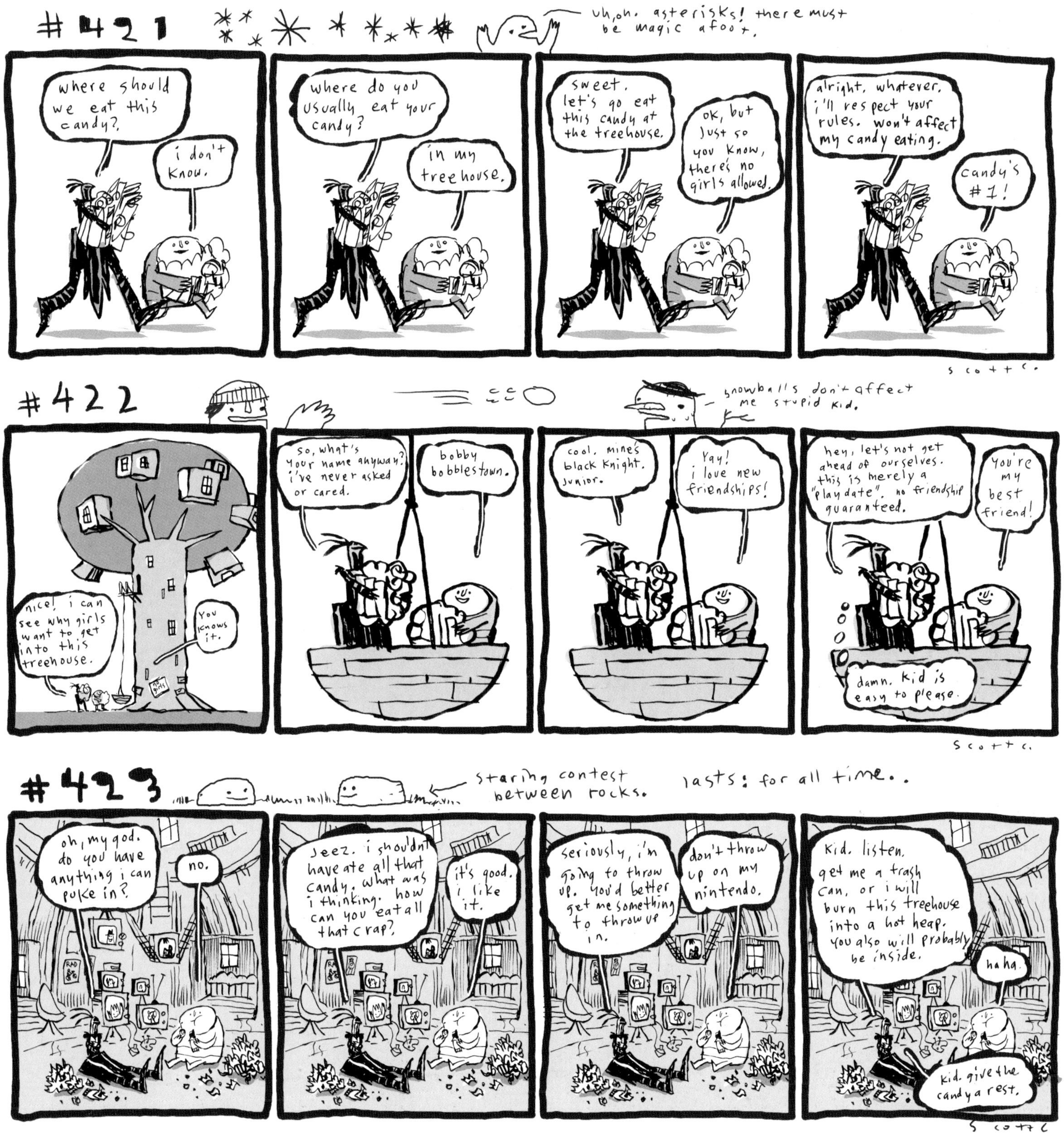
#421
uh, oh. asterisks! there must be magic afoot.
where should we eat this candy?.
i don't know.
where do you usually eat your candy?
in my treehouse.
sweet. let's go eat this candy at the treehouse.
ok, but just so you know, there's no girls allowed.
alright, whatever. i'll respect your rules. won't affect my candy eating.
candy's #1!
scott c.
#422
snowballs don't affect me stupid kid.
nice! i can see why girls want to get into this treehouse.
you knows it.
so, what's your name anyway? i've never asked or cared.
bobby bobblestown.
cool. mine's black knight. junior.
yay! i love new friendships!
hey, let's not get ahead of ourselves. this is merely a "playdate". no friendship guaranteed.
you're my best friend!
damn. kid is easy to please.
scott c.
#423
staring contest between rocks. lasts: for all time..
oh, my god. do you have anything i can puke in?
no.
jeez. i shouldn't have ate all that candy. what was i thinking. how can you eat all that crap?
it's good. i like it.
seriously, i'm going to throw up. you'd better get me something to throw up in.
don't throw up on my nintendo.
kid. listen. get me a trash can, or i will burn this treehouse into a hot heap. you also will probably be inside.
haha.
kid. give the candy a rest.
scott c

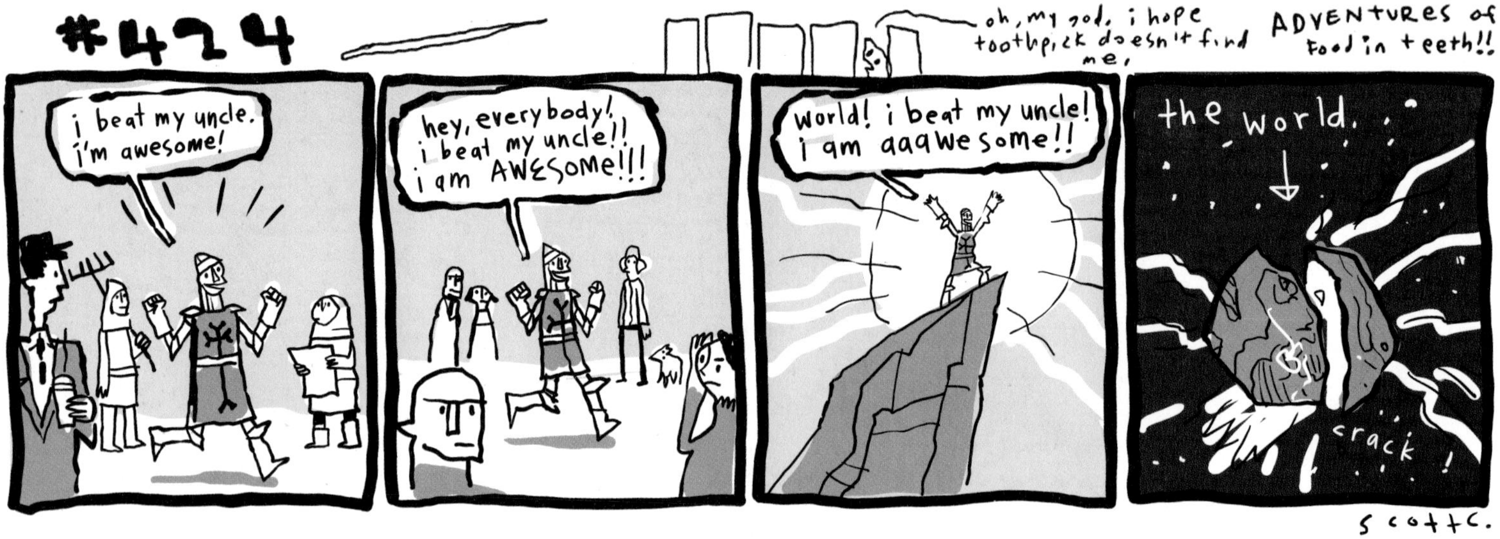
#424
oh, my god, i hope toothpick doesn't find me.
ADVENTURES of food in teeth!!
i beat my uncle. i'm awesome!
hey, everybody! i beat my uncle!! i am AWESOME!!!
world! i beat my uncle! i am aaawesome!!
the world.
crack!
scott c.

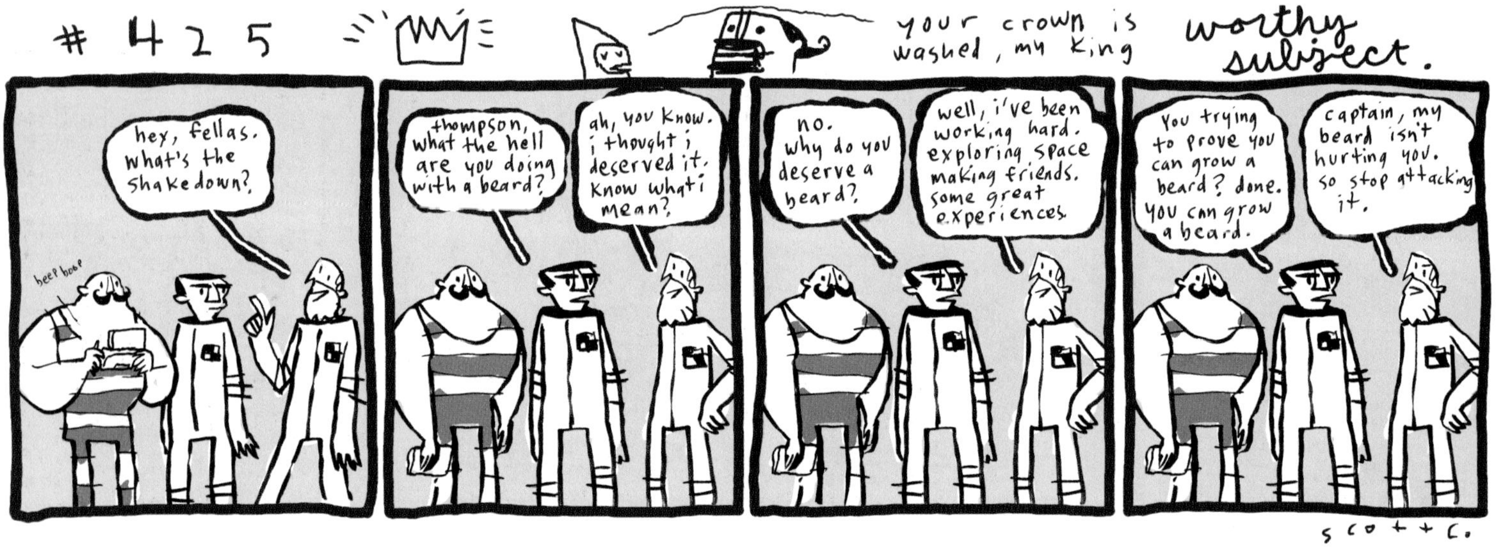
#425
your crown is washed, my king
worthy subject.
hey, fellas. what's the shakedown?
beep boop
thompson, what the hell are you doing with a beard?
ah, you know. i thought i deserved it. know what i mean?
no. why do you deserve a beard?
well, i've been working hard. exploring space making friends. some great experiences.
you trying to prove you can grow a beard? done. you can grow a beard.
captain, my beard isn't hurting you. so stop attacking it.
scott c.

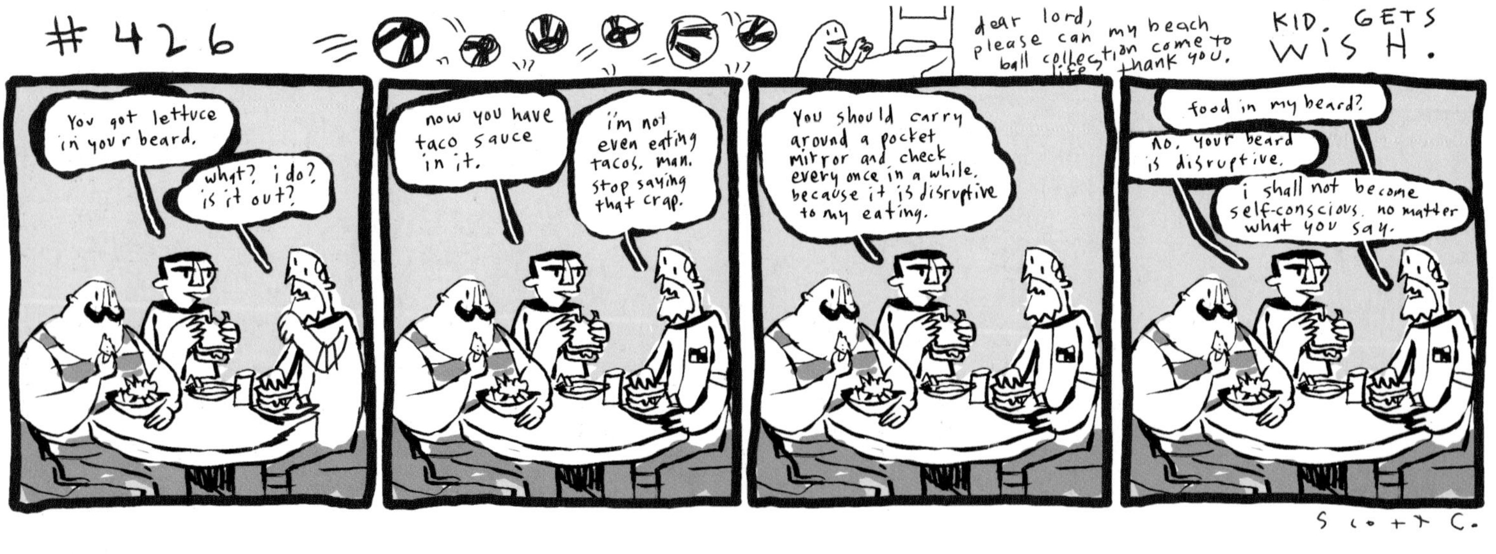
#426
dear lord, please can my beach ball collection come to life? thank you.
KID. GETS WISH.
you got lettuce in your beard.
what? i do? is it out?
now you have taco sauce in it.
i'm not even eating tacos, man. stop saying that crap.
you should carry around a pocket mirror and check every once in a while. because it is disruptive to my eating.
food in my beard?
no. your beard is disruptive.
i shall not become self-conscious. no matter what you say.
scott c.

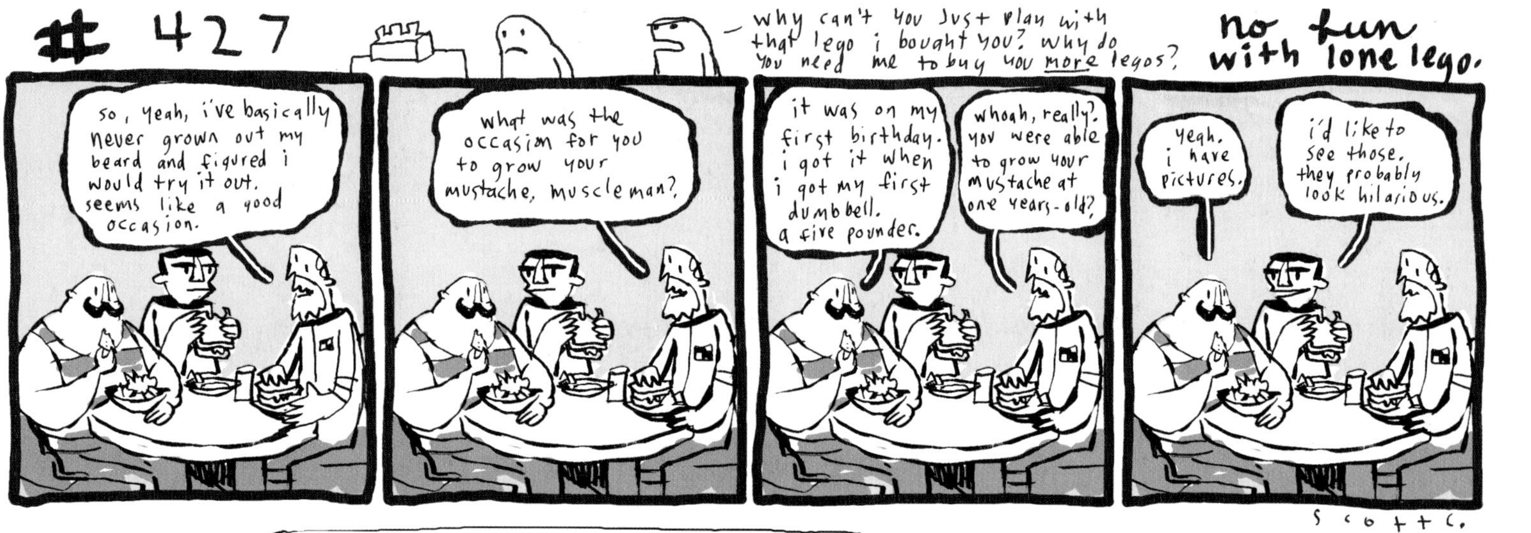

#427
why can't you just play with that lego i bought you? why do you need me to buy you more legos?
no fun with lone lego.
so, yeah, i've basically never grown out my beard and figured i would try it out. seems like a good occasion.
what was the occasion for you to grow your mustache, muscleman?
it was on my first birthday. i got it when i got my first dumbbell. a five pounder.
whoah, really? you were able to grow your mustache at one years-old?
yeah. i have pictures.
i'd like to see those. they probably look hilarious.
scott c.

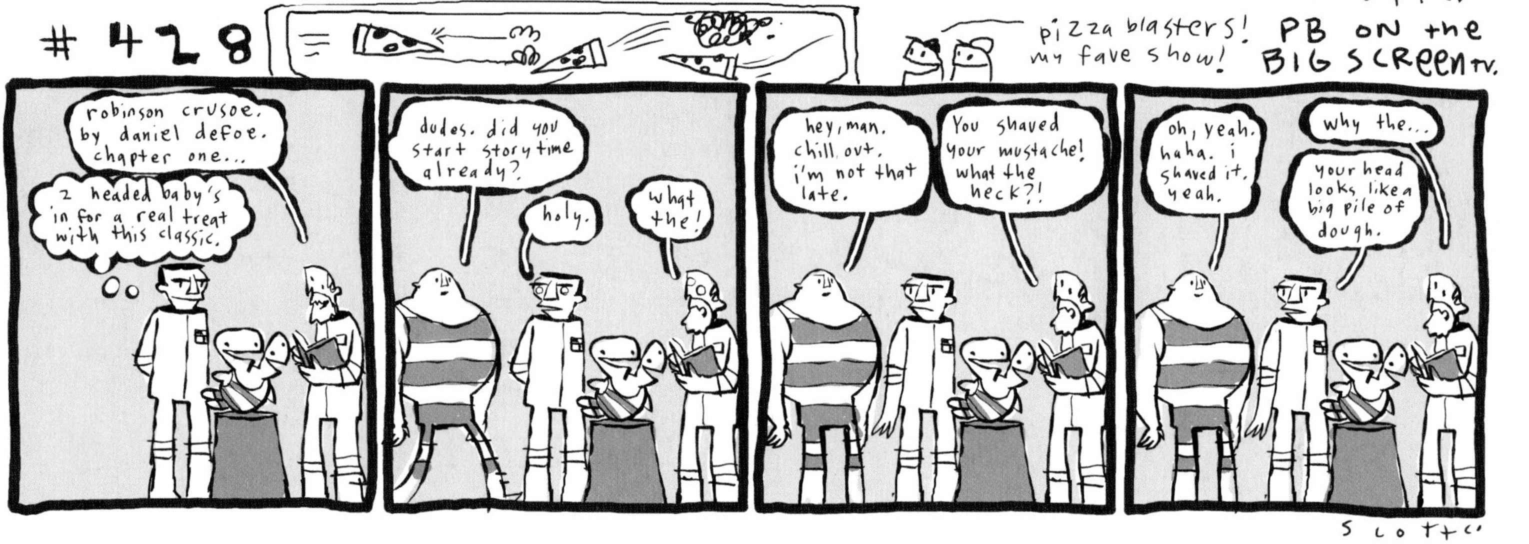

#428
pizza blasters! my fave show!
PB on the BIG SCREEN TV.
robinson crusoe, by daniel defoe. chapter one...
2 headed baby's in for a real treat with this classic.
dudes. did you start story time already?
holy.
what the!
hey, man. chill out. i'm not that late.
you shaved your mustache! what the heck?!
oh, yeah. haha. i shaved it. yeah.
why the...
your head looks like a big pile of dough.
scott c.

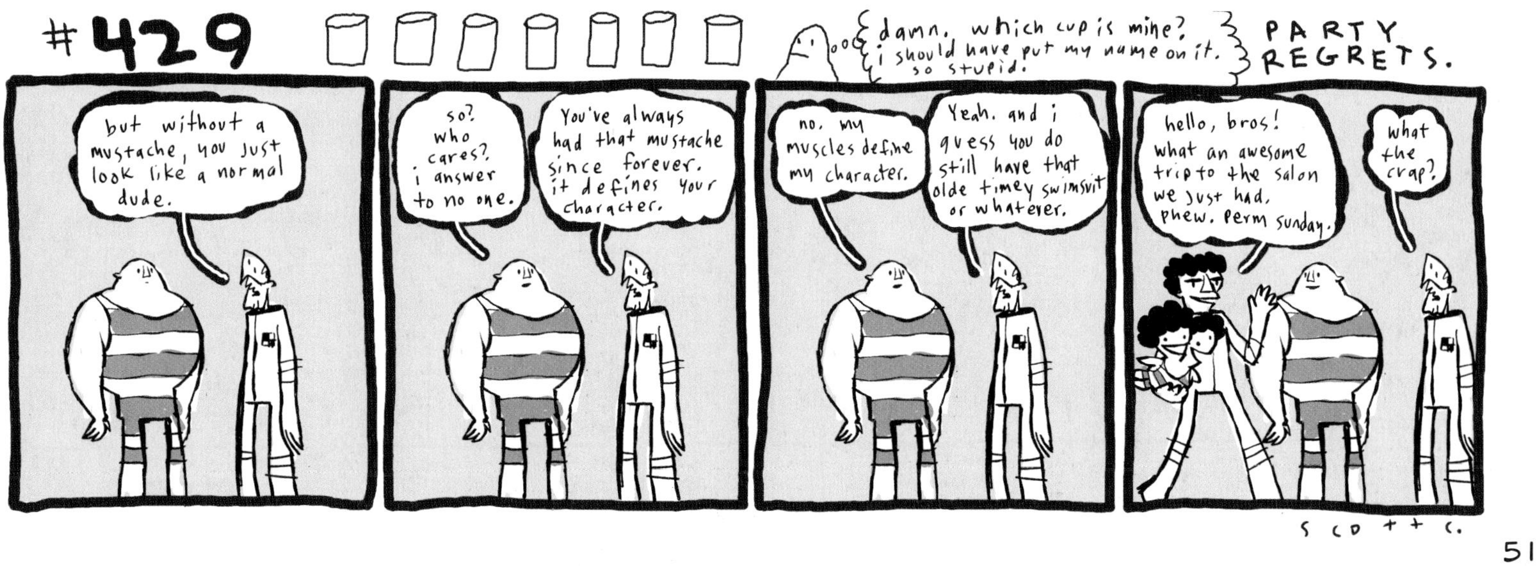

#429
damn. which cup is mine? i should have put my name on it. so stupid.
PARTY REGRETS.
but without a mustache, you just look like a normal dude.
so? who cares? i answer to no one.
you've always had that mustache since forever. it defines your character.
no. my muscles define my character.
yeah. and i guess you do still have that olde timey swimsuit or whatever.
hello, bros! what an awesome trip to the salon we just had. phew. perm sunday.
what the crap?
scott c.

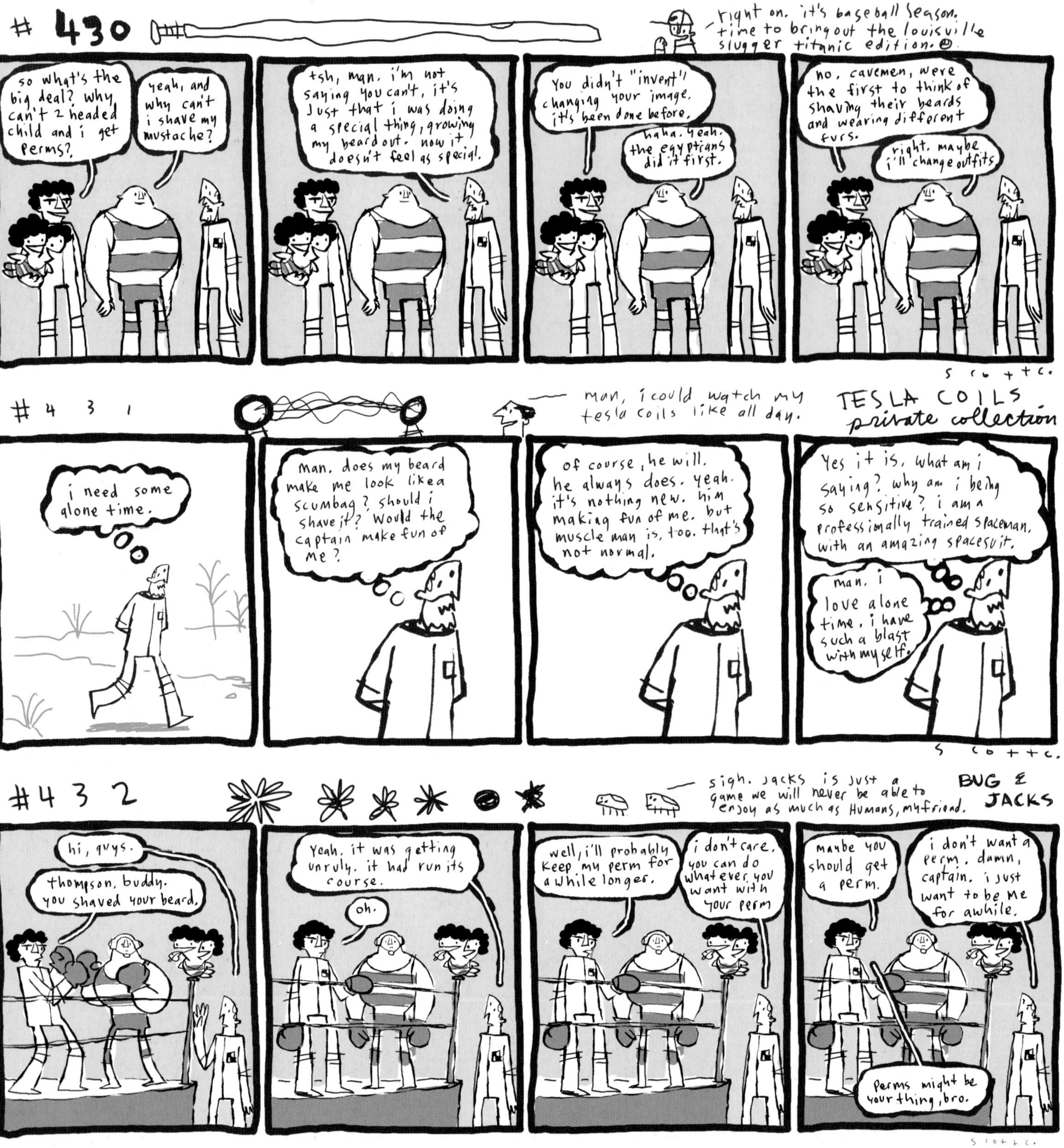

430
right on. it's baseball season. time to bring out the louisville slugger titanic edition.
so what's the big deal? why can't 2 headed child and i get perms?
yeah, and why can't i shave my mustache?
tsh, man. i'm not saying you can't, it's just that i was doing a special thing, growing my beard out. now it doesn't feel as special.
You didn't "invent" changing your image. it's been done before.
haha. yeah. the egyptians did it first.
no, cavemen, were the first to think of shaving their beards and wearing different furs.
right. maybe i'll change outfits.
scott c.
4 3 1
man, i could watch my tesla coils like all day.
TESLA COILS
private collection
i need some alone time.
man. does my beard make me look like a scumbag? should i shave it? would the captain make fun of me?
of course, he will. he always does. yeah. it's nothing new. him making fun of me. but muscle man is, too. that's not normal.
Yes it is. what am i saying? why am i being so sensitive? i am a professionally trained spaceman, with an amazing spacesuit.
man. i love alone time. i have such a blast with myself.
scott c.
4 3 2
sigh. jacks is just a game we will never be able to enjoy as much as humans, my friend.
BUG & JACKS
hi, guys.
thompson, buddy. you shaved your beard.
Yeah. it was getting unruly. it had run its course.
oh.
well, i'll probably keep my perm for a while longer.
i don't care. you can do whatever you want with your perm
maybe you should get a perm.
i don't want a perm. damn, captain. i just want to be me for awhile.
Perms might be your thing, bro.
scott c.

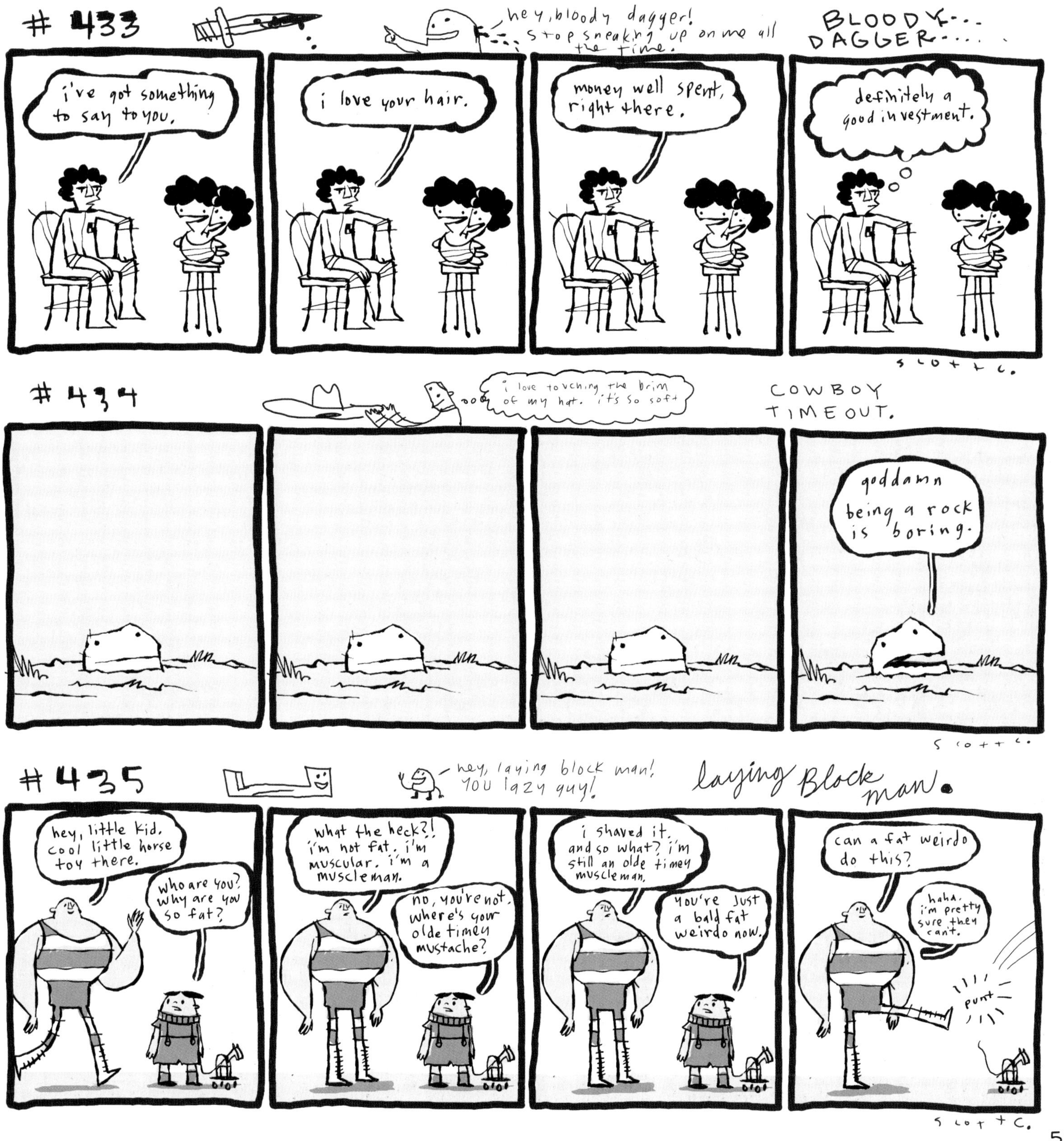

433
hey, bloody dagger! stop sneaking up on me all the time.
BLOODY DAGGER....
i've got something to say to you.
i love your hair.
money well spent, right there.
definitely a good investment.
scott c.
434
i love touching the brim of my hat. it's so soft
COWBOY TIMEOUT.
goddamn being a rock is boring.
scott c.
435
hey, laying block man! you lazy guy!
laying Block man.
hey, little kid. cool little horse toy there.
who are you? why are you so fat?
what the heck?! i'm not fat. i'm muscular. i'm a muscleman.
no, you're not. where's your olde timey mustache?
i shaved it. and so what? i'm still an olde timey muscleman.
you're just a bald fat weirdo now.
can a fat weirdo do this?
haha. i'm pretty sure they can't.
punt
scott c.

#436

hi, the suitcasers. the most organized duo.

the backpacks are looking sad.

Panel 1: i have finally invented "the rock stick".

Panel 2: no, wait. it shall be called "sharp stick".

Panel 3: stupid sounding. "stabbing rock". "throwing rock". wait, sharp should be in there somehow.

Panel 4: "the sharp stabber". "the sharp rocker".

i can't wait to go hunting. eventually.

Scott C.

#437 the Eating Lesson (demoed by knight)

i've always wondered!

Panel 1: first off, choose a sandwich. then eat it with your mouth.

Panel 2: wash it down with some sort of cold drink.

Panel 3: then afterwards, brush the crap out of your teeth to make sure no sandwich lingers.

Panel 4: for dessert, spray some Binaca® in your mouth and go talk to your friends. refreshed!

end of lesson!

Scott C.

#438

monster family is distracted by the T.V. perfect time to escape.

MONSTER FAMILY loses dude.

Panel 1: i'm thinking about embarking on another space mission, thompson, but don't quote me on that.

yes, captain.

Panel 2: i said don't quote me on that. you're not writing that down are you?

oh, no. i'm just drawing.

Panel 3: drawing? drawing what?

i don't know really. just a design i guess.

Panel 4: you mean like scribbly nonsense? why don't you draw something awesome. like a jet.

because i'm just drawing whatever comes out. it's relaxing.

but my talking should be relaxing.

Scott C.

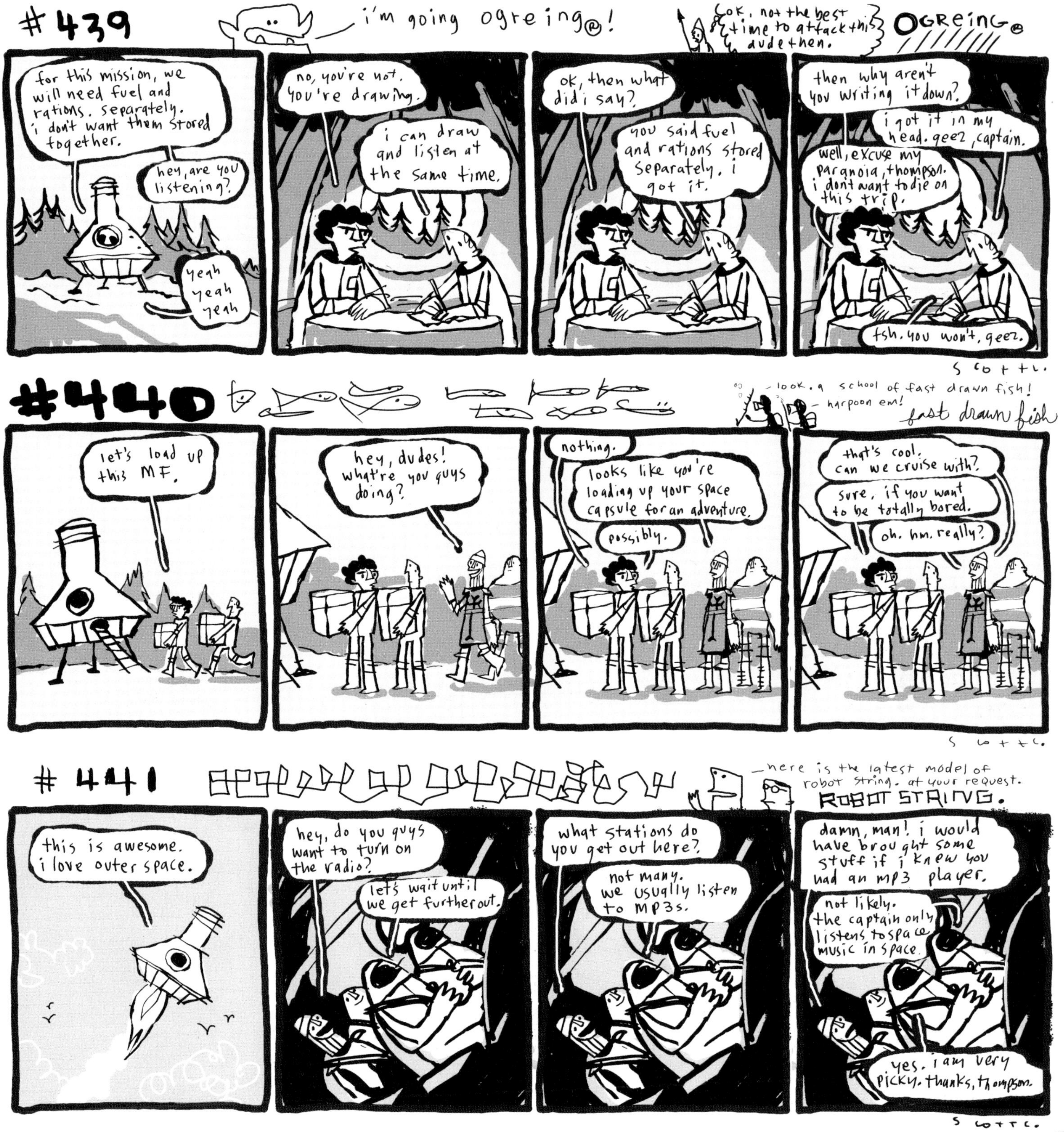
#439
i'm going ogreing®!
ok, not the best time to attack this dude then.
OGREING®
for this mission, we will need fuel and rations. separately. i don't want them stored together.
hey, are you listening?
yeah yeah yeah
no, you're not. you're drawing.
i can draw and listen at the same time.
ok, then what did i say?
you said fuel and rations stored separately. i got it.
then why aren't you writing it down?
i got it in my head. geez, captain.
well, excuse my paranoia, thompson. i don't want to die on this trip.
tsh. you won't. geez.
scott c.
#440
look. a school of fast drawn fish!
harpoon em!
fast drawn fish
let's load up this MF.
hey, dudes! what're you guys doing?
nothing.
looks like you're loading up your space capsule for an adventure.
possibly.
that's cool. can we cruise with?
sure, if you want to be totally bored.
oh. hm. really?
scott c.
#441
here is the latest model of robot string. at your request.
ROBOT STRING.
this is awesome. i love outer space.
hey, do you guys want to turn on the radio?
let's wait until we get further out.
what stations do you get out here?
not many. we usually listen to mp3s.
damn, man! i would have brought some stuff if i knew you had an mp3 player.
not likely. the captain only listens to space music in space.
yes. i am very picky. thanks, thompson.
scott c.

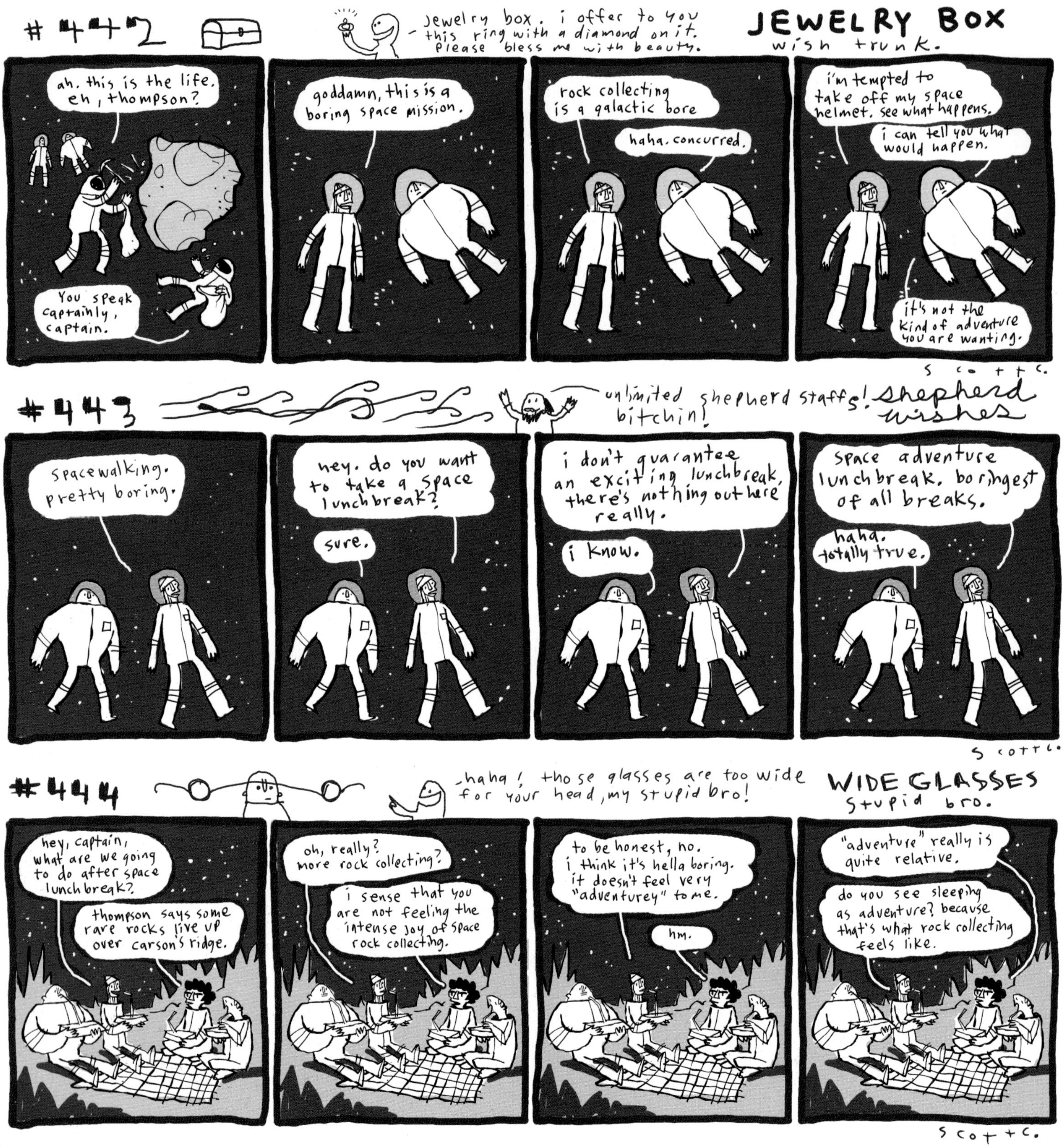
#442
jewelry box. i offer to you this ring with a diamond on it. Please bless me with beauty.
JEWELRY BOX
wish trunk.
ah. this is the life. eh, thompson?
You speak captainly, captain.
goddamn, this is a boring space mission.
rock collecting is a galactic bore
haha. concurred.
i'm tempted to take off my space helmet. see what happens.
i can tell you what would happen.
it's not the kind of adventure you are wanting.
scott c.
#443
unlimited shepherd staffs! bitchin!
shepherd wishes
spacewalking. pretty boring.
hey. do you want to take a space lunchbreak?
sure.
i don't guarantee an exciting lunchbreak, there's nothing out here really.
i know.
space adventure lunchbreak, boringest of all breaks.
haha. totally true.
scott c.
#444
-haha! those glasses are too wide for your head, my stupid bro!
WIDE GLASSES
stupid bro.
hey, captain, what are we going to do after space lunchbreak?
thompson says some rare rocks live up over carson's ridge.
oh, really? more rock collecting?
i sense that you are not feeling the intense joy of space rock collecting.
to be honest, no. i think it's hella boring. it doesn't feel very "adventurey" to me.
hm.
"adventure" really is quite relative.
do you see sleeping as adventure? because that's what rock collecting feels like.
scott c.

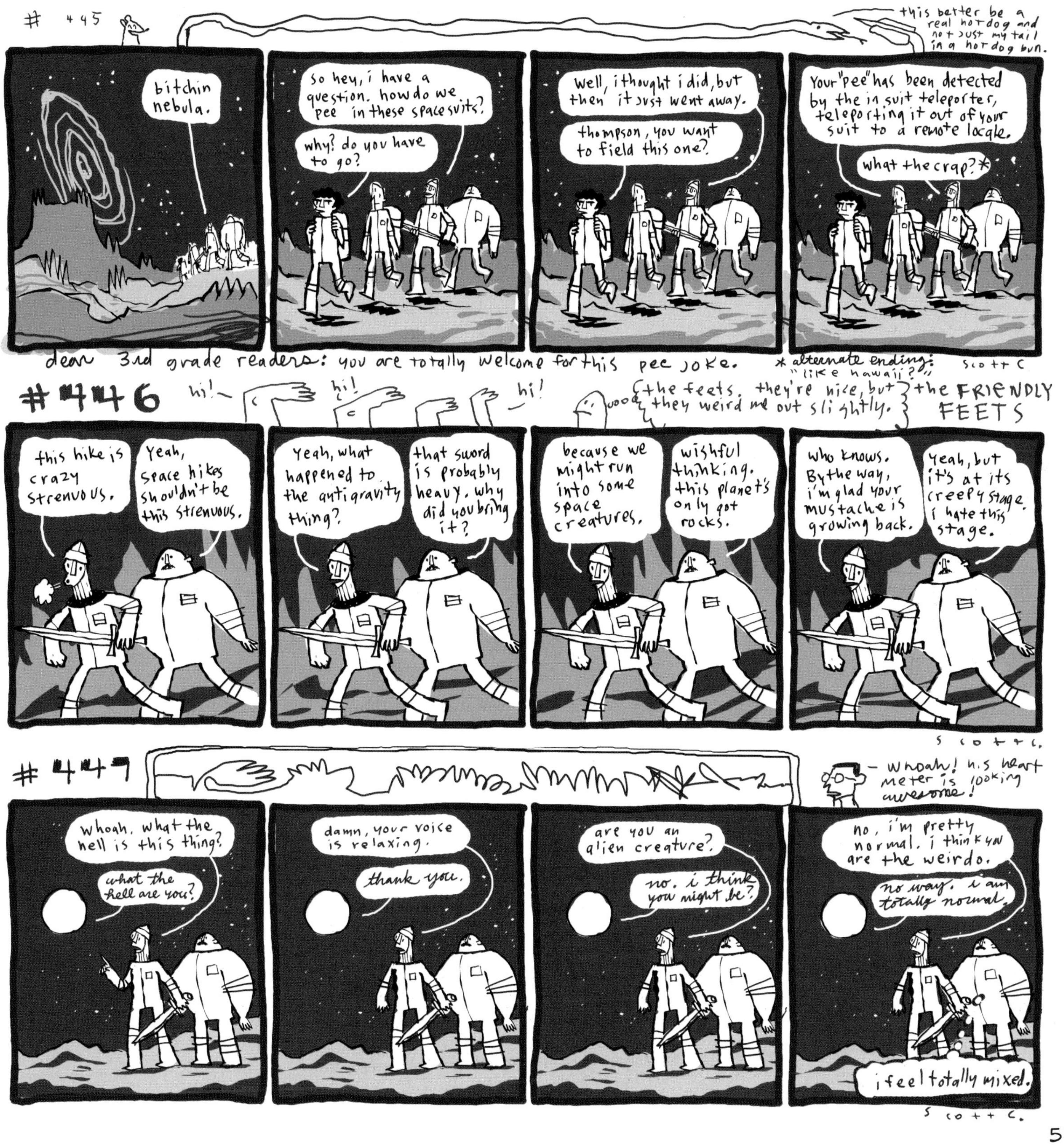

445
this better be a real hot dog and not just my tail in a hot dog bun.
bitchin nebula.
so hey, i have a question. how do we pee in these spacesuits?
why? do you have to go?
Well, i thought i did, but then it just went away.
thompson, you want to field this one?
Your "pee" has been detected by the in suit teleporter, teleporting it out of your suit to a remote locale.
what the crap?*
dear 3rd grade readers: you are totally welcome for this pee joke.
* alternate ending: "like hawaii?"
scott c
#446
hi!
hi!
hi!
oooo
the feets, they're nice, but they weird me out slightly.
the FRIENDLY FEETS
this hike is crazy strenuous.
Yeah, space hikes shouldn't be this strenuous.
Yeah, what happened to the antigravity thing?
that sword is probably heavy. why did you bring it?
because we might run into some space creatures.
wishful thinking. this planet's only got rocks.
who knows. By the way, i'm glad your mustache is growing back.
Yeah, but it's at its creepy stage. i hate this stage.
scott c.
#447
Whoah! his heart meter is looking awesome!
Whoah. what the hell is this thing?
what the hell are you?
damn, your voice is relaxing.
thank you.
are you an alien creature?
no. i think you might be?
no, i'm pretty normal. i think you are the weirdo.
no way. i am totally normal.
i feel totally mixed.
scott c.

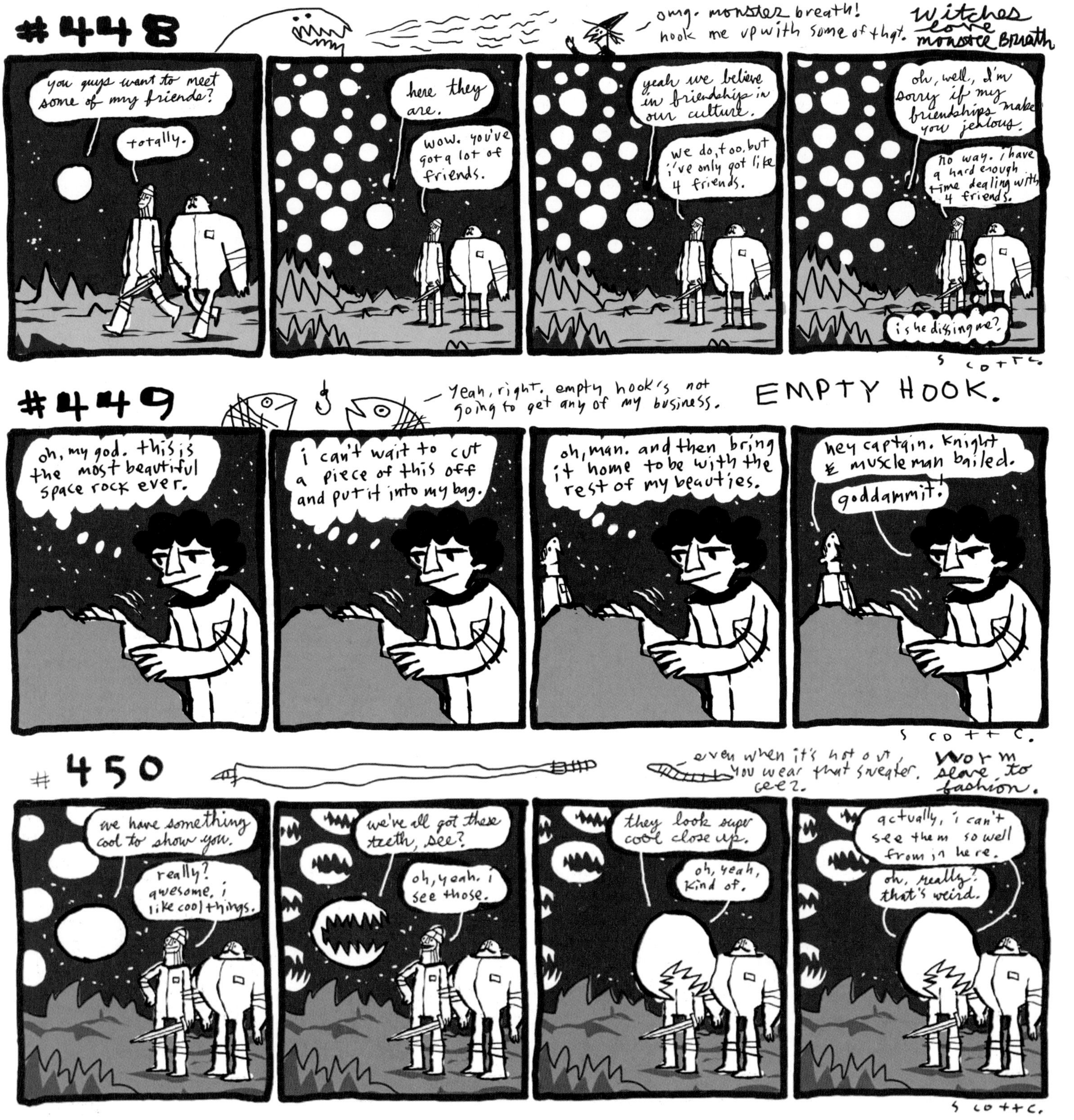
#448
— omg. monster breath! hook me up with some of that.
Witches love monster Breath
you guys want to meet some of my friends?
totally.
here they are.
wow. you've got a lot of friends.
yeah we believe in friendships in our culture.
we do, too, but i've only got like 4 friends.
oh, well, i'm sorry if my friendships make you jealous.
no way. i have a hard enough time dealing with 4 friends.
is he dissing me?
scott c.
#449
— Yeah, right. empty hook's not going to get any of my business.
EMPTY HOOK.
oh, my god. this is the most beautiful space rock ever.
i can't wait to cut a piece of this off and put it into my bag.
oh, man. and then bring it home to be with the rest of my beauties.
hey captain. knight & muscleman bailed.
goddammit!
scott c.
#450
— even when it's not out, you wear that sweater. geez.
Worm slave to fashion.
we have something cool to show you.
really? awesome. i like cool things.
we've all got these teeth, see?
oh, yeah. i see those.
they look super cool close up.
oh, yeah, kind of.
actually, i can't see them so well from in here.
oh, really? that's weird.
scott c.

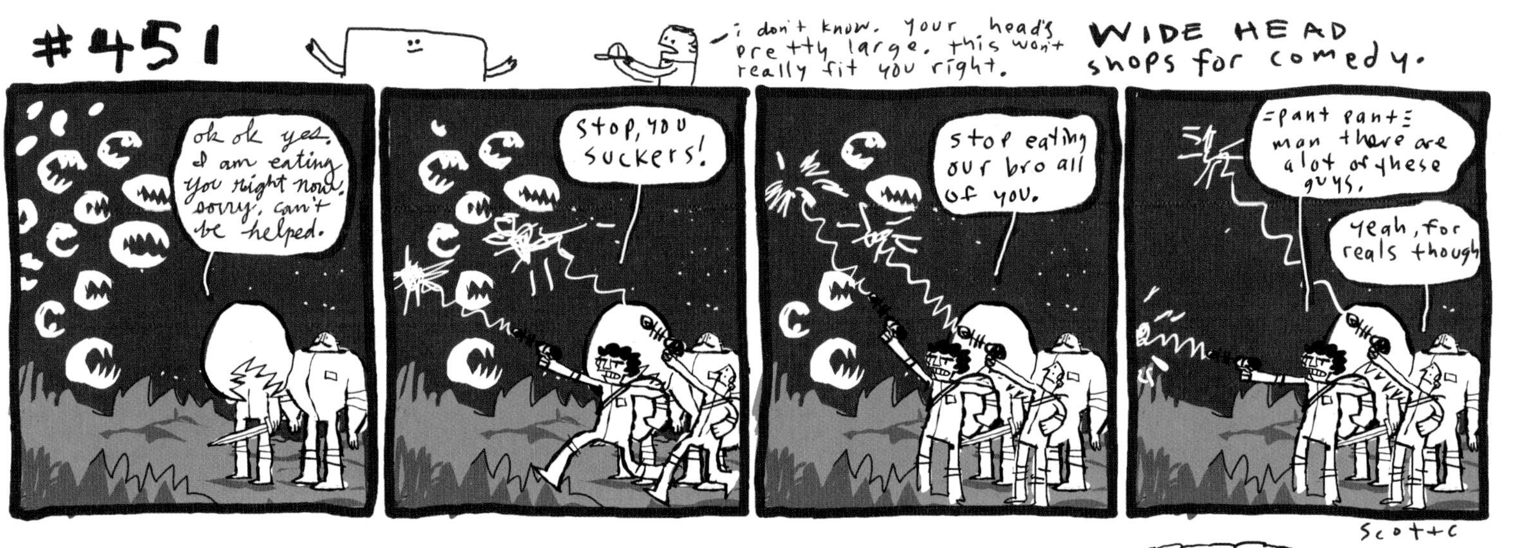
#451
i don't know. your head's pretty large. this won't really fit you right.
WIDE HEAD shops for comedy.
ok ok yes. I am eating you right now. sorry, can't be helped.
Stop, you suckers!
stop eating our bro all of you.
=pant pant= man there are alot of these guys.
yeah, for reals though
scott c

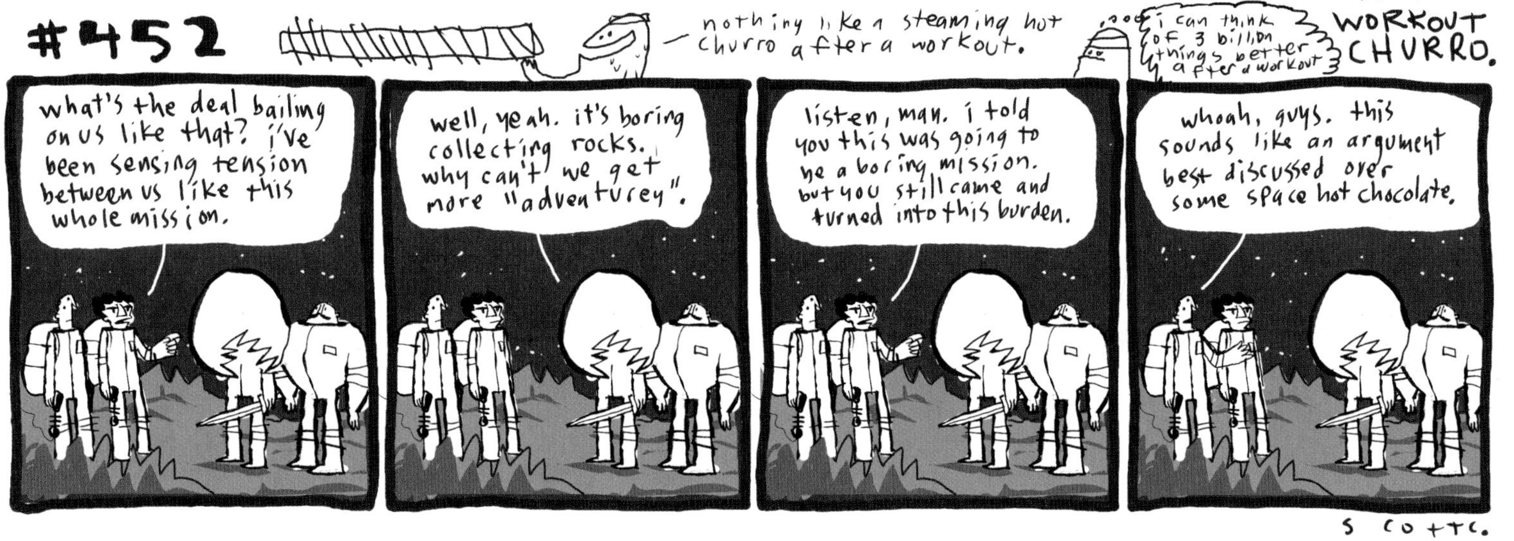
#452
nothing like a steaming hot churro after a workout.
i can think of 3 billion things better after a workout
WORKOUT CHURRO.
what's the deal bailing on us like that? i've been sensing tension between us like this whole mission.
well, yeah. it's boring collecting rocks. why can't we get more "adventurey".
listen, man. i told you this was going to be a boring mission. but you still came and turned into this burden.
whoah, guys. this sounds like an argument best discussed over some space hot chocolate.
scott c.

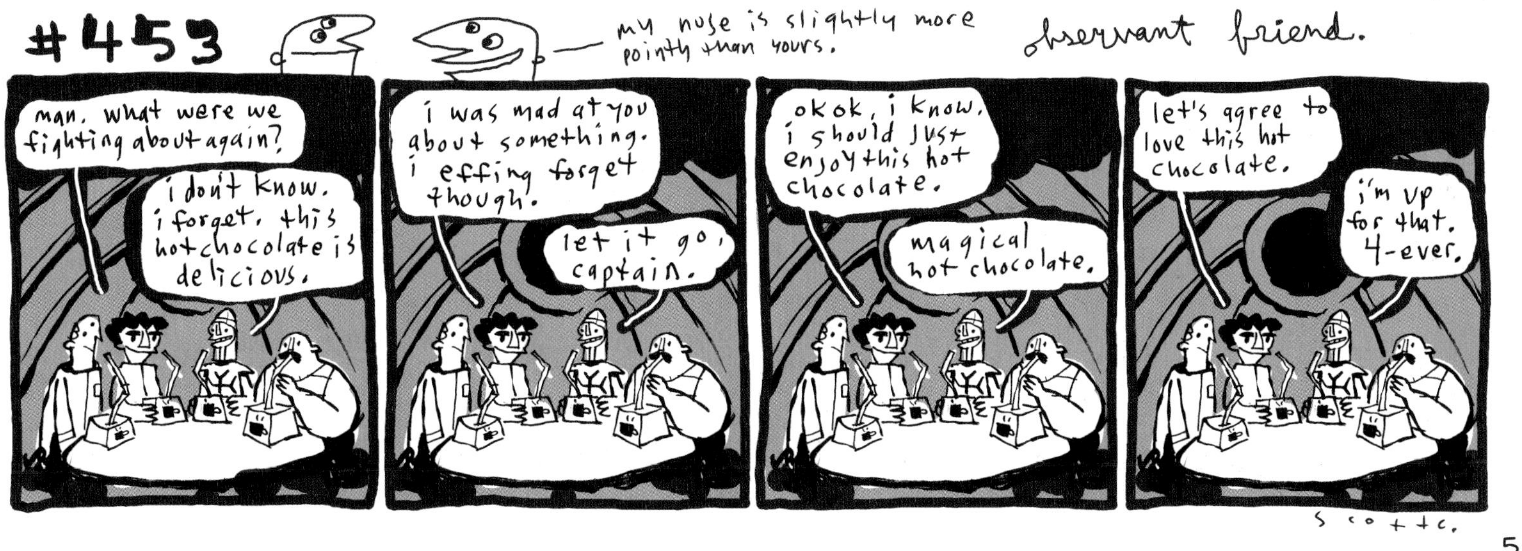
#453
my nose is slightly more pointy than yours.
observant friend.
man. what were we fighting about again?
i don't know. i forget. this hot chocolate is delicious.
i was mad at you about something. i effing forget though.
let it go, captain.
ok ok, i know. i should just enjoy this hot chocolate.
magical hot chocolate.
let's agree to love this hot chocolate.
i'm up for that. 4-ever.
scott c.

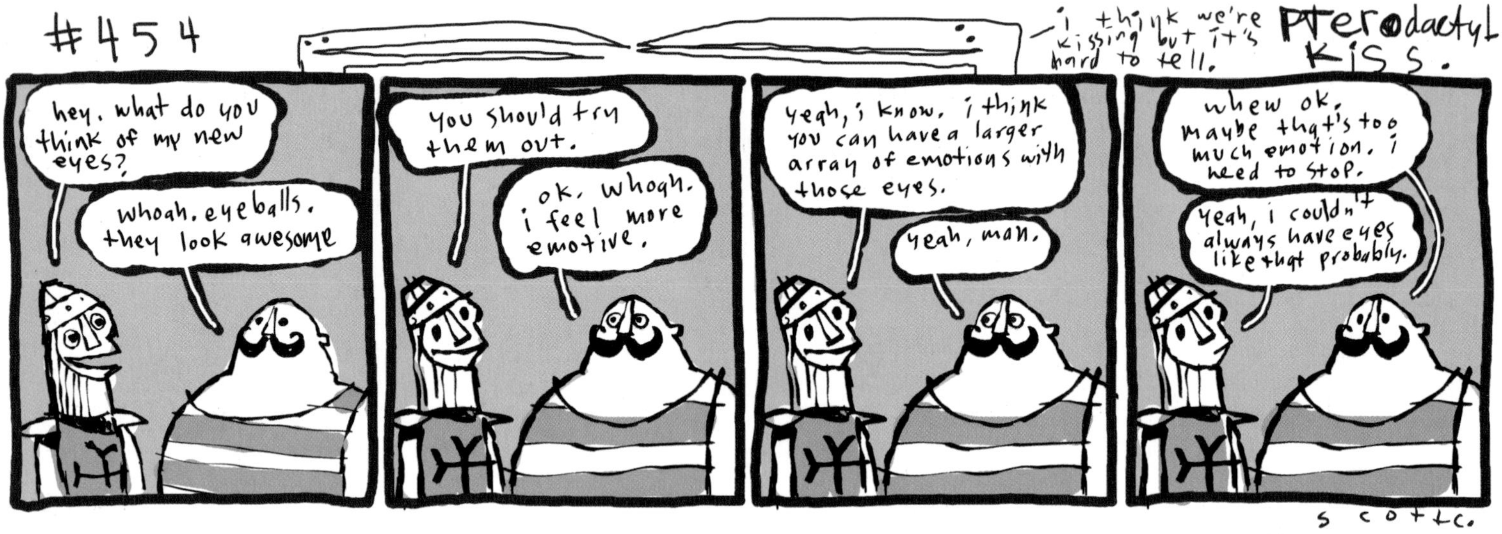
#454
i think we're kissing but it's hard to tell.
Pterodactyl Kiss.
hey. what do you think of my new eyes?
whoah. eyeballs. they look awesome
you should try them out.
ok. whoah. i feel more emotive.
yeah, i know. i think you can have a larger array of emotions with those eyes.
yeah, man.
whew ok. maybe that's too much emotion. i need to stop.
yeah, i couldn't always have eyes like that probably.
scott c.

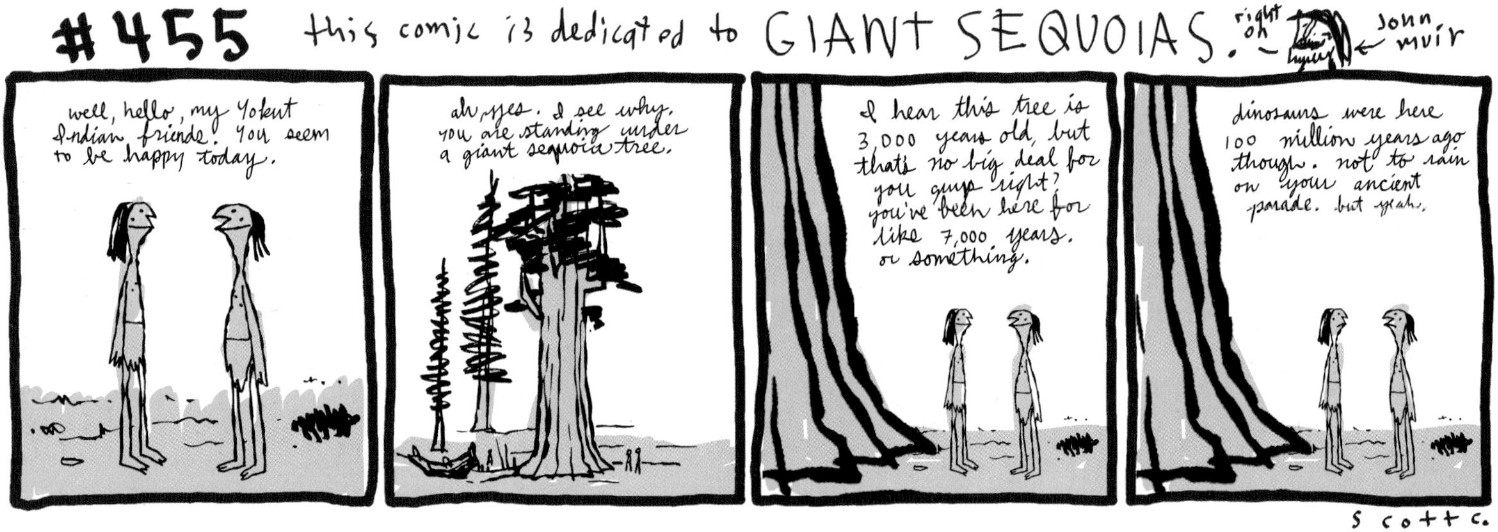
#455
this comic is dedicated to GIANT SEQUOIAS.
right on
John Muir
well, hello, my Yokut Indian friend. You seem to be happy today.
ah, yes. I see why. you are standing under a giant sequoia tree.
I hear this tree is 3,000 years old, but that's no big deal for you guys right? you've been here for like 7,000 years. or something.
dinosaurs were here 100 million years ago though. not to rain on your ancient parade. but yeah.
scott c.

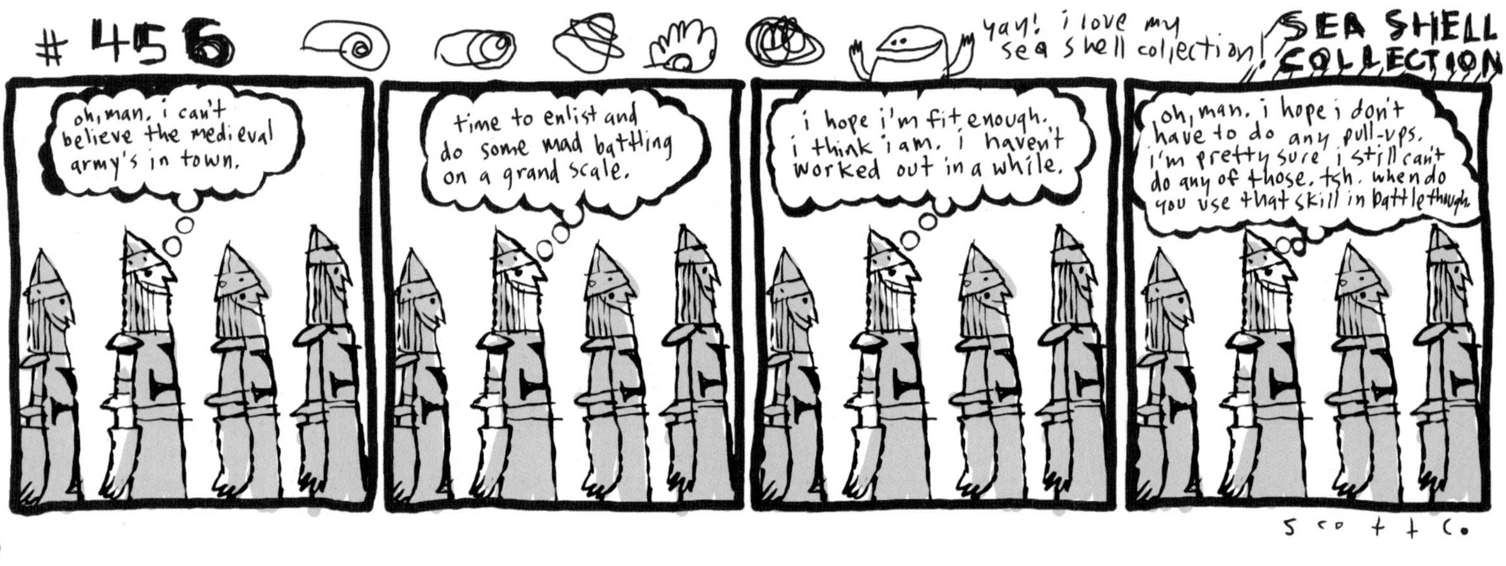
#456
yay! i love my sea shell collection!
SEA SHELL COLLECTION
oh, man. i can't believe the medieval army's in town.
time to enlist and do some mad battling on a grand scale.
i hope i'm fit enough. i think i am. i haven't worked out in a while.
oh, man. i hope i don't have to do any pull-ups. i'm pretty sure i still can't do any of those. tsh. when do you use that skill in battle though.
scott c.

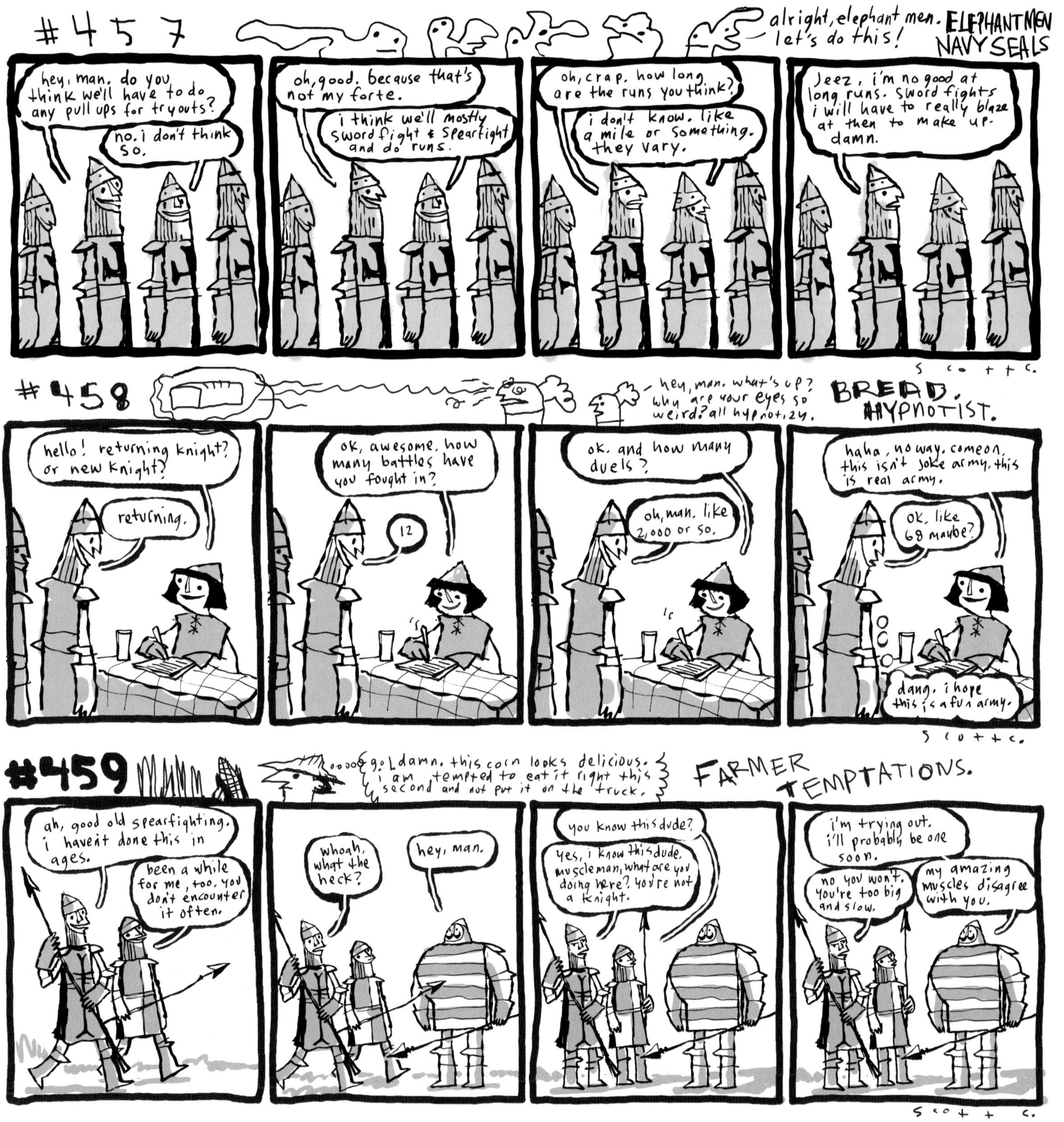
#457
alright, elephant men. let's do this!
ELEPHANTMEN NAVY SEALS
hey, man. do you think we'll have to do any pull ups for tryouts?
no. i don't think so.
oh, good. because that's not my forte.
i think we'll mostly swordfight & spearfight and do runs.
oh, crap. how long are the runs you think?
i don't know. like a mile or something. they vary.
Jeez, i'm no good at long runs. sword fights i will have to really blaze at then to make up- damn.
scott c.
#458
- hey, man. what's up? why are your eyes so weird? all hypnotizy.
BREAD. HYPNOTIST.
hello! returning knight? or new knight?
returning.
ok, awesome. how many battles have you fought in?
12
ok. and how many duels?
oh, man. like 2,000 or so.
haha, no way. come on. this isn't joke army. this is real army.
ok, like 68 maybe?
dang. i hope this is a fun army.
scott c.
#459
goldamn. this corn looks delicious. i am tempted to eat it right this second and not put it on the truck.
FARMER TEMPTATIONS.
ah, good old spearfighting. i haven't done this in ages.
been a while for me, too. you don't encounter it often.
whoah, what the heck?
hey, man.
you know this dude?
yes, i know this dude. muscleman, what are you doing here? you're not a knight.
i'm trying out. i'll probably be one soon.
no you won't. you're too big and slow.
my amazing muscles disagree with you.
scott c.

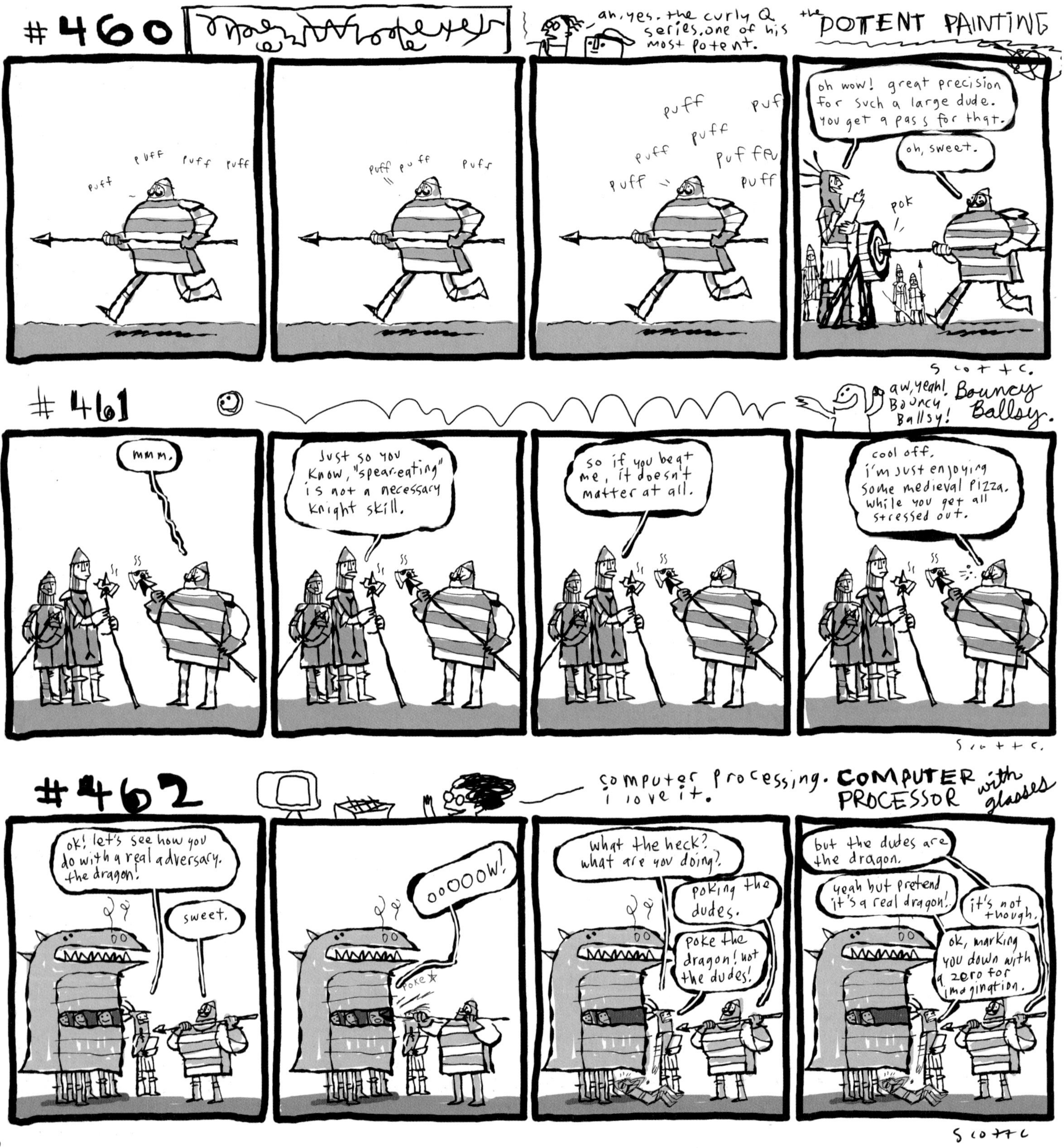

#460
ah, yes. the curly Q series. one of his most potent.
the POTENT PAINTING
puff puff puff puff
puff puff puff
puff puff puff puff puff puff puff puff
oh wow! great precision for such a large dude. you get a pass for that.
oh, sweet.
pok
scott c.
#461
aw, yeah! Bouncy Ballsy!
Bouncy Ballsy.
mmm.
just so you know, "spear-eating" is not a necessary knight skill.
so if you beat me, it doesn't matter at all.
cool off. i'm just enjoying some medieval pizza. while you get all stressed out.
scott c.
#462
computer processing. i love it.
COMPUTER PROCESSOR with glasses
ok! let's see how you do with a real adversary. the dragon!
sweet.
ooOOOW!
poke
what the heck? what are you doing?
poking the dudes.
poke the dragon! not the dudes!
but the dudes are the dragon.
yeah but pretend it's a real dragon!
it's not though.
ok, marking you down with a zero for imagination.
scott c

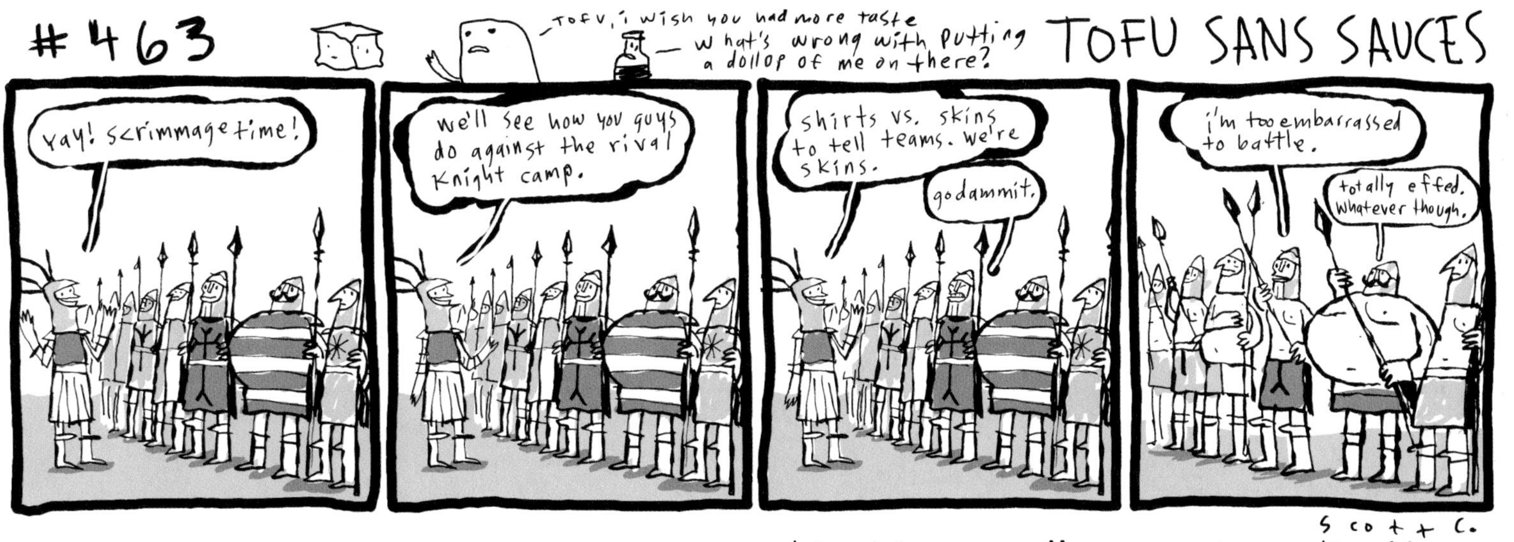
#463
TOFU SANS SAUCES
- tofu, i wish you had more taste
- what's wrong with putting a dollop of me on there?
yay! scrimmage time!
we'll see how you guys do against the rival knight camp.
shirts vs. skins to tell teams. we're skins.
godammit.
i'm too embarrassed to battle.
totally effed. whatever though.
scott c.

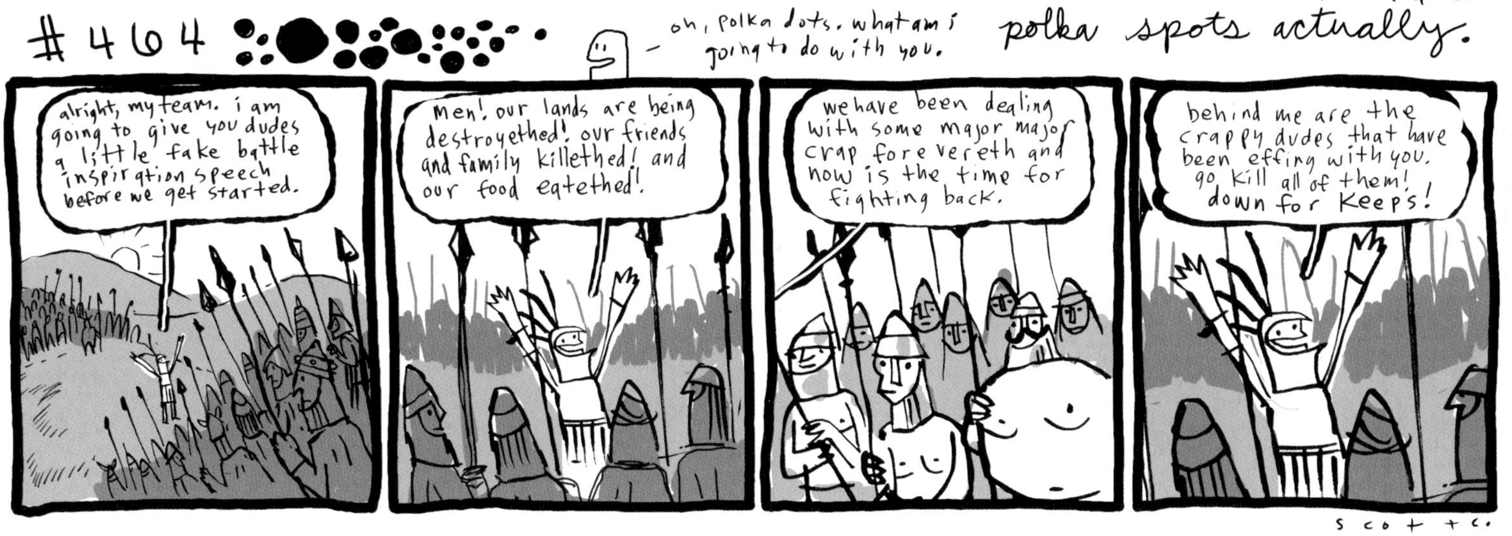
#464
- oh, polka dots. what am i going to do with you.
polka spots actually.
alright, my team. i am going to give you dudes a little fake battle inspiration speech before we get started.
men! our lands are being destroyethed! our friends and family killethed! and our food eatethed!
we have been dealing with some major major crap forevereth and now is the time for fighting back.
behind me are the crappy dudes that have been effing with you. go kill all of them! down for keeps!
scott c.

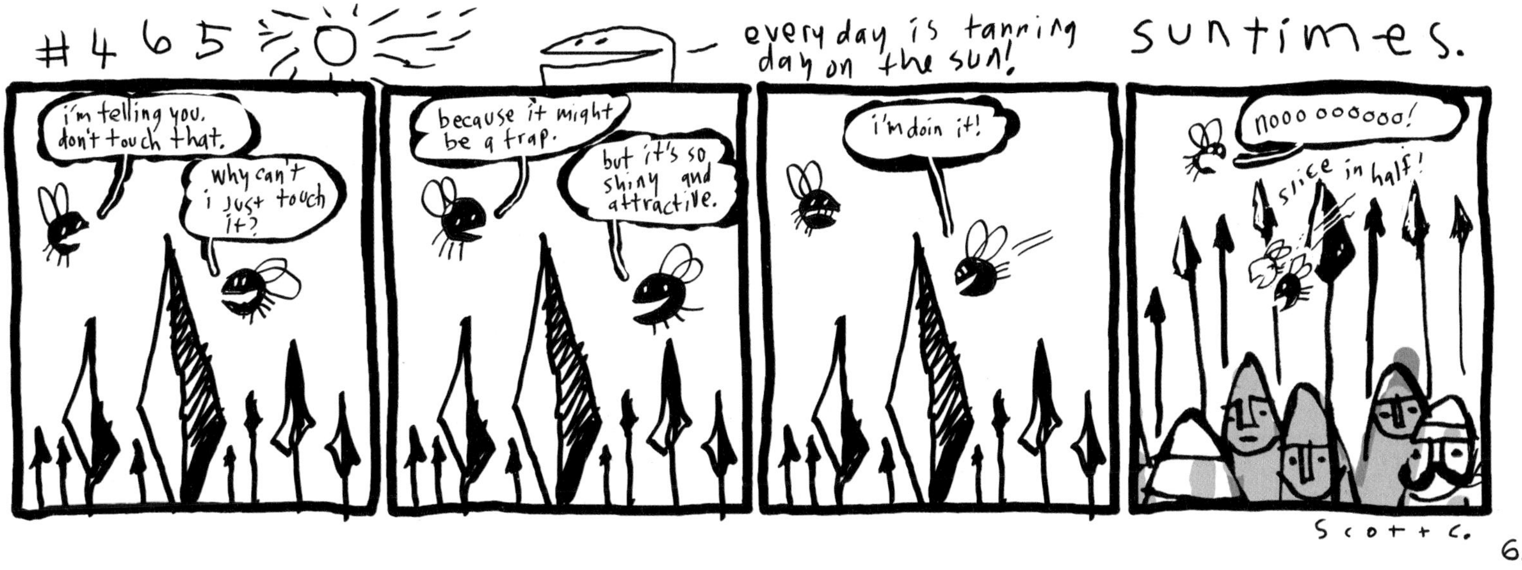
#465
- everyday is tanning day on the sun!
suntimes.
i'm telling you. don't touch that.
why can't i just touch it?
because it might be a trap.
but it's so shiny and attractive.
i'm doin it!
nooo oooooo!
slice in half!
scott c.

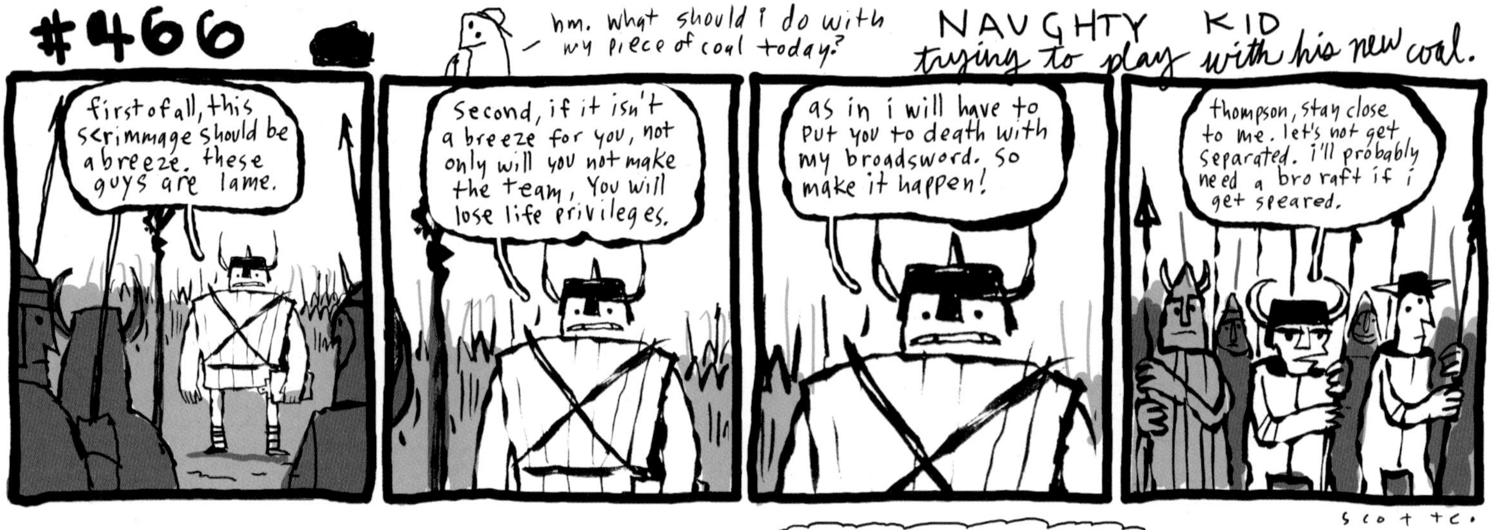
#466
hm. what should i do with my piece of coal today?
NAUGHTY KID trying to play with his new coal.
first of all, this scrimmage should be a breeze. these guys are lame.
Second, if it isn't a breeze for you, not only will you not make the team, You will lose life privileges.
as in i will have to put you to death with my broadsword. So make it happen!
thompson, stay close to me. let's not get separated. i'll probably need a bro raft if i get speared.
scott c.

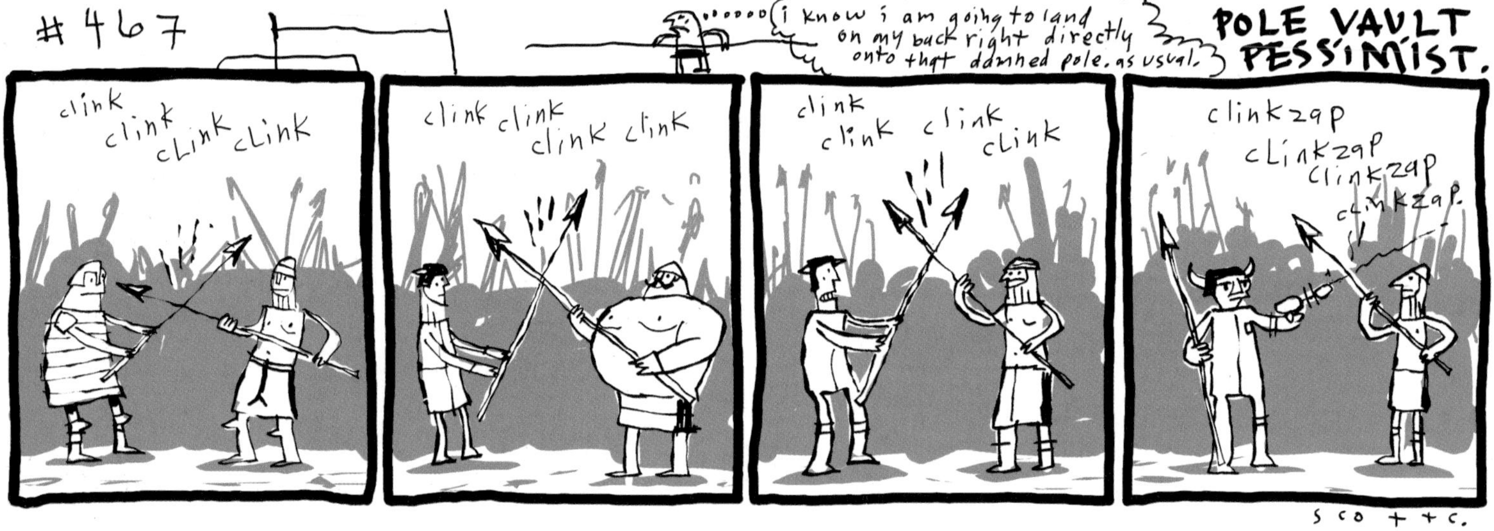
#467
i know i am going to land on my back right directly onto that damned pole. as usual.
POLE VAULT PESSIMIST.
clink clink clink clink
clink clink clink clink
clink clink clink clink
clinkzap clinkzap clinkzap clinkzap.
scott c.

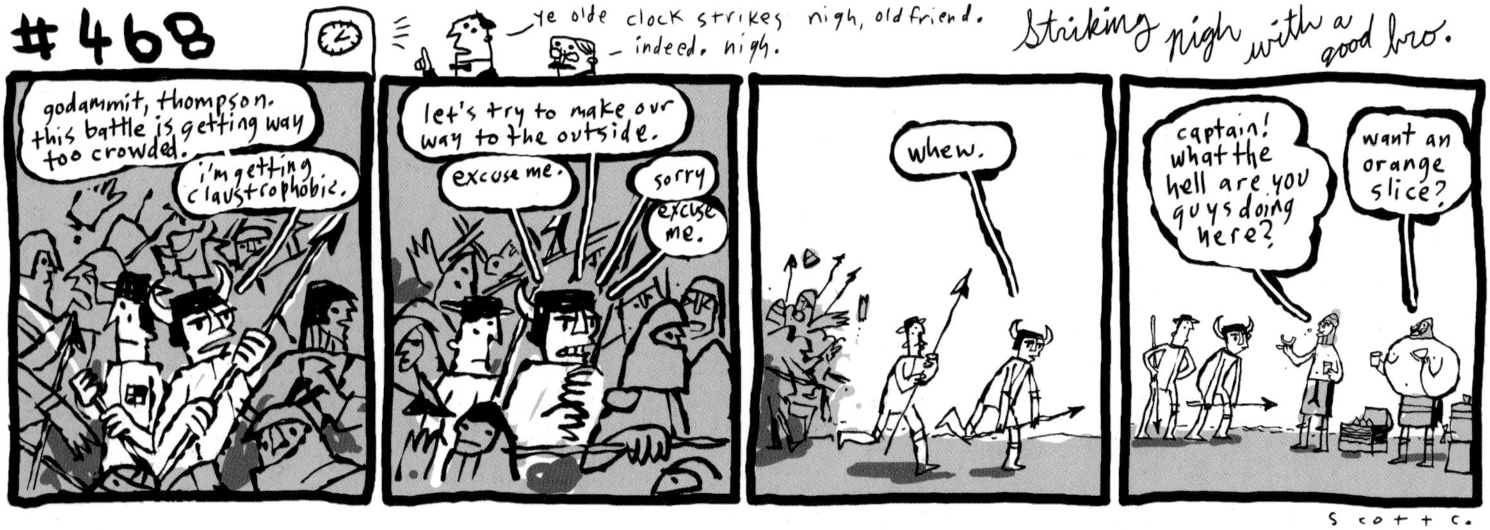
#468
ye olde clock strikes nigh, old friend.
indeed. nigh.
Striking nigh with a good bro.
godammit, thompson. this battle is getting way too crowded.
i'm getting claustrophobic.
let's try to make our way to the outside.
excuse me.
sorry
excuse me.
whew.
captain! what the hell are you guys doing here?
want an orange slice?
scott c.

WEREWOLF & WOLF MAN
full moon bro-out!

Panel 1: oh, man. these orange slices taste amazing.

Panel 2: captain, you still haven't answered my question as to why you two are trying to be knights.

Panel 3: are we eating these orange slices to get some quick vitamin C for our battling? or quick sugar?

Panel 4: what? / how'd you get to be captain of your own ship? / hey, man! it's a capsule! not a ship.

470

 whoah, these ten commandments are a tough read. i have to keep going back and rereading crap. my wandering mind.

Moses checking out his new 10 commandments

SCOTT C.

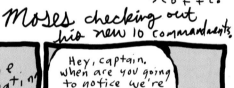 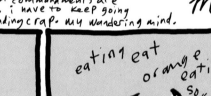

Panel 1: eat eat eating eating

Panel 2:

Panel 3: eating eat orange eating sounds

Panel 4: Hey, captain. when are you going to notice we're staring you down? / yeah, stop ignoring us.

scott c.

---

471 un-popped

RETURN of the popcorn heads!

Panel 1: knight, we allowed you to try out the world of the spaceman* why can we not try out the world of the knight?

Panel 2: tsh. well, for one we were all out in space alone. Here you're acting crazy in front of all my knighting friends.

Panel 3: knight, i suggest you get over yourself. there is a good chance that we are better at knighting than you. / maybe in your dreams.

Panel 4: hey, thompson. you've been working on that orange slice for awhile. you even eating it? / yeah. i'm just sucking on it now.

see #440 for the start of that spaceman world dabbling.

SCOTT C.

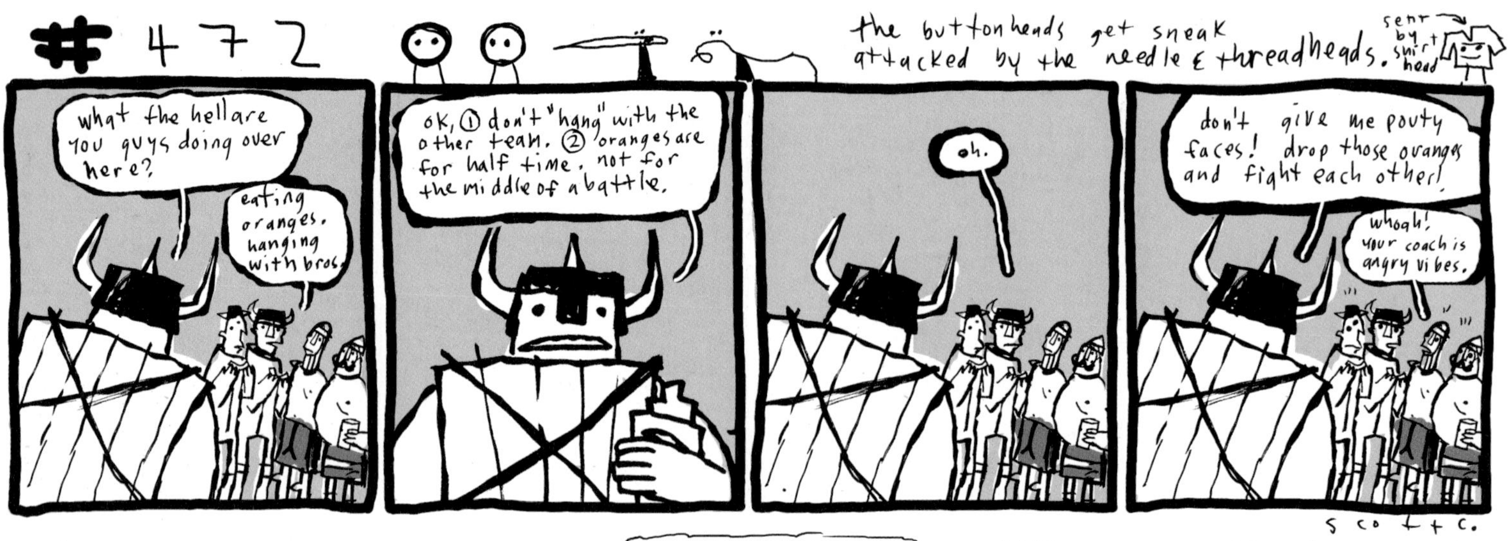
#472
the buttonheads get sneak attacked by the needle & threadheads.
sent by t shirt head
what the hell are you guys doing over here?
eating oranges. hanging with bros.
ok, ① don't "hang" with the other team. ② oranges are for half time. not for the middle of a battle.
oh.
don't give me pouty faces! drop those oranges and fight each other!
whoah! your coach is angry vibes.
scott c.

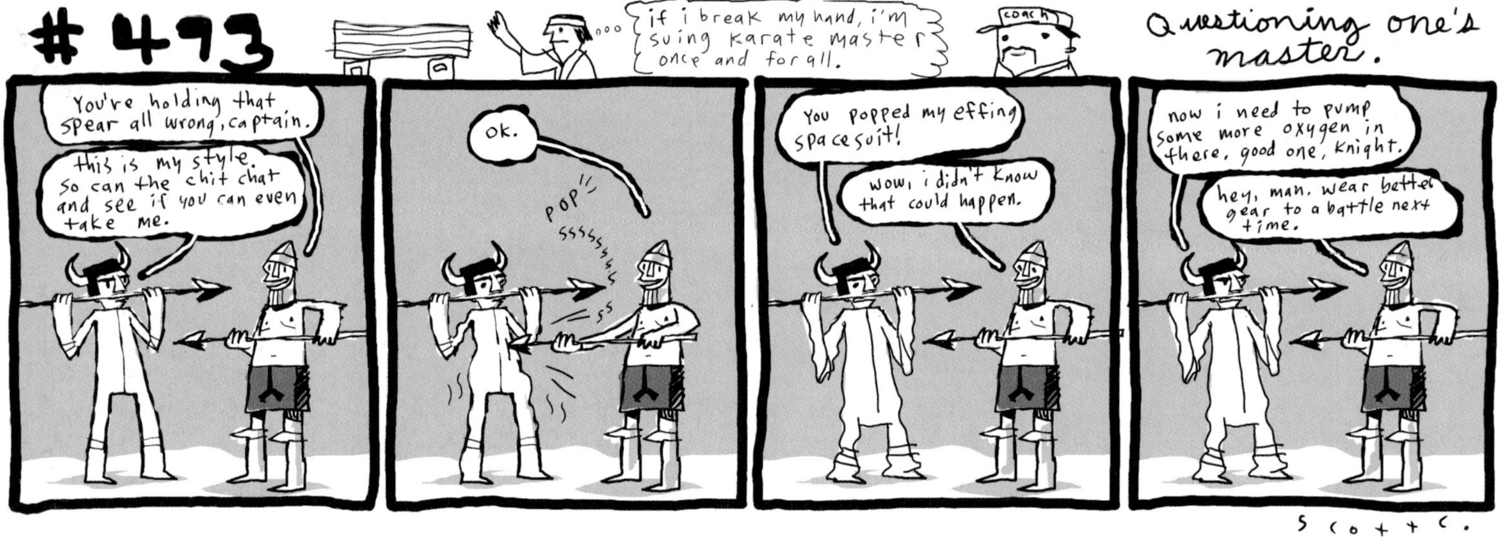
#493
if i break my hand, i'm suing karate master once and for all.
coach
Questioning one's master.
You're holding that spear all wrong, captain.
this is my style. so can the chit chat and see if you can even take me.
ok.
POP
sssssss
You popped my effing spacesuit!
wow, i didn't know that could happen.
now i need to pump some more oxygen in there. good one, knight.
hey, man. wear better gear to a battle next time.
scott c.

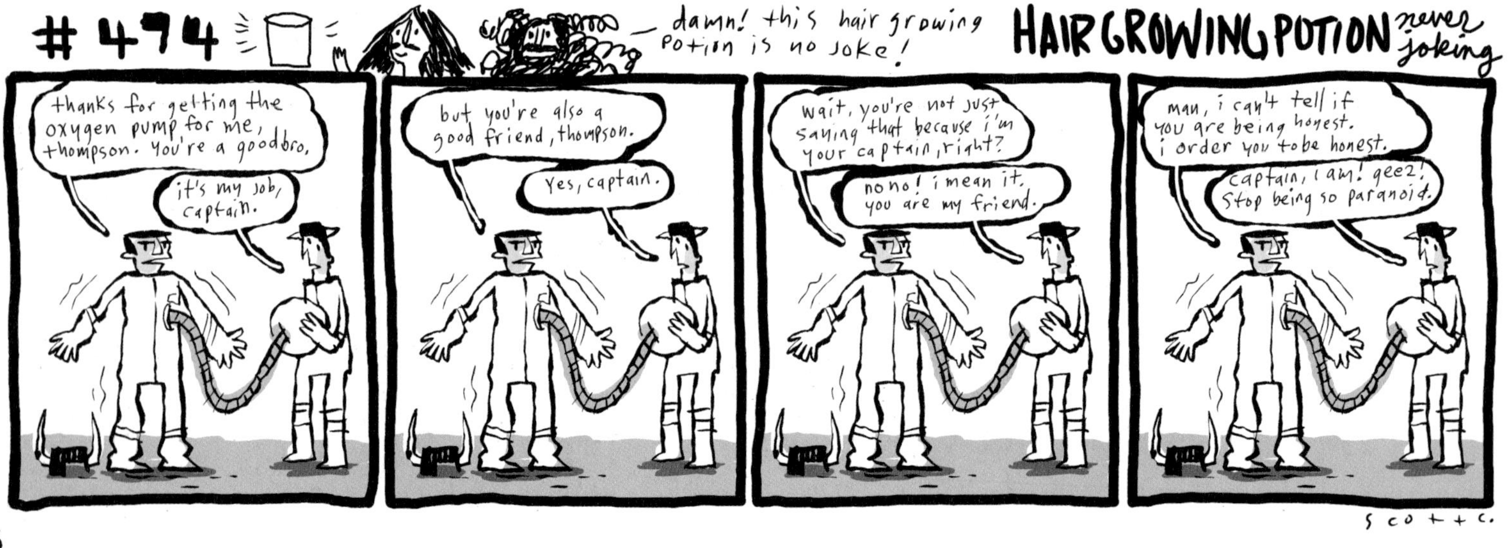
#494
damn! this hair growing potion is no joke!
HAIR GROWING POTION never joking
thanks for getting the oxygen pump for me, thompson. You're a good bro.
it's my job, captain.
but you're also a good friend, thompson.
Yes, captain.
wait, you're not just saying that because i'm your captain, right?
no no! i mean it. you are my friend.
man, i can't tell if you are being honest. i order you to be honest.
captain, i am! geez! stop being so paranoid.
scott c.

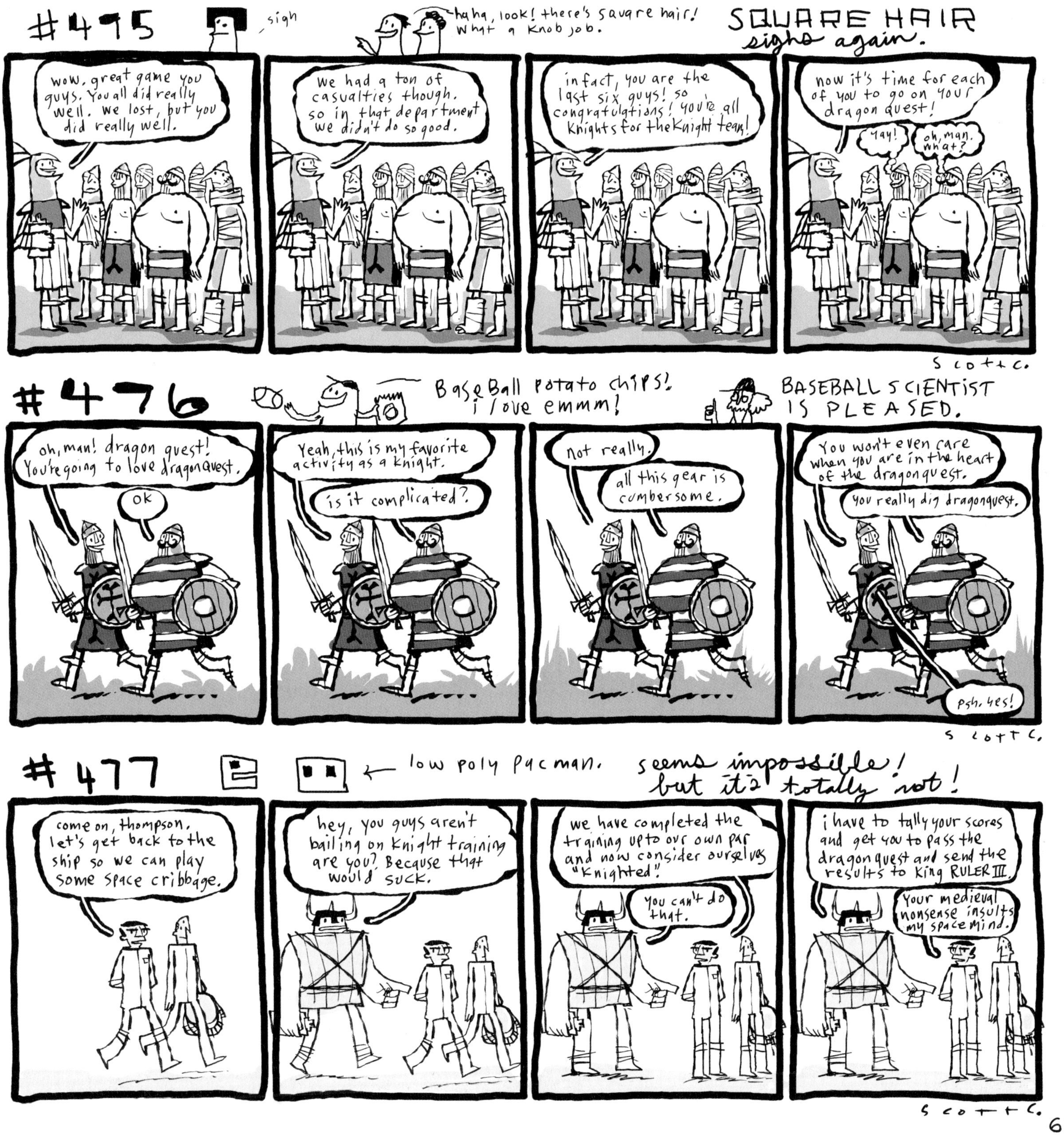
#475
sigh
haha, look! there's square hair! What a knob job.
SQUARE HAIR sighs again.
wow, great game you guys. You all did really well. we lost, but you did really well.
We had a ton of casualties though. so in that department we didn't do so good.
in fact, you are the last six guys! so congratulations! You're all Knights for the Knight team!
now it's time for each of you to go on your dragon quest!
Yay!
oh, man. what?
Scott C.
#476
Baseball potato chips! i love emmm!
BASEBALL SCIENTIST IS PLEASED.
oh, man! dragon quest! You're going to love dragonquest.
ok
Yeah, this is my favorite activity as a knight.
is it complicated?
not really.
all this gear is cumbersome.
You won't even care when you are in the heart of the dragonquest.
You really dig dragonquest.
psh, yes!
Scott C.
#477
low poly pacman.
seems impossible! but it's totally not!
come on, thompson, let's get back to the ship so we can play some space cribbage.
hey, you guys aren't bailing on knight training are you? Because that would suck.
we have completed the training up to our own par and now consider ourselves "Knighted".
You can't do that.
i have to tally your scores and get you to pass the dragonquest and send the results to King RULER III.
Your medieval nonsense insults my space mind.
Scott C.

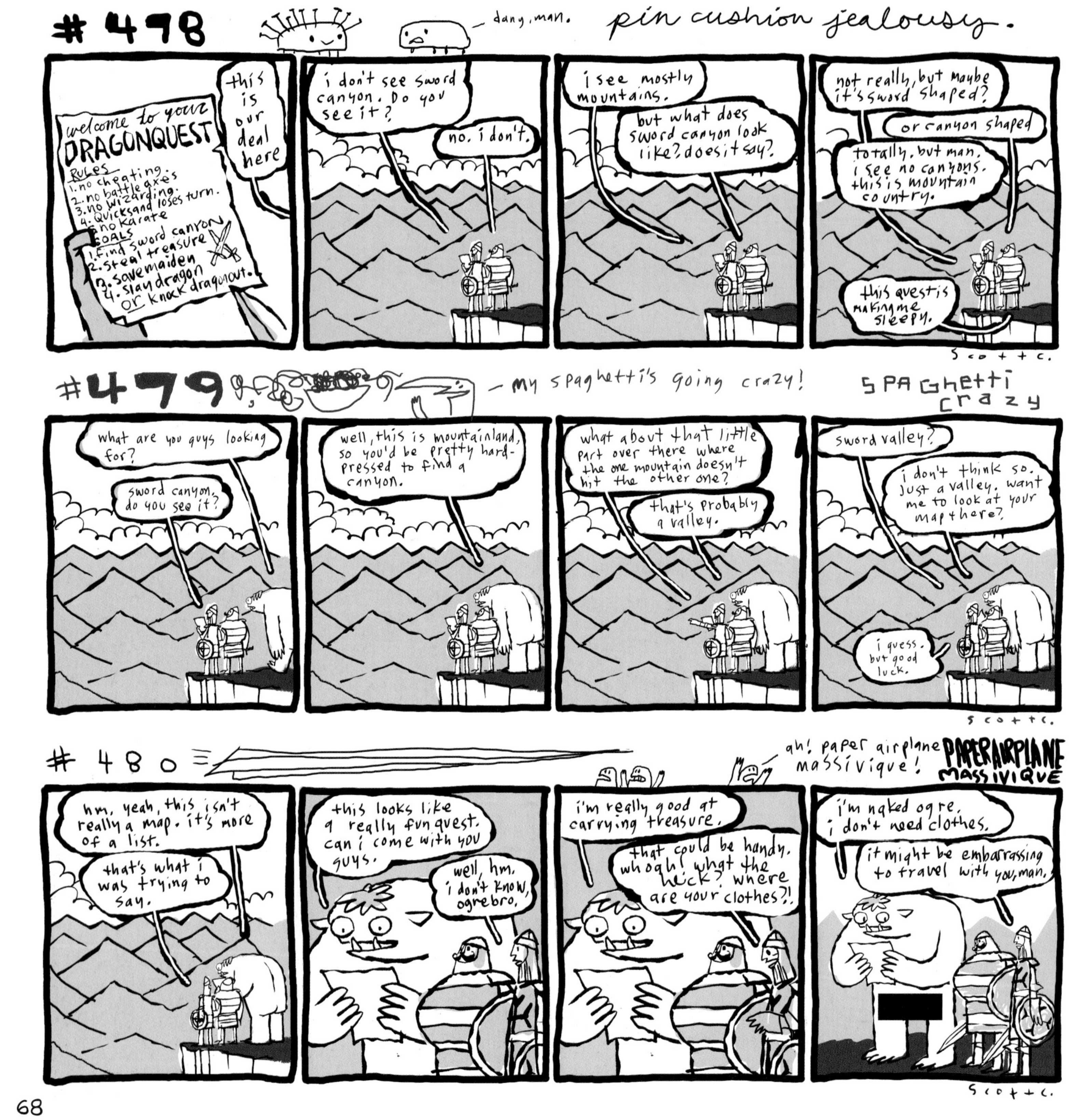

#478
— dang, man.
pin cushion jealousy.
welcome to your DRAGONQUEST
RULES
1. no cheating
2. no battle axe's
3. no wizarding.
4. Quicksand loses turn.
5. no karate
GOALS
1. find sword canyon
2. steal treasure
3. save maiden
4. slay dragon or knock dragon out.
this is our deal here
i don't see sword canyon. Do you see it?
no. i don't.
i see mostly mountains.
but what does sword canyon look like? does it say?
not really, but maybe it's sword shaped?
or canyon shaped
totally, but man, i see no canyons. this is mountain country.
this quest is making me sleepy.
scott c.
#479
— my spaghetti's going crazy!
SPAGHETTI CRAZY
what are you guys looking for?
sword canyon. do you see it?
well, this is mountainland, so you'd be pretty hard-pressed to find a canyon.
what about that little part over there where the one mountain doesn't hit the other one?
that's probably a valley.
sword valley?
i don't think so. just a valley. want me to look at your map there?
i guess. but good luck.
scott c.
#480
ah! paper airplane massivique!
PAPER AIRPLANE MASSIVIQUE
hm, yeah, this isn't really a map. it's more of a list.
that's what i was trying to say.
this looks like a really fun quest. can i come with you guys.
well, hm, i don't know, ogrebro.
i'm really good at carrying treasure.
that could be handy. whoah! what the heck? where are your clothes?!
i'm naked ogre. i don't need clothes.
it might be embarrassing to travel with you, man.
scott c.

#481

rectangle bug and circle bug! best friends forever.

triangle bug's comin to throw a wrench in the friendship works!

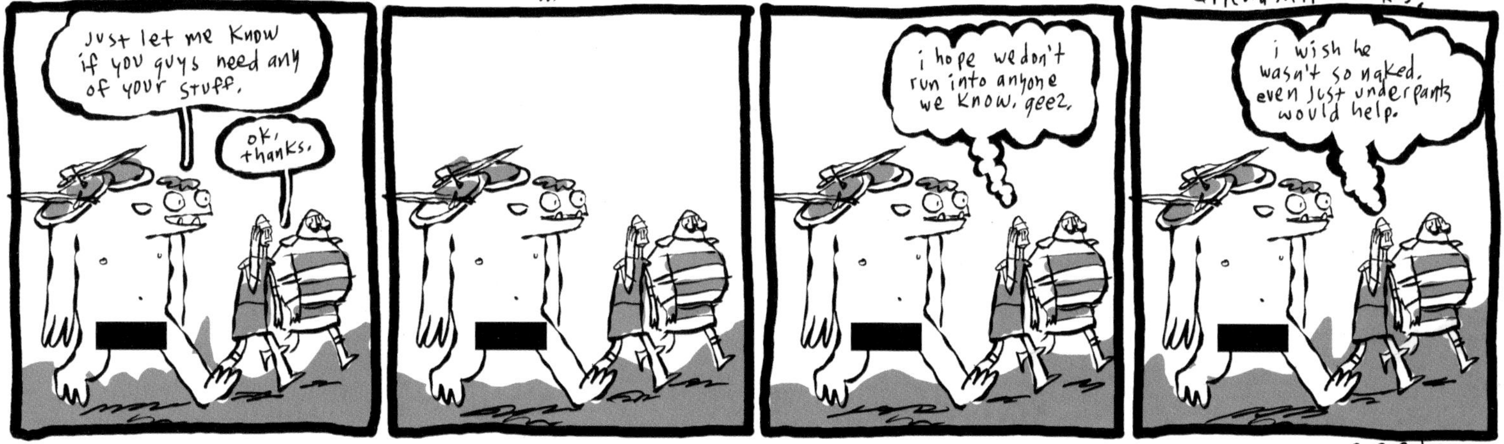

just let me know if you guys need any of your stuff.
ok, thanks.
i hope we don't run into anyone we know, geez.
i wish he wasn't so naked. even just underpants would help.

scott c.

#482

sugar rocks!

salt rocks!

chocolate rocks!

normal rocks.

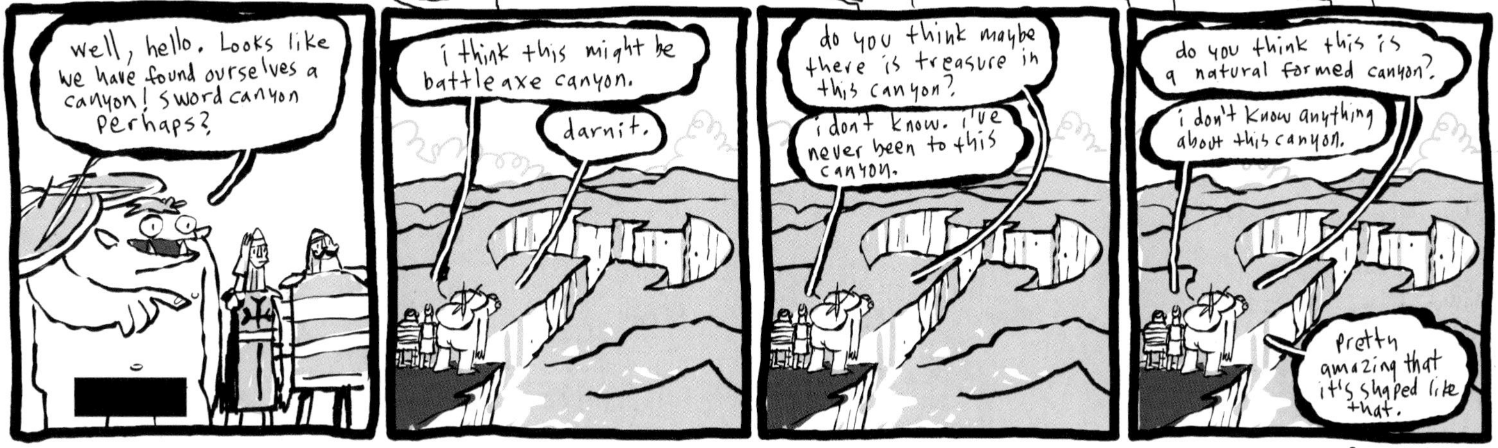

well, hello. looks like we have found ourselves a canyon! sword canyon perhaps?
i think this might be battleaxe canyon.
darnit.
do you think maybe there is treasure in this canyon?
i don't know. i've never been to this canyon.
do you think this is a natural formed canyon?
i don't know anything about this canyon.
pretty amazing that it's shaped like that.

scott c.

#483

well, i definitely want an evil hat. so shape and color are a big deal for me i think.

DEMONWITCH shopping frenzy!

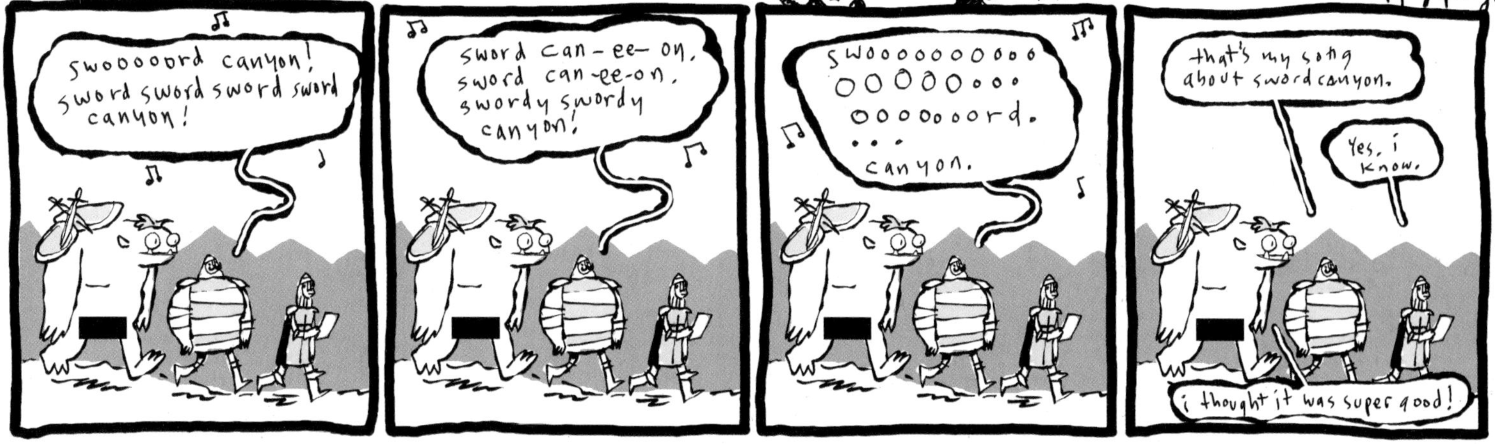

swoooord canyon! sword sword sword sword canyon!
sword can-ee-on, sword can-ee-on, swordy swordy canyon!
swoooooooooo OOOOOooo ooooooord. . . . canyon.
that's my song about sword canyon.
yes, i know.
i thought it was super good!

scott c.

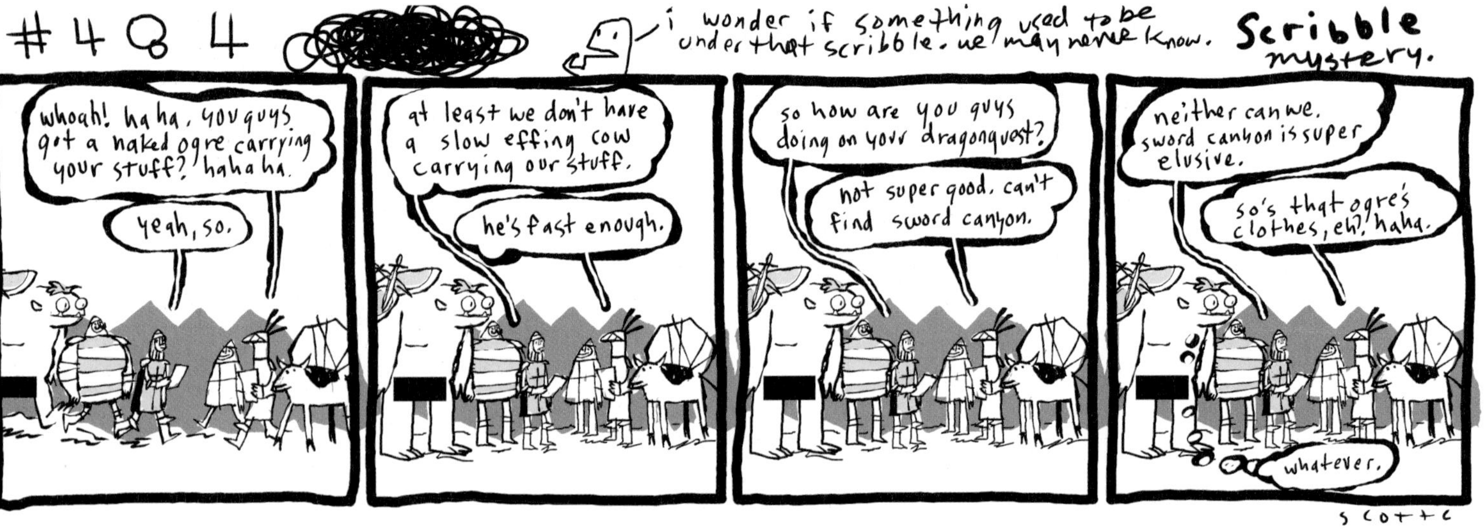
#484
i wonder if something used to be under that scribble. we may never know.
Scribble mystery.
whoah! haha, you guys got a naked ogre carrying your stuff? hahaha.
yeah, so.
at least we don't have a slow effing cow carrying our stuff.
he's fast enough.
so how are you guys doing on your dragonquest?
not super good. can't find sword canyon.
neither can we. sword canyon is super elusive.
so's that ogre's clothes, eh? haha.
whatever.
scott c.

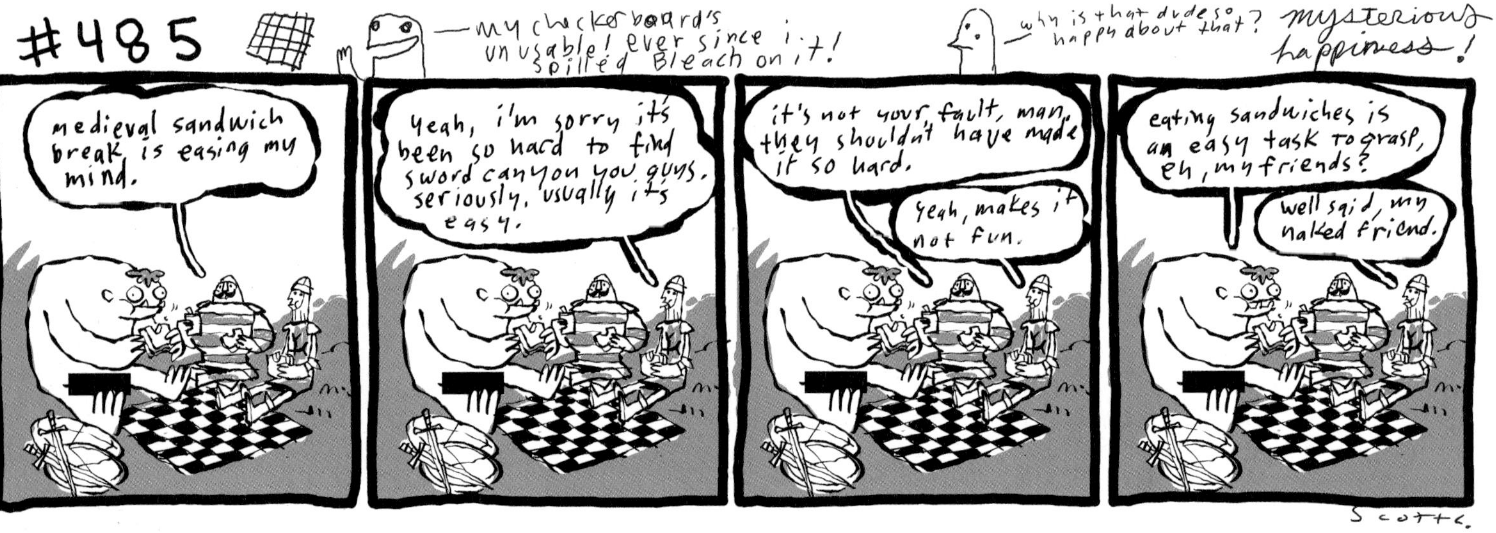
#485
my checkerboard's unusable! ever since i spilled bleach on it!
why is that dude so happy about that?
mysterious happiness!
medieval sandwich break is easing my mind.
yeah, i'm sorry it's been so hard to find sword canyon you guys. seriously. usually it's easy.
it's not your fault, man. they shouldn't have made it so hard.
yeah, makes it not fun.
eating sandwiches is an easy task to grasp, eh, my friends?
well said, my naked friend.
scott c.

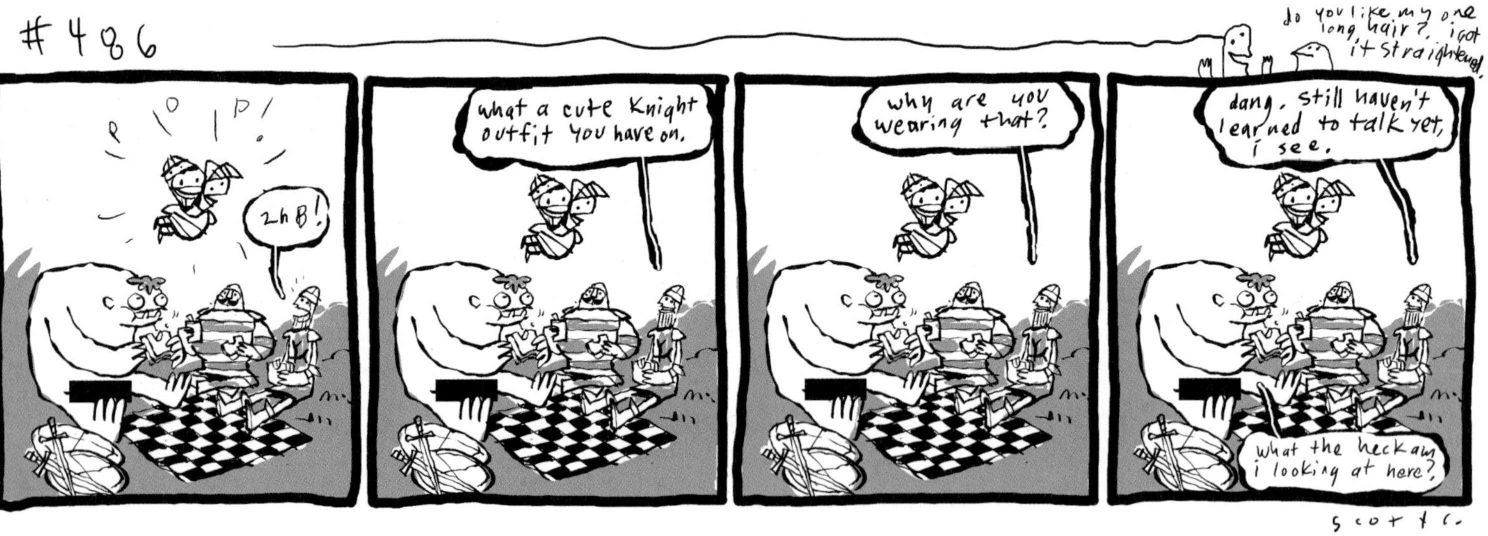
#486
do you like my one long hair? i got it straightened!
POP!
2hB!
what a cute knight outfit you have on.
why are you wearing that?
dang. still haven't learned to talk yet, i see.
what the heck am i looking at here?
scott c.

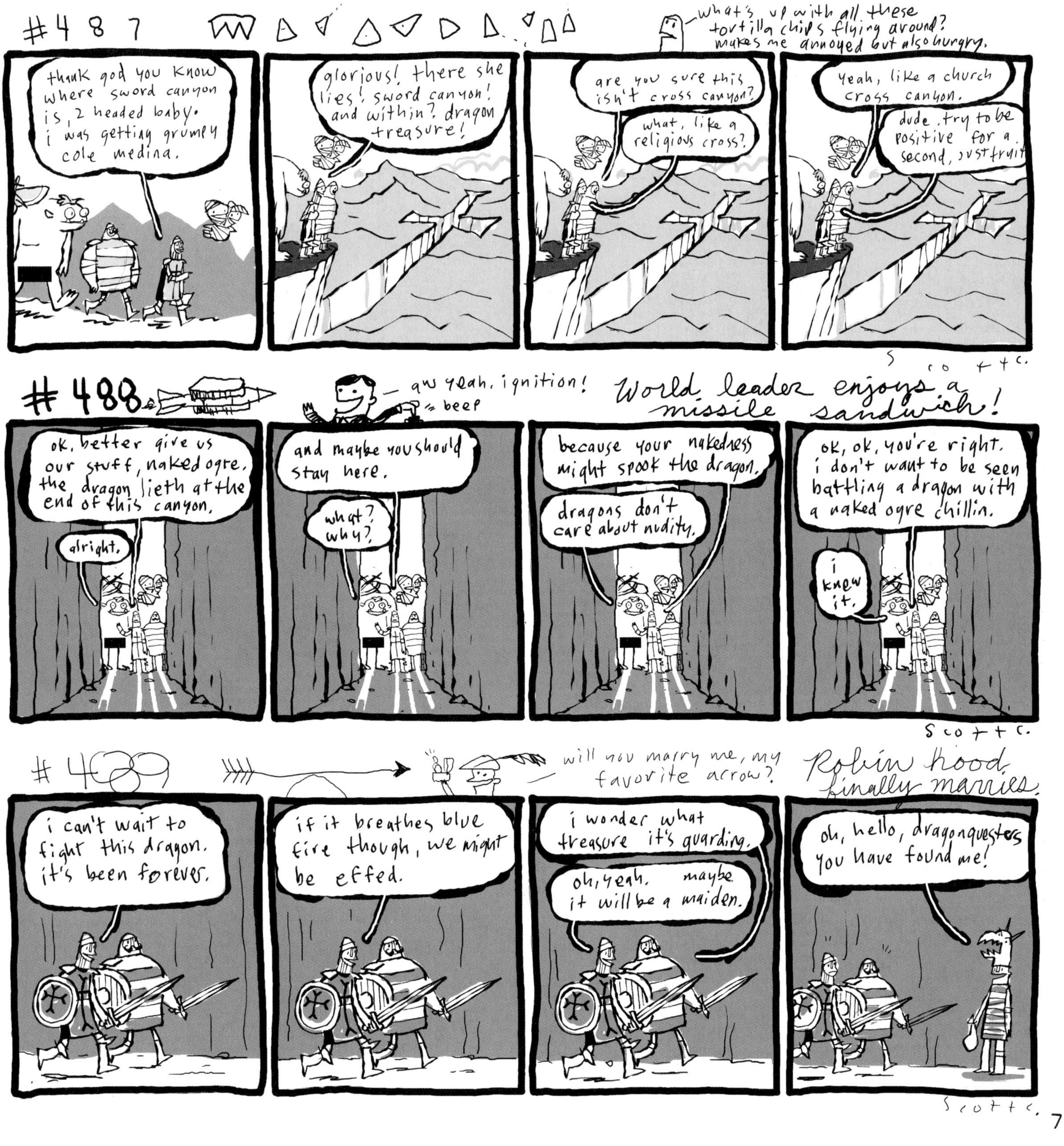
#487
what's up with all these tortilla chips flying around? makes me annoyed but also hungry.
thank god you know where sword canyon is, 2 headed baby. i was getting grumpy cole medina.
glorious! there she lies! sword canyon! and within? dragon treasure!
are you sure this isn't cross canyon?
what, like a religious cross?
yeah, like a church cross canyon.
dude, try to be positive for a second, just fruit
scott c.
#488
aw yeah, ignition!
beep
World leader enjoys a missile sandwich!
ok, better give us our stuff, naked ogre. the dragon lieth at the end of this canyon.
alright.
and maybe you should stay here.
what? why?
because your nakedness might spook the dragon.
dragons don't care about nudity.
ok, ok, you're right. i don't want to be seen battling a dragon with a naked ogre chillin.
i knew it.
scott c.
#489
will you marry me, my favorite arrow?
Robin hood finally marries.
i can't wait to fight this dragon. it's been forever.
if it breathes blue fire though, we might be effed.
i wonder what treasure it's guarding.
oh, yeah. maybe it will be a maiden.
oh, hello, dragonquesters you have found me!
scott c.

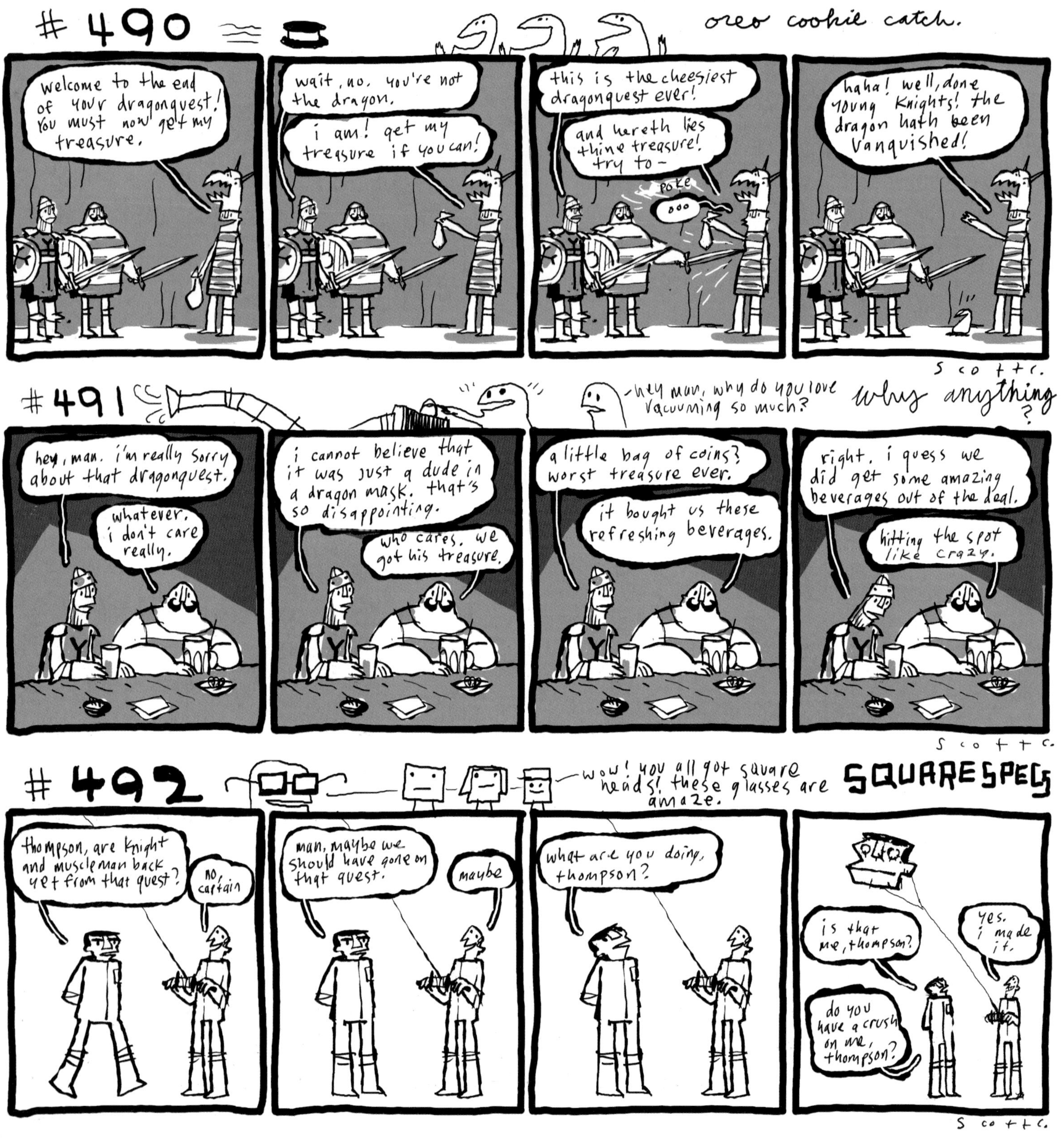
#490
oreo cookie catch.
welcome to the end of your dragonquest! you must now get my treasure.
wait, no. you're not the dragon.
i am! get my treasure if you can!
this is the cheesiest dragonquest ever!
and hereth lies thine treasure! try to -
POKE
ooo
haha! well, done young knights! the dragon hath been vanquished!
scott c.
#491
-hey man, why do you love vacuuming so much?
why anything?
hey, man. i'm really sorry about that dragonquest.
whatever. i don't care really.
i cannot believe that it was just a dude in a dragon mask. that's so disappointing.
who cares. we got his treasure.
a little bag of coins? worst treasure ever.
it bought us these refreshing beverages.
right. i guess we did get some amazing beverages out of the deal.
hitting the spot like crazy.
scott c.
#492
-wow! you all got square heads! these glasses are amaze.
SQUARESPECS
thompson, are knight and muscleman back yet from that quest?
no, captain
man, maybe we should have gone on that quest.
maybe
what are you doing, thompson?
is that me, thompson?
yes. i made it.
do you have a crush on me, thompson?
scott c.

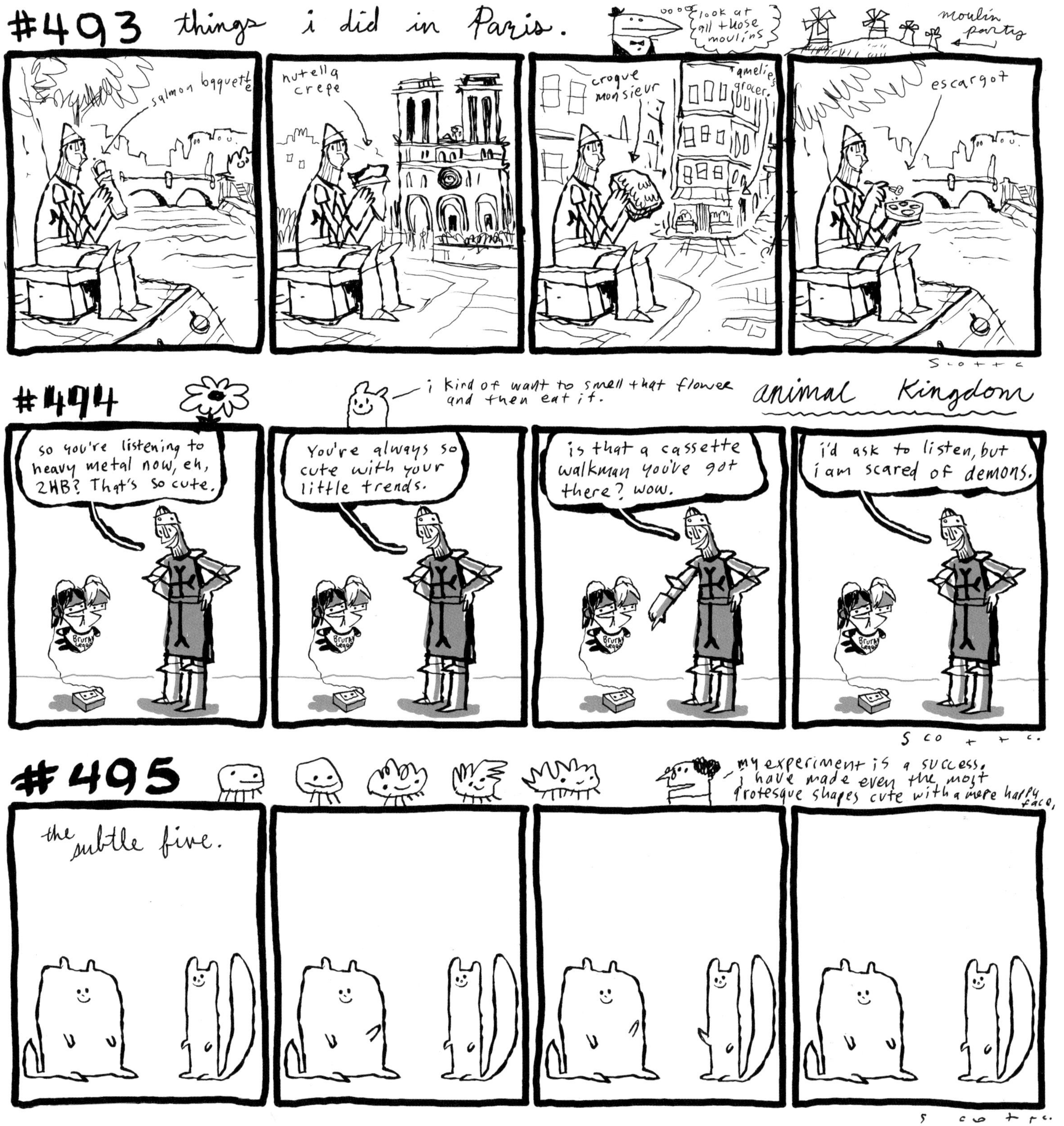
#493 things i did in Paris.
oooo look at all those moulins
moulin party
salmon baguette
nutella crepe
croque monsieur
amelie's grocer.
escargot
scott c
#494
i kind of want to smell that flower and then eat it.
animal kingdom
so you're listening to heavy metal now, eh, 2HB? That's so cute.
You're always so cute with your little trends.
is that a cassette walkman you've got there? wow.
i'd ask to listen, but i am scared of demons.
Brutal Legend
scott c.
#495
my experiment is a success. i have made even the most grotesque shapes cute with a mere happy face,
the subtle five.
scott c.

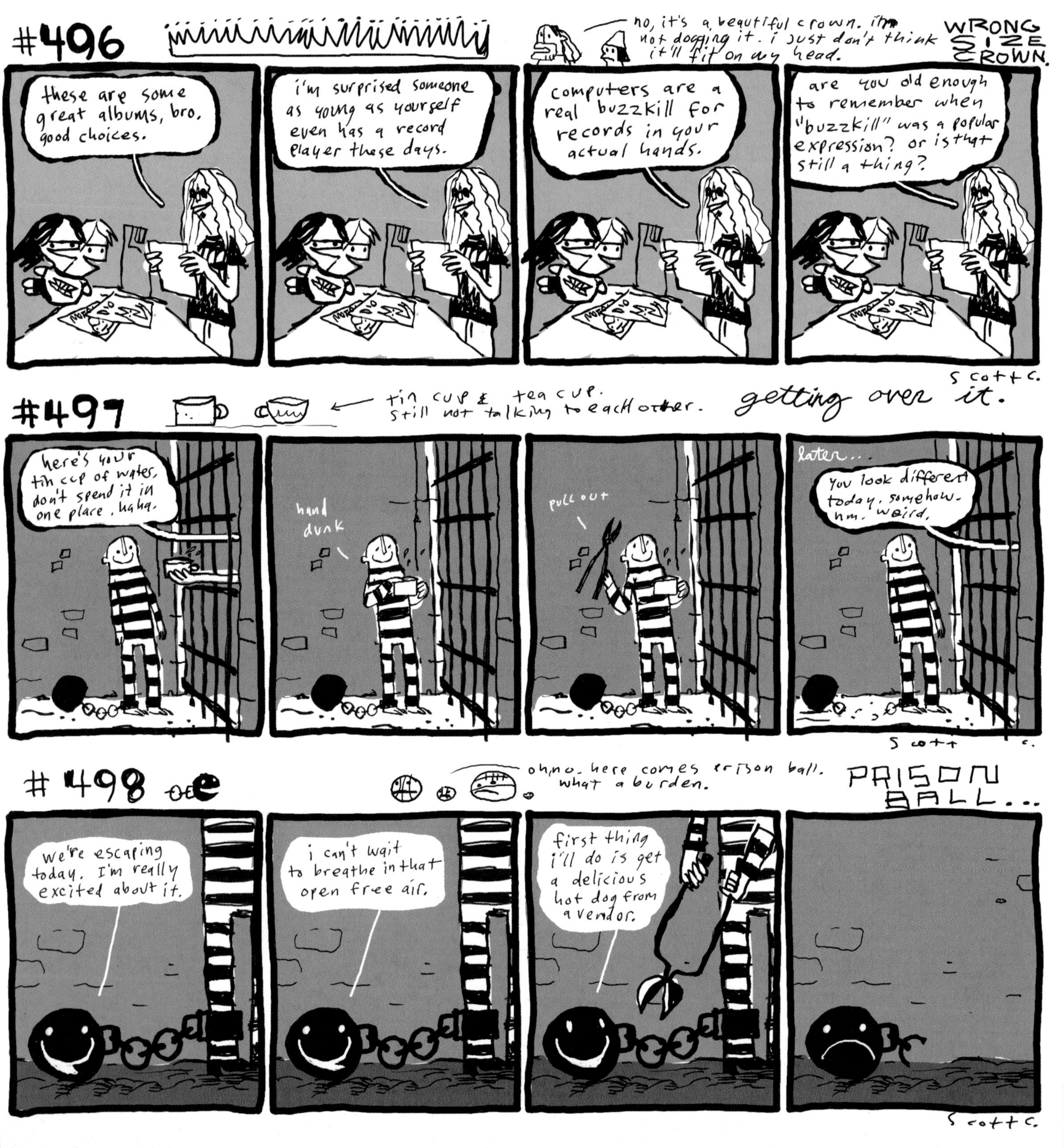
#496
no, it's a beautiful crown. i'm not dogging it. i just don't think it'll fit on my head.
WRONG SIZE CROWN.
these are some great albums, bro, good choices.
i'm surprised someone as young as yourself even has a record player these days.
computers are a real buzzkill for records in your actual hands.
are you old enough to remember when "buzzkill" was a popular expression? or is that still a thing?
scott c.
#497
tin cup & tea cup. still not talking to each other.
getting over it.
here's your tin cup of water, don't spend it in one place, haha.
hand dunk
pull out
later...
you look different today, somehow. hm. weird.
scott c.
#498
oh, no. here comes prison ball. what a burden.
PRISON BALL...
we're escaping today. I'm really excited about it.
i can't wait to breathe in that open free air.
first thing i'll do is get a delicious hot dog from a vendor.
scott c.

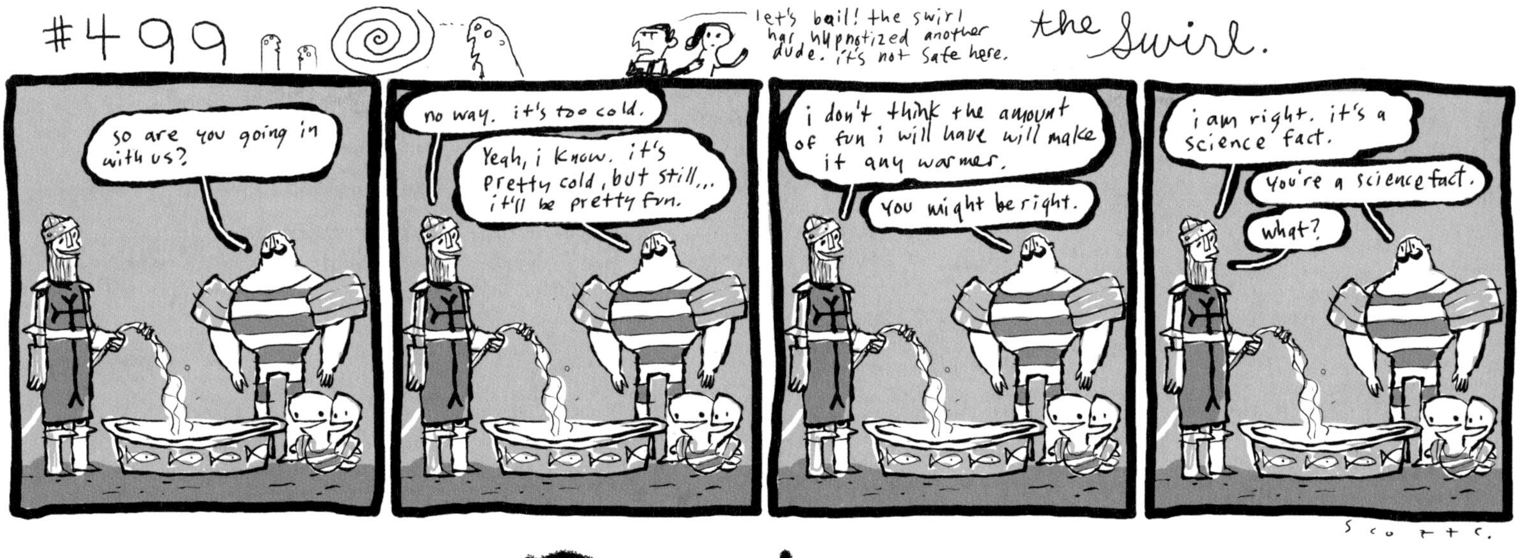
#499
let's bail! the swirl has hypnotized another dude. it's not safe here.
the Swirl.
so are you going in with us?
no way. it's too cold.
Yeah, i know. it's pretty cold, but still... it'll be pretty fun.
i don't think the amount of fun i will have will make it any warmer.
you might be right.
i am right. it's a science fact.
You're a science fact.
what?
scott c.

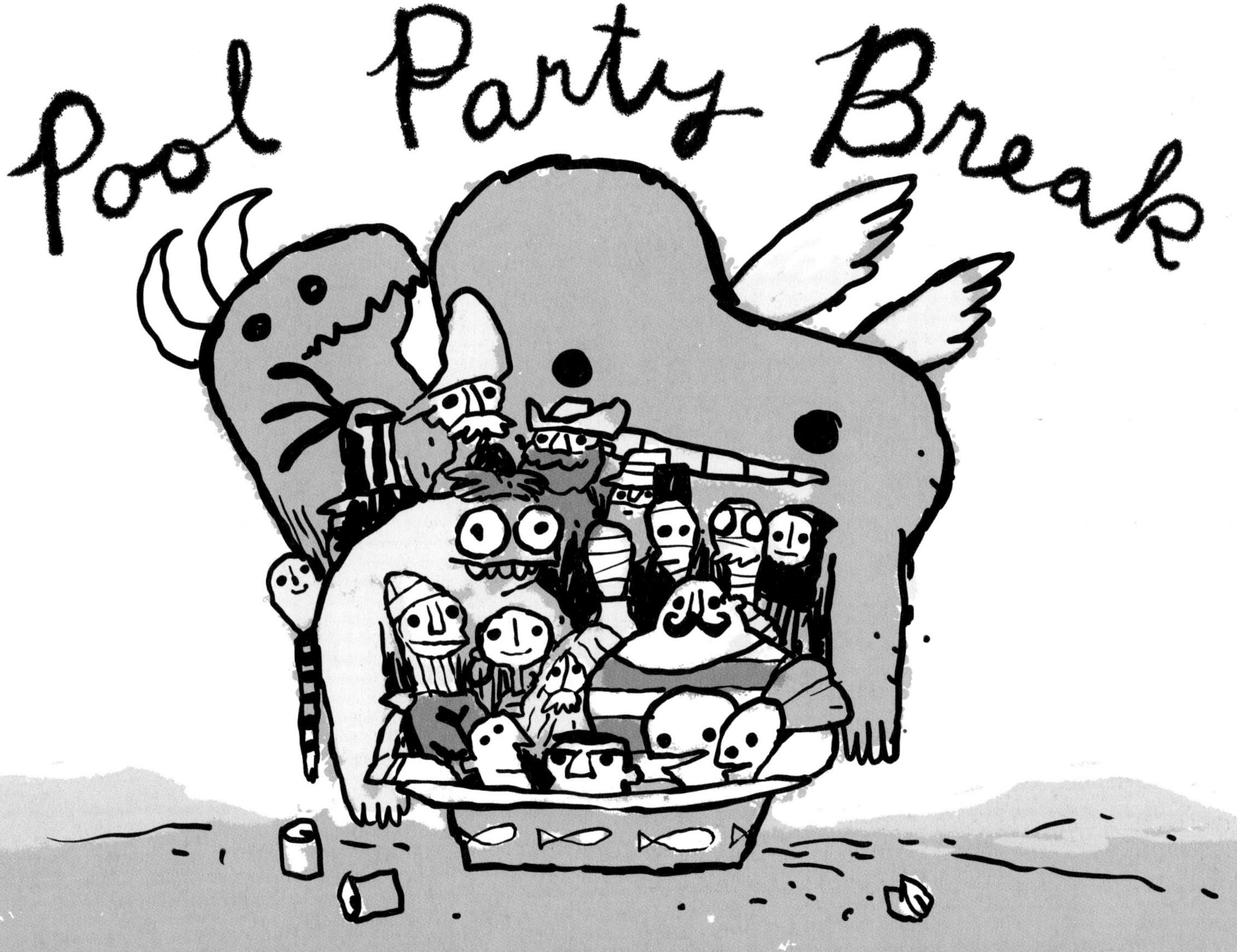
Pool Party Break

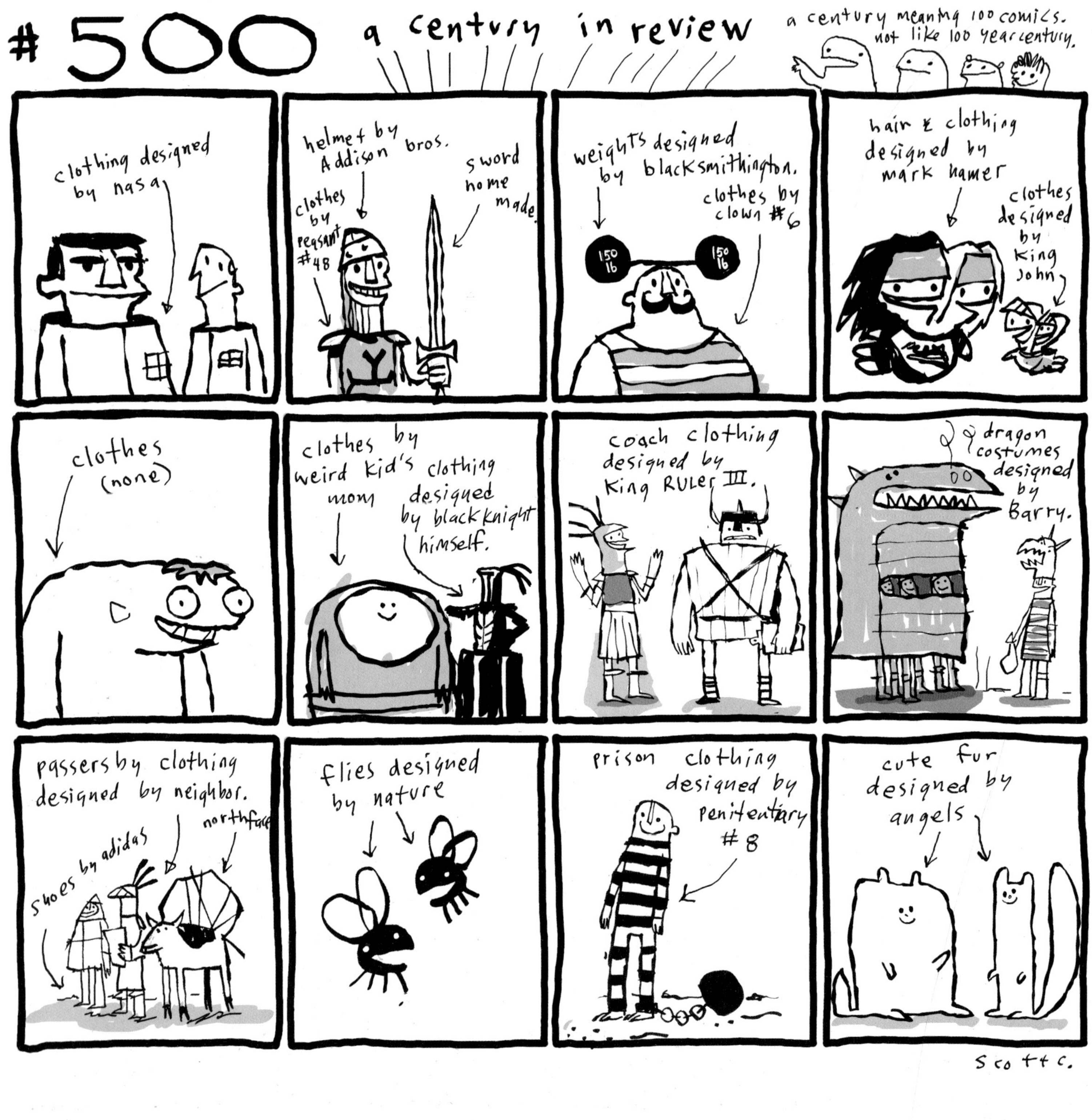
#500 a century in review
a century meaning 100 comics. not like 100 year century.
clothing designed by nasa
helmet by Addison bros.
clothes by peasant #48
sword home made.
weights designed by blacksmithington.
150 lb
150 lb
clothes by clown #6
hair & clothing designed by mark hamer
clothes designed by King John
clothes (none)
clothes by weird kid's mom
clothing designed by black knight himself.
coach clothing designed by King RULER III.
dragon costumes designed by Barry.
passersby clothing designed by neighbor.
shoes by adidas
northfac
flies designed by nature
prison clothing designed by penitentiary #8
cute fur designed by angels
scott c.

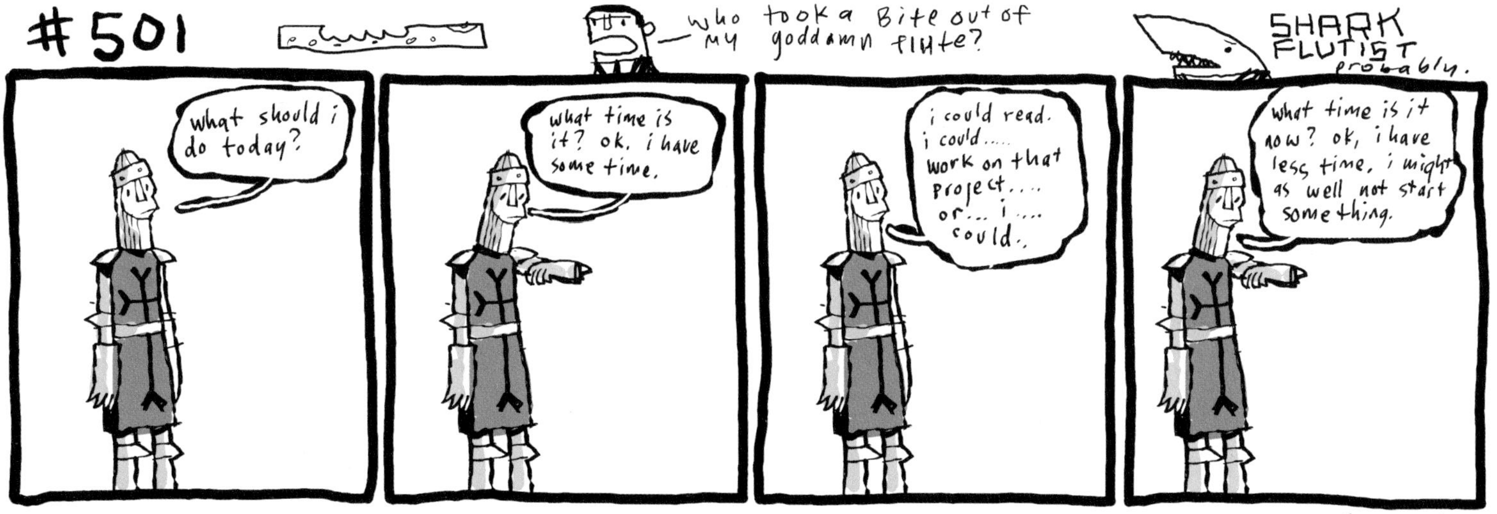
#501
who took a bite out of my goddamn flute?
SHARK FLUTIST probably.
what should i do today?
what time is it? ok, i have some time.
i could read. i could..... work on that project.... or... i.... could..
what time is it now? ok, i have less time, i might as well not start something.
scott c.

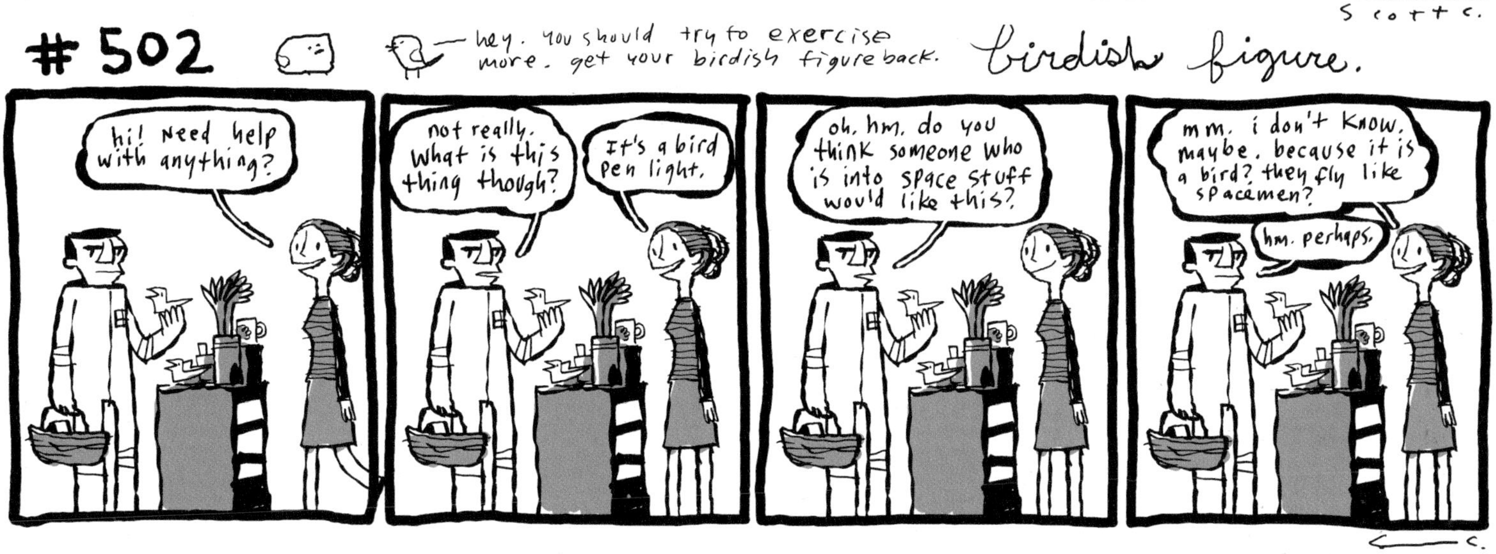
#502
hey. you should try to exercise more. get your birdish figure back.
birdish figure.
hi! need help with anything?
not really. what is this thing though?
It's a bird pen light.
oh. hm. do you think someone who is into space stuff would like this?
mm. i don't know. maybe. because it is a bird? they fly like spacemen?
hm. perhaps.
c.

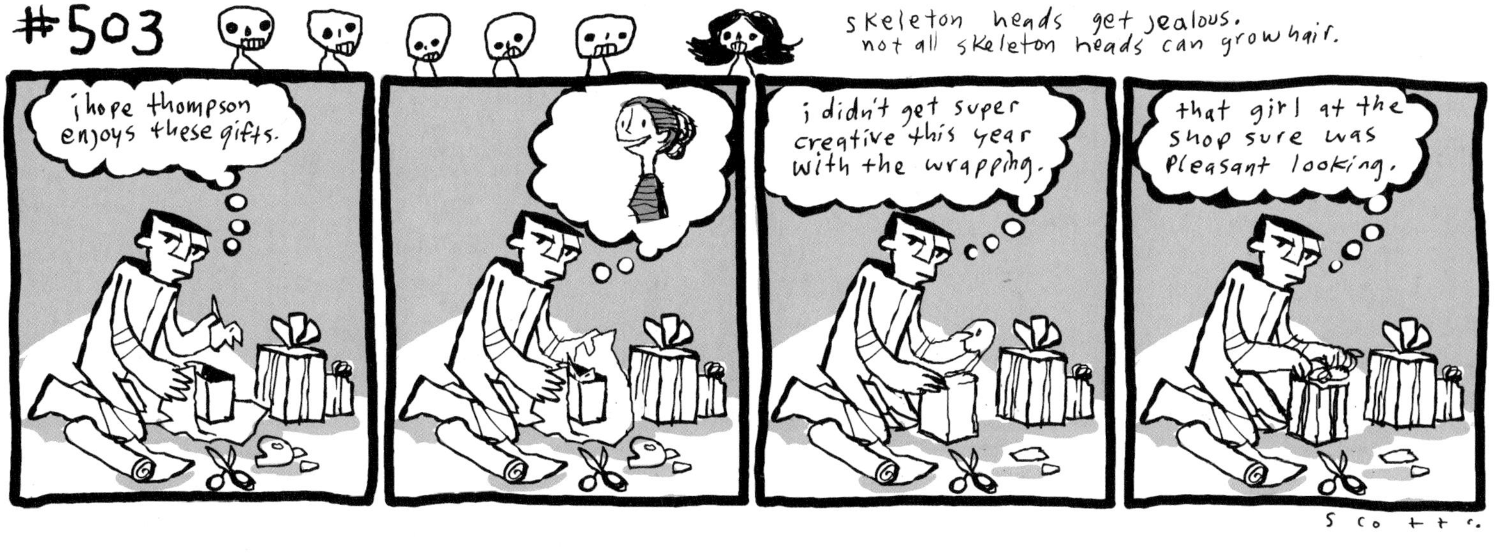
#503
skeleton heads get jealous. not all skeleton heads can grow hair.
i hope thompson enjoys these gifts.
i didn't get super creative this year with the wrapping.
that girl at the shop sure was pleasant looking.
scott c.

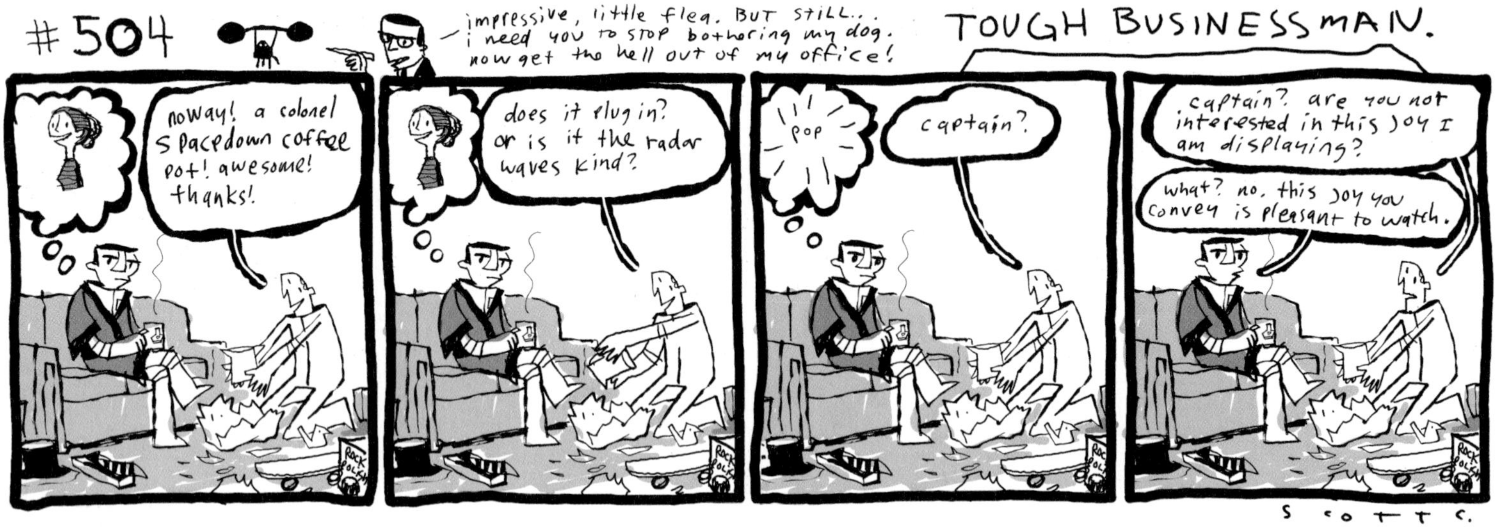
#504
impressive, little flea. BUT STILL.. i need you to stop bothering my dog. now get the hell out of my office!
TOUGH BUSINESSMAN.
noway! a colonel Spacedown coffee pot! awesome! thanks!
does it plug in? or is it the radar waves kind?
pop
captain?
captain? are you not interested in this joy I am displaying?
what? no. this joy you convey is pleasant to watch.
SCOTT C.

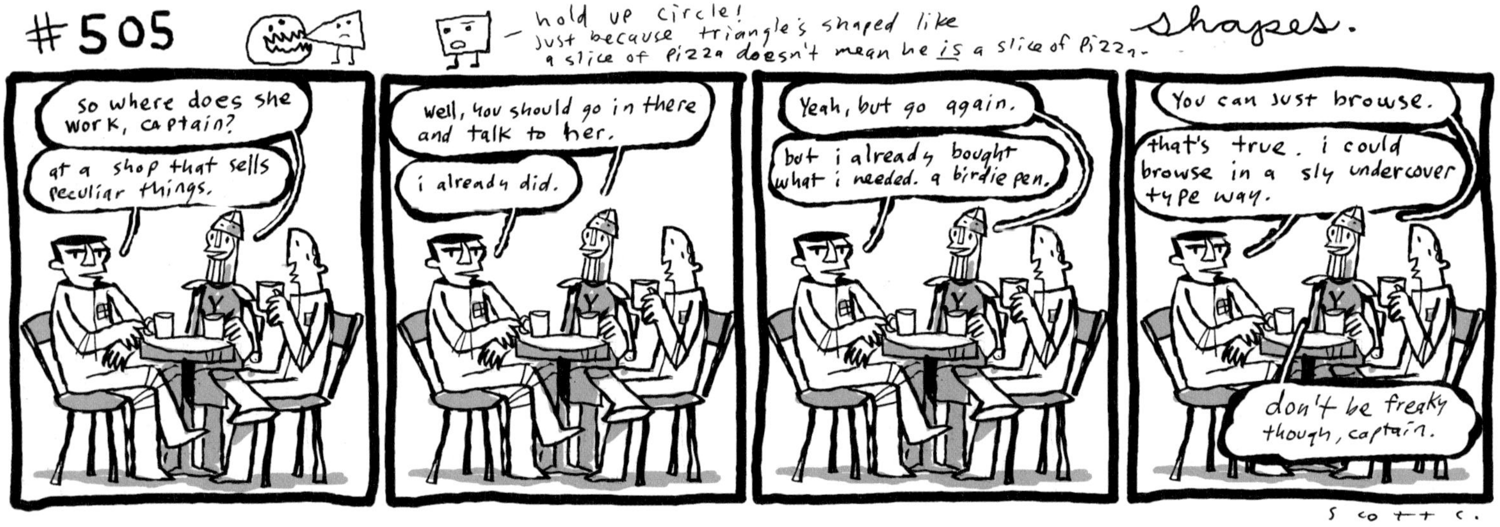
#505
hold up circle! just because triangle's shaped like a slice of pizza doesn't mean he is a slice of pizza.
shapes.
so where does she work, captain?
at a shop that sells peculiar things.
well, you should go in there and talk to her.
i already did.
Yeah, but go again.
but i already bought what i needed. a birdie pen.
You can just browse.
that's true. i could browse in a sly undercover type way.
don't be freaky though, captain.
SCOTT C.

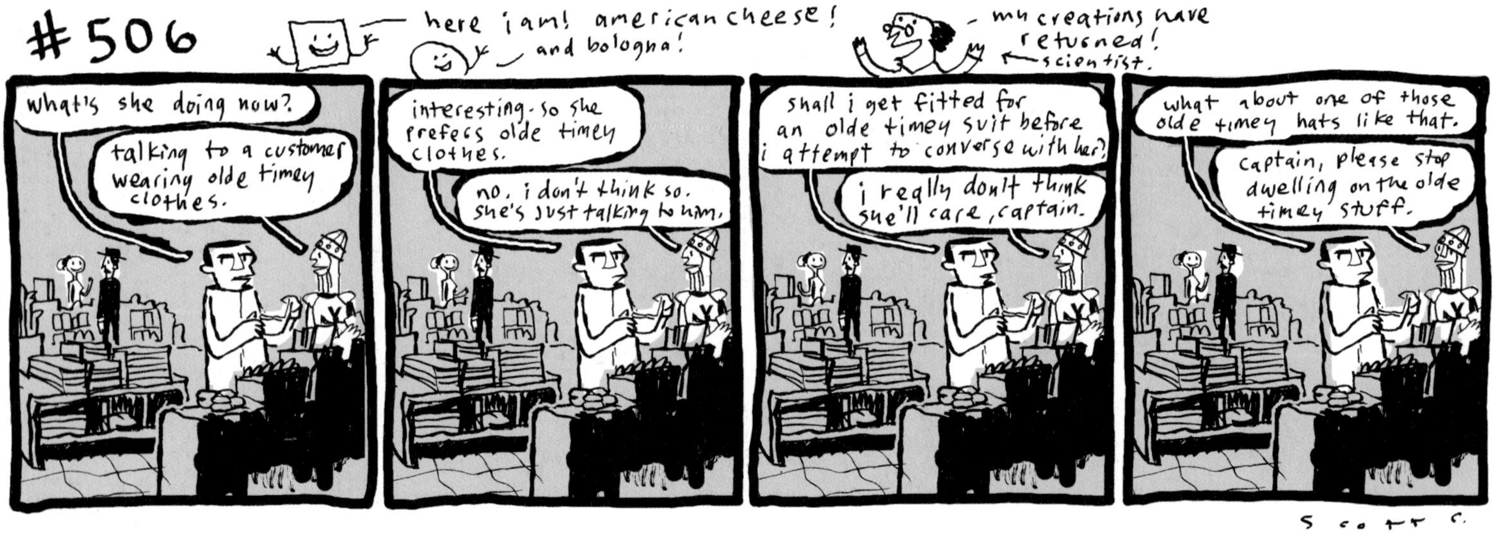
#506
here i am! american cheese!
and bologna!
my creations have returned!
scientist.
what's she doing now?
talking to a customer wearing olde timey clothes.
interesting. so she prefers olde timey clothes.
no. i don't think so. she's just talking to him.
shall i get fitted for an olde timey suit before i attempt to converse with her?
i really don't think she'll care, captain.
what about one of those olde timey hats like that.
captain, please stop dwelling on the olde timey stuff.
SCOTT C.

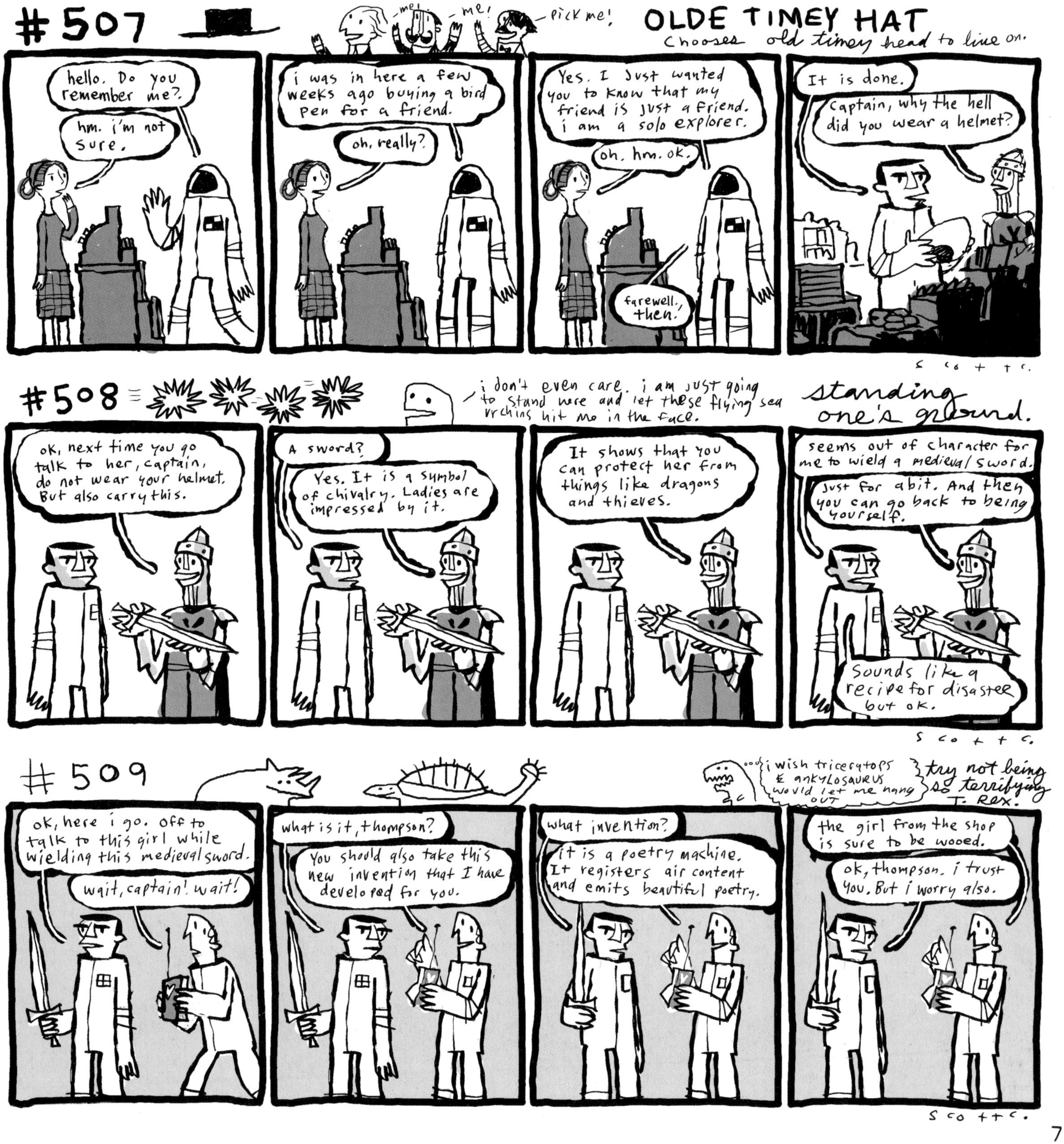
#507
-me!
-me!
-pick me!
OLDE TIMEY HAT
chooses old timey head to live on.
hello. Do you remember me?
hm. i'm not sure.
i was in here a few weeks ago buying a bird pen for a friend.
oh, really?
Yes. I just wanted you to know that my friend is just a friend. i am a solo explorer.
oh. hm. ok.
farewell, then.
It is done.
captain, why the hell did you wear a helmet?
scott c.
#508
i don't even care. i am just going to stand here and let these flying sea urchins hit me in the face.
standing one's ground.
ok, next time you go talk to her, captain, do not wear your helmet. But also carry this.
A sword?
Yes. It is a symbol of chivalry. Ladies are impressed by it.
It shows that you can protect her from things like dragons and thieves.
seems out of character for me to wield a medieval sword.
Just for a bit. And then you can go back to being yourself.
Sounds like a recipe for disaster but ok.
scott c.
#509
i wish triceratops & ankylosaurus would let me hang out
try not being so terrifying T. Rex.
ok, here i go. off to talk to this girl while wielding this medieval sword.
wait, captain! wait!
what is it, thompson?
You should also take this new invention that I have developed for you.
what invention?
it is a poetry machine. It registers air content and emits beautiful poetry.
the girl from the shop is sure to be wooed.
ok, thompson. i trust you. But i worry also.
scott c.

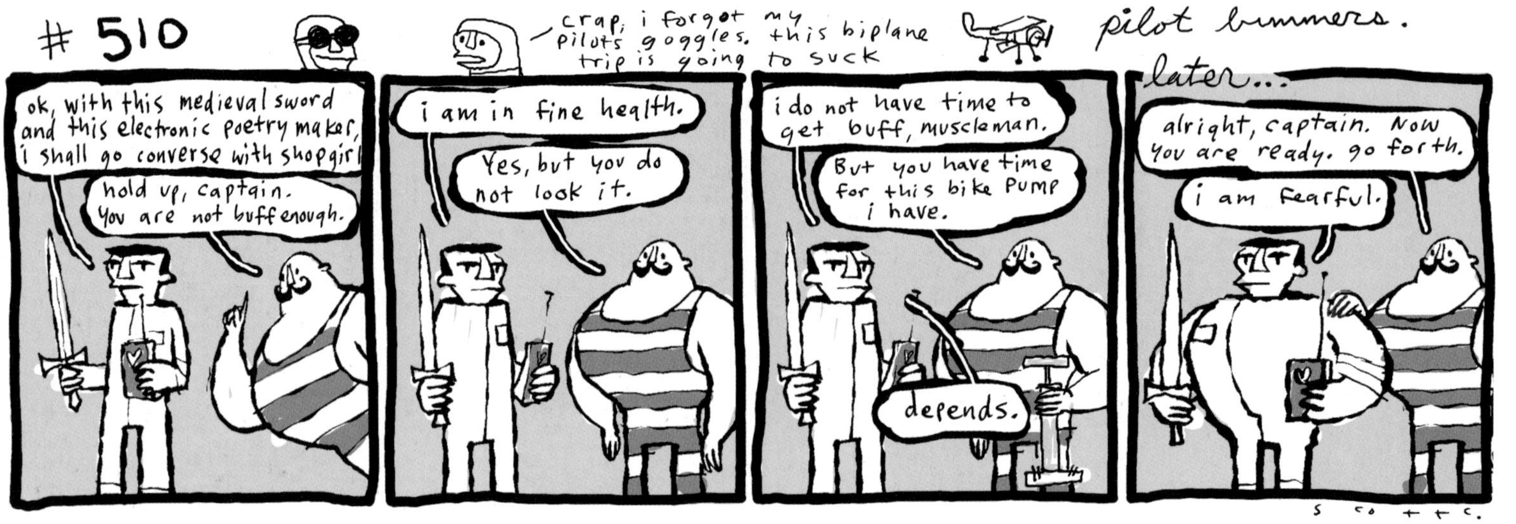

510
crap, i forgot my pilots goggles. this biplane trip is going to suck
pilot bummers.
ok, with this medieval sword and this electronic poetry maker, i shall go converse with shopgirl
hold up, captain. You are not buff enough.
i am in fine health.
Yes, but you do not look it.
i do not have time to get buff, muscleman.
But you have time for this bike pump i have.
depends.
later...
alright, captain. Now you are ready. go forth.
i am fearful.
scott c.

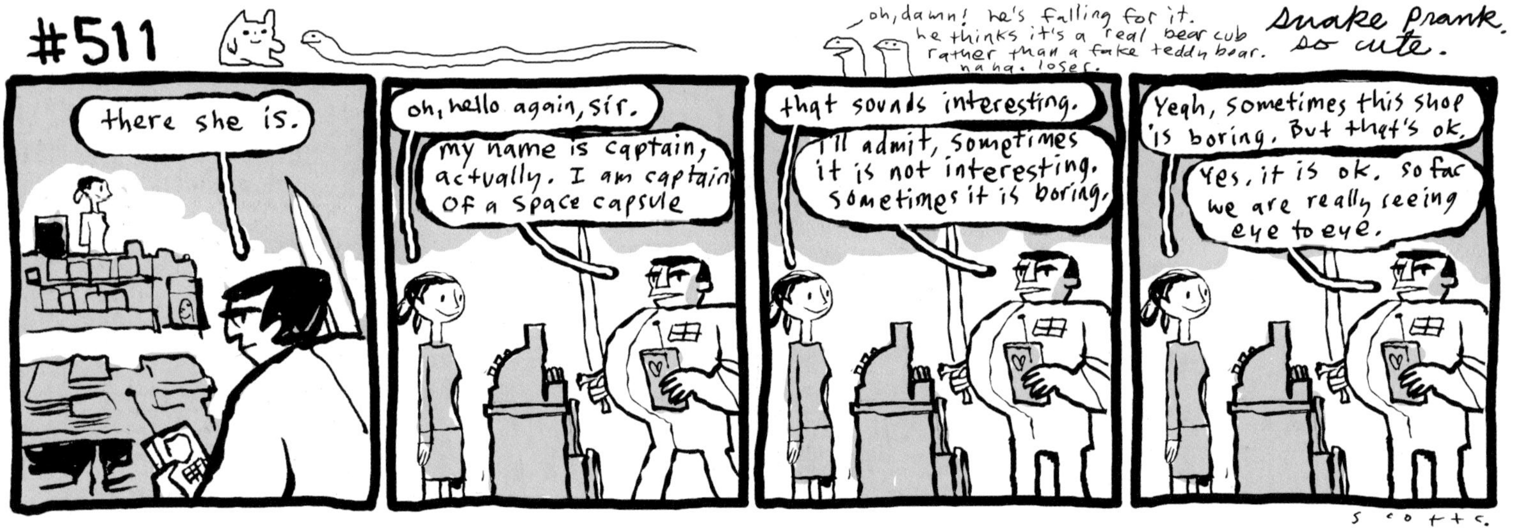

#511
oh, damn! he's falling for it. he thinks it's a real bear cub rather than a fake teddy bear. haha. loser.
snake prank. so cute.
there she is.
oh, hello again, sir.
my name is captain, actually. I am captain of a space capsule
that sounds interesting.
i'll admit, sometimes it is not interesting. sometimes it is boring.
Yeah, sometimes this shop is boring. But that's ok.
Yes, it is ok. so far we are really seeing eye to eye.
scott c.

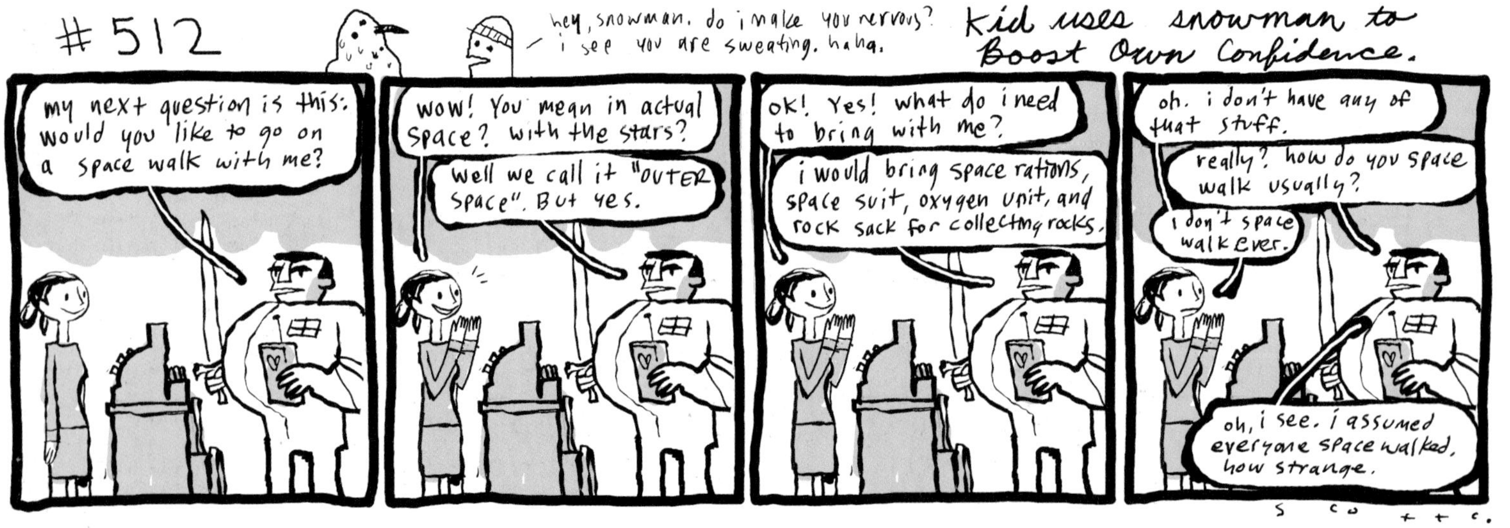

512
hey, snowman. do i make you nervous? i see you are sweating. haha.
Kid uses snowman to Boost Own Confidence.
my next question is this: would you like to go on a space walk with me?
wow! You mean in actual space? with the stars?
Well we call it "OUTER SPACE". But yes.
ok! Yes! what do i need to bring with me?
i would bring space rations, space suit, oxygen unit, and rock sack for collecting rocks.
oh. i don't have any of that stuff.
really? how do you space walk usually?
i don't space walk ever.
oh, i see. i assumed everyone space walked. how strange.
scott c.

#513

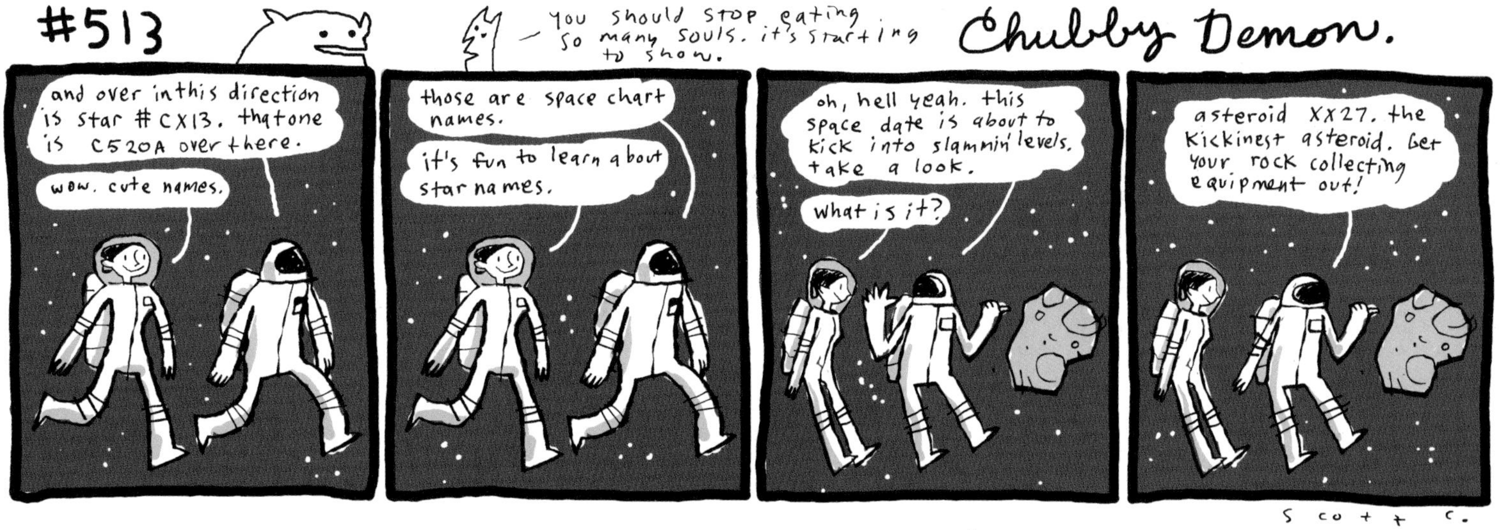
you should stop eating so many souls. it's starting to show.
Chubby Demon.
and over in this direction is star #CX13. that one is C520A over there.
wow. cute names.
those are space chart names.
it's fun to learn about star names.
oh, hell yeah. this space date is about to kick into slammin' levels. take a look.
what is it?
asteroid XX27. the kickinest asteroid. get your rock collecting equipment out!
scott c.

#514

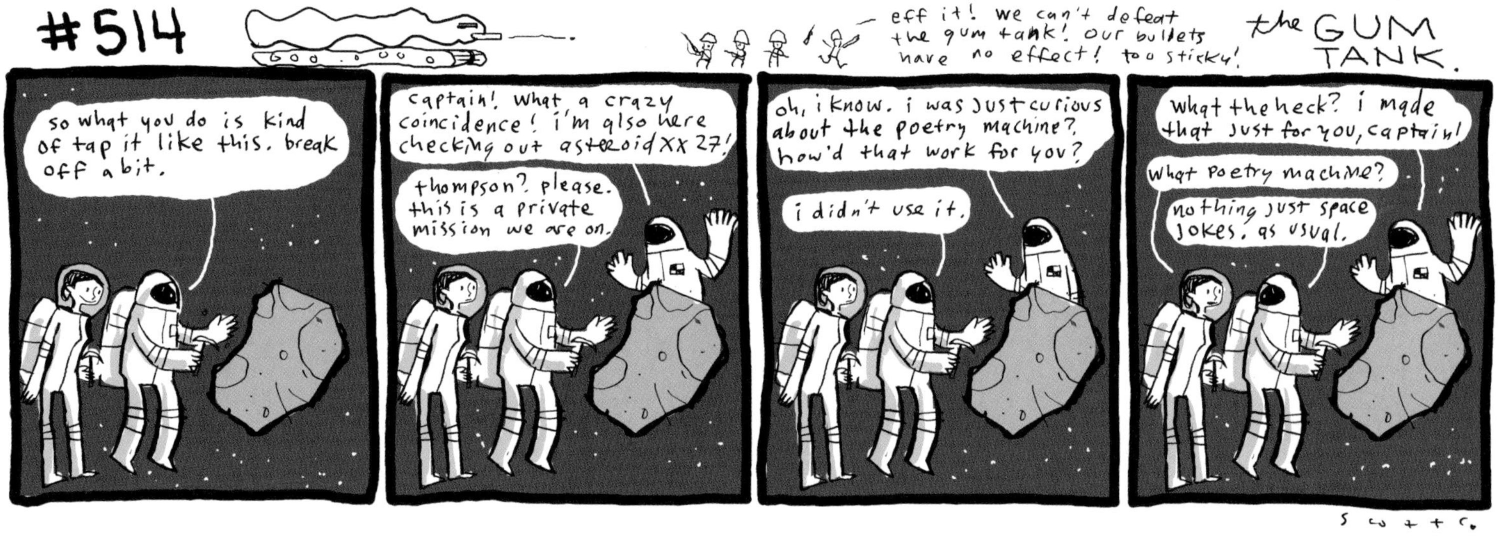
eff it! we can't defeat the gum tank! our bullets have no effect! too sticky!
the GUM TANK.
so what you do is kind of tap it like this. break off a bit.
captain! what a crazy coincidence! i'm also here checking out asteroid XX 27!
thompson? please. this is a private mission we are on.
oh, i know. i was just curious about the poetry machine? how'd that work for you?
i didn't use it.
what the heck? i made that just for you, captain!
what poetry machine?
nothing just space jokes, as usual.
scott c.

#515

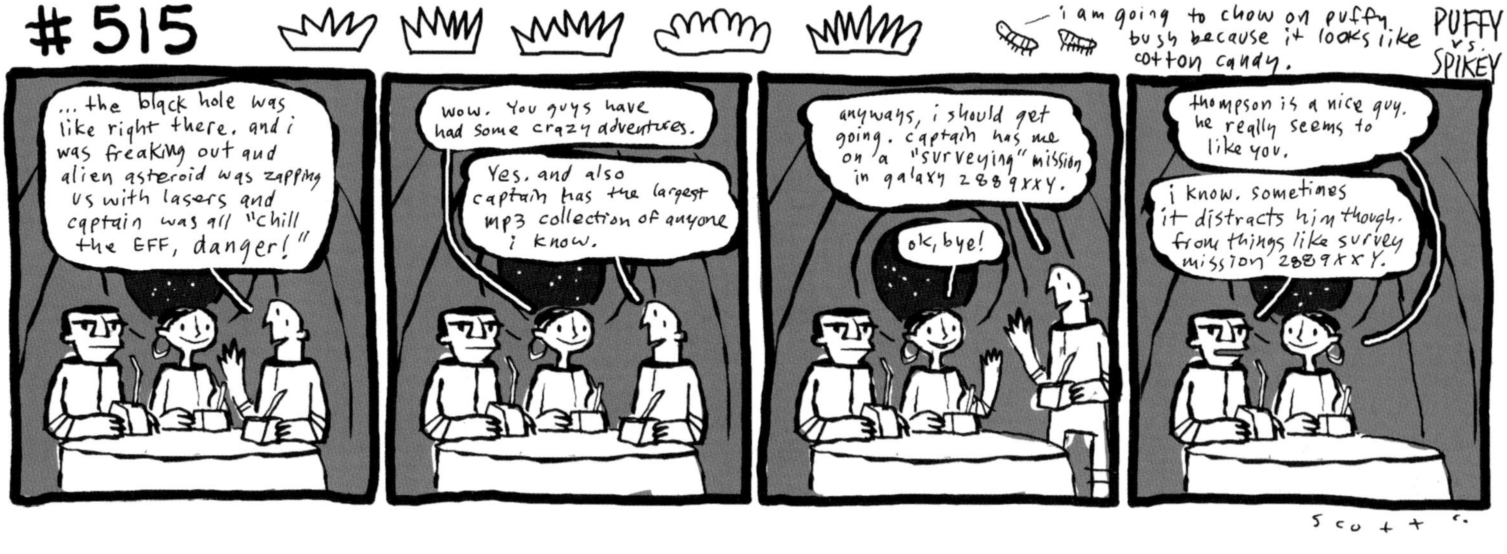
i am going to chow on puffy bush because it looks like cotton candy.
PUFFY vs. SPIKEY
... the black hole was like right there, and i was freaking out and alien asteroid was zapping us with lasers and captain was all "chill the EFF, danger!"
wow. you guys have had some crazy adventures.
yes. and also captain has the largest mp3 collection of anyone i know.
anyways, i should get going. captain has me on a "surveying" mission in galaxy 2889XXY.
ok, bye!
thompson is a nice guy. he really seems to like you.
i know. sometimes it distracts him though. from things like survey mission 2889XXY.
scott c.

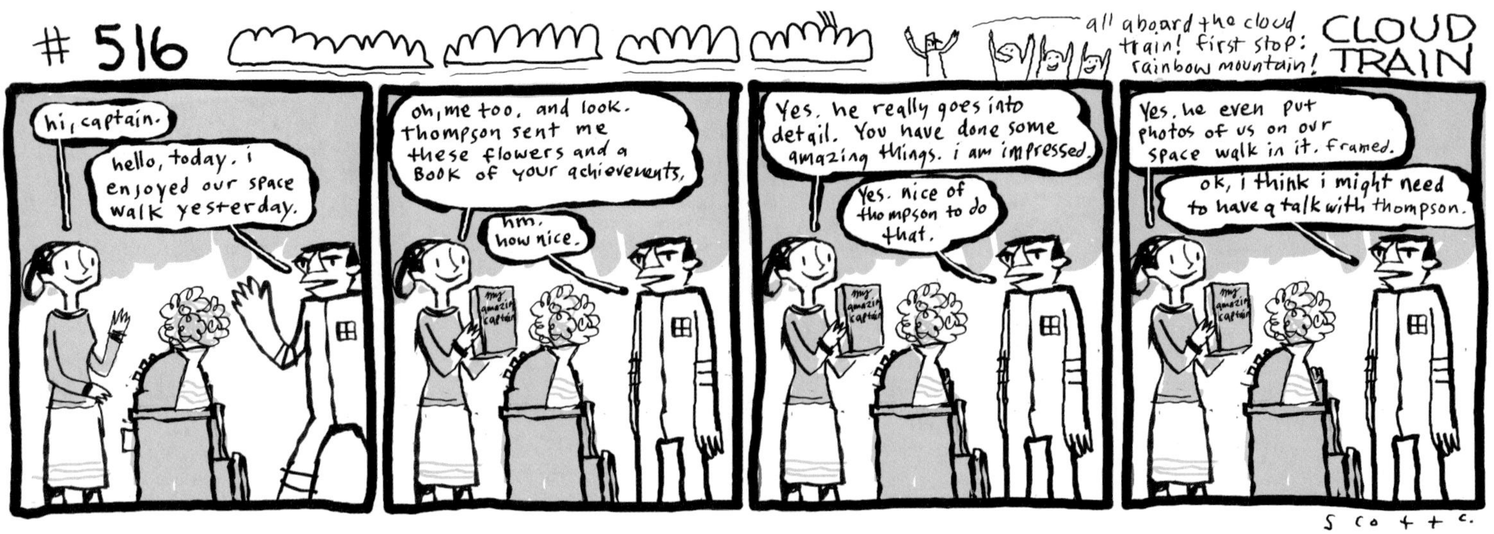
#516
all aboard the cloud train! first stop: rainbow mountain!
CLOUD TRAIN
hi, captain.
hello, today. i enjoyed our space walk yesterday.
oh, me too. and look. thompson sent me these flowers and a book of your achievements.
hm. how nice.
my amazing captain
Yes. he really goes into detail. You have done some amazing things. i am impressed.
Yes. nice of thompson to do that.
Yes. he even put photos of us on our space walk in it. framed.
ok, i think i might need to have a talk with thompson.
scott c.

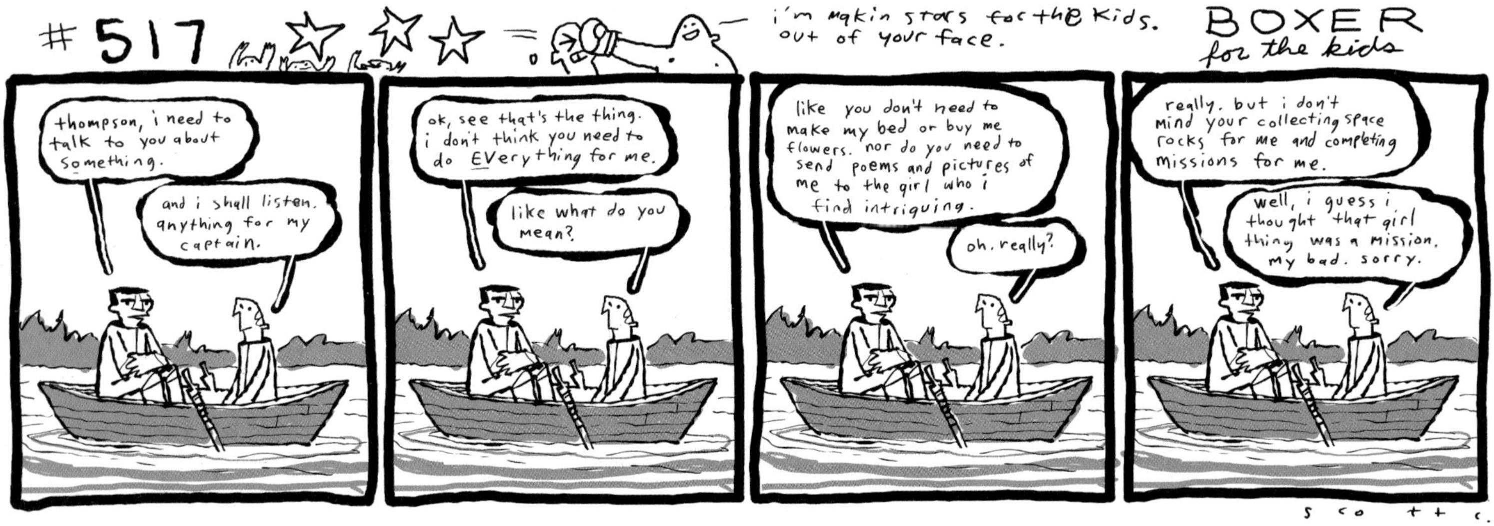
#517
i'm makin stars for the kids. out of your face.
BOXER for the kids
thompson, i need to talk to you about something.
and i shall listen. anything for my captain.
ok, see that's the thing. i don't think you need to do EVerything for me.
like what do you mean?
like you don't need to make my bed or buy me flowers. nor do you need to send poems and pictures of me to the girl who i find intriguing.
oh. really?
really. but i don't mind your collecting space rocks for me and completing missions for me.
well, i guess i thought that girl thing was a mission. my bad. sorry.
scott c.

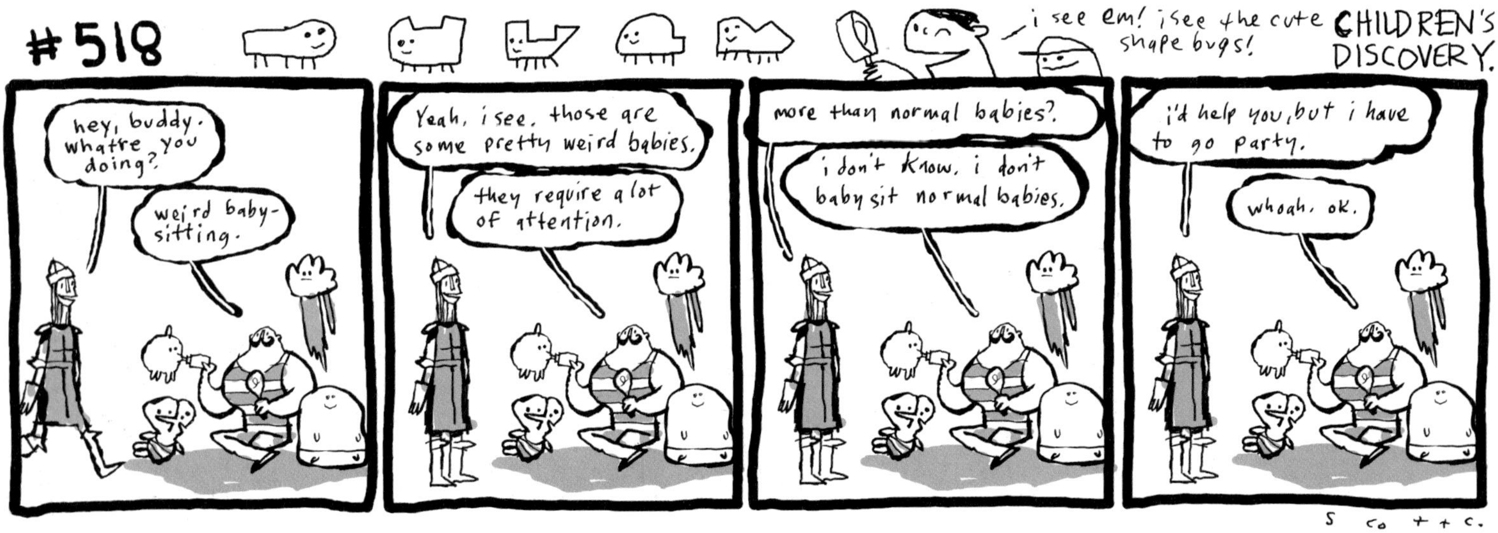
#518
i see em! i see the cute shape bugs!
CHILDREN'S DISCOVERY.
hey, buddy. whatre you doing?
weird baby-sitting.
Yeah, i see. those are some pretty weird babies.
they require a lot of attention.
more than normal babies?
i don't know. i don't babysit normal babies.
i'd help you, but i have to go party.
whoah. ok.
scott c.

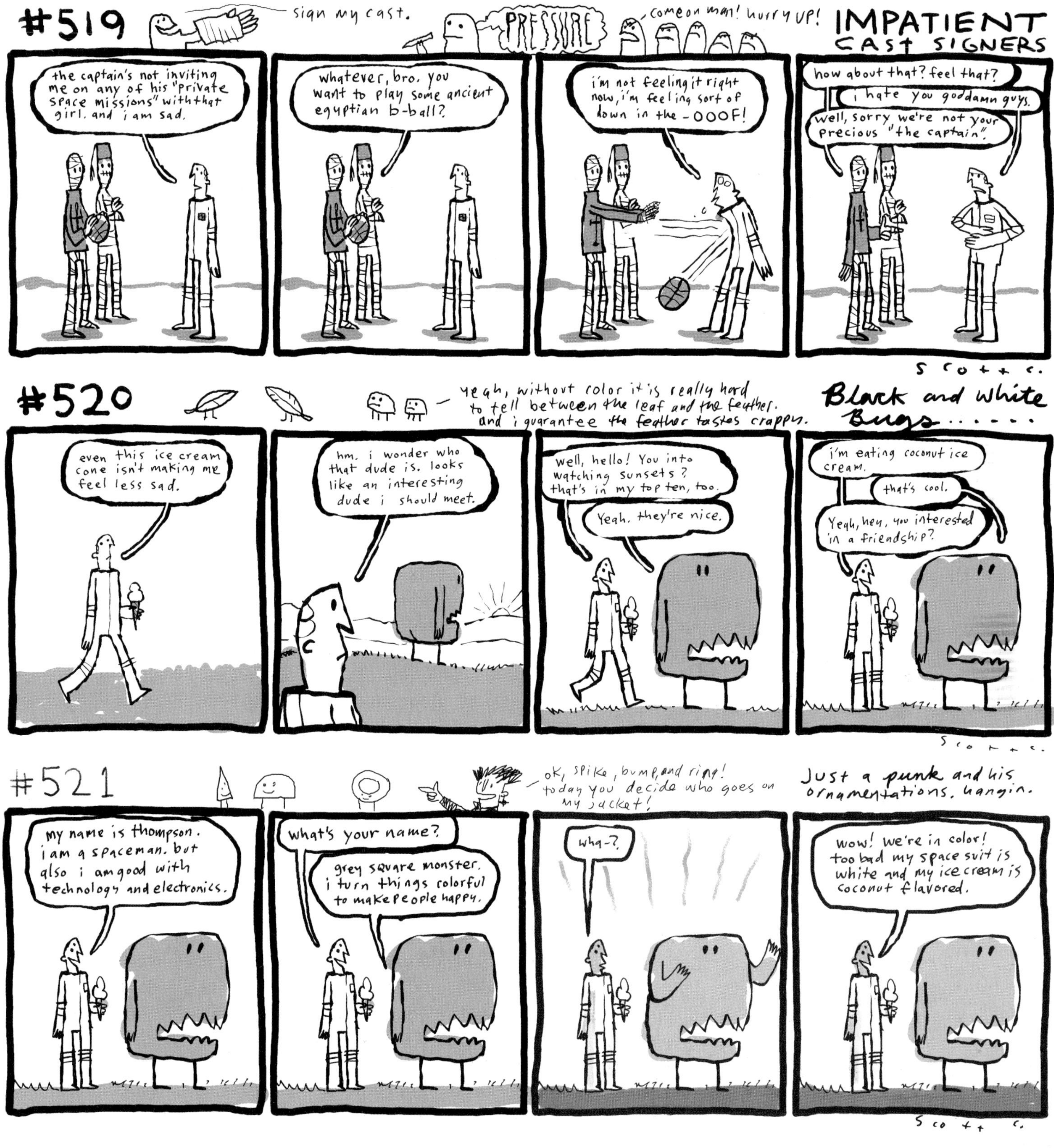

#519
sign my cast.
PRESSURE
come on man! hurry up!
IMPATIENT CAST SIGNERS
the captain's not inviting me on any of his "private space missions" with that girl. and i am sad.
whatever, bro. you want to play some ancient egyptian b-ball?
i'm not feeling it right now, i'm feeling sort of down in the - OOOF!
how about that? feel that?
i hate you goddamn guys.
well, sorry we're not your precious "the captain".
scott c.
#520
yeah, without color it is really hard to tell between the leaf and the feather. and i guarantee the feather tastes crappy.
Black and White Bugs.....
even this ice cream cone isn't making me feel less sad.
hm. i wonder who that dude is. looks like an interesting dude i should meet.
well, hello! You into watching sunsets? that's in my top ten, too.
Yeah. they're nice.
i'm eating coconut ice cream.
that's cool.
Yeah, hey. you interested in a friendship?
scott c.
#521
ok, spike, bump, and ring! today you decide who goes on my jacket!
Just a punk and his ornamentations, hangin.
my name is thompson. i am a spaceman. but also i am good with technology and electronics.
what's your name?
grey square monster. i turn things colorful to make people happy.
wha-?
wow! we're in color! too bad my space suit is white and my ice cream is coconut flavored.
scott c.

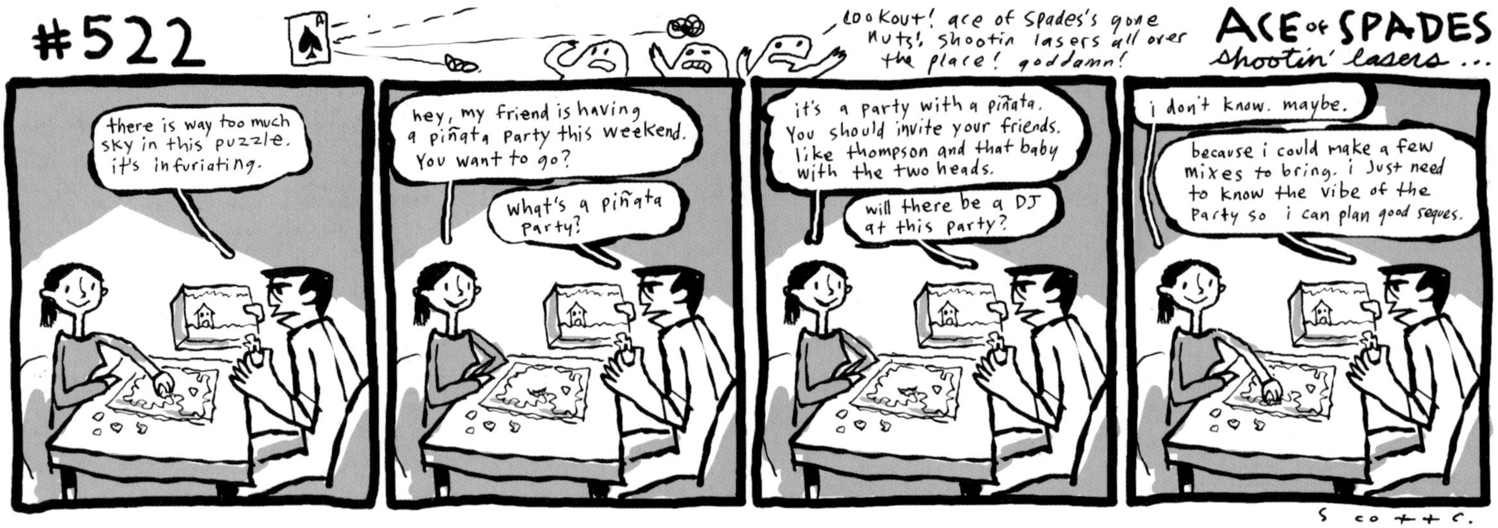
#522
lookout! ace of spades's gone nuts! shootin lasers all over the place! goddamn!
ACE OF SPADES shootin' lasers...
there is way too much sky in this puzzle. it's infuriating.
hey, my friend is having a piñata party this weekend. You want to go?
What's a piñata party?
it's a party with a piñata. You should invite your friends. like thompson and that baby with the two heads.
will there be a DJ at this party?
i don't know. maybe.
because i could make a few mixes to bring. i just need to know the vibe of the party so i can plan good seques.
scott c.

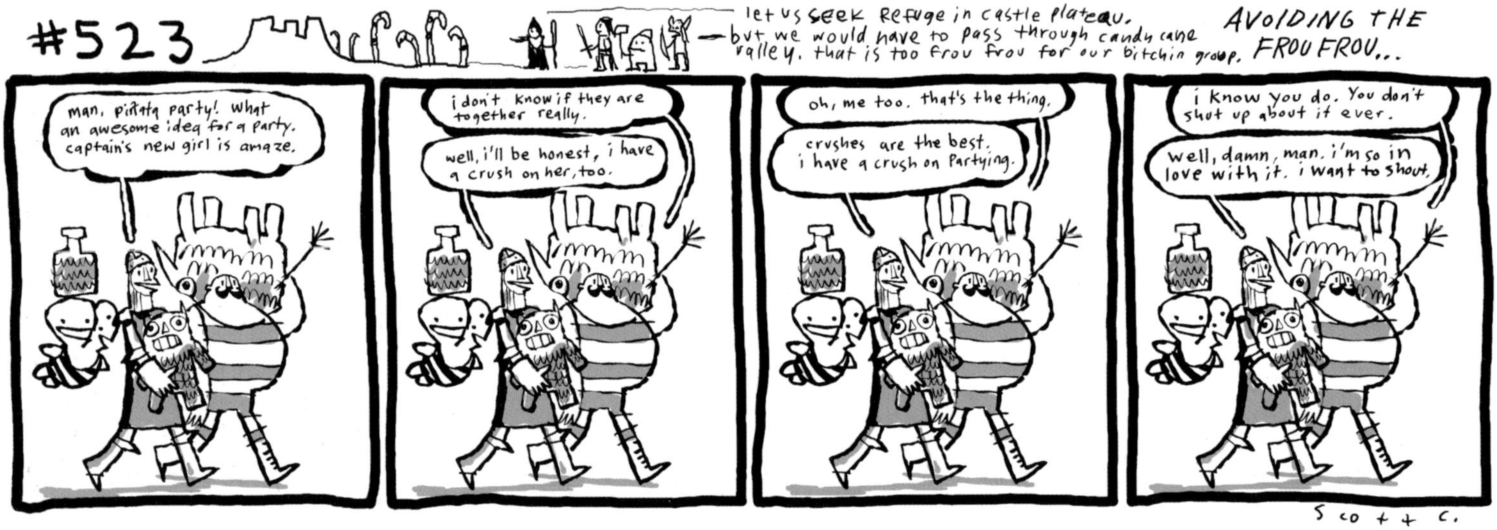
#523
let us seek refuge in castle plateau.
but we would have to pass through candy cane valley. that is too frou frou for our bitchin group.
AVOIDING THE FROU FROU...
man, piñata party! what an awesome idea for a party. captain's new girl is amaze.
i don't know if they are together really.
well, i'll be honest, i have a crush on her, too.
oh, me too. that's the thing.
crushes are the best. i have a crush on partying.
i know you do. You don't shut up about it ever.
well, damn, man. i'm so in love with it. i want to shout.
scott c.

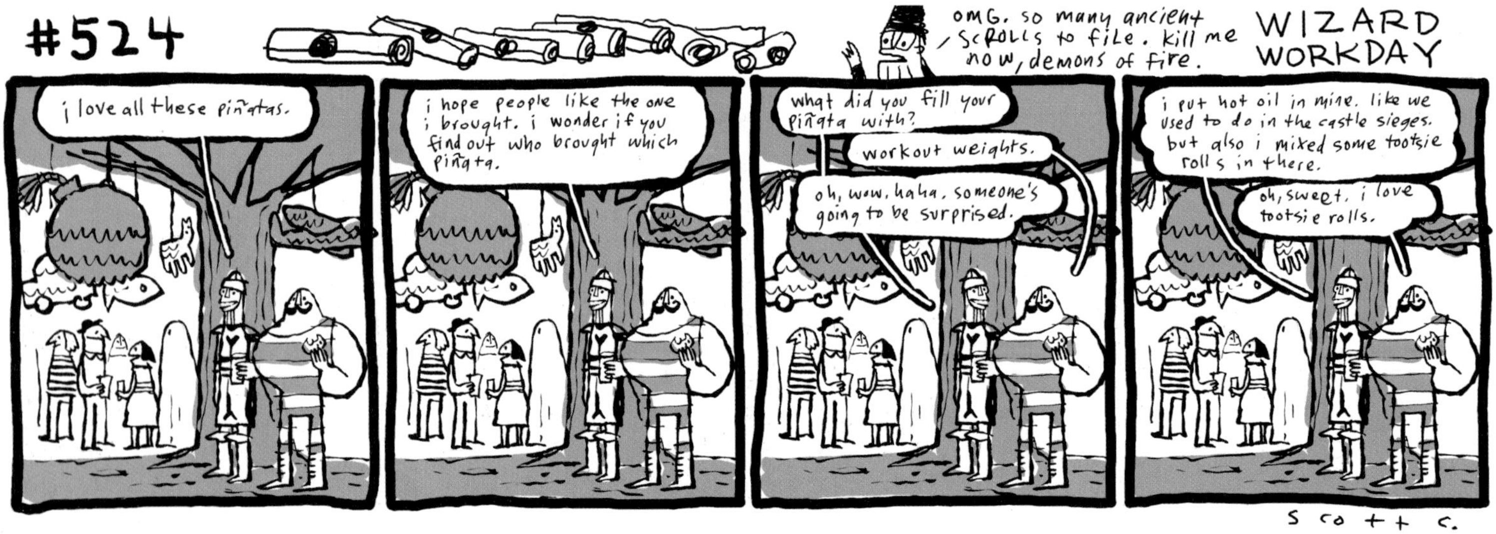
#524
OMG. so many ancient scrolls to file. kill me now, demons of fire.
WIZARD WORKDAY
i love all these piñatas.
i hope people like the one i brought. i wonder if you find out who brought which piñata.
what did you fill your piñata with?
workout weights.
oh, wow, haha. someone's going to be surprised.
i put hot oil in mine. like we used to do in the castle sieges. but also i mixed some tootsie rolls in there.
oh, sweet. i love tootsie rolls.
scott c.

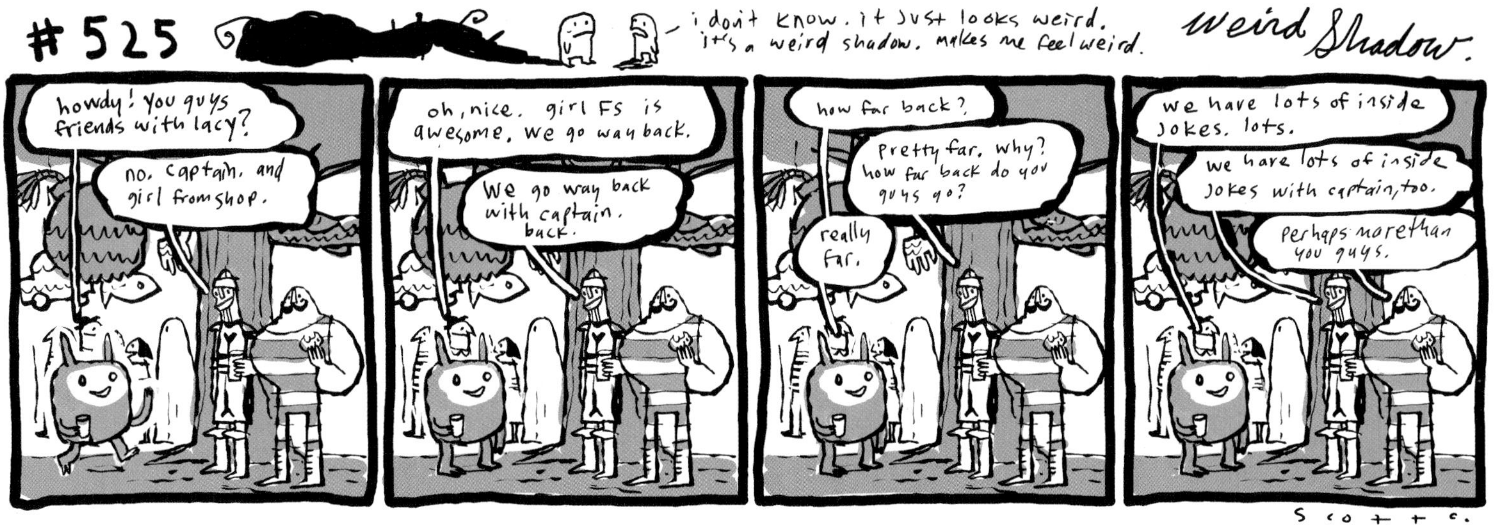
#525
i don't know. it just looks weird. it's a weird shadow. makes me feel weird.
weird Shadow.
howdy! you guys friends with lacy?
no. captain. and girl from shop.
oh, nice. girl FS is awesome. we go way back.
we go way back with captain. back.
how far back?
pretty far. why? how far back do you guys go?
really far.
we have lots of inside jokes. lots.
we have lots of inside jokes with captain, too.
perhaps more than you guys.
scott c.

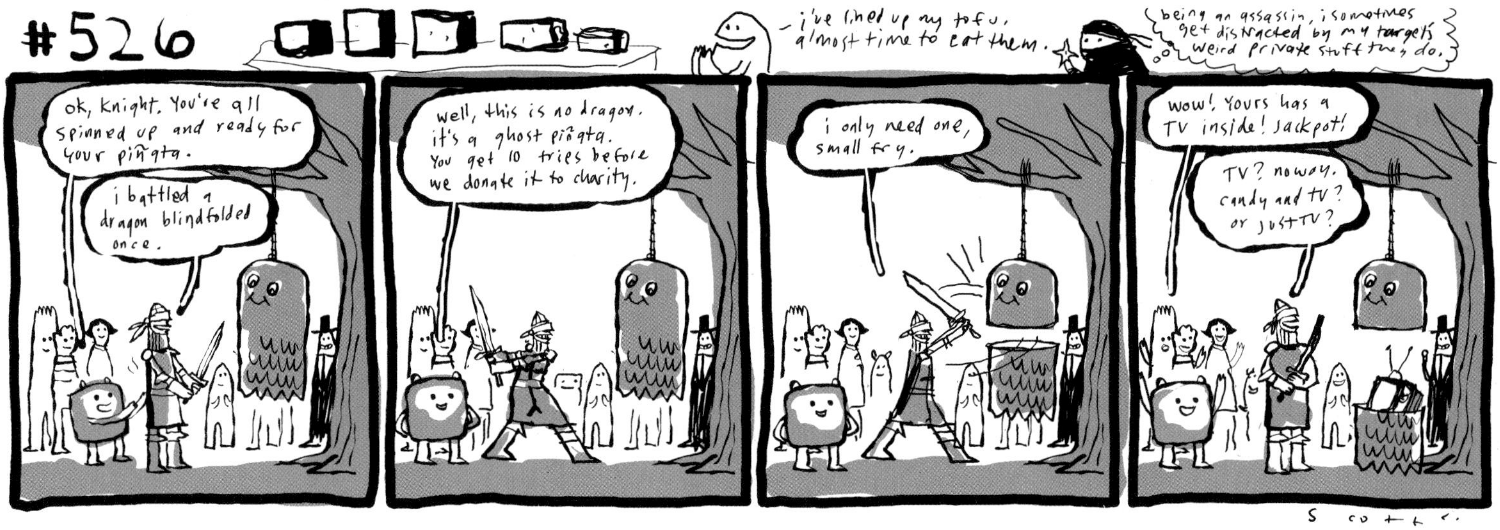
#526
i've lined up my tofu, almost time to eat them.
being an assassin, i sometimes get distracted by my target's weird private stuff they do.
ok, knight. you're all spinned up and ready for your piñata.
i battled a dragon blindfolded once.
well, this is no dragon. it's a ghost piñata. you get 10 tries before we donate it to charity.
i only need one, small fry.
wow! yours has a TV inside! jackpot!
TV? no way. candy and TV? or just TV?
scott c.

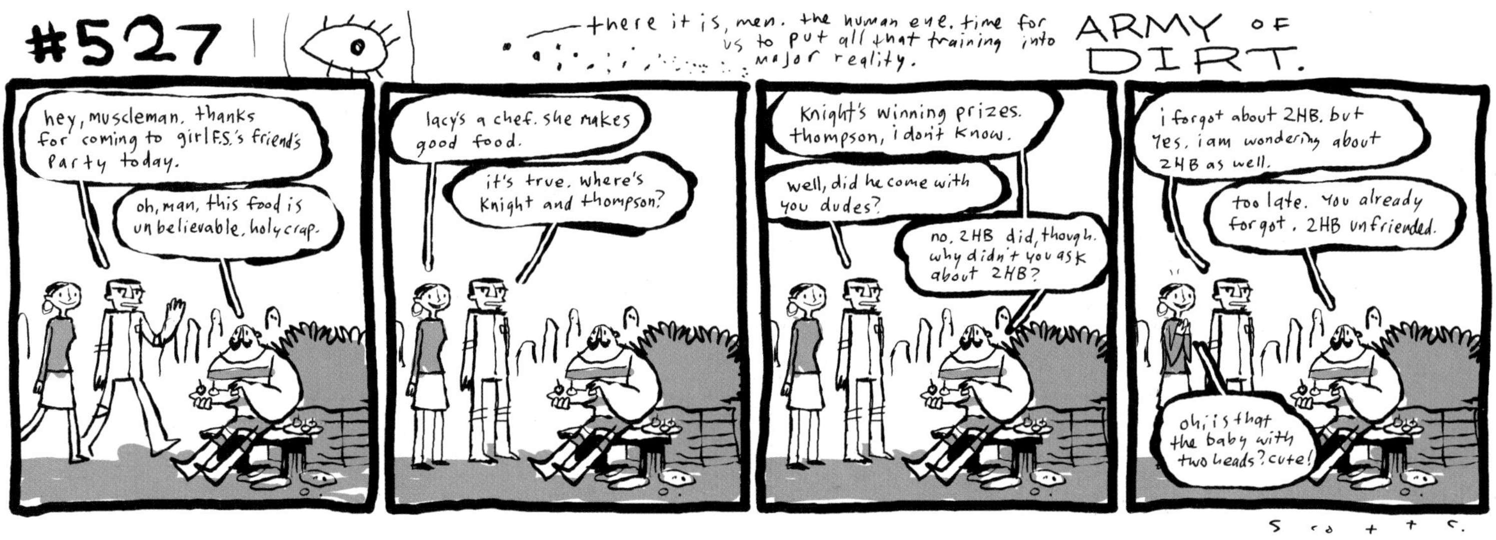
#527
there it is, men. the human eye. time for us to put all that training into major reality.
ARMY OF DIRT.
hey, muscleman. thanks for coming to girl F.S.'s friend's party today.
oh, man. this food is unbelievable. holy crap.
lacy's a chef. she makes good food.
it's true. where's knight and thompson?
knight's winning prizes. thompson, i don't know.
well, did he come with you dudes?
no. 2HB did, though. why didn't you ask about 2HB?
i forgot about 2HB. but yes. i am wondering about 2HB as well.
too late. you already forgot. 2HB unfriended.
oh! is that the baby with two heads? cute!
scott c.

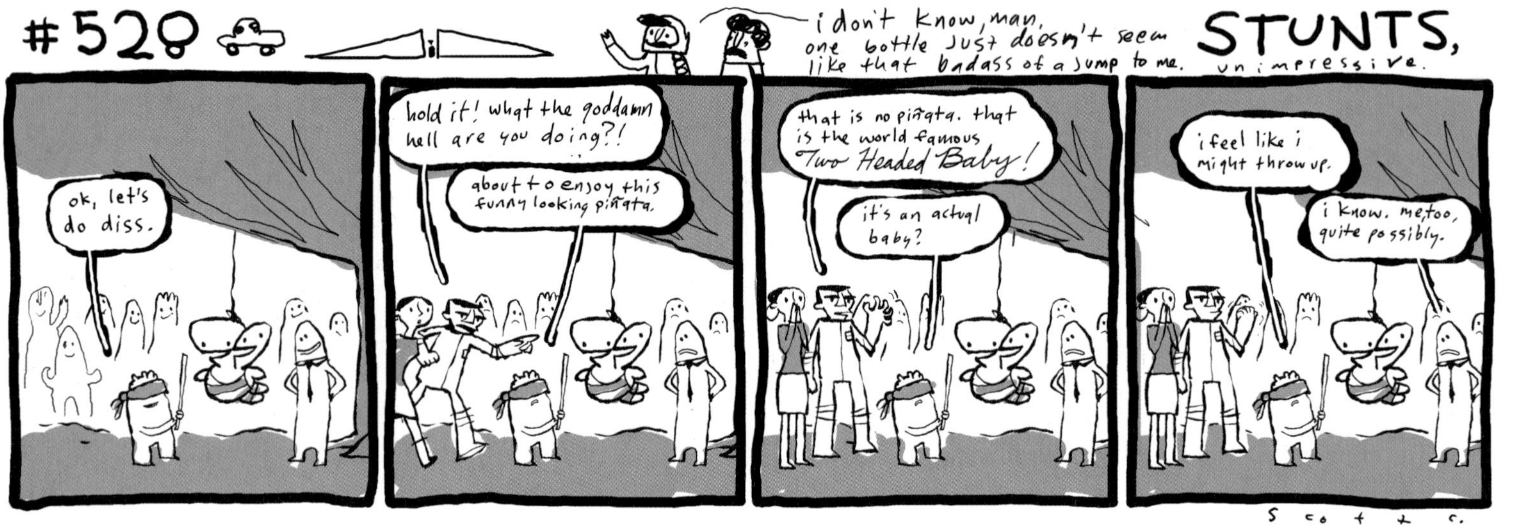
#528
i don't know, man. one bottle just doesn't seem like that badass of a jump to me.
STUNTS, unimpressive.
ok, let's do diss.
hold it! what the goddamn hell are you doing?!
about to enjoy this funny looking piñata.
that is no piñata. that is the world famous Two Headed Baby!
it's an actual baby?
i feel like i might throw up.
i know. me, too, quite possibly.
scott c.

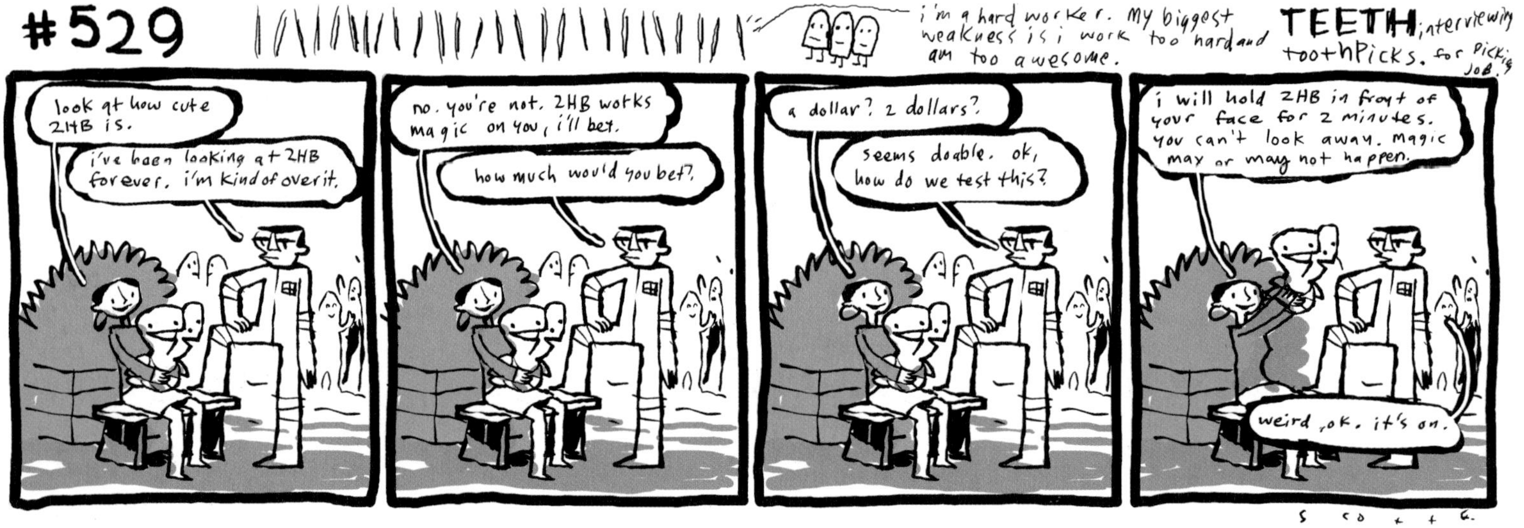
#529
i'm a hard worker. My biggest weakness is i work too hard and am too awesome.
TEETH interviewing toothpicks. for picking job.
look at how cute 2HB is.
i've been looking at 2HB forever. i'm kind of over it.
no. you're not. 2HB works magic on you, i'll bet.
how much would you bet?
a dollar? 2 dollars?
seems doable. ok, how do we test this?
i will hold 2HB in front of your face for 2 minutes. you can't look away. magic may or may not happen.
weird, ok. it's on.
scott c.

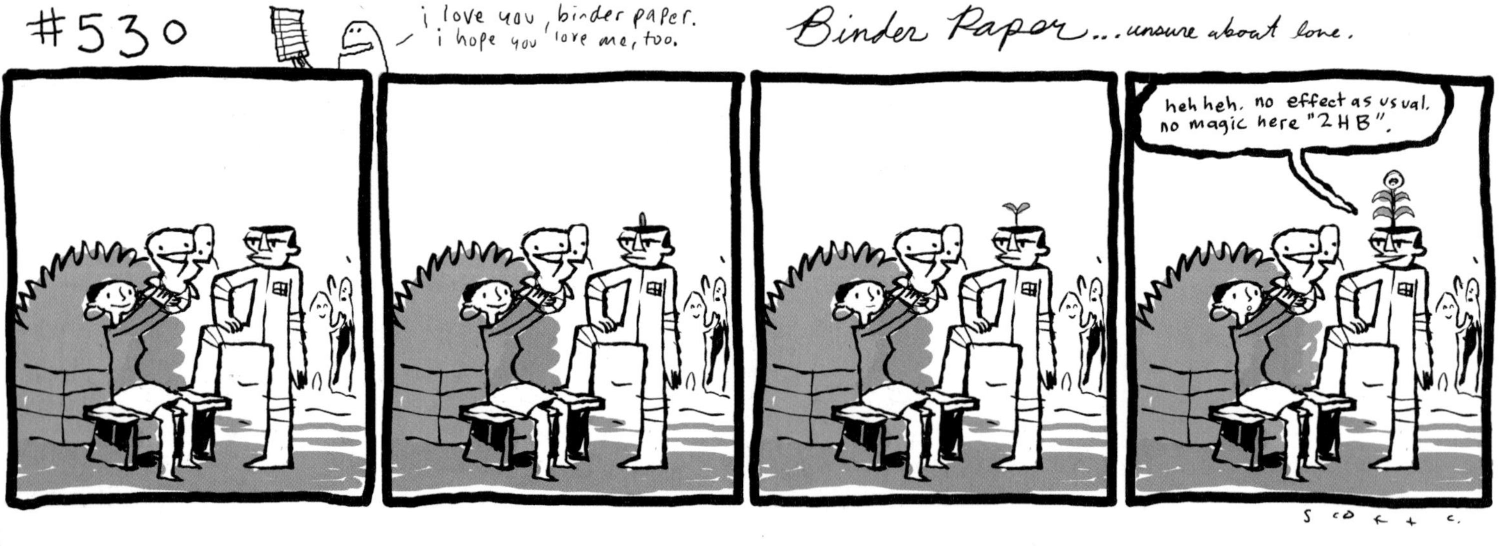
#530
i love you, binder paper. i hope you love me, too.
Binder Paper... unsure about love.
heh heh. no effect as usual. no magic here "2HB".
scott c.

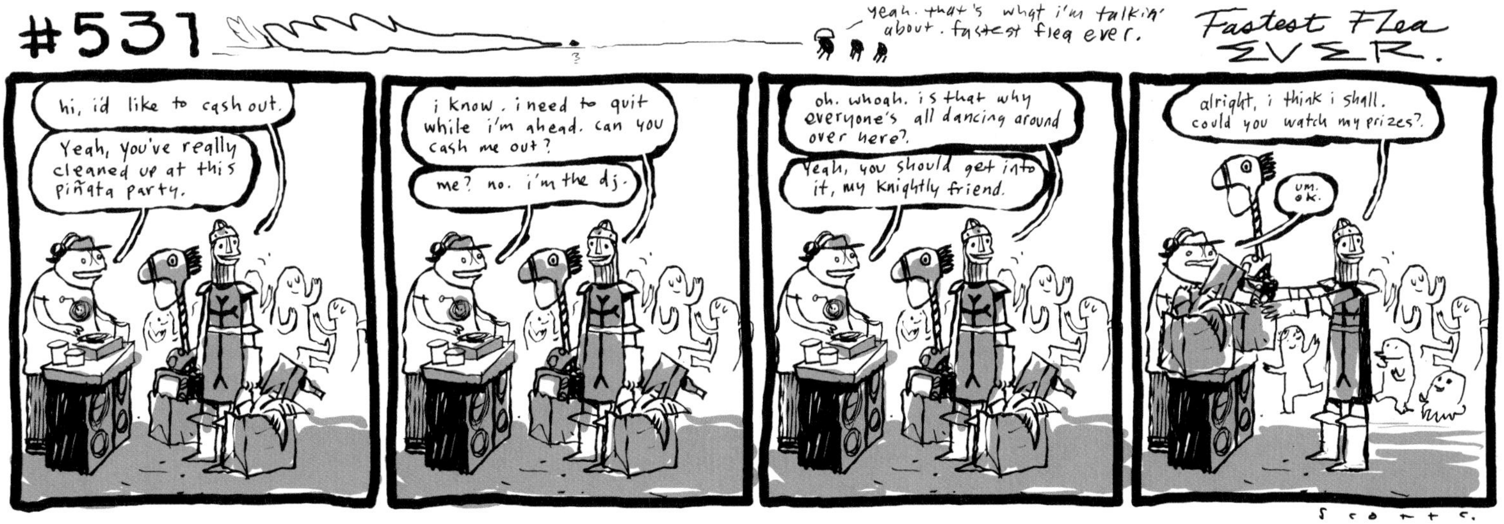
#531
yeah. that's what i'm talkin' about. fastest flea ever.
Fastest Flea EVER.
hi, i'd like to cash out.
Yeah, you've really cleaned up at this piñata party.
i know. i need to quit while i'm ahead. can you cash me out?
me? no. i'm the dj.
oh. whoah. is that why everyone's all dancing around over here?.
Yeah, you should get into it, my knightly friend.
alright, i think i shall. could you watch my prizes?.
um. ok.
scott c.

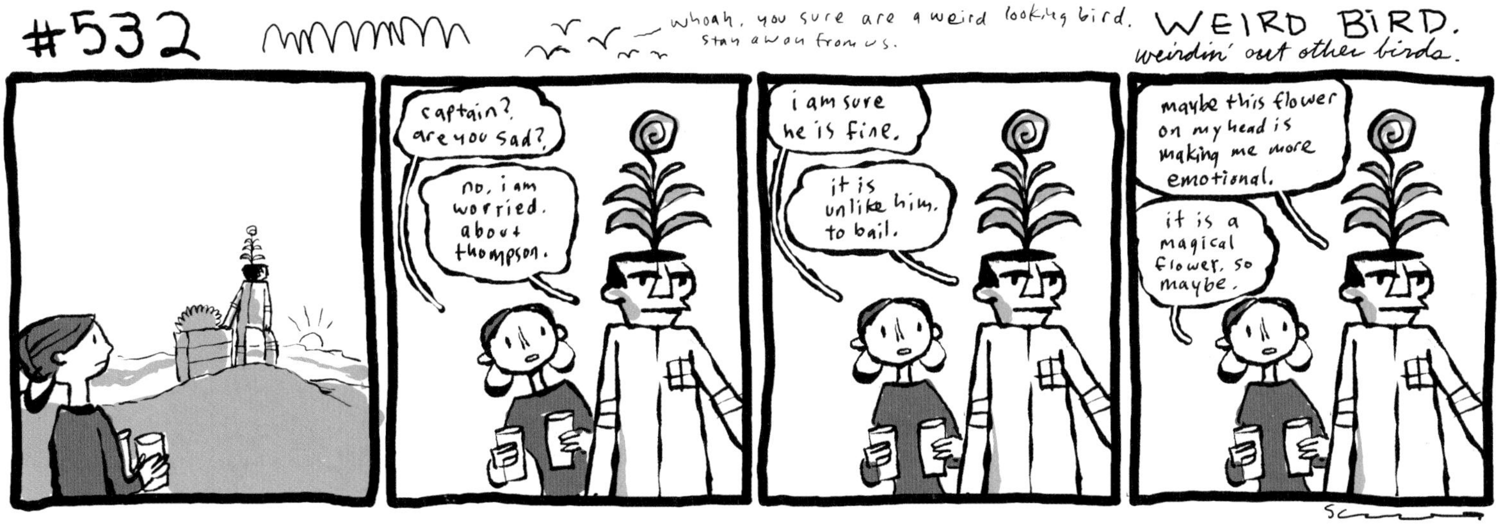
#532
whoah. you sure are a weird looking bird. stay away from us.
WEIRD BIRD. weirdin' out other birds.
captain? are you sad?
no. i am worried. about thompson.
i am sure he is fine.
it is unlike him. to bail.
maybe this flower on my head is making me more emotional.
it is a magical flower, so maybe.

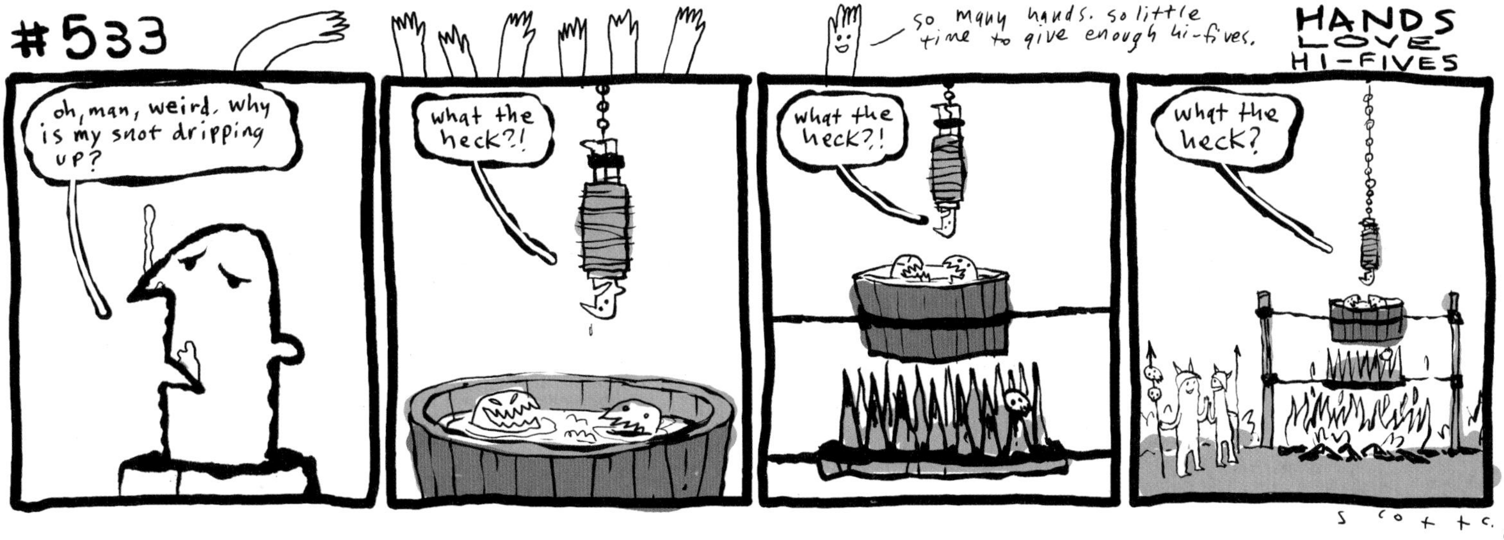
#533
so many hands. so little time to give enough hi-fives.
HANDS LOVE HI-FIVES
oh, man, weird. why is my snot dripping up?
what the heck?!
what the heck?!
what the heck?
scott c.

#534

-SOUP!

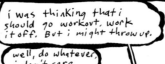 soup can head misses the soup that used to be in his head. his whole life soup has been in his head.

EMPTY SOUP can head.

Panel 1:
ok, god, knight. i'm so full. what should i do?

Panel 2:
what do you mean? how should i know what you should do? go on a diet.

hm. maybe.

Panel 3:
i was thinking that i should go workout, work it off. but i might throw up.

well, do whatever, i don't care.

Panel 4:
well, i figured you were my friend, and friends care. but my mistake.

hey, man. i'm trying to impress this crew with my dancing. so scoot.

scott c.

#535

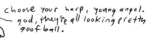 choose your harp, young angel. god, they're all looking pretty goofball.

goofball harps. (all they got.)

Panel 1:
is this the guy?

this is the guy.

Panel 2:
tigerface here says that you are a master at the piñata.

perhaps. who's asking.

Panel 3:
i am known as lacy. and this is my piñata party that you have mastered.

holy! your food is amazing! it's made me fat!

Panel 4:
listen. i have a piñata that i feel you cannot defeat. it is filled with immense treasures.

what... the... h?

p.s. i am glad you enjoyed the food, chubby dude.

scott c.

#536

 - well, good morning igor. your eye is exceptionally bulgy today.

Dr. Frankenstein super polite. (pre-monster. because after the monster, he gets pretty aggro.) -vated.

Panel 1:
it is called "IRON DEATH" and it is the most feared of all piñatas. no one can defeat it.

Panel 2:
it is made of thick iron and is filled with something grand, i hear from legend.

Panel 3:
what do you think, piñata master? think you can defeat IRON DEATH? and collect its riches?

Panel 4:
well, if i smash it open, is everyone going to bum rush all the stuff that falls out? because that would not be worth it.

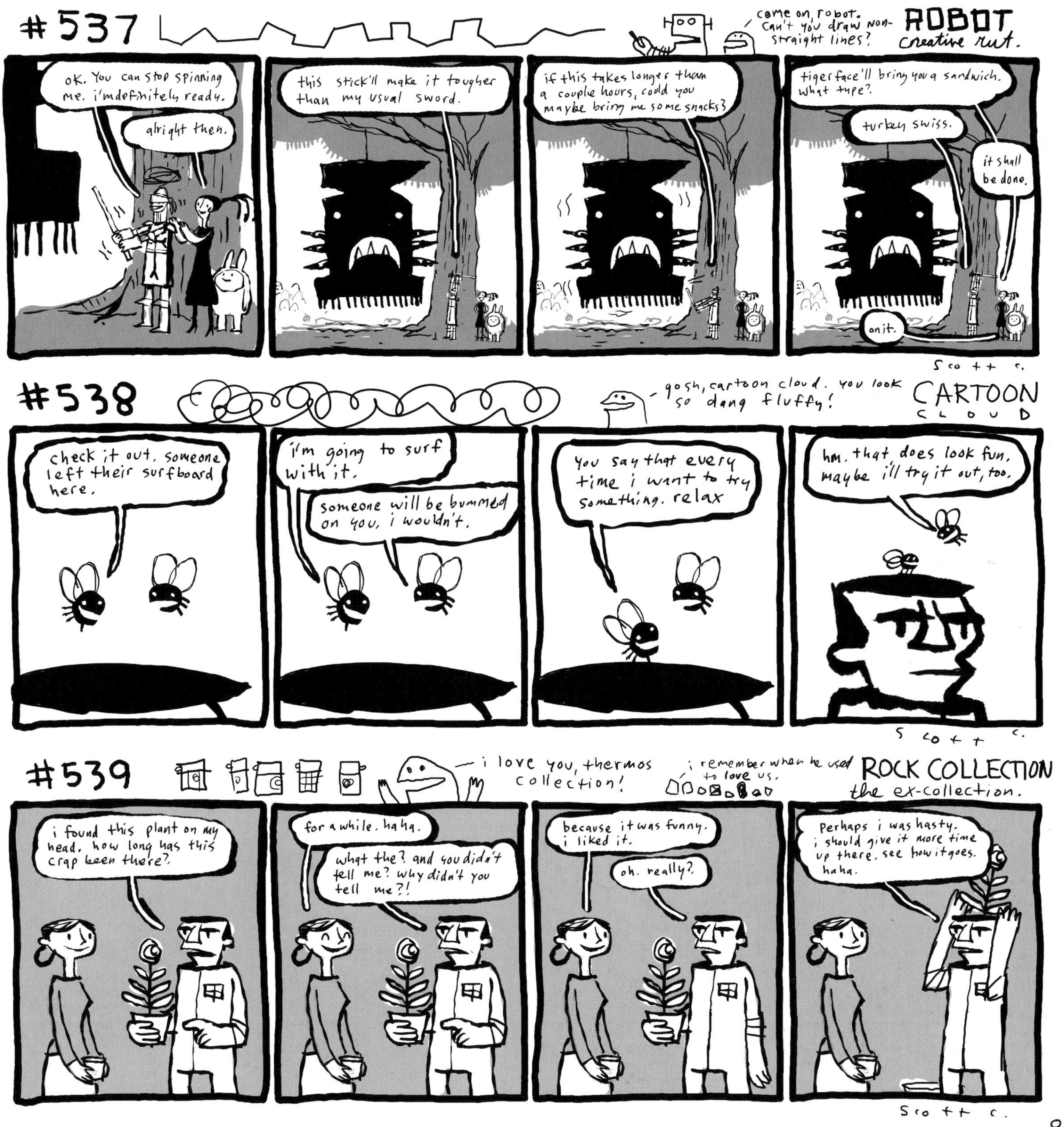
#537
come on, robot. can't you draw non-straight lines?
ROBOT
creative rut.
ok. you can stop spinning me. i'm definitely ready.
alright then.
this stick'll make it tougher than my usual sword.
if this takes longer than a couple hours, could you maybe bring me some snacks?
tigerface'll bring you a sandwich. what type?
turkey swiss.
it shall be done.
on it.
scott c.
#538
gosh, cartoon cloud. you look so dang fluffy!
CARTOON
CLOUD
check it out. someone left their surfboard here.
i'm going to surf with it.
someone will be bummed on you, i wouldn't.
you say that every time i want to try something. relax
hm. that does look fun. maybe i'll try it out, too.
scott c.
#539
i love you, thermos collection!
i remember when he used to love us.
ROCK COLLECTION
the ex-collection.
i found this plant on my head. how long has this crap been there?
for a while. haha.
what the? and you didn't tell me? why didn't you tell me?!
because it was funny. i liked it.
oh. really?
perhaps i was hasty. i should give it more time up there. see how it goes. haha.
scott c.

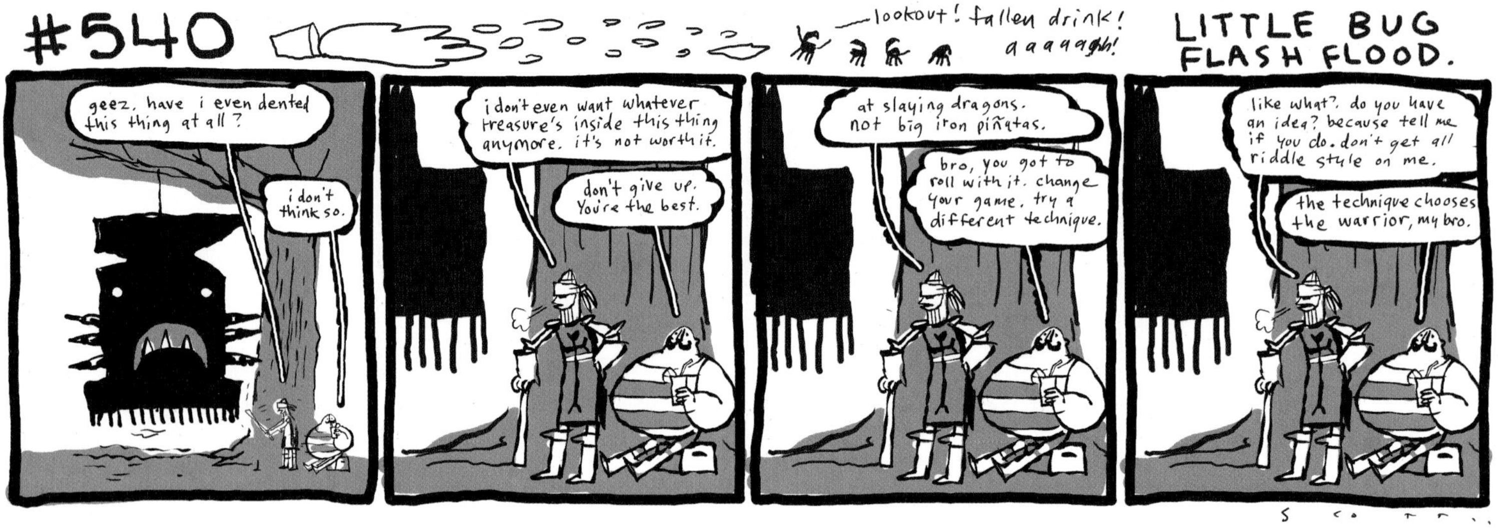
#540
lookout! fallen drink!
aaaaaagh!
LITTLE BUG FLASH FLOOD.
geez, have i even dented this thing at all?
i don't think so.
i don't even want whatever treasure's inside this thing anymore. it's not worth it.
don't give up. You're the best.
at slaying dragons. not big iron piñatas.
bro, you got to roll with it. change your game. try a different technique.
like what?. do you have an idea? because tell me if you do. don't get all riddle style on me.
the technique chooses the warrior, my bro.

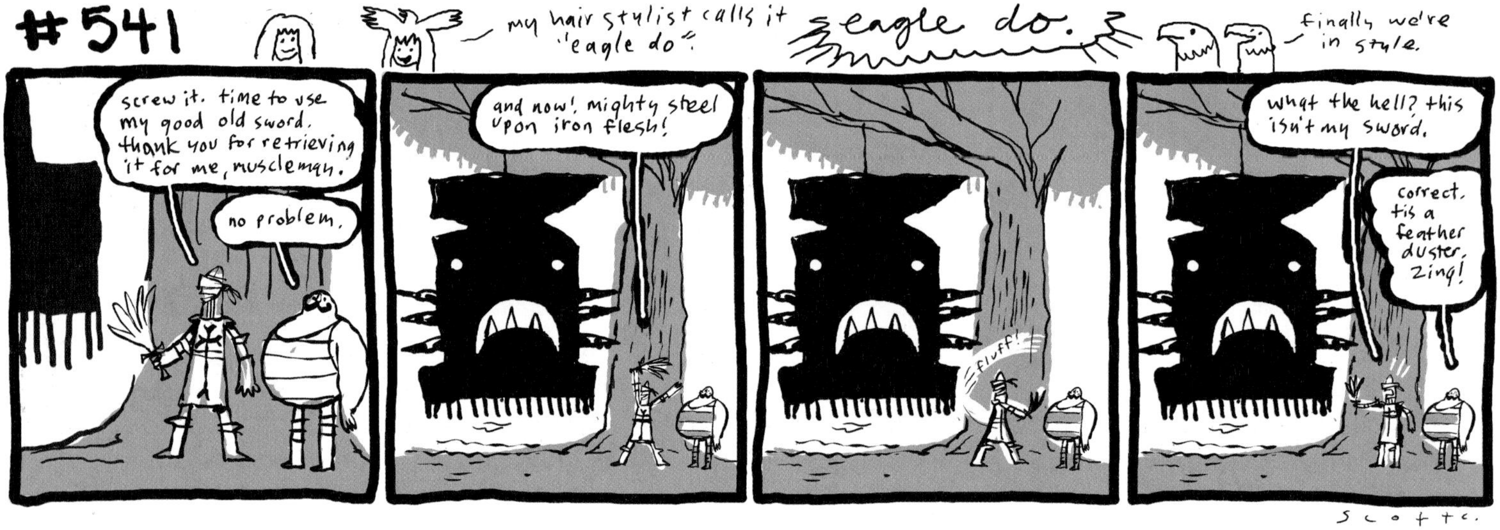
#541
my hair stylist calls it "eagle do".
eagle do.
finally we're in style.
screw it. time to use my good old sword. thank you for retrieving it for me, muscleman.
no problem.
and now! mighty steel upon iron flesh!
FLUFF!
what the hell? this isn't my sword.
correct. tis a feather duster. Zing!
scott c.

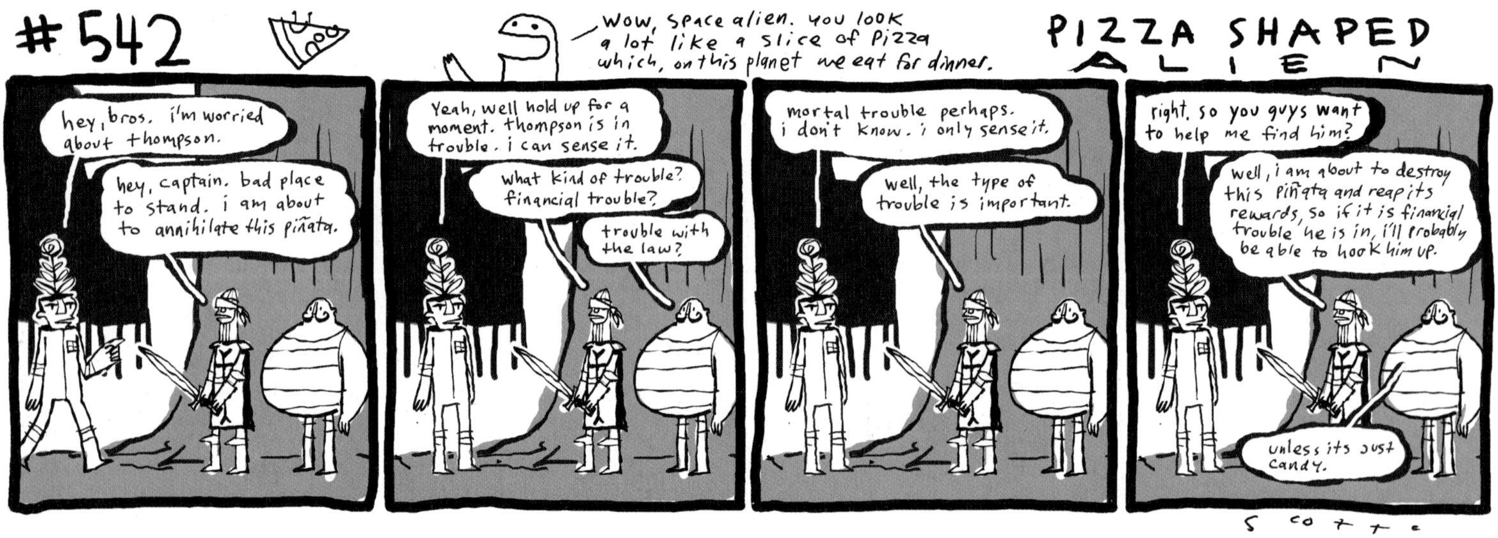
#542
wow, space alien. you look a lot like a slice of pizza which, on this planet we eat for dinner.
PIZZA SHAPED ALIEN
hey, bros. i'm worried about thompson.
hey, captain. bad place to stand. i am about to annihilate this piñata.
Yeah, well hold up for a moment. thompson is in trouble. i can sense it.
what kind of trouble? financial trouble?
trouble with the law?
mortal trouble perhaps. i don't know. i only sense it.
well, the type of trouble is important.
right. so you guys want to help me find him?
well, i am about to destroy this piñata and reap its rewards, so if it is financial trouble he is in, i'll probably be able to hook him up.
unless its just candy.
scott c.

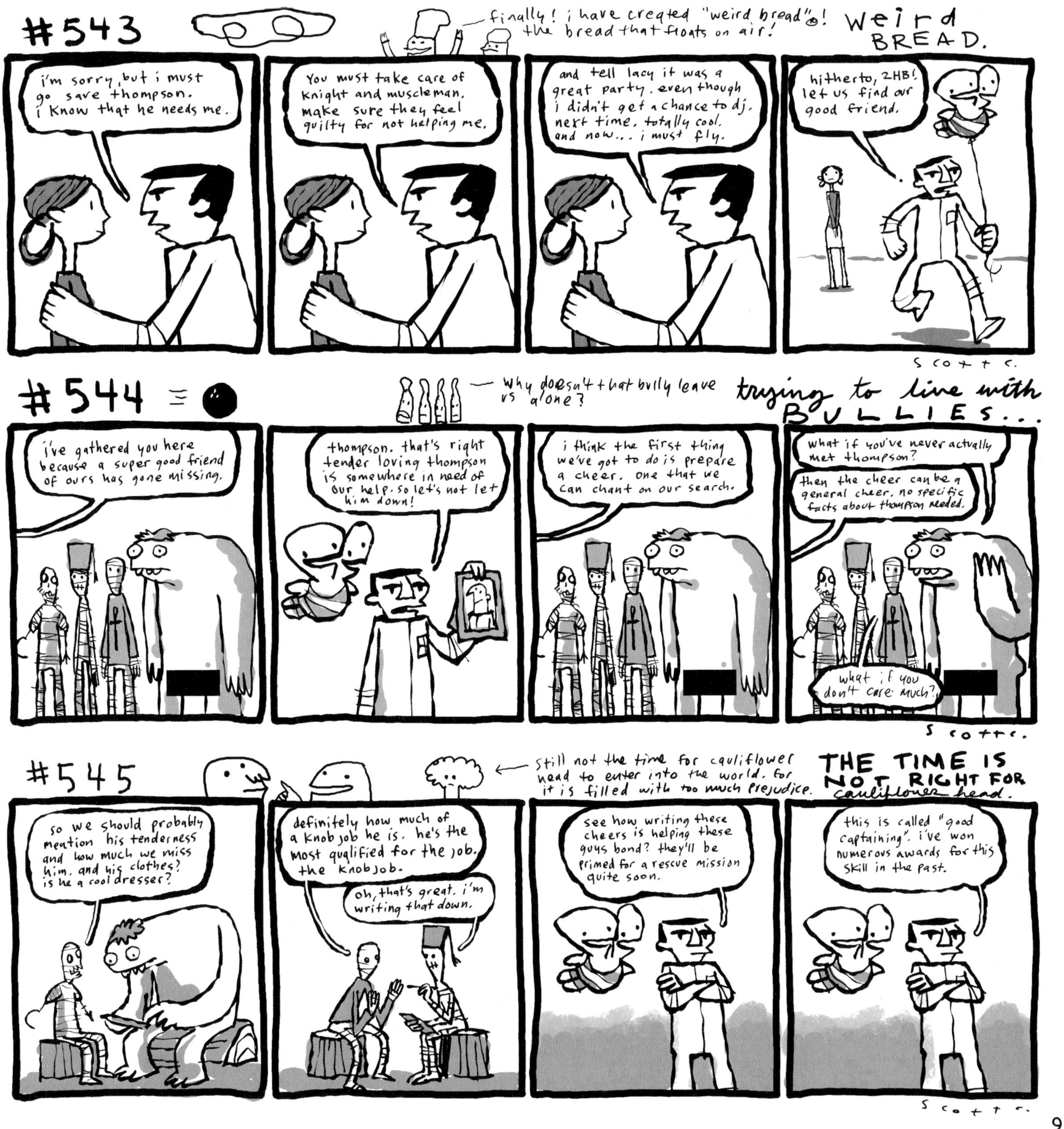
#543
finally! i have created "weird bread"®! the bread that floats on air!
weird BREAD.
i'm sorry, but i must go save thompson. i know that he needs me.
You must take care of knight and muscleman, make sure they feel guilty for not helping me.
and tell lacy it was a great party, even though i didn't get a chance to dj. next time, totally cool. and now... i must fly.
hitherto, 2HB! let us find our good friend.
scott c.
#544
why doesn't that bully leave us alone?
trying to live with BULLIES...
i've gathered you here because a super good friend of ours has gone missing.
thompson. that's right tender loving thompson is somewhere in need of our help. so let's not let him down!
i think the first thing we've got to do is prepare a cheer. one that we can chant on our search.
what if you've never actually met thompson?
then the cheer can be a general cheer. no specific facts about thompson needed.
what if you don't care much?
scott c.
#545
still not the time for cauliflower head to enter into the world. for it is filled with too much prejudice.
THE TIME IS NOT RIGHT FOR cauliflower head.
so we should probably mention his tenderness and how much we miss him. and his clothes? is he a cool dresser?
definitely how much of a knob job he is. he's the most qualified for the job. the knobjob.
oh, that's great. i'm writing that down.
see how writing these cheers is helping these guys bond? they'll be primed for a rescue mission quite soon.
this is called "good captaining". i've won numerous awards for this skill in the past.
scott c.

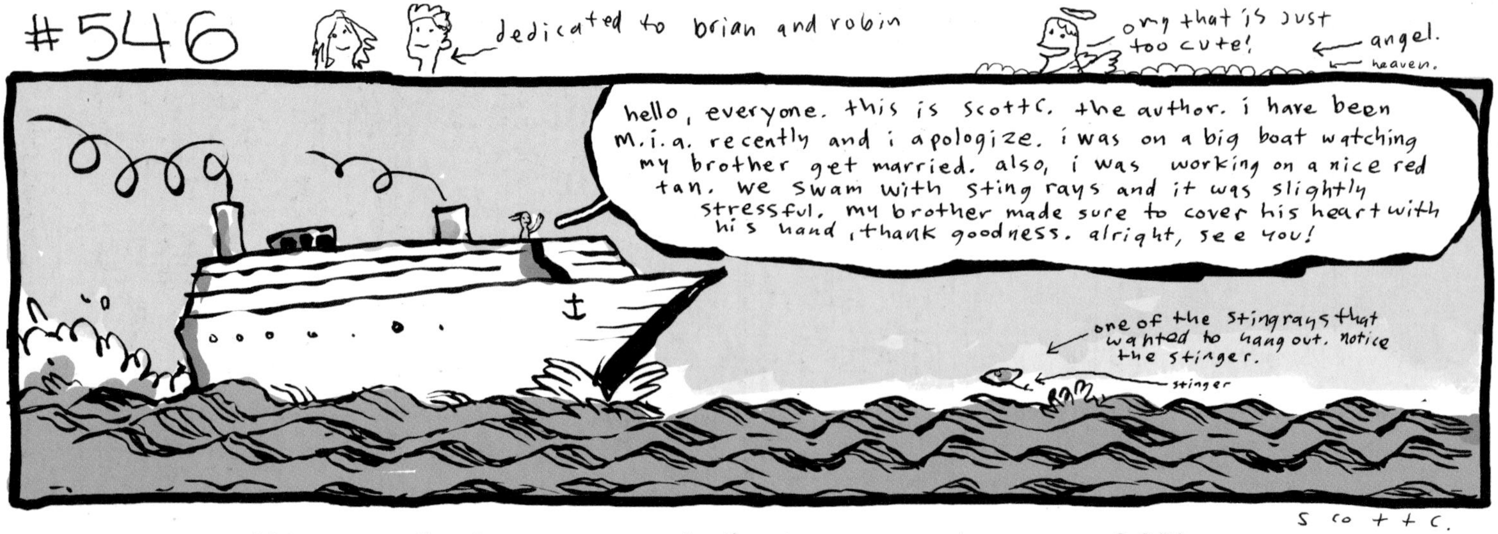
#546
dedicated to brian and robin
omg that is just too cute!
angel.
heaven.
hello, everyone. this is scott c. the author. i have been m.i.a. recently and i apologize. i was on a big boat watching my brother get married. also, i was working on a nice red tan. we swam with sting rays and it was slightly stressful. my brother made sure to cover his heart with his hand, thank goodness. alright, see you!
one of the stingrays that wanted to hang out. notice the stinger.
stinger
scott c.

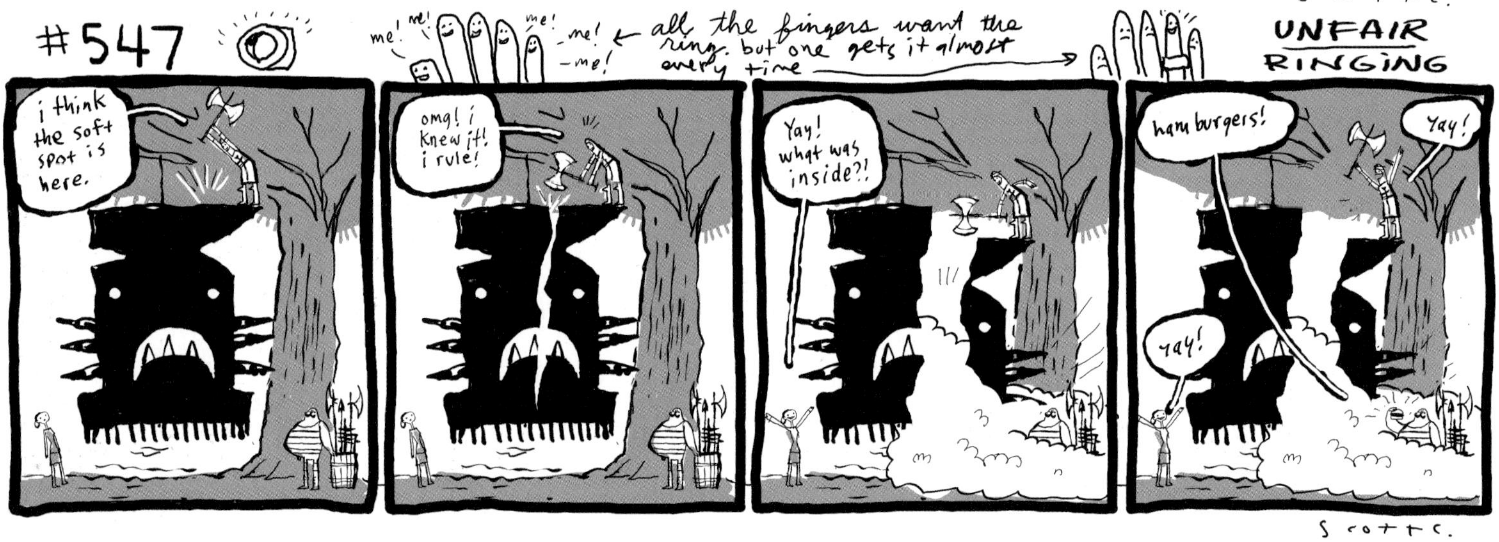
#547
me! me! me! me! me!
all the fingers want the ring. but one gets it almost every time
UNFAIR RINGING
i think the soft spot is here.
omg! i knew it! i rule!
Yay! what was inside?!
hamburgers!
Yay!
yay!
scott c.

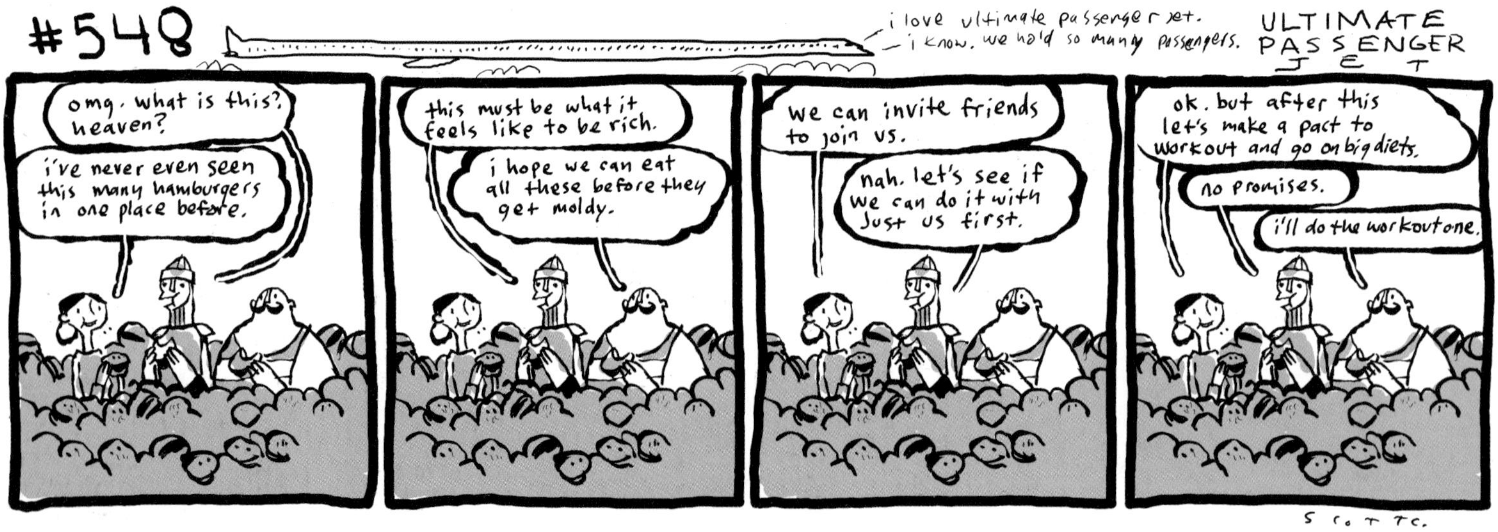
#548
i love ultimate passenger jet.
i know. we hold so many passengers.
ULTIMATE PASSENGER JET
omg. what is this? heaven?
i've never even seen this many hamburgers in one place before.
this must be what it feels like to be rich.
i hope we can eat all these before they get moldy.
we can invite friends to join us.
nah. let's see if we can do it with just us first.
ok. but after this let's make a pact to workout and go on big diets.
no promises.
i'll do the workout one.
scott c.

#549

- you've changed. i can't identify with you anymore. ← double decker checker getting scolded by old bro who actually is a little jealous because he wasn't the one to be "kinged", as they say.

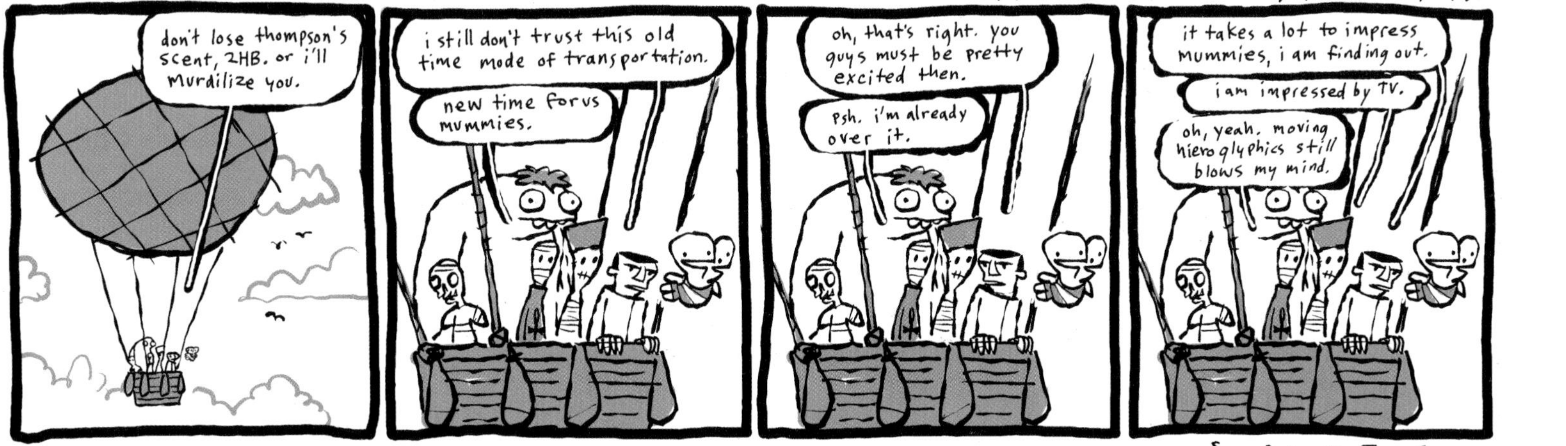

don't lose thompson's scent, 2HB. or i'll murdilize you.
i still don't trust this old time mode of transportation.
new time for us mummies.
oh, that's right. you guys must be pretty excited then.
psh. i'm already over it.
it takes a lot to impress mummies, i am finding out.
i am impressed by TV.
oh, yeah. moving hieroglyphics still blows my mind.

s c o t t c.

#550

- no, i like the mustache itself. i just think you have it on upside down is all

upside down mustache

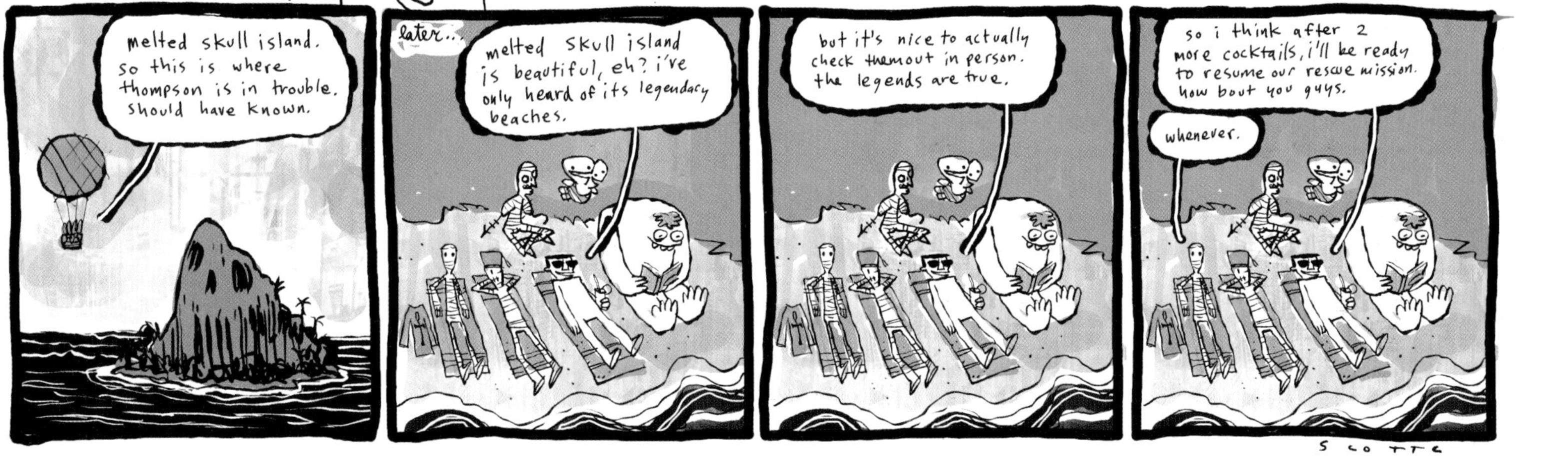

melted skull island. so this is where thompson is in trouble. should have known.
later...
melted skull island is beautiful, eh? i've only heard of its legendary beaches.
but it's nice to actually check them out in person. the legends are true.
so i think after 2 more cocktails, i'll be ready to resume our rescue mission. how bout you guys.
whenever.

s c o t t c

#551 [redacted]

- oh, no. not tar again. tar again

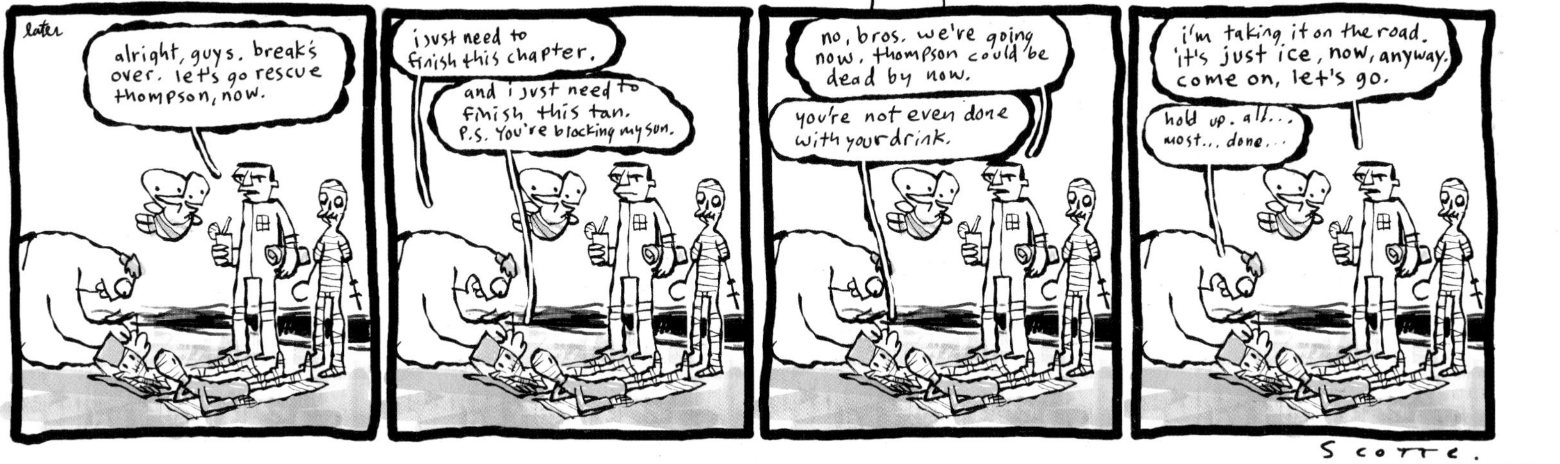

later
alright, guys. break's over. let's go rescue thompson, now.
i just need to finish this chapter.
and i just need to finish this tan. P.S. you're blocking my son.
no, bros. we're going now. thompson could be dead by now.
you're not even done with your drink.
i'm taking it on the road. it's just ice, now, anyway. come on, let's go.
hold up. al... most... done...

s c o t t c.

#552

← speeding bullet meets silver bullet. two very famous bullets.

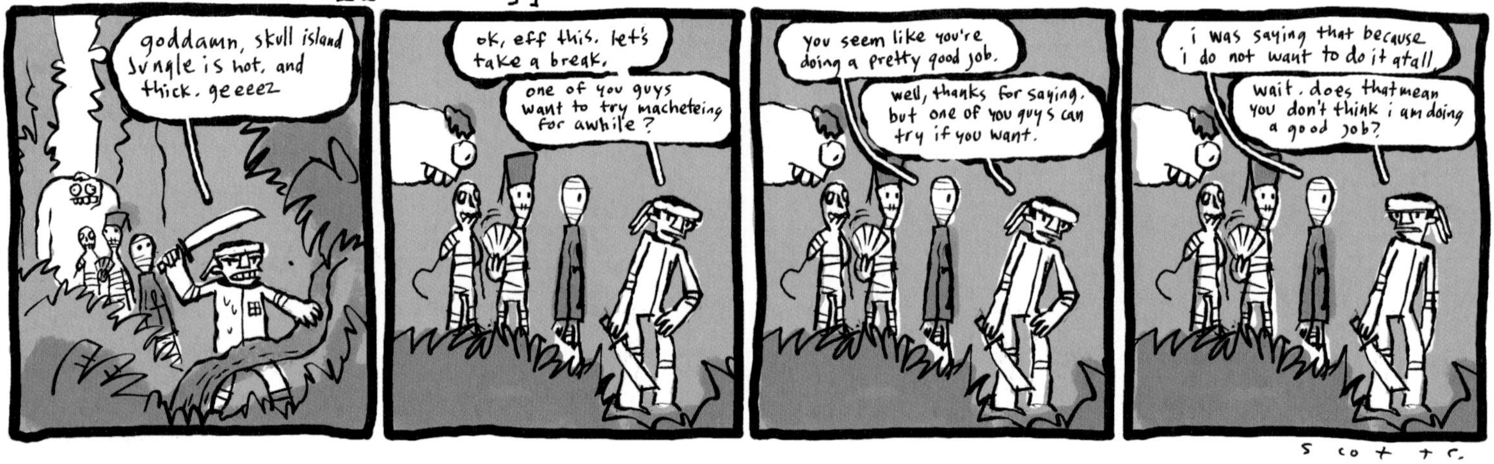
goddamn, skull island jungle is hot, and thick. geeeez
ok, eff this. let's take a break.
one of you guys want to try macheteing for awhile?
you seem like you're doing a pretty good job.
well, thanks for saying. but one of you guys can try if you want.
i was saying that because i do not want to do it atall.
wait. does that mean you don't think i am doing a good job?
scott c.

#553

the dancin' flames! (choreography group)

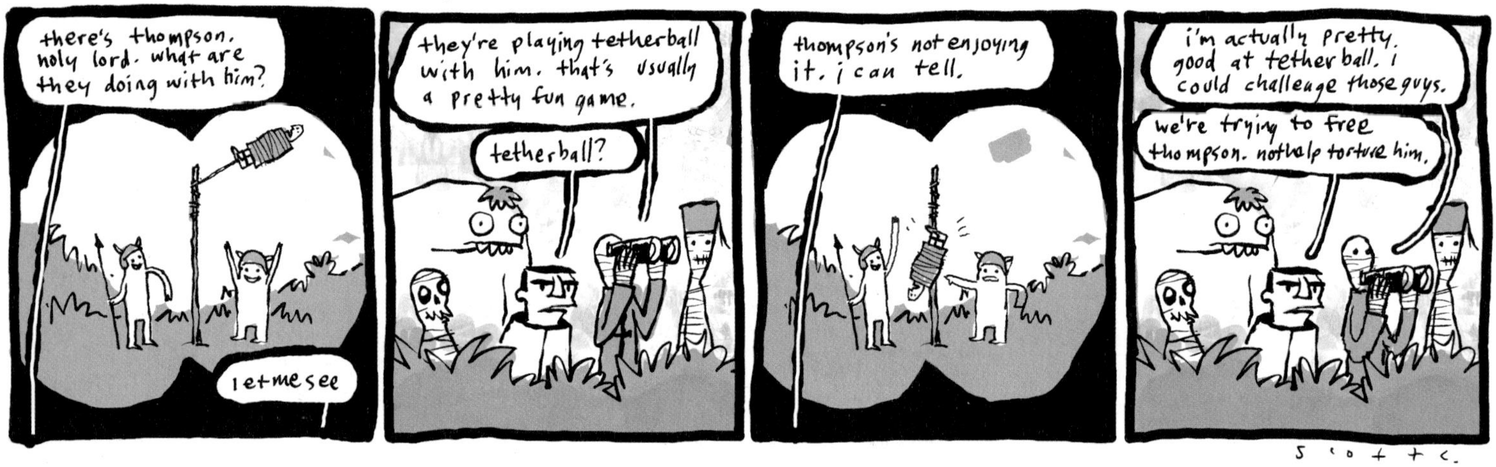
there's thompson. holy lord. what are they doing with him?
let me see
they're playing tetherball with him. that's usually a pretty fun game.
tetherball?
thompson's not enjoying it. i can tell.
i'm actually pretty good at tetherball. i could challenge those guys.
we're trying to free thompson. not help torture him.
scott c.

#554

— nice of pacman to sacrifice himself so we can catch a ghost.
— yeah, he's a good guy.

GHOST TRAP.

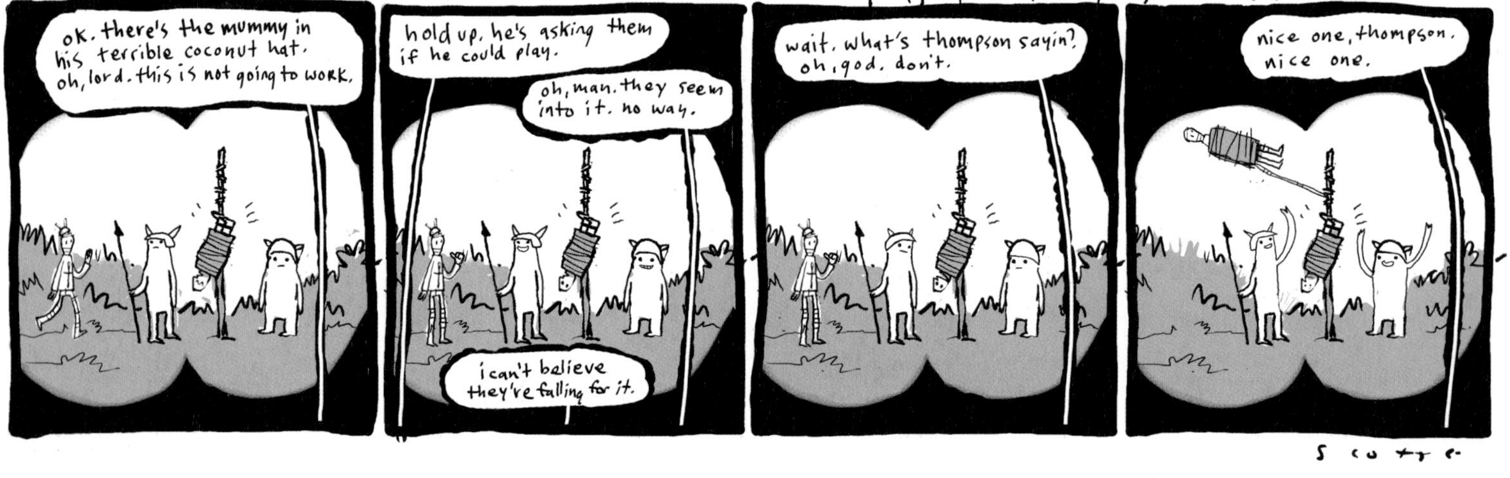
ok. there's the mummy in his terrible coconut hat. oh, lord. this is not going to work.
hold up, he's asking them if he could play.
oh, man. they seem into it. no way.
i can't believe they're falling for it.
wait. what's thompson sayin? oh, god. don't.
nice one, thompson. nice one.
scott c.

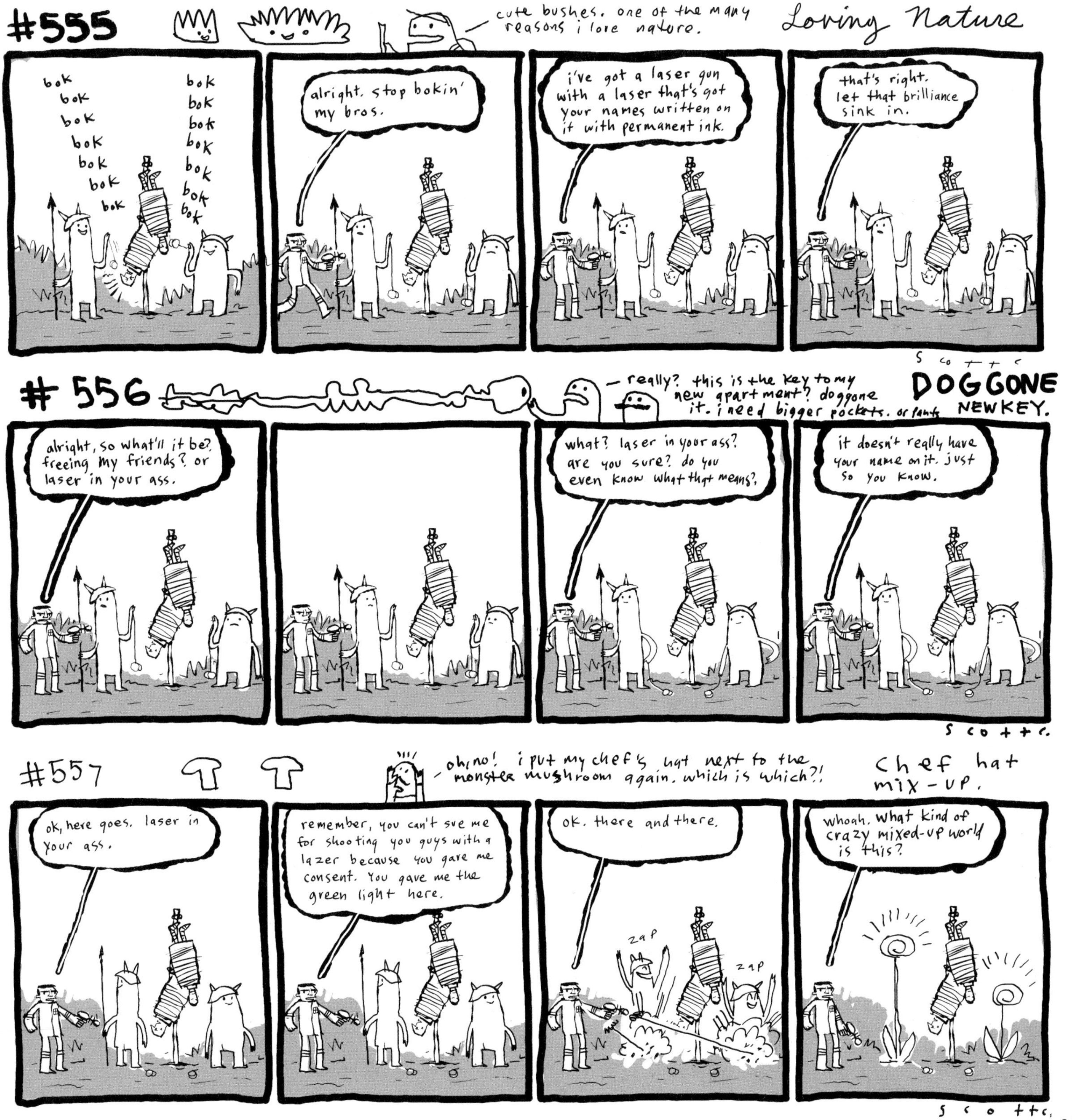

#555
cute bushes. one of the many reasons i love nature.
Loving Nature
bok bok bok bok bok bok bok
bok bok bok bok bok bok bok
alright. stop bokin' my bros.
i've got a laser gun with a laser that's got your names written on it with permanent ink.
that's right. let that brilliance sink in.
scott c.
#556
really? this is the key to my new apartment? doggone it. i need bigger pockets. or pants
DOGGONE NEWKEY.
alright, so what'll it be? freeing my friends? or laser in your ass.
what? laser in your ass? are you sure? do you even know what that means?
it doesn't really have your name on it. just so you know.
scott c.
#557
oh, no! i put my chef's hat next to the monster mushroom again. which is which?!
chef hat mix-up.
ok, here goes. laser in your ass.
remember, you can't sue me for shooting you guys with a lazer because you gave me consent. You gave me the green light here.
ok. there and there.
zap
zap
whoah. what kind of crazy mixed-up world is this?
scott c.

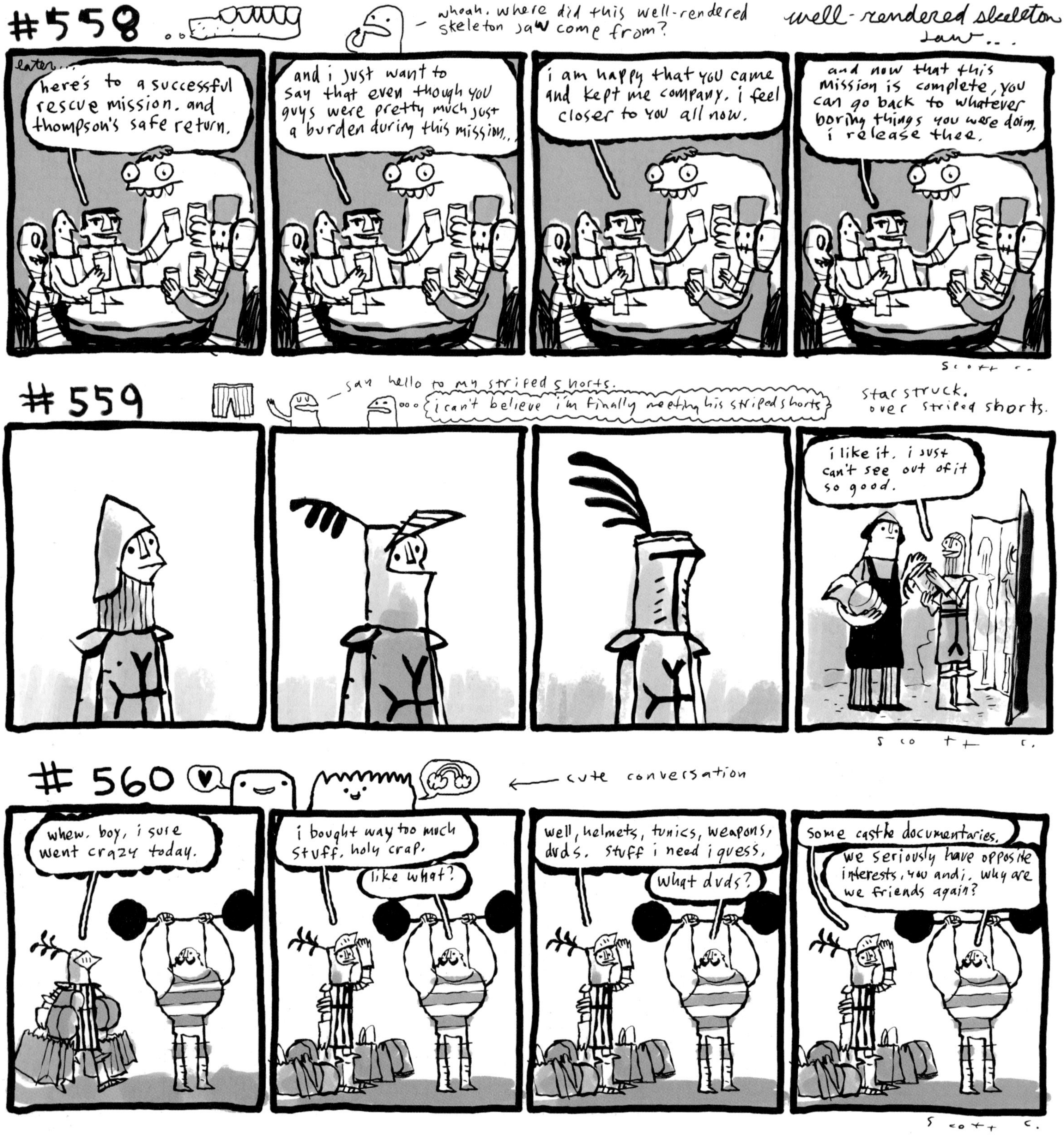
#558
whoah. where did this well-rendered skeleton jaw come from?
well-rendered skeleton jaw...
later...
here's to a successful rescue mission. and thompson's safe return.
and i just want to say that even though you guys were pretty much just a burden during this mission..
i am happy that you came and kept me company. i feel closer to you all now.
and now that this mission is complete, you can go back to whatever boring things you were doing, i release thee.
scott c.
#559
say hello to my striped shorts.
i can't believe i'm finally meeting his striped shorts
starstruck. over striped shorts.
i like it. i just can't see out of it so good.
scott c.
#560
cute conversation
whew. boy, i sure went crazy today.
i bought way too much stuff. holy crap.
like what?
well, helmets, tunics, weapons, dvds. stuff i need i guess.
what dvds?
some castle documentaries.
we seriously have opposite interests, you and i. why are we friends again?
scott c.

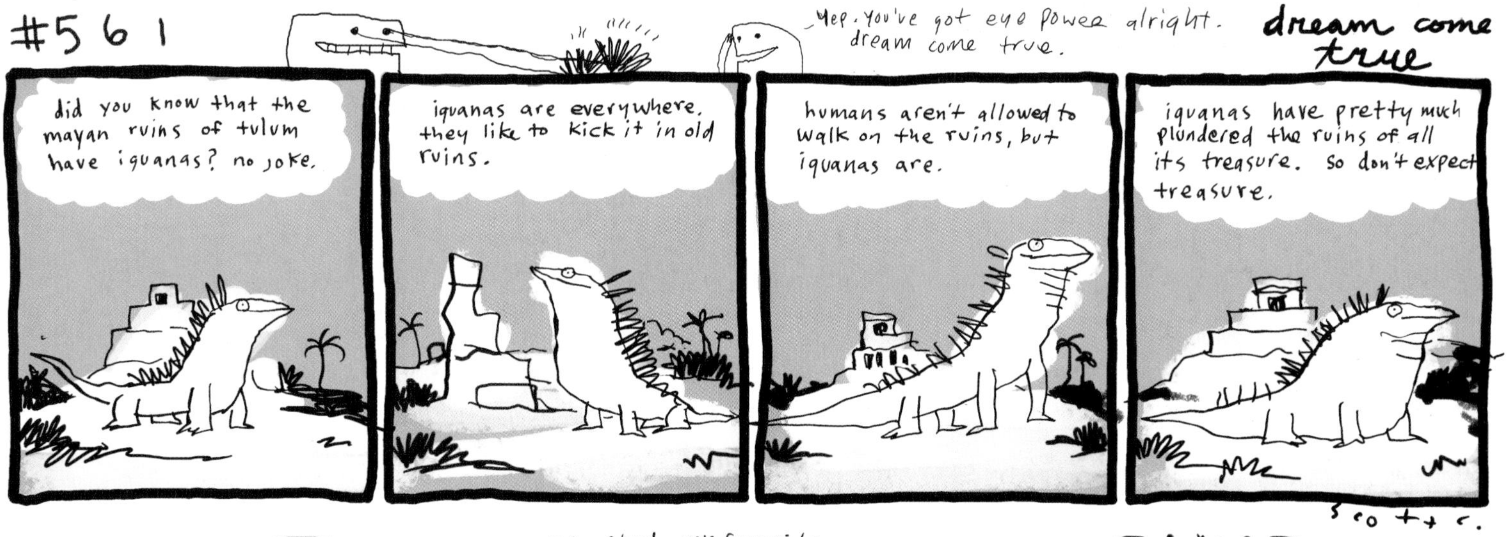
#561
Yep. You've got eye power alright. dream come true.
dream come true
did you know that the mayan ruins of tulum have iguanas? no joke.
iguanas are everywhere. they like to kick it in old ruins.
humans aren't allowed to walk on the ruins, but iguanas are.
iguanas have pretty much plundered the ruins of all its treasure. So don't expect treasure.
scott c.

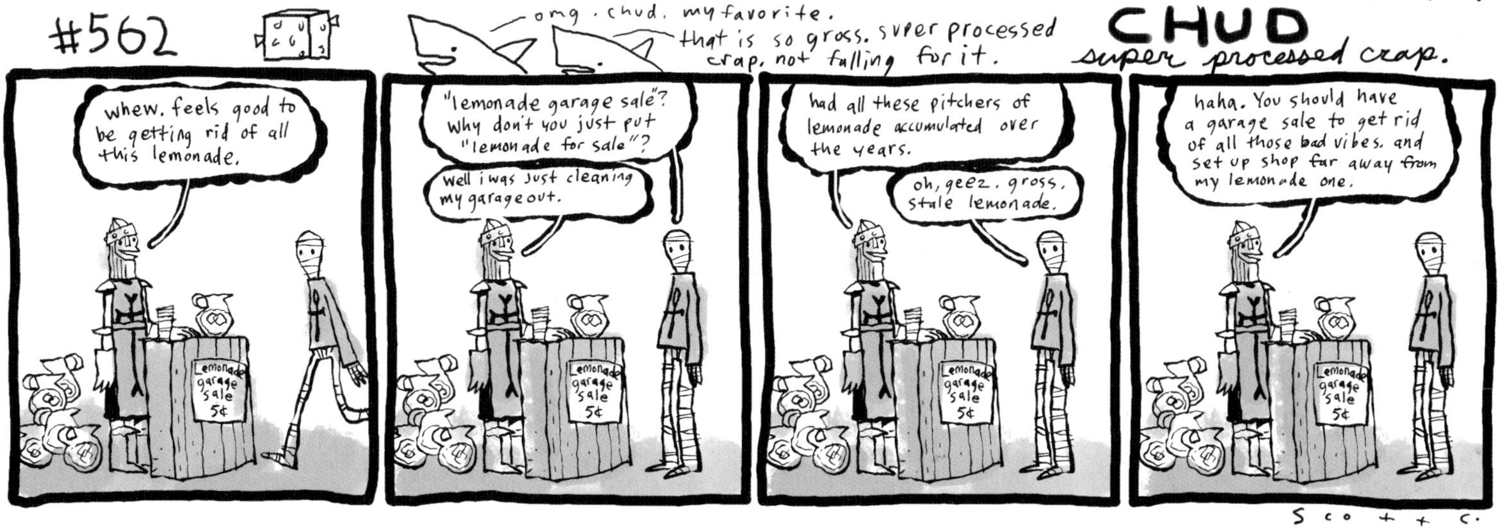
#562
omg. chud. my favorite.
that is so gross. super processed crap. not falling for it.
CHUD
super processed crap.
whew. feels good to be getting rid of all this lemonade.
Lemonade garage sale 5¢
"lemonade garage sale"? why don't you just put "lemonade for sale"?
well i was just cleaning my garage out.
had all these pitchers of lemonade accumulated over the years.
oh, geez. gross. stale lemonade.
haha. You should have a garage sale to get rid of all those bad vibes. and set up shop far away from my lemonade one.
scott c.

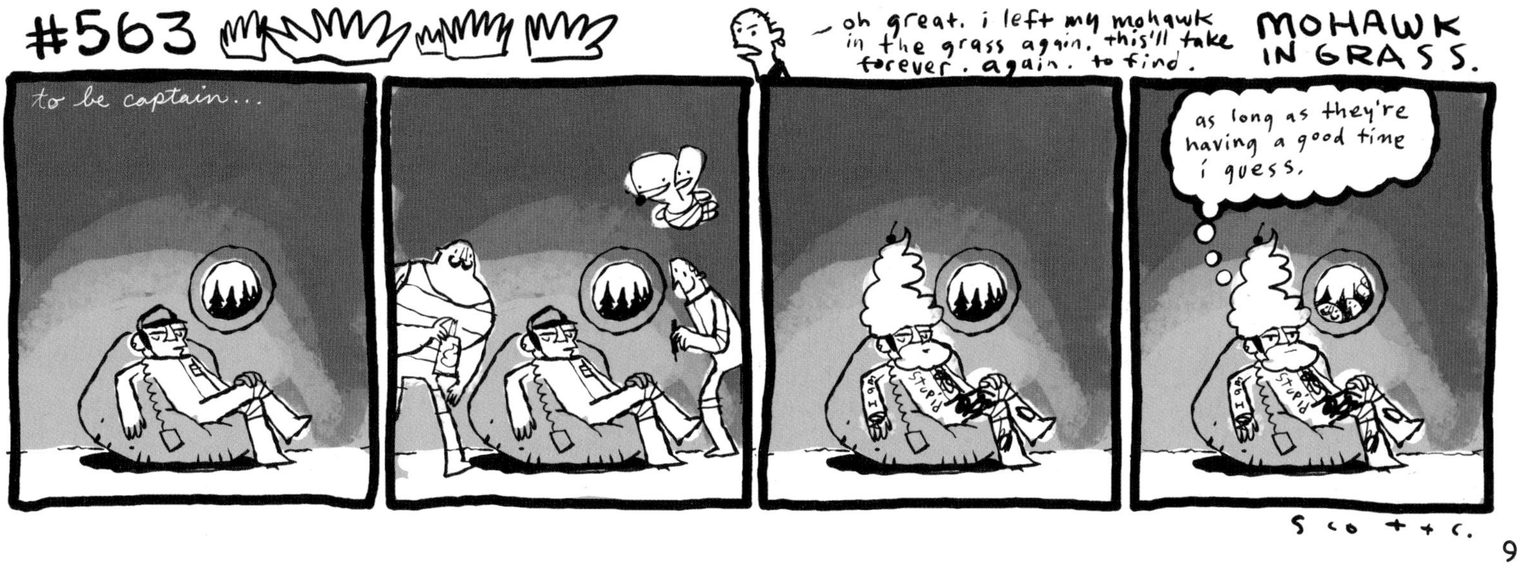
#563
oh great. i left my mohawk in the grass again. this'll take forever. again. to find.
MOHAWK IN GRASS.
to be captain...
as long as they're having a good time i guess.
STUPID
scott c.

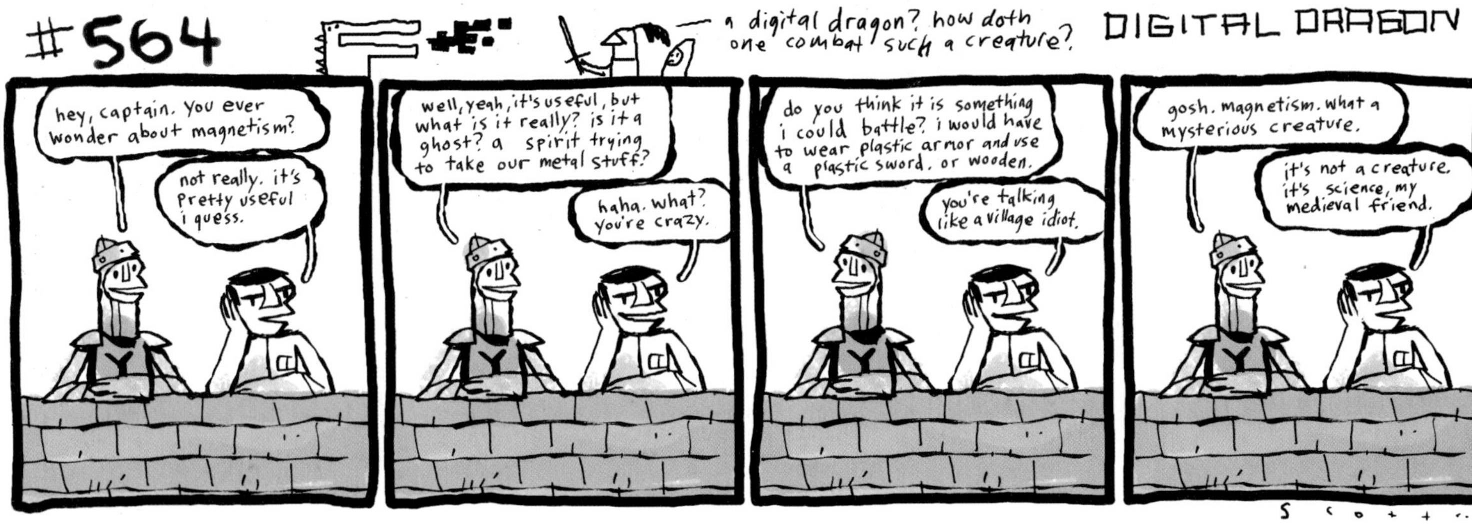

#564
—a digital dragon? how doth one combat such a creature?
DIGITAL DRAGON
hey, captain. you ever wonder about magnetism?
not really. it's pretty useful i guess.
well, yeah, it's useful, but what is it really? is it a ghost? a spirit trying to take our metal stuff?
haha. what? you're crazy.
do you think it is something i could battle? i would have to wear plastic armor and use a plastic sword. or wooden.
you're talking like a village idiot.
gosh. magnetism. what a mysterious creature.
it's not a creature. it's science, my medieval friend.
scott c.

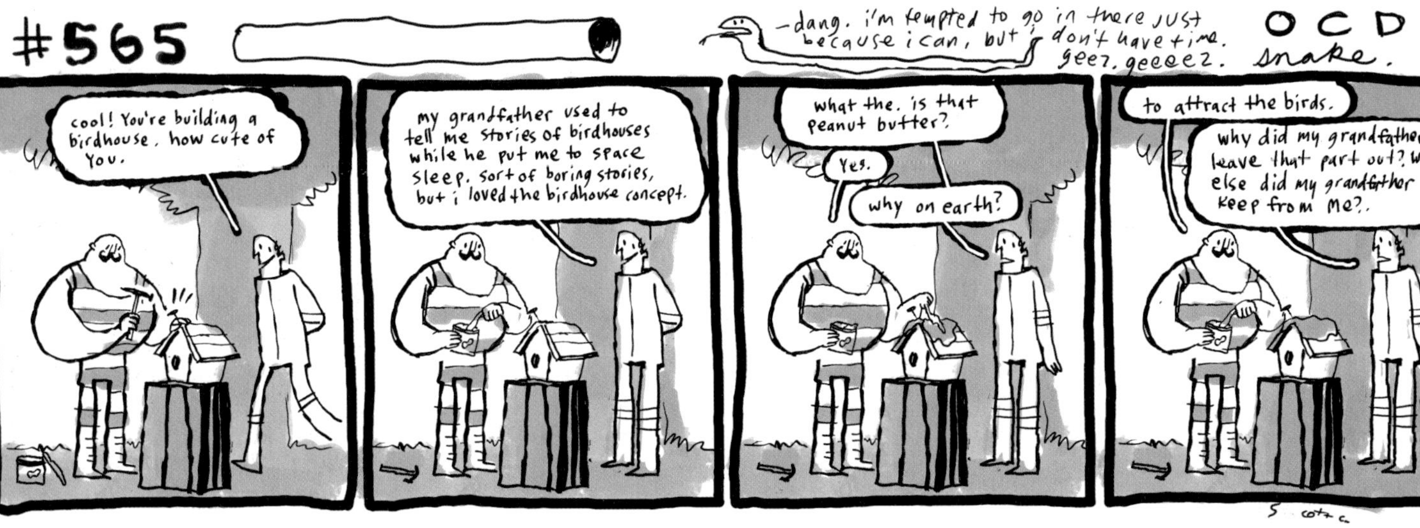

#565
—dang. i'm tempted to go in there just because i can, but i don't have time. geez. geeeez.
OCD snake.
cool! you're building a birdhouse. how cute of you.
my grandfather used to tell me stories of birdhouses while he put me to sleep. sort of boring stories, but i loved the birdhouse concept.
what the. is that peanut butter?
yes.
why on earth?
to attract the birds.
why did my grandfather leave that part out? what else did my grandfather keep from me?.
scott c.

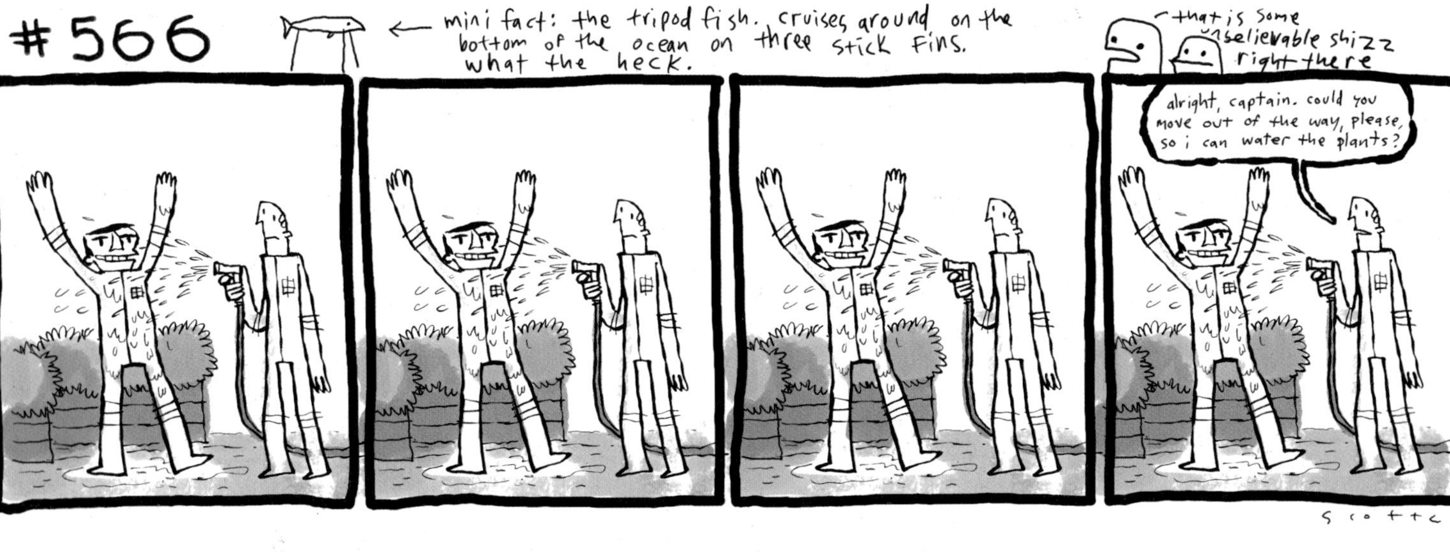

#566
← mini fact: the tripod fish. cruises around on the bottom of the ocean on three stick fins. what the heck.
—that is some unbelievable shizz right there
alright, captain. could you move out of the way, please, so i can water the plants?
scott c.

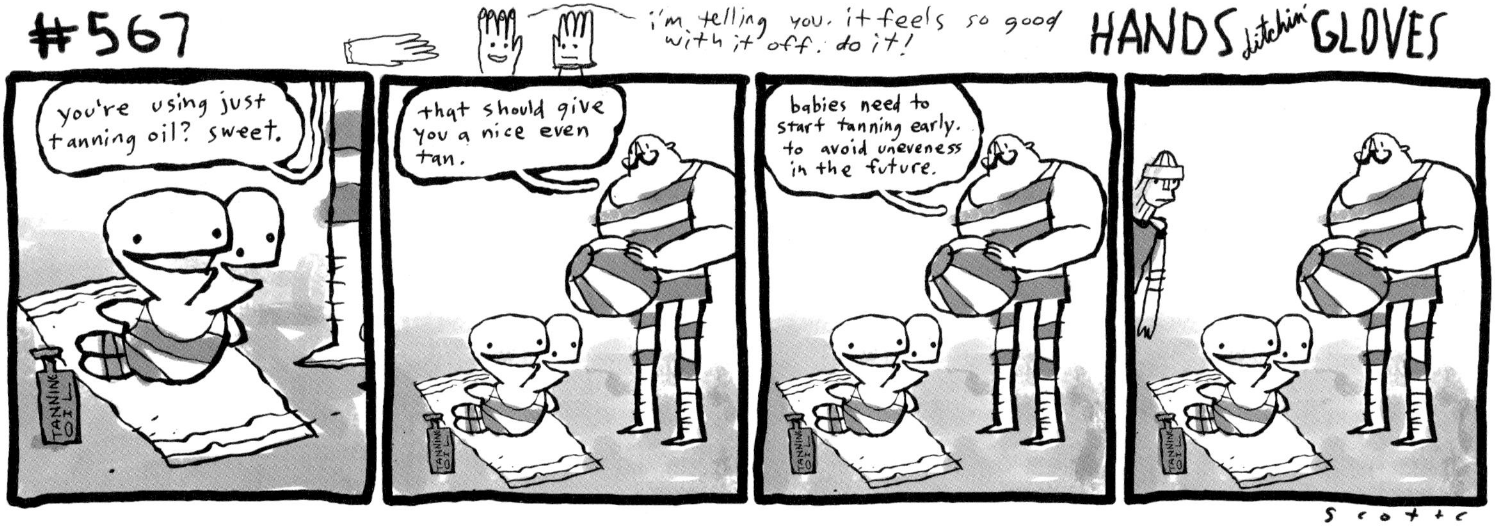
#567
i'm telling you. it feels so good with it off. do it!
HANDS ditchin' GLOVES
you're using just tanning oil? sweet.
TANNING OIL
that should give you a nice even tan.
babies need to start tanning early. to avoid uneveness in the future.
scott c

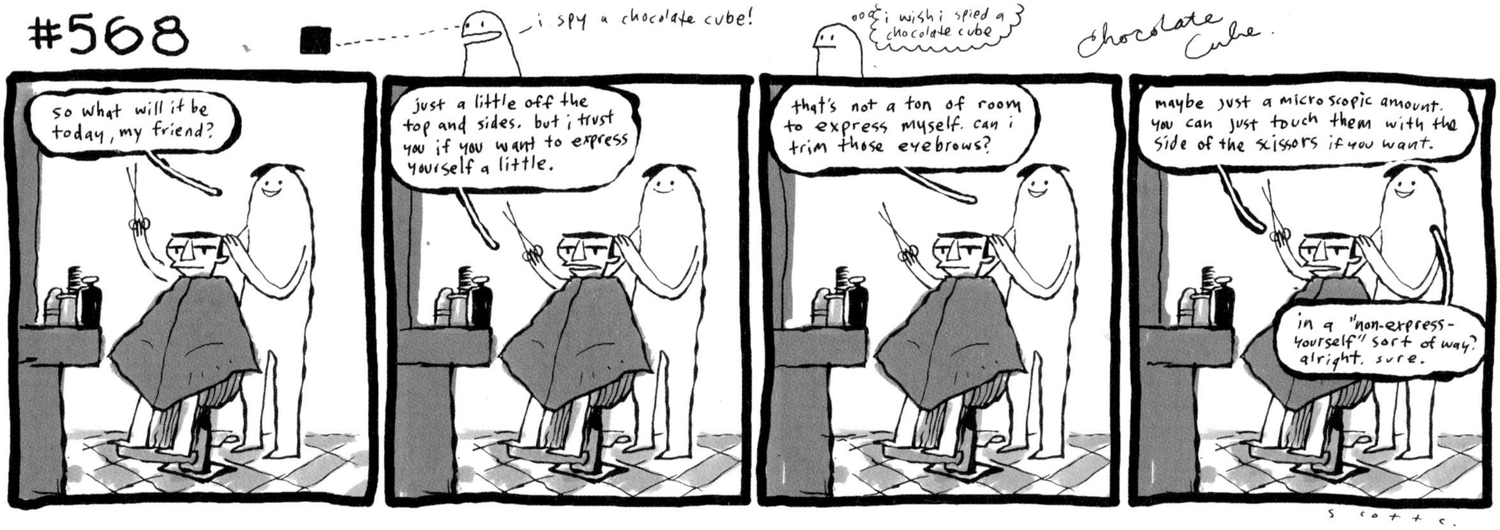
#568
i spy a chocolate cube!
ooo { i wish i spied a chocolate cube }
Chocolate Cube.
so what will it be today, my friend?
just a little off the top and sides. but i trust you if you want to express yourself a little.
that's not a ton of room to express myself. can i trim those eyebrows?
maybe just a microscopic amount. you can just touch them with the side of the scissors if you want.
in a "non-express-yourself" sort of way? alright. sure.
scott c.

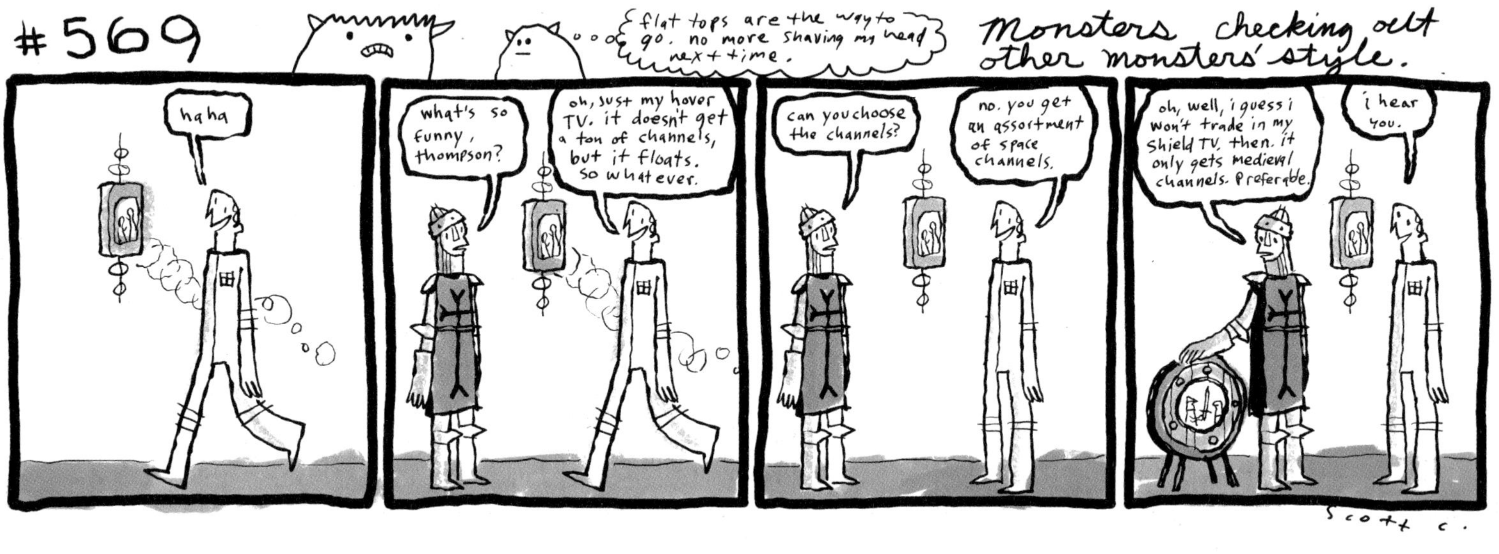
#569
ooo { flat tops are the way to go. no more shaving my head next time. }
Monsters checking out other monsters' style.
haha
what's so funny, thompson?
oh, just my hover TV. it doesn't get a ton of channels, but it floats. so whatever.
can you choose the channels?
no. you get an assortment of space channels.
oh, well, i guess i won't trade in my Shield TV, then. it only gets medieval channels. Preferable.
i hear you.
scott c.

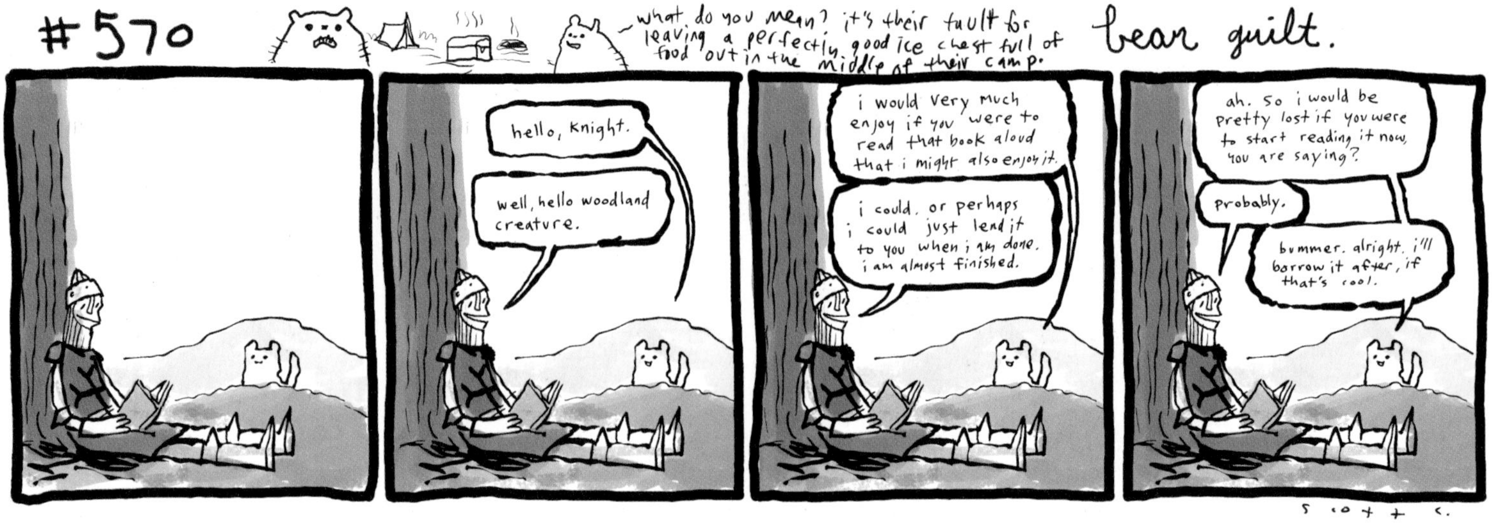

#570
what do you mean? it's their fault for leaving a perfectly good ice chest full of food out in the middle of their camp.
bear guilt.
hello, knight.
well, hello woodland creature.
i would very much enjoy if you were to read that book aloud that i might also enjoy it.
i could, or perhaps i could just lend it to you when i am done. i am almost finished.
ah. so i would be pretty lost if you were to start reading it now, you are saying?
probably.
bummer. alright. i'll borrow it after, if that's cool.
scott c.

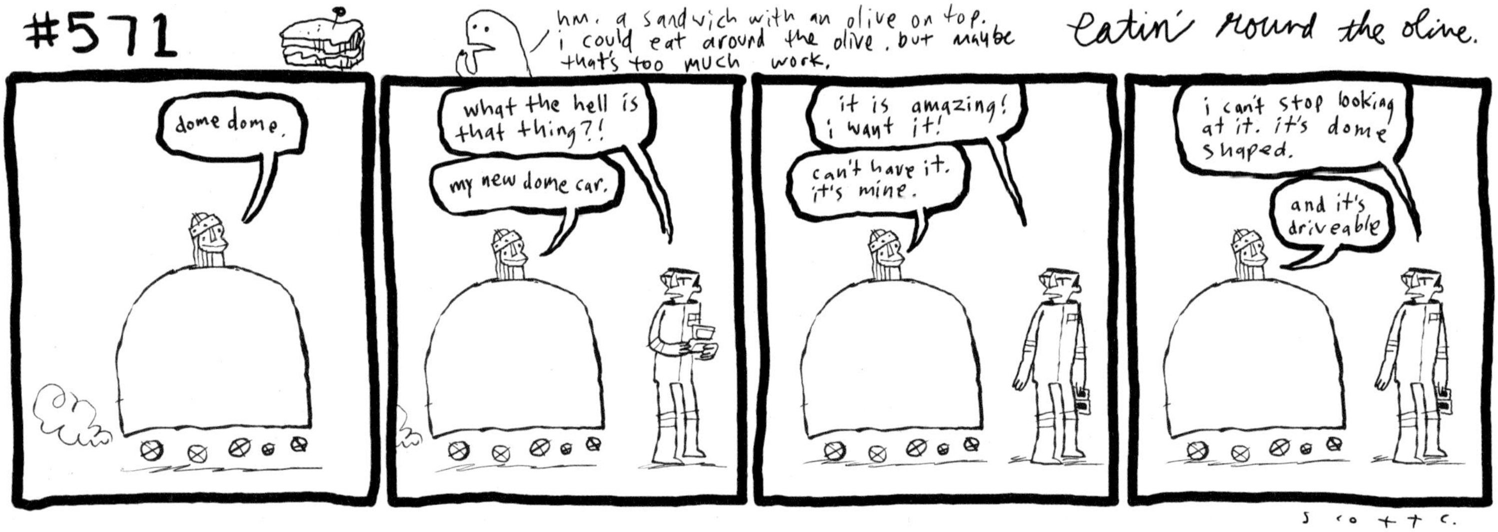

#571
hm. a sandwich with an olive on top. i could eat around the olive, but maybe that's too much work.
eatin' round the olive.
dome dome.
what the hell is that thing?!
my new dome car.
it is amazing! i want it!
can't have it. it's mine.
i can't stop looking at it. it's dome shaped.
and it's driveable
scott c.

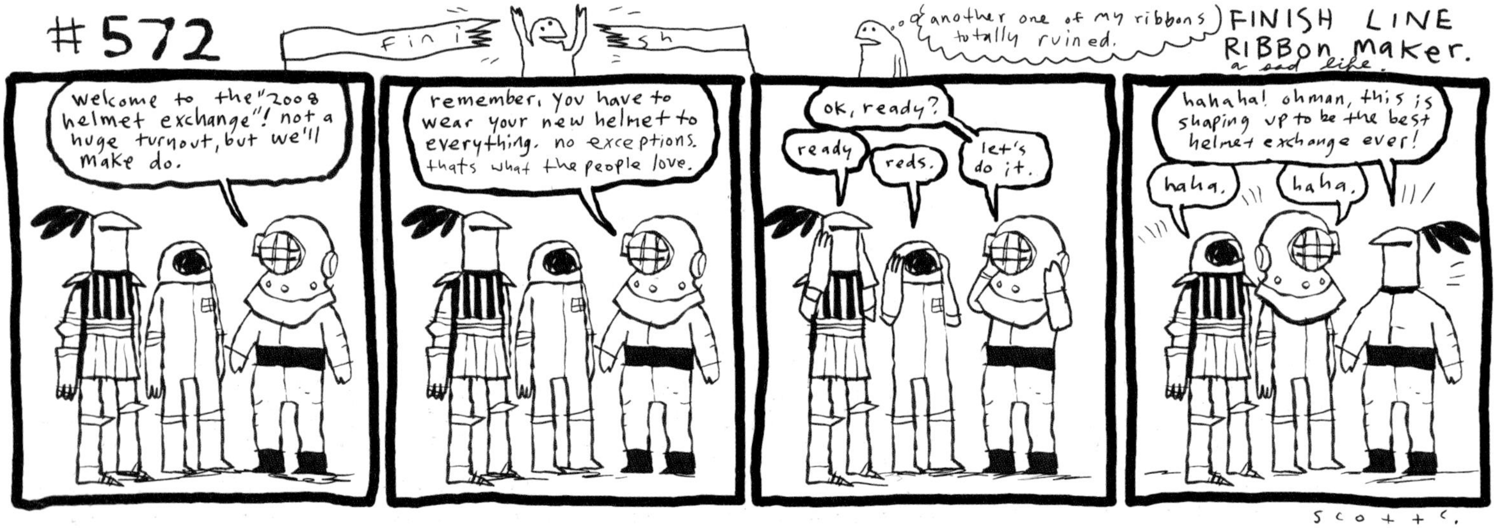

#572
fini
sh
another one of my ribbons totally ruined.
FINISH LINE RIBBON maker.
a sad life.
welcome to the "2008 helmet exchange"! not a huge turnout, but we'll make do.
remember, you have to wear your new helmet to everything. no exceptions. thats what the people love.
ok, ready?
ready
reds.
let's do it.
hahaha! ohman, this is shaping up to be the best helmet exchange ever!
haha.
haha.
scott c.

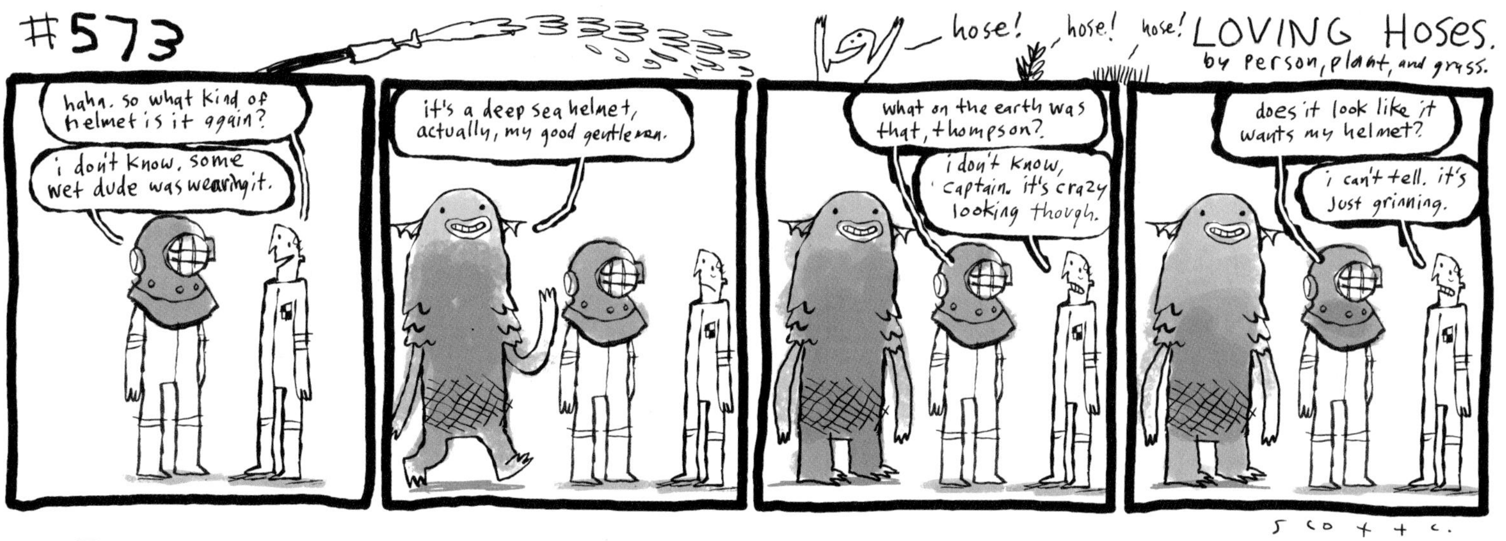
#573
hose!
hose!
hose!
LOVING HOSES.
by person, plant, and grass.
haha. so what kind of helmet is it again?
i don't know. some wet dude was wearing it.
it's a deep sea helmet, actually, my good gentlemen.
what on the earth was that, thompson?
i don't know, captain. it's crazy looking though.
does it look like it wants my helmet?
i can't tell. it's just grinning.
scott c.

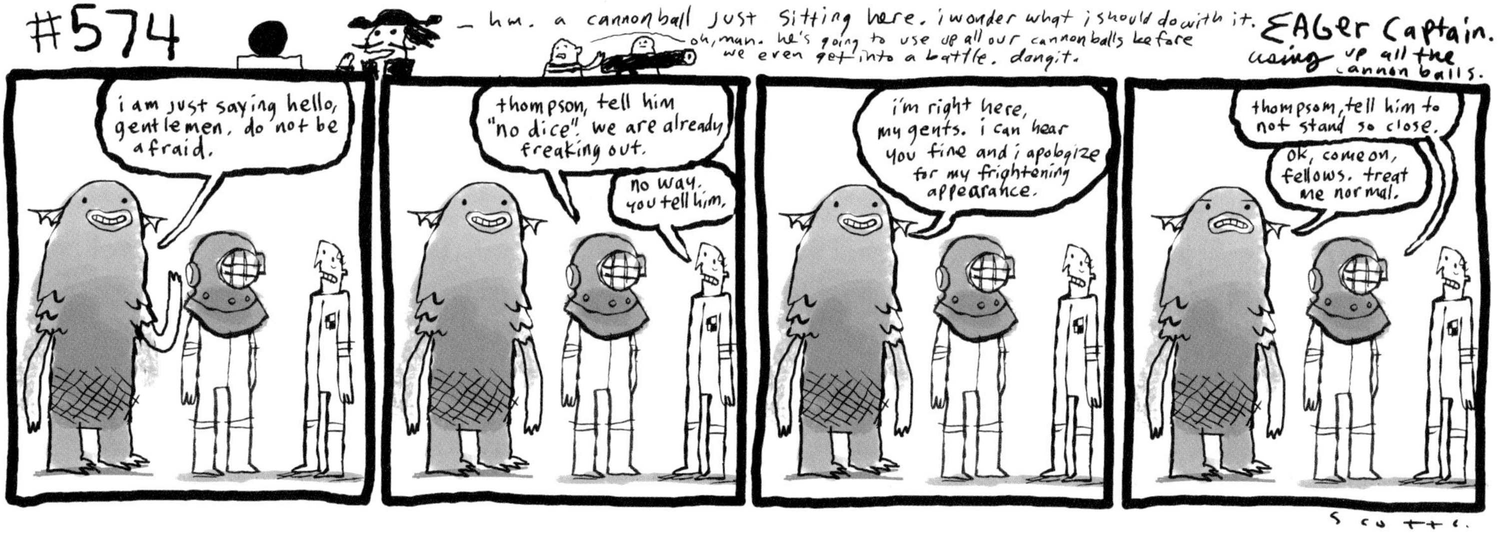
#574
hm. a cannonball just sitting here. i wonder what i should do with it.
oh, man. he's going to use up all our cannonballs before we even get into a battle. dangit.
EAGER Captain. using up all the cannon balls.
i am just saying hello, gentlemen. do not be afraid.
thompson, tell him "no dice". we are already freaking out.
no way. you tell him.
i'm right here, my gents. i can hear you fine and i apologize for my frightening appearance.
thompsom, tell him to not stand so close.
ok, come on, fellows. treat me normal.
scott c.

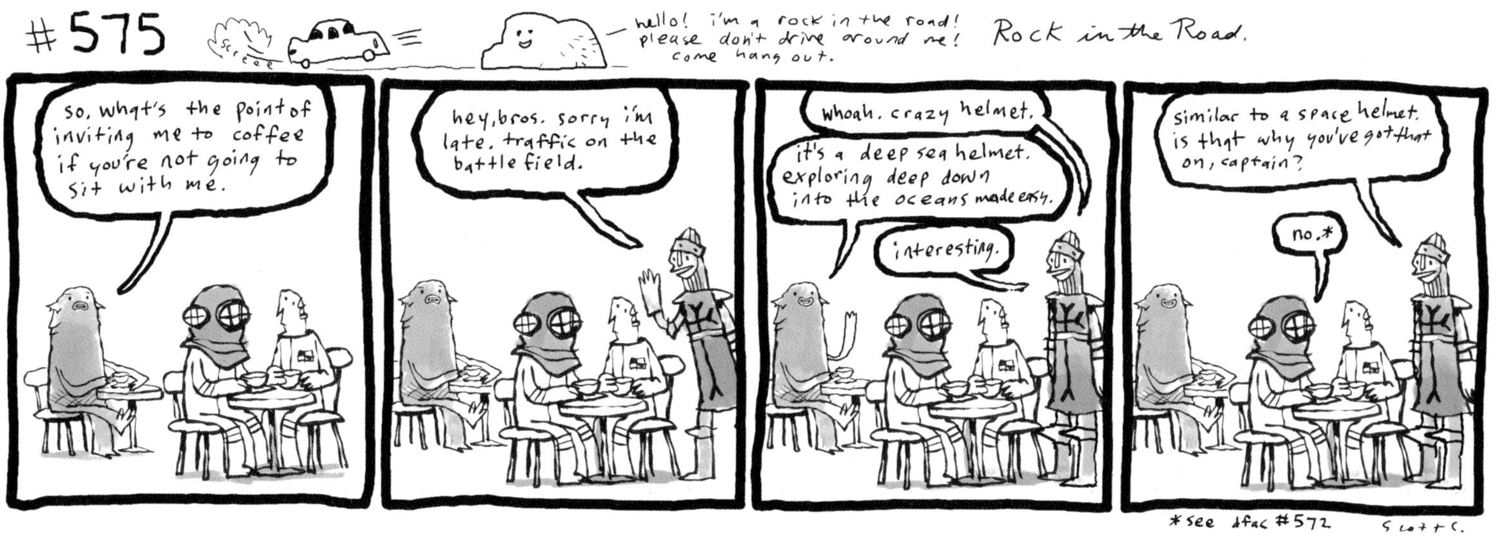
#575
screeee
hello! i'm a rock in the road! please don't drive around me! come hang out.
Rock in the Road.
so, what's the point of inviting me to coffee if you're not going to sit with me.
hey, bros. sorry i'm late. traffic on the battle field.
whoah. crazy helmet.
it's a deep sea helmet. exploring deep down into the oceans made easy.
interesting.
similar to a space helmet. is that why you've got that on, captain?
no.*
*see dfac #572
scott c.

#576 — realistic teeth? omg. what dragon doth intimidate me. DRAGON with realistic teeth.

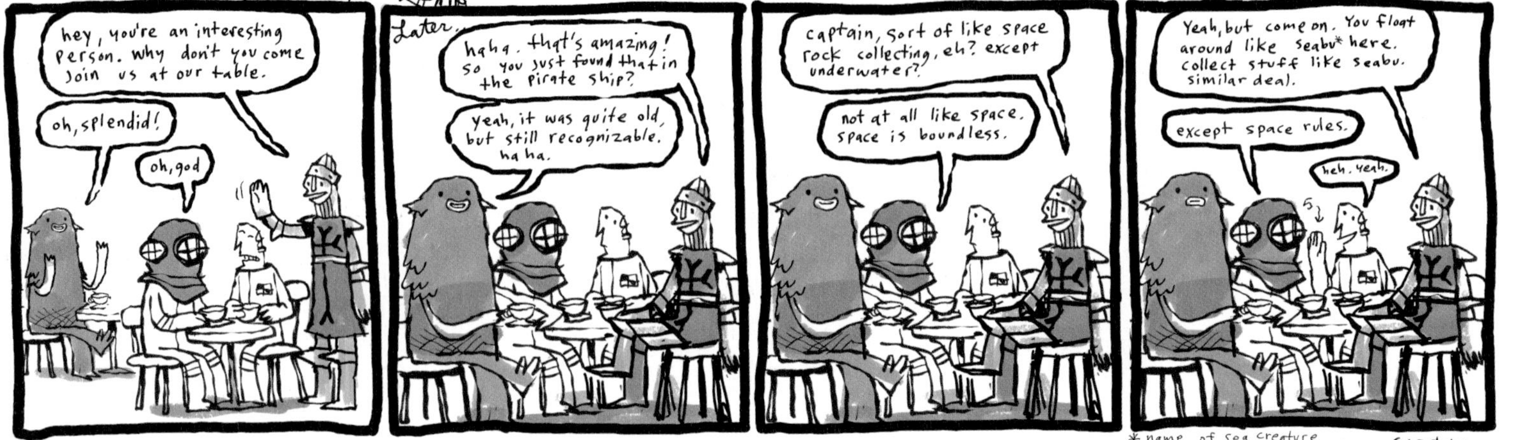
hey, you're an interesting person. why don't you come join us at our table.
oh, splendid!
oh, god
Later...
haha. that's amazing! so you just found that in the pirate ship?
yeah, it was quite old, but still recognizable. ha ha.
captain, sort of like space rock collecting, eh? except underwater?
not at all like space. space is boundless.
Yeah, but come on. You float around like Seabu* here. collect stuff like Seabu. similar deal.
except space rules.
heh. yeah.

* name of sea creature with which they are sharing coffee. scott c

#577 — whaddup, skeleton head! — ooo those guys have so much in common — WISHING for things in common.

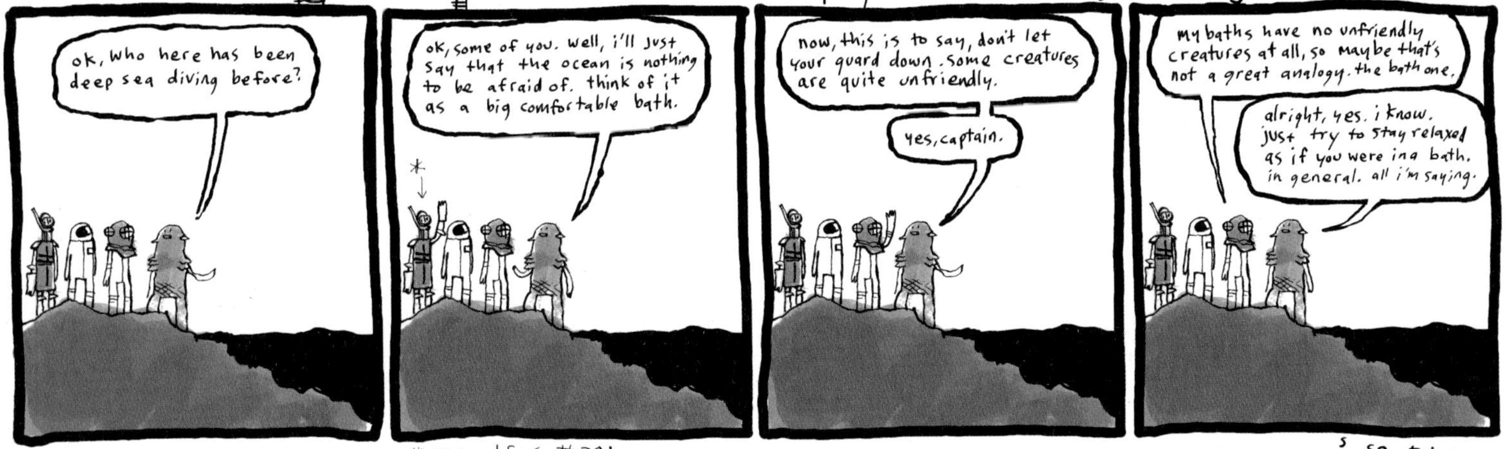
ok, who here has been deep sea diving before?
ok, some of you. well, i'll just say that the ocean is nothing to be afraid of. think of it as a big comfortable bath.
now, this is to say, don't let your guard down. some creatures are quite unfriendly.
yes, captain.
my baths have no unfriendly creatures at all, so maybe that's not a great analogy. the bath one.
alright, yes. i know. just try to stay relaxed as if you were in a bath. in general. all i'm saying.

*see dfac #391 scott c.

#578 — oh, great. here comes that wheel again. just rolling. Rolling by Wheel.

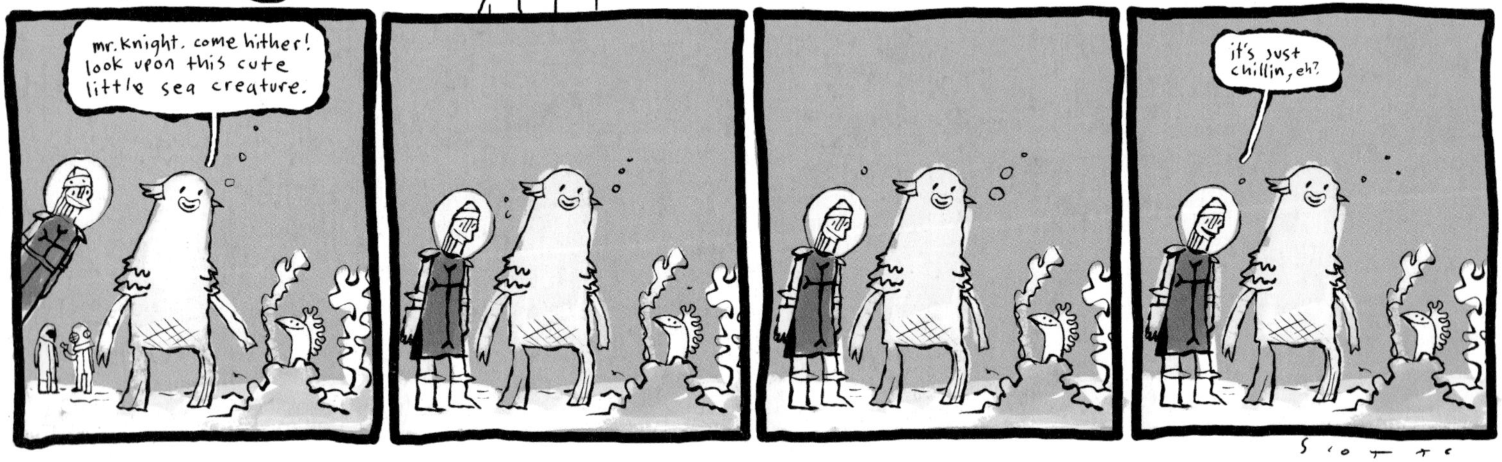
mr. knight. come hither! look upon this cute little sea creature.
it's just chillin, eh?

scott c

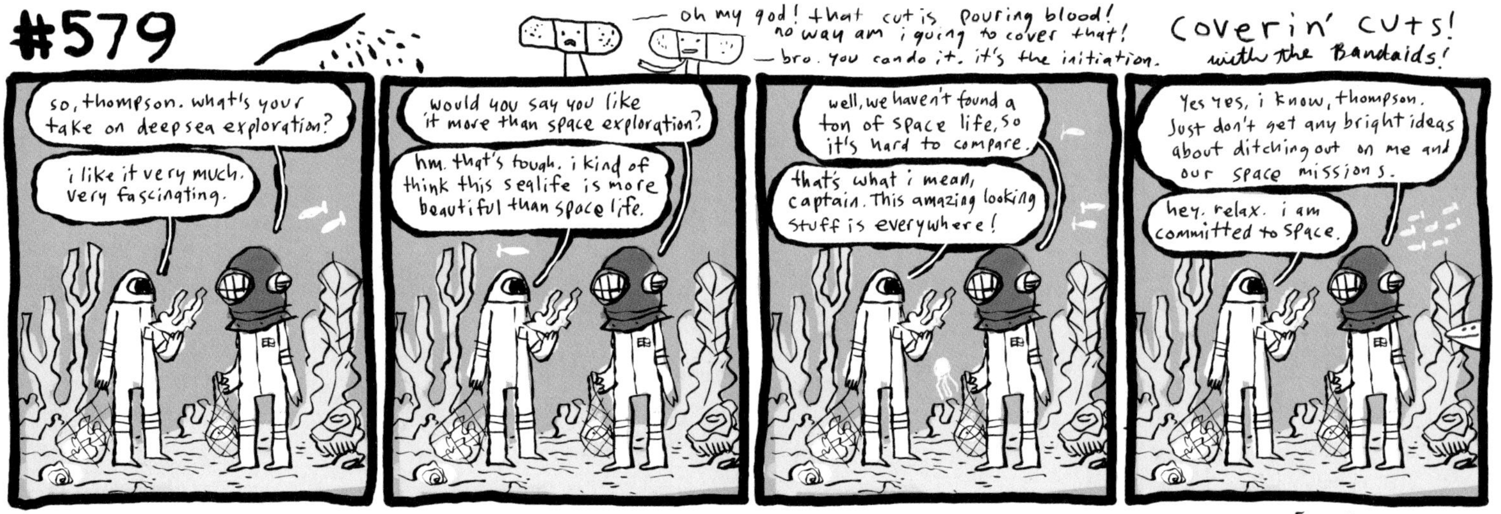

#579
oh my god! that cut is pouring blood! no way am i going to cover that!
bro. you can do it. it's the initiation.
coverin' cuts! with the Bandaids!
so, thompson. what's your take on deepsea exploration?
i like it very much. very fascinating.
would you say you like it more than space exploration?
hm. that's tough. i kind of think this sealife is more beautiful than space life.
well, we haven't found a ton of space life, so it's hard to compare.
that's what i mean, captain. This amazing looking stuff is everywhere!
Yes yes, i know, thompson. Just don't get any bright ideas about ditching out on me and our space missions.
hey. relax. i am committed to space.

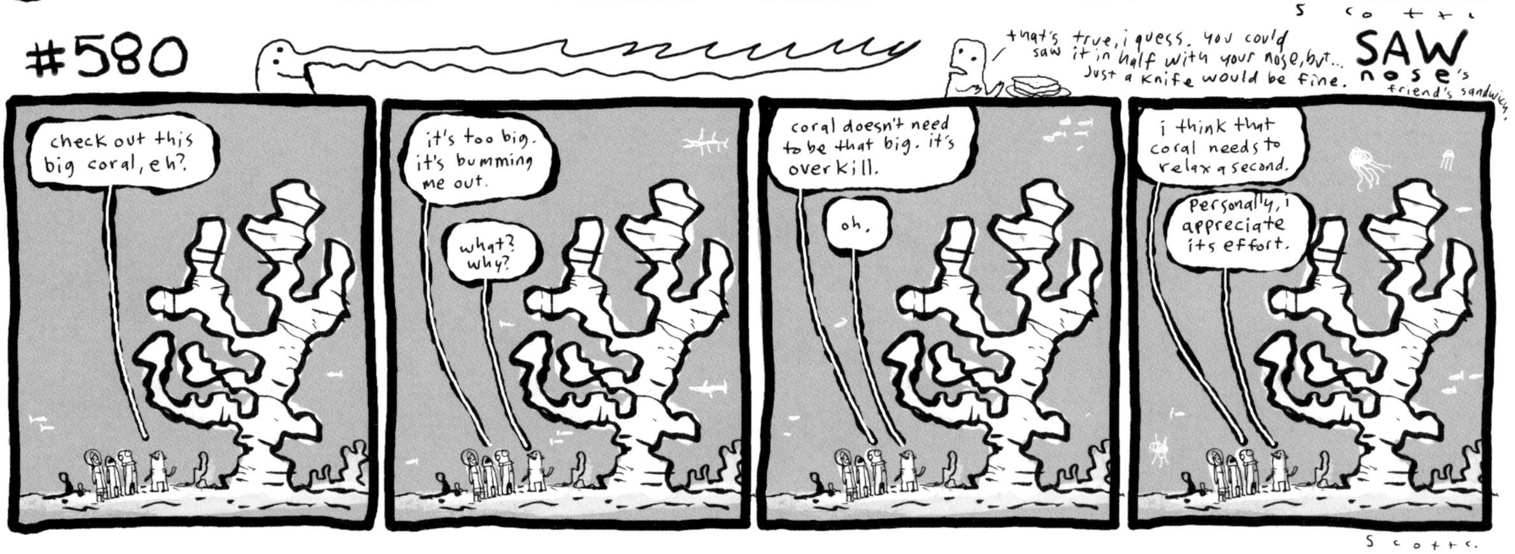

#580
scott c.
that's true, i guess. you could saw it in half with your nose, but... just a knife would be fine.
SAW nose's friend's sandwich.
check out this big coral, eh?
it's too big. it's bumming me out.
what? why?
coral doesn't need to be that big. it's overkill.
oh.
i think that coral needs to relax a second.
Personally, i appreciate its effort.
scott c.

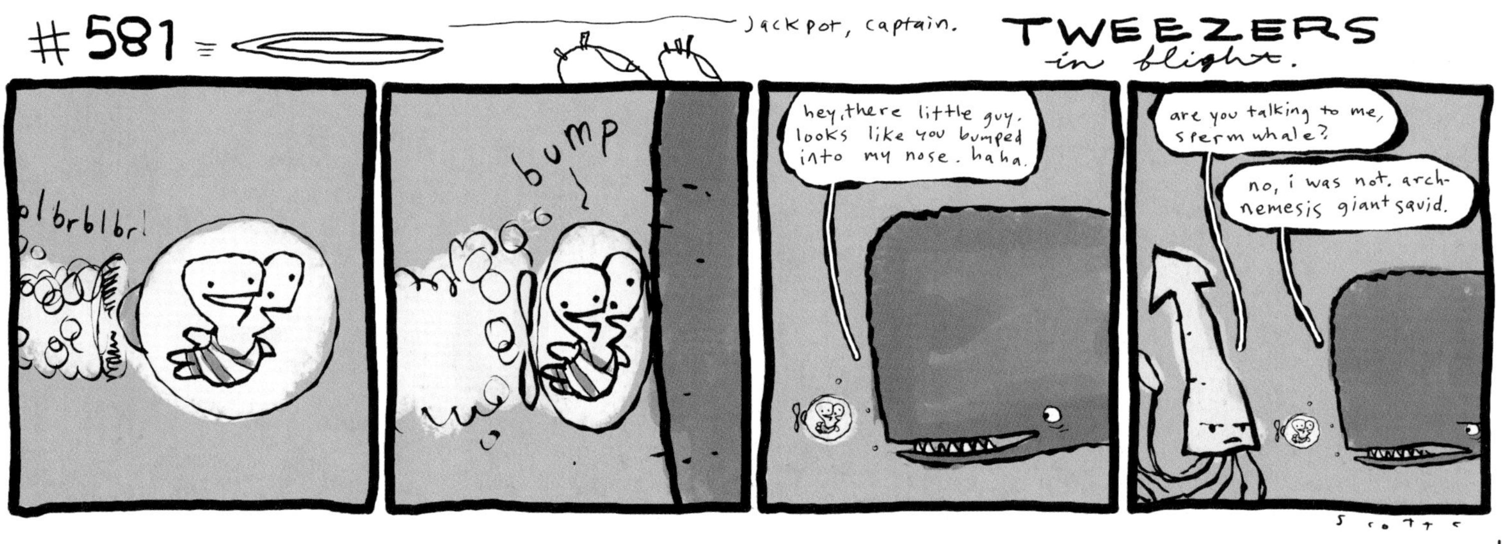

#581
Jackpot, captain.
TWEEZERS in flight.
blbrblbr!
bump
hey, there little guy. looks like you bumped into my nose. haha.
are you talking to me, sperm whale?
no, i was not, arch-nemesis giant squid.
scott c.

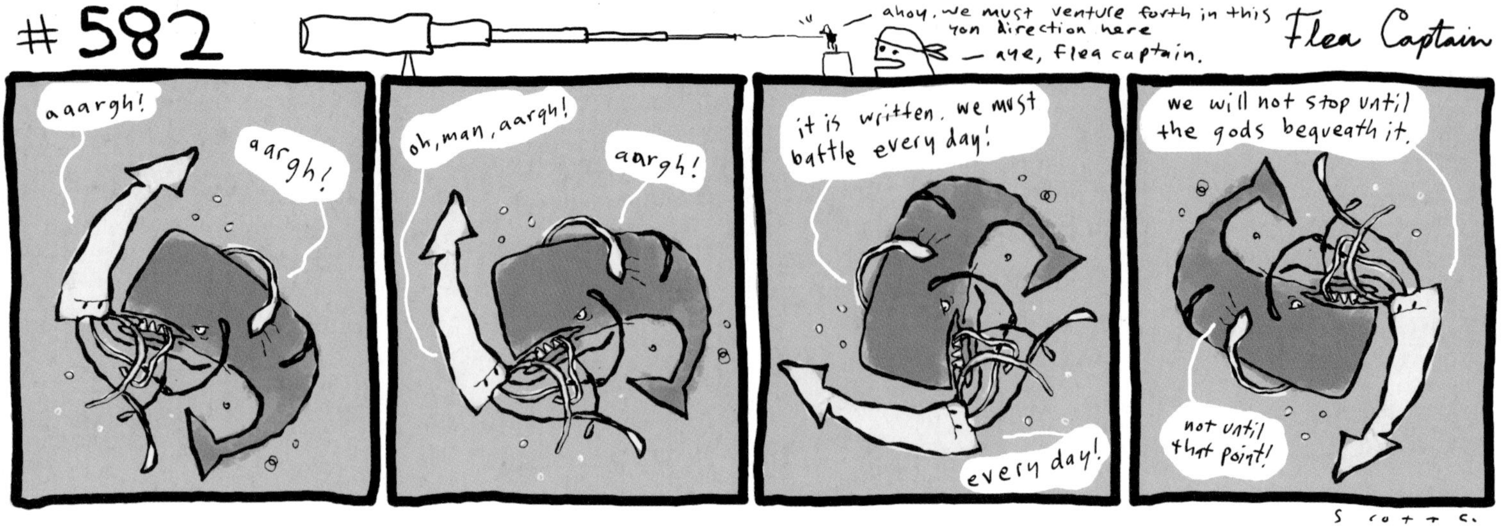
#582
— ahoy, we must venture forth in this yon direction here
— aye, flea captain.
Flea Captain
aaargh!
aargh!
oh, man, aargh!
aargh!
it is written, we must battle every day!
every day!
we will not stop until the gods bequeath it.
not until that point!
scott c.

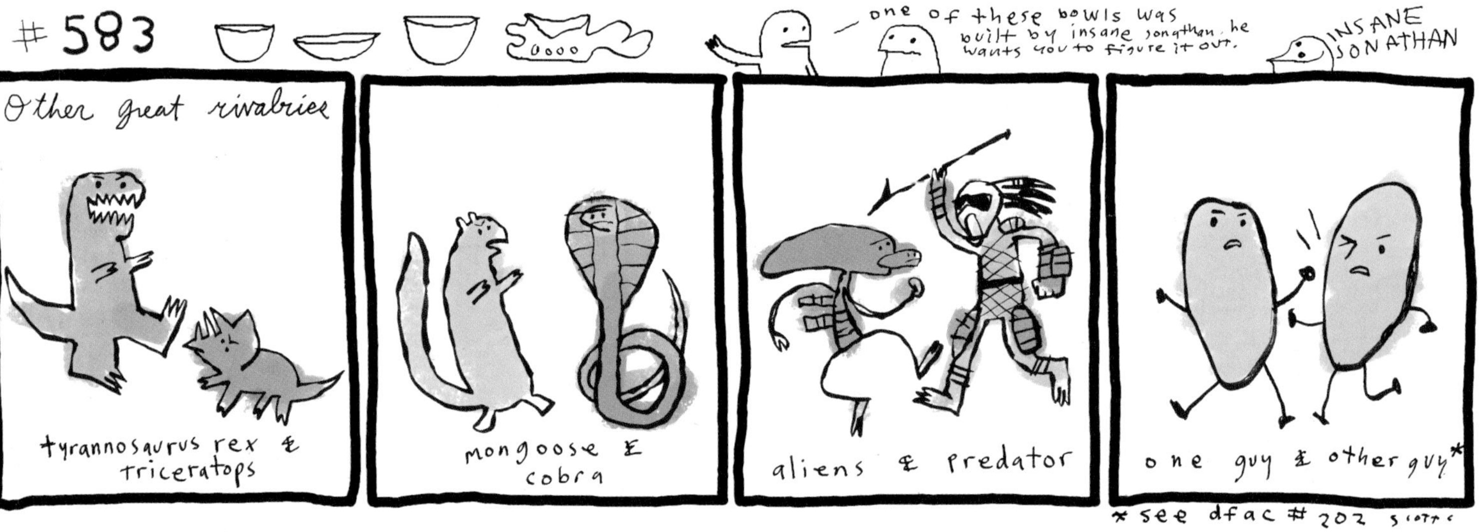
#583
— one of these bowls was built by insane jonathan. he wants you to figure it out.
INSANE JONATHAN
Other great rivalries
tyrannosaurus rex & triceratops
mongoose & cobra
aliens & predator
one guy & other guy*
*see dfac #202
scott c

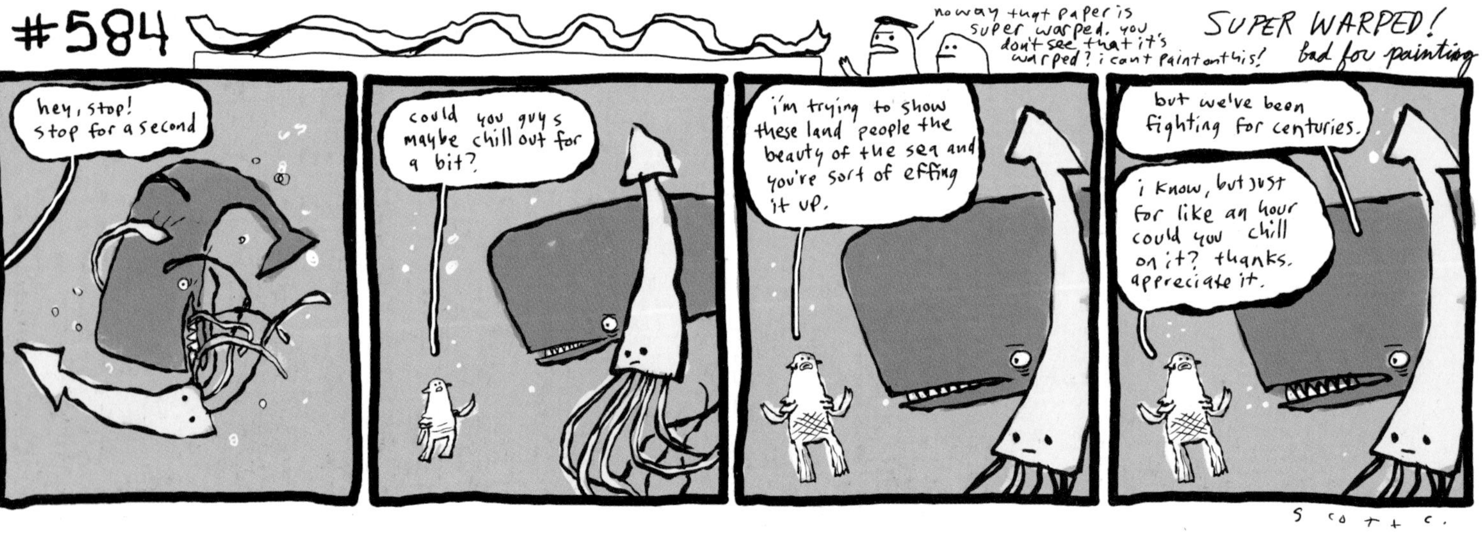
#584
no way that paper is super warped. you don't see that it's warped? i cant paint on this!
SUPER WARPED! bad for painting
hey, stop! stop for a second
could you guys maybe chill out for a bit?
i'm trying to show these land people the beauty of the sea and you're sort of effing it up.
but we've been fighting for centuries.
i know, but just for like an hour could you chill on it? thanks. appreciate it.
scott c.

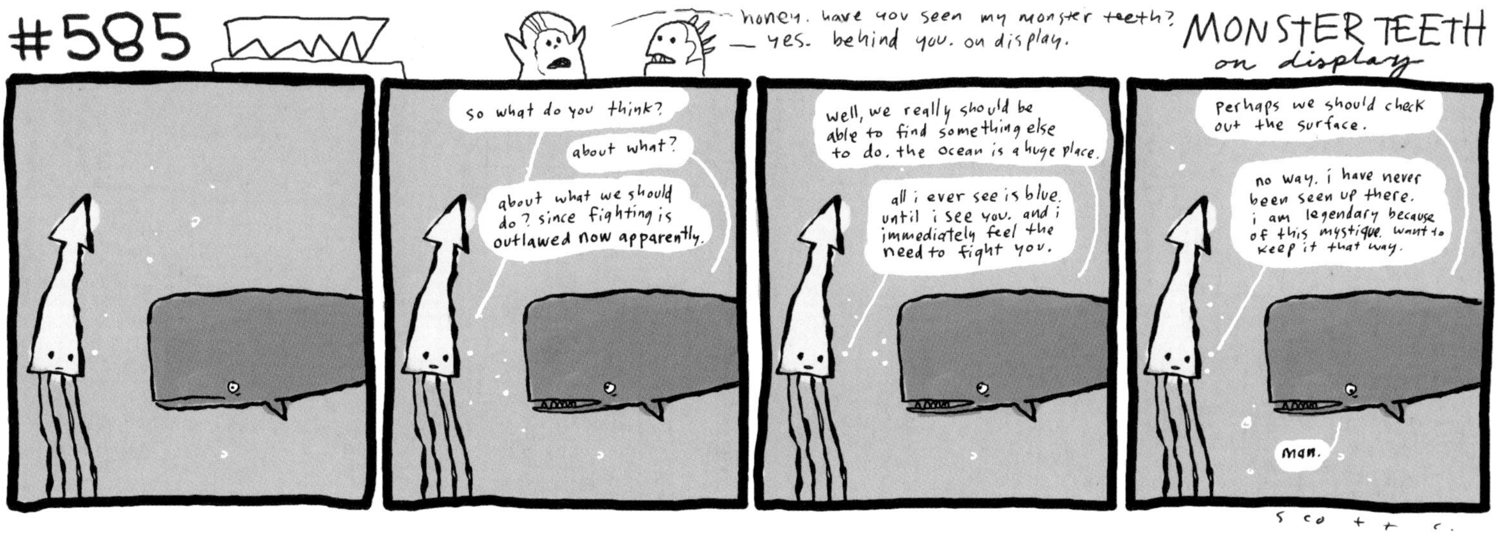

#585
— honey. have you seen my monster teeth?
— yes. behind you. on display.
MONSTER TEETH
on display
so what do you think?
about what?
about what we should do? since fighting is outlawed now apparently.
well, we really should be able to find something else to do. the ocean is a huge place.
all i ever see is blue. until i see you. and i immediately feel the need to fight you.
perhaps we should check out the surface.
no way. i have never been seen up there. i am legendary because of this mystique. want to keep it that way.
man.
scott c.

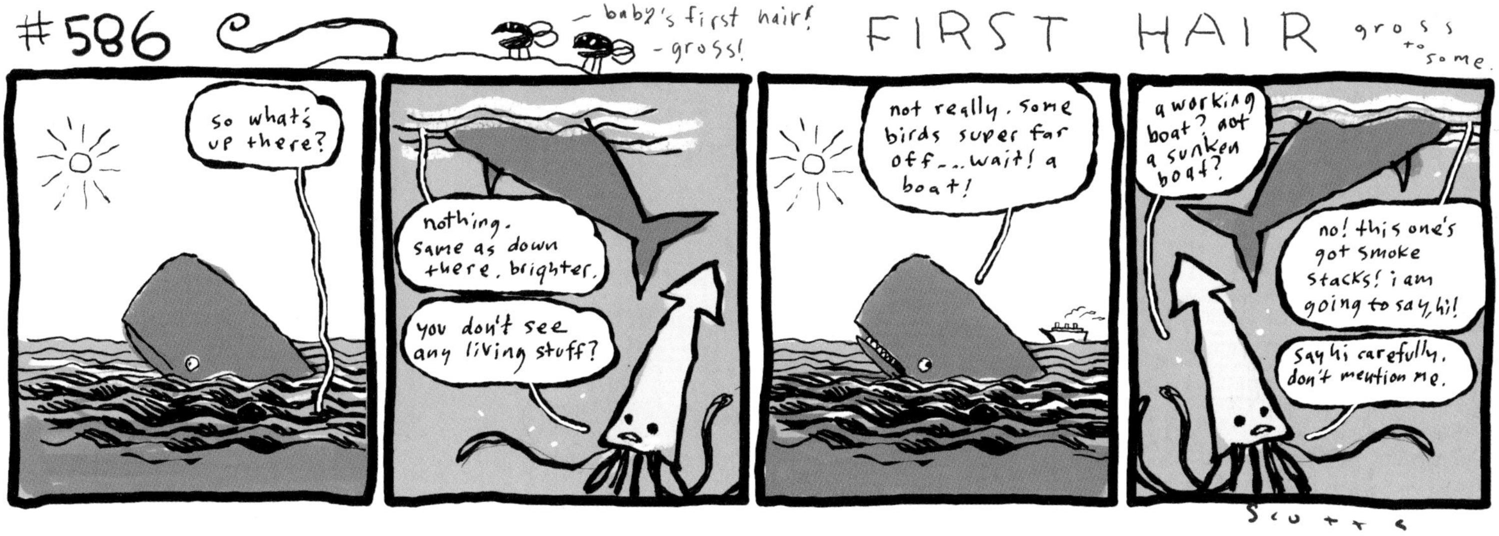

#586
— baby's first hair!
— gross!
FIRST HAIR
gross to some.
so what's up there?
nothing. same as down there, brighter.
you don't see any living stuff?
not really. some birds super far off... wait! a boat!
a working boat? not a sunken boat?
no! this one's got smoke stacks! i am going to say hi!
say hi carefully. don't mention me.
scott c.

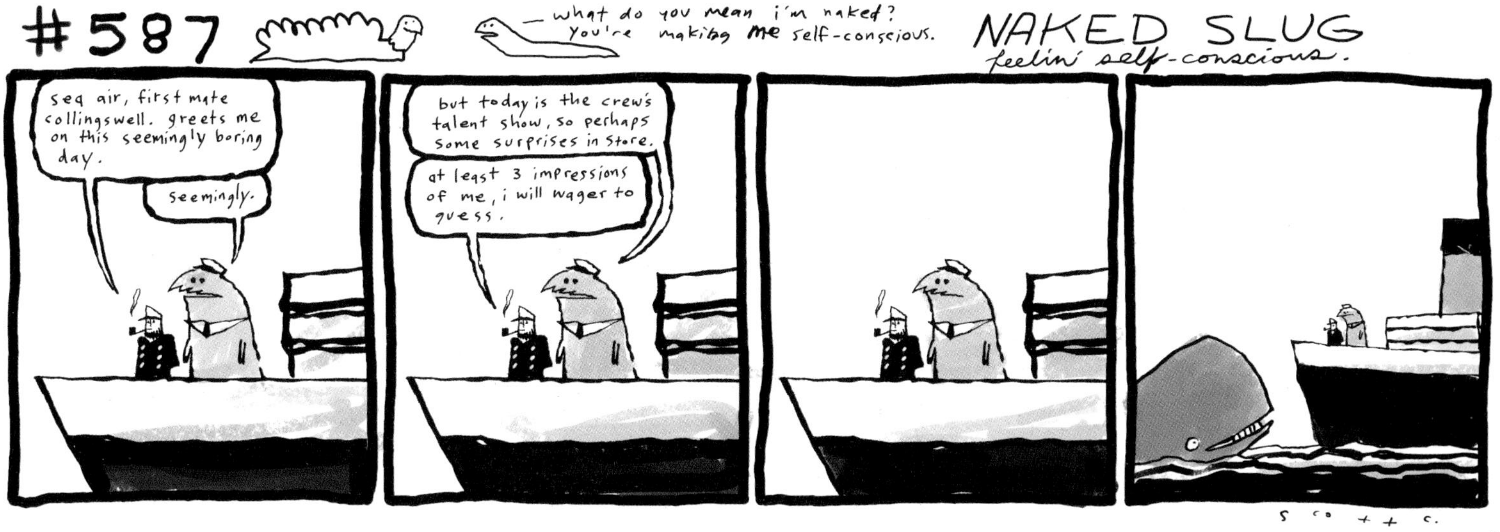

#587
— what do you mean i'm naked?
you're making me self-conscious.
NAKED SLUG
feelin' self-conscious.
sea air, first mate collingswell. greets me on this seemingly boring day.
seemingly.
but today is the crew's talent show, so perhaps some surprises in store.
at least 3 impressions of me, i will wager to guess.
scott c.

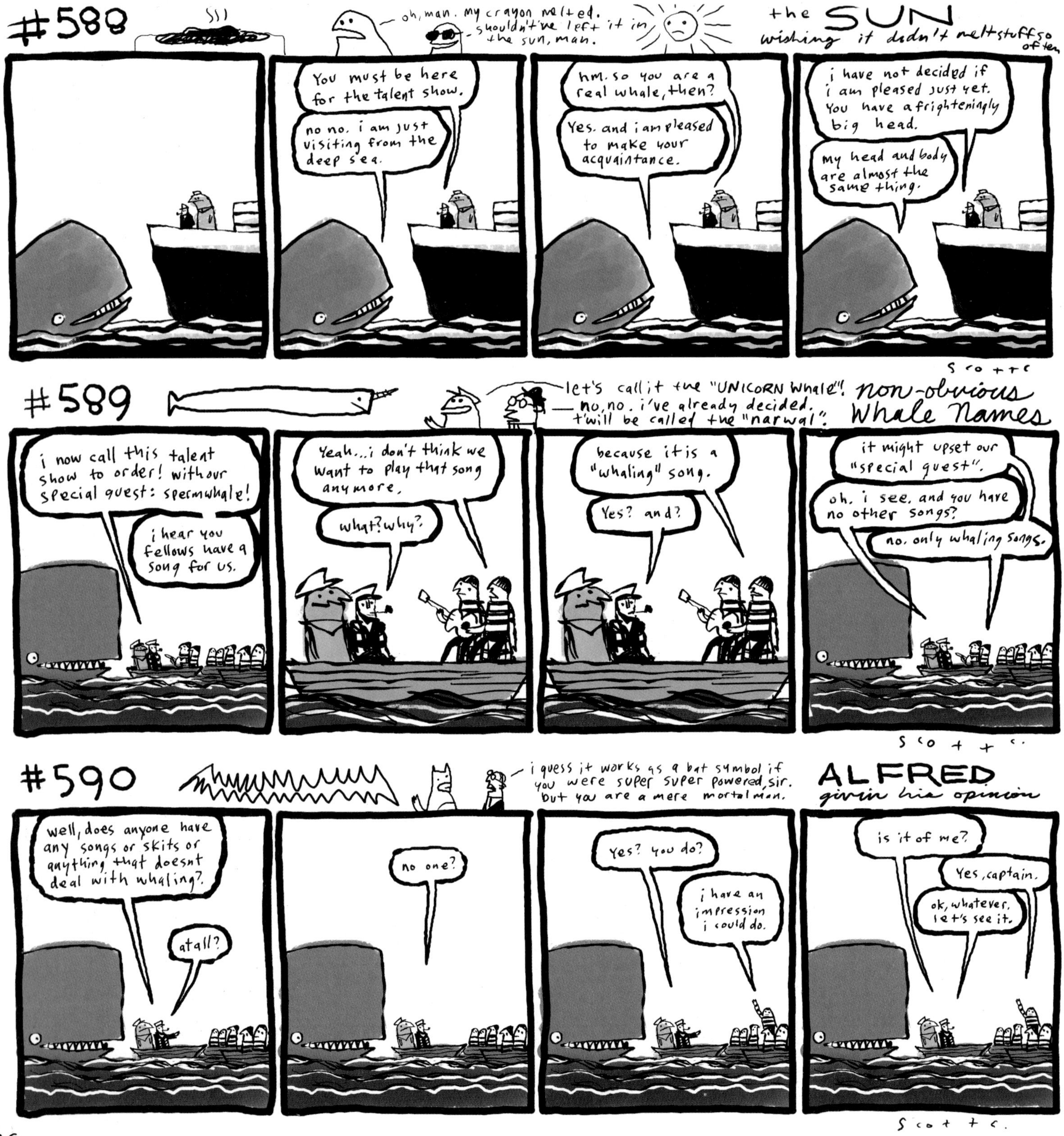
#588
oh, man. my crayon melted.
shouldn't've left it in the sun, man.
the SUN
wishing it didn't melt stuff so often
You must be here for the talent show.
no no. i am just visiting from the deep sea.
hm. so you are a real whale, then?
Yes. and i am pleased to make your acquaintance.
i have not decided if i am pleased just yet. You have a frighteningly big head.
My head and body are almost the same thing.
scott c
#589
let's call it the "UNICORN whale"!
no, no. i've already decided. t'will be called the "narwal".
non-obvious Whale Names
i now call this talent show to order! with our special guest: spermwhale!
i hear you fellows have a song for us.
Yeah... i don't think we want to play that song anymore.
what? why?
because it is a "whaling" song.
Yes? and?
it might upset our "special guest".
oh. i see. and you have no other songs?
no. only whaling songs.
scott c.
#590
i guess it works as a bat symbol if you were super super powered, sir. but you are a mere mortal man.
ALFRED
givin his opinion
well, does anyone have any songs or skits or anything that doesnt deal with whaling?
atall?
no one?
Yes? you do?
i have an impression i could do.
is it of me?
Yes, captain.
ok, whatever. let's see it.
scott c.

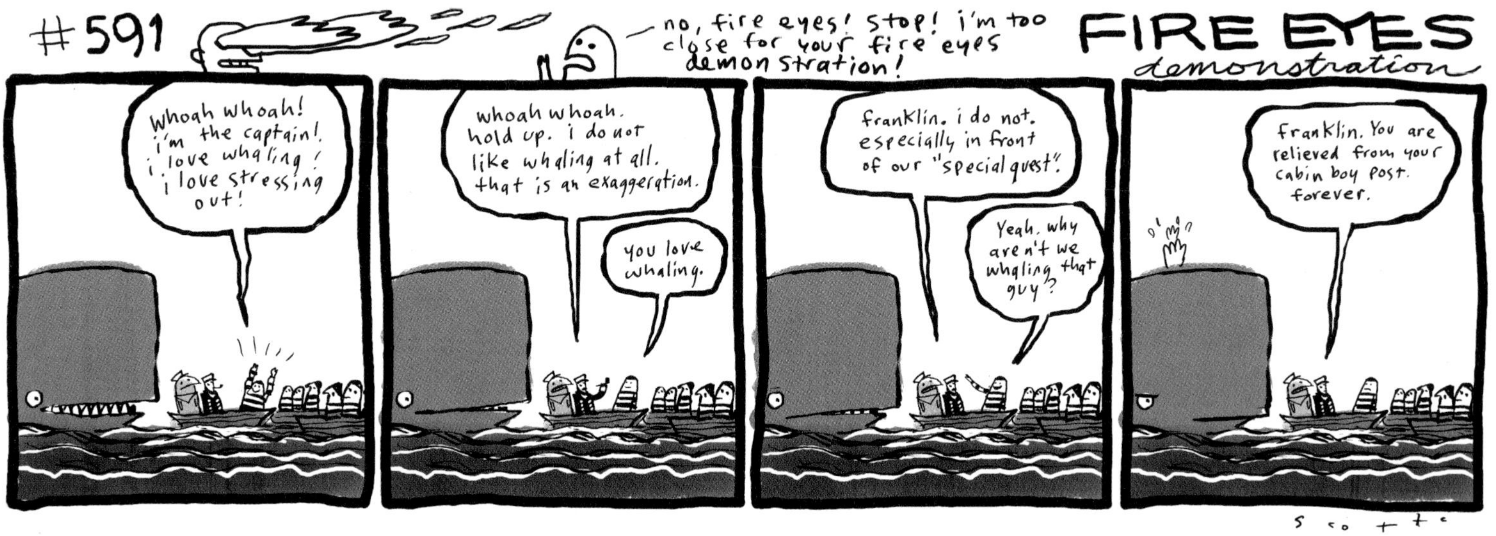
#591
no, fire eyes! stop! i'm too close for your fire eyes demonstration!
FIRE EYES demonstration
whoah whoah! i'm the captain! i love whaling! i love stressing out!
whoah whoah. hold up. i do not like whaling at all. that is an exaggeration.
you love whaling.
franklin. i do not. especially in front of our "special guest".
Yeah. why aren't we whaling that guy?
Franklin. You are relieved from your cabin boy post. forever.
scott c.

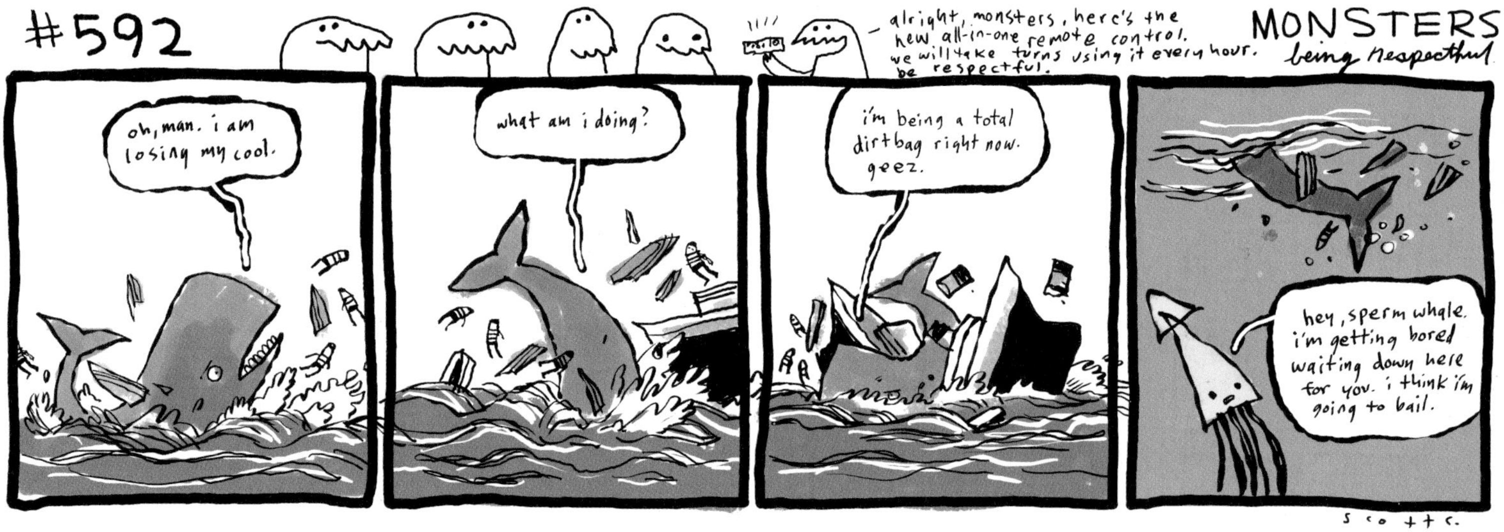
#592
alright, monsters, here's the new all-in-one remote control. we will take turns using it every hour. be respectful.
MONSTERS being respectful
oh, man. i am losing my cool.
what am i doing?
i'm being a total dirtbag right now. geez.
hey, sperm whale. i'm getting bored waiting down here for you. i think i'm going to bail.
scott c.

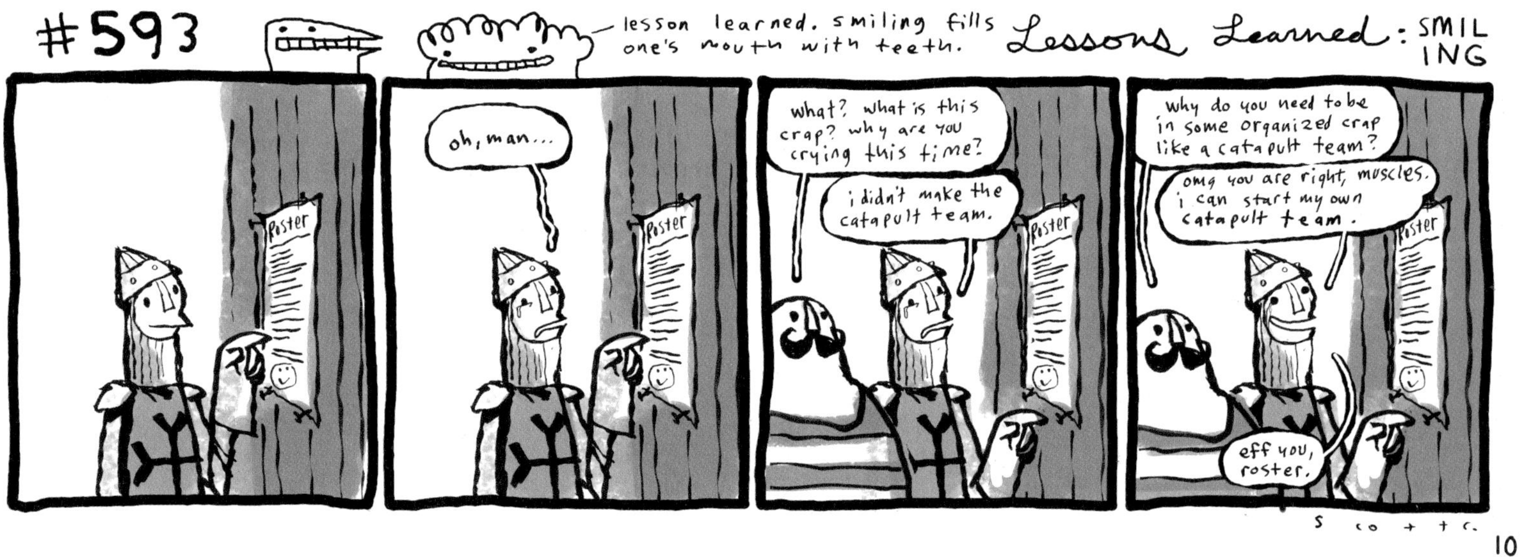
#593
lesson learned. smiling fills one's mouth with teeth.
Lessons Learned: SMILING
Roster
oh, man...
what? what is this crap? why are you crying this time?
i didn't make the catapult team.
why do you need to be in some organized crap like a catapult team?
omg you are right, muscles. i can start my own catapult team.
eff you, roster.
scott c.

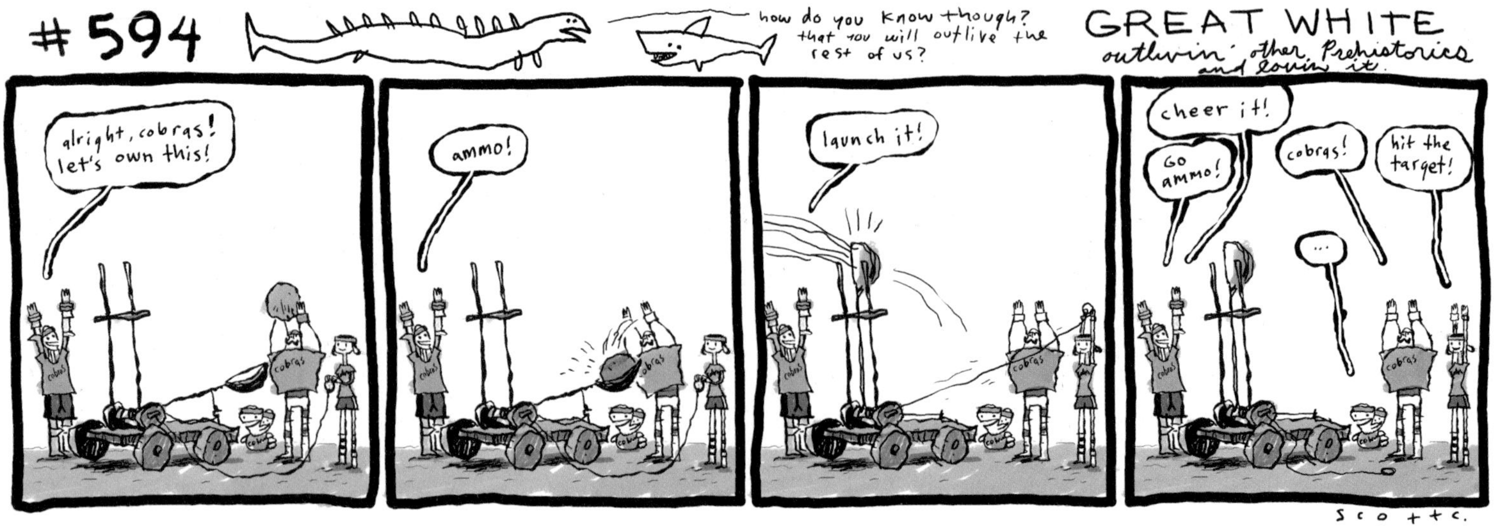
#594
how do you know though? that you will outlive the rest of us?
GREAT WHITE
outlivin' other Prehistorics and lovin' it.
alright, cobras! let's own this!
ammo!
launch it!
cheer it!
Go ammo!
cobras!
hit the target!
...
scott c.

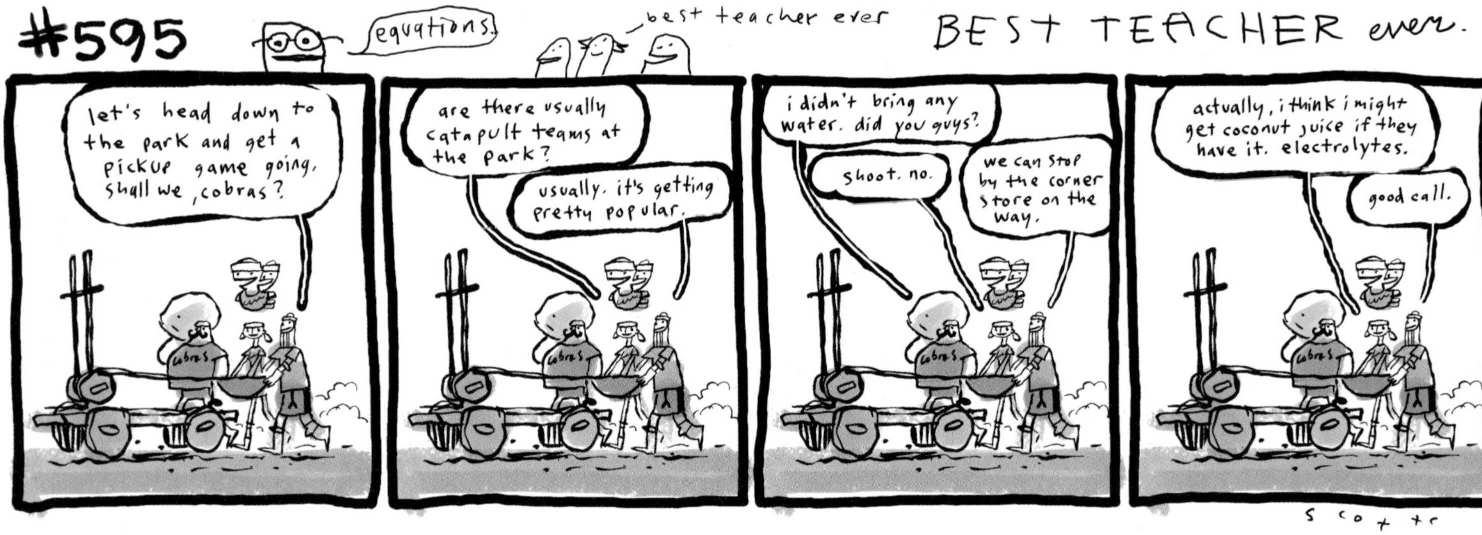
#595
equations.
best teacher ever
BEST TEACHER ever.
let's head down to the park and get a pickup game going, shall we, cobras?
are there usually catapult teams at the park?
usually. it's getting pretty popular.
i didn't bring any water. did you guys?
shoot. no.
we can stop by the corner store on the way.
actually, i think i might get coconut juice if they have it. electrolytes.
good call.
scott c.

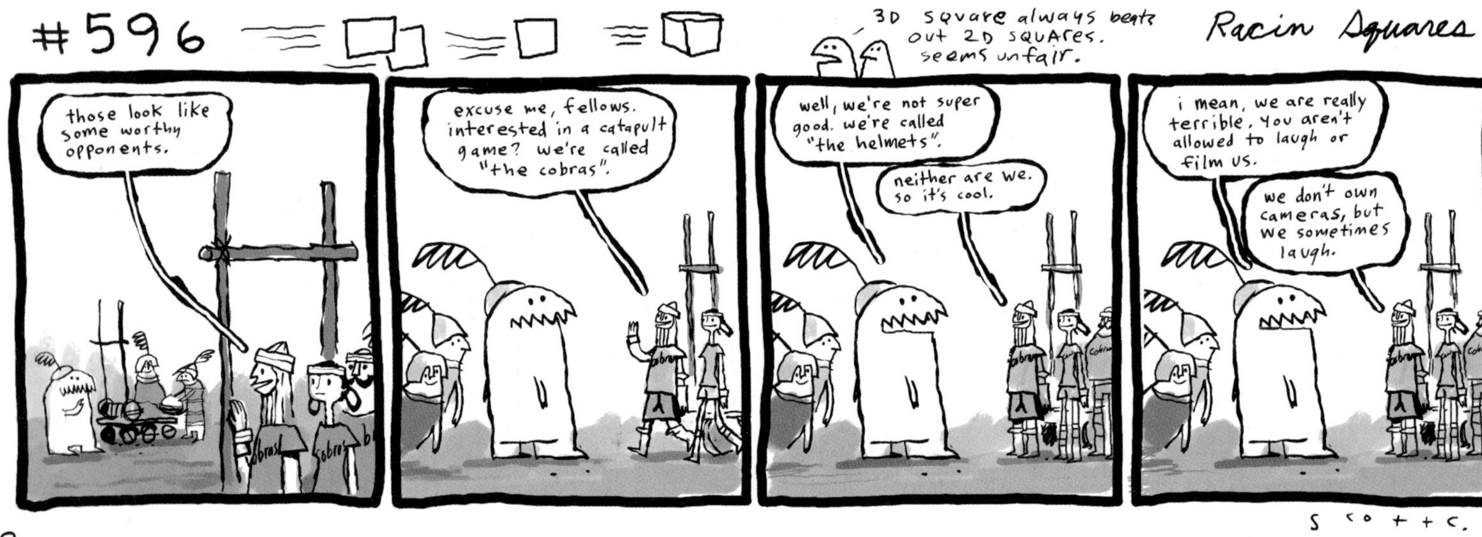
#596
3D square always beats out 2D squares. seems unfair.
Racin Squares
those look like some worthy opponents.
excuse me, fellows. interested in a catapult game? we're called "the cobras".
well, we're not super good. we're called "the helmets".
neither are we. so it's cool.
i mean, we are really terrible. You aren't allowed to laugh or film us.
we don't own cameras, but we sometimes laugh.
scott c.

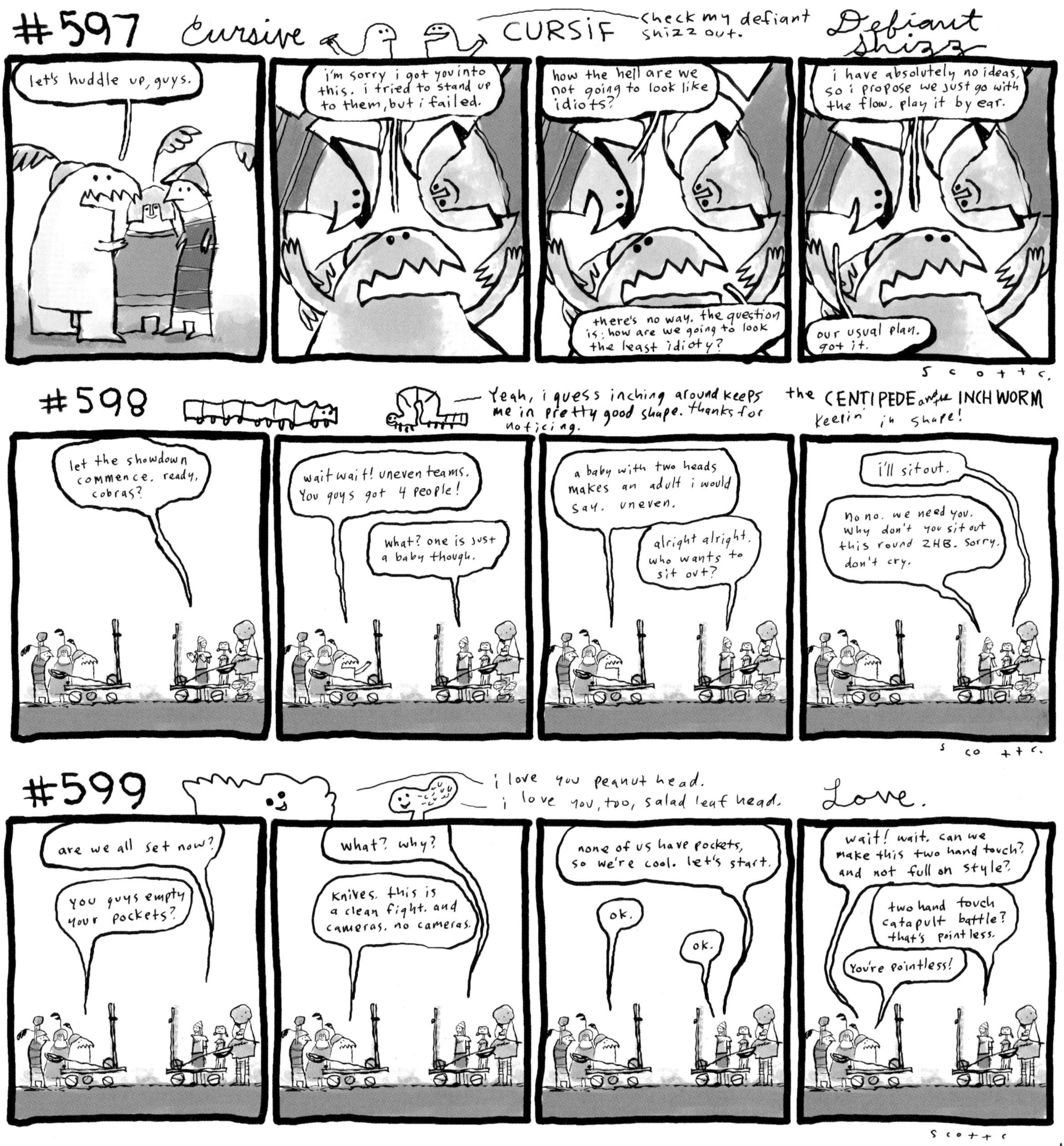

#597
Cursive
CURSIF
check my defiant shizz out.
Defiant Shizz
let's huddle up, guys.
i'm sorry i got you into this. i tried to stand up to them, but i failed.
how the hell are we not going to look like idiots?
there's no way. the question is; how are we going to look the least idioty?
i have absolutely no ideas, so i propose we just go with the flow. play it by ear.
our usual plan. got it.
scott c.
#598
Yeah, i guess inching around keeps me in pretty good shape. thanks for noticing.
the CENTIPEDE and the INCHWORM keepin' in shape!
let the showdown commence. ready, cobras?
wait wait! uneven teams. You guys got 4 people!
what? one is just a baby though.
a baby with two heads makes an adult i would say. uneven.
alright alright. who wants to sit out?
i'll sit out.
No no. we need you. why don't you sit out this round 2HB. Sorry. don't cry.
scott c.
#599
i love you peanut head.
i love you, too, salad leaf head.
Love.
are we all set now?
you guys empty your pockets?
what? why?
Knives. this is a clean fight. and cameras. no cameras.
none of us have pockets, so we're cool. let's start.
ok.
ok.
wait! wait. can we make this two hand touch? and not full on style?
two hand touch catapult battle? that's pointless.
You're pointless!
scott c

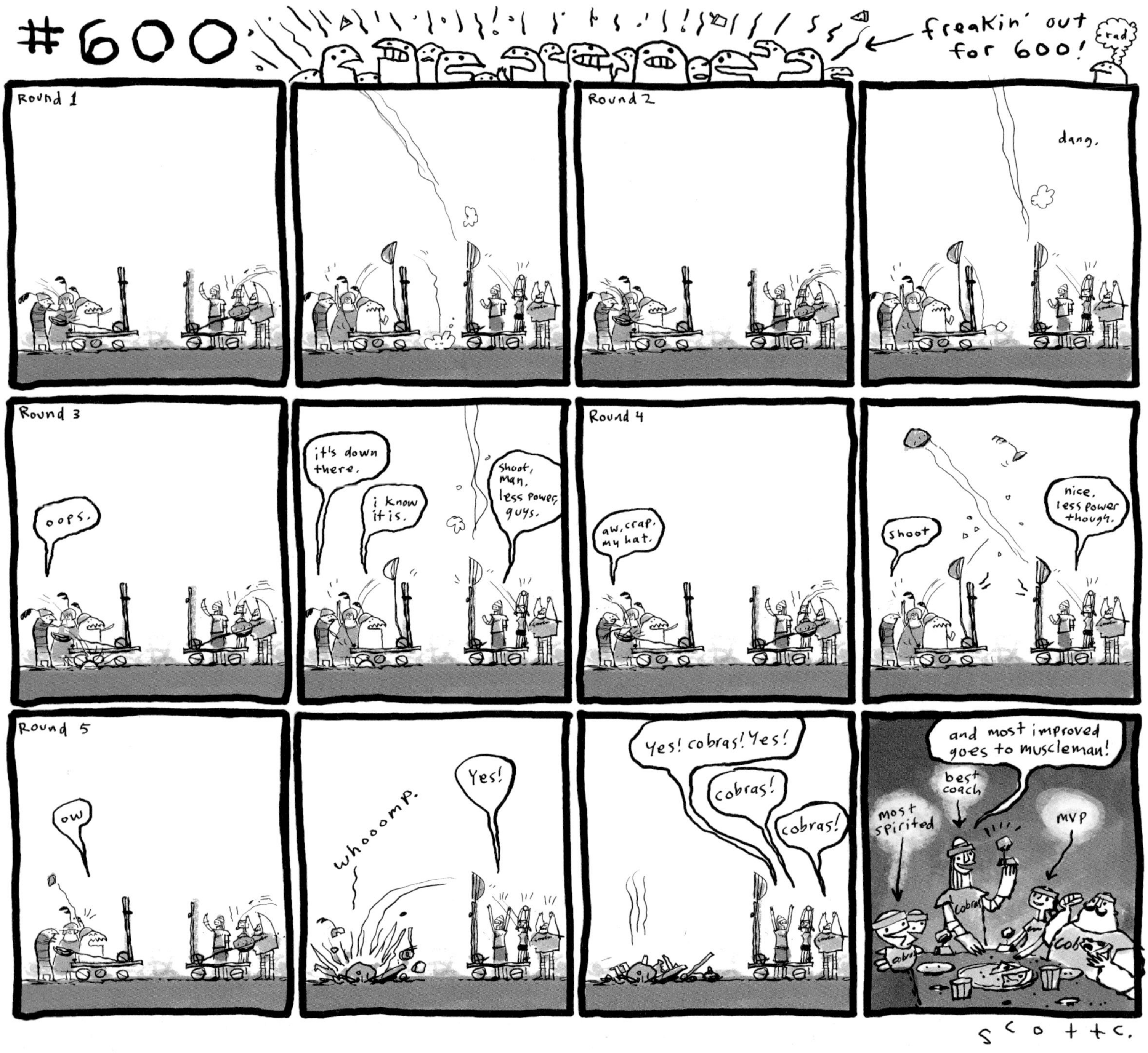
#600
freakin' out for 600!
rad
Round 1
Round 2
dang.
Round 3
oops.
it's down there.
i know it is.
Shoot, man. less power, guys.
Round 4
aw, crap. my hat.
shoot
nice. less power though.
Round 5
ow
whooomp.
Yes!
Yes! cobras! Yes!
cobras!
cobras!
and most improved goes to muscleman!
best coach
most spirited
MVP
scott c.

BONUS CONTENT!

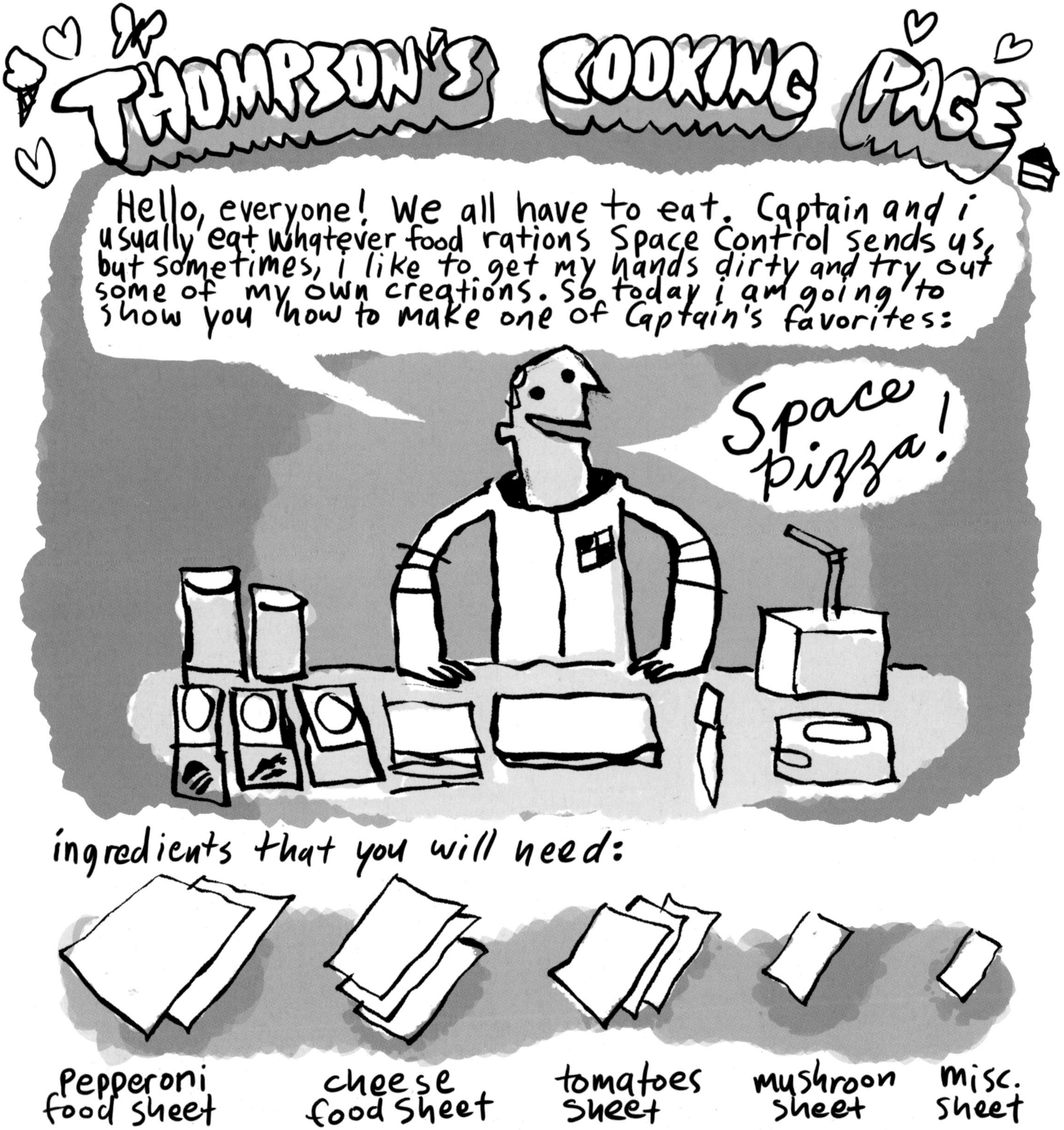
THOMPSON'S COOKING PAGE
Hello, everyone! We all have to eat. Captain and i usually eat whatever food rations Space Control sends us, but sometimes, i like to get my hands dirty and try out some of my own creations. So today i am going to show you how to make one of Captain's favorites:
Space pizza!
ingredients that you will need:
pepperoni food sheet
cheese food sheet
tomatoes sheet
mushroon sheet
misc. sheet

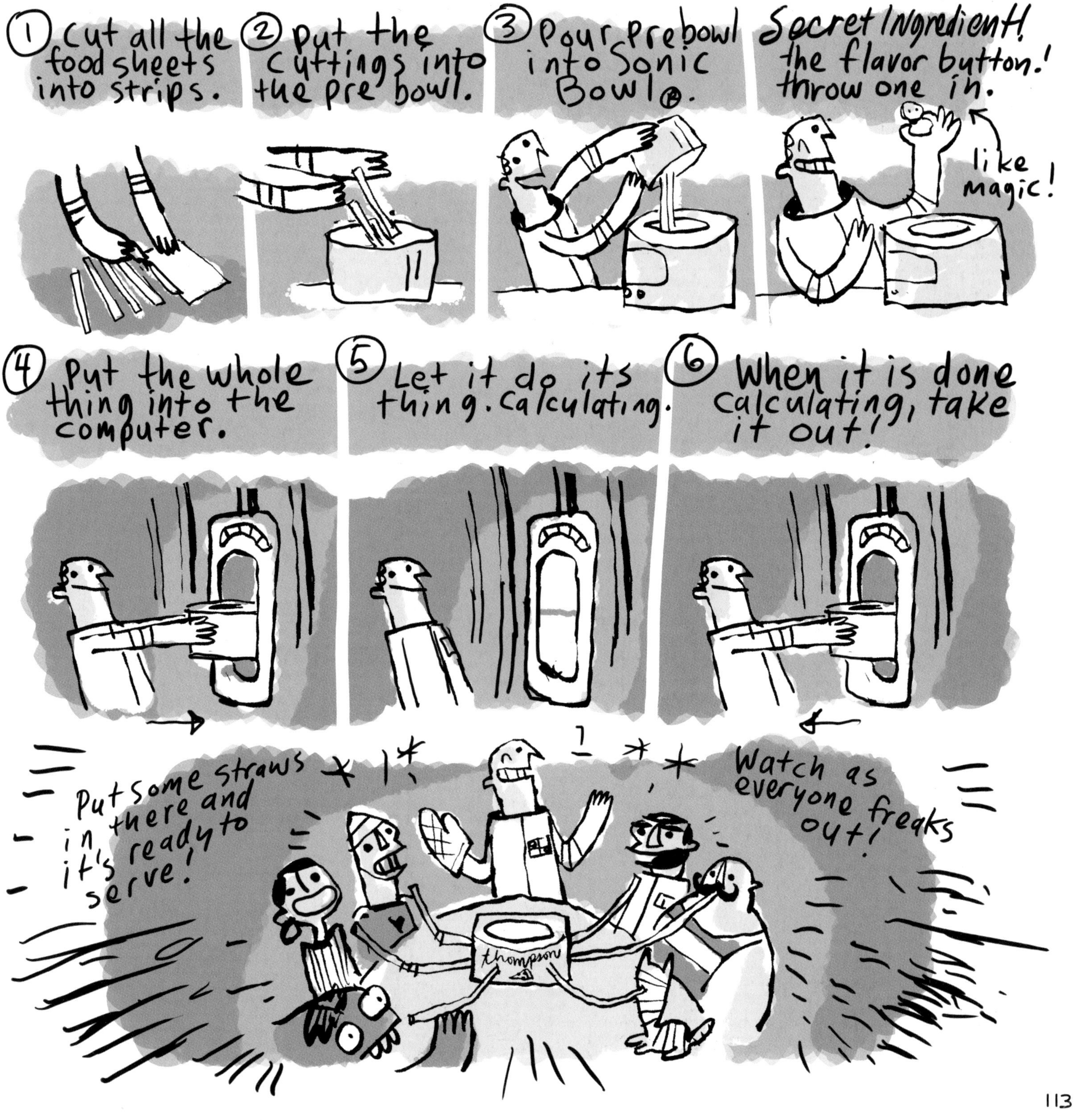

1 Cut all the food sheets into strips.
2 put the cuttings into the pre bowl.
3 Pour prebowl into Sonic Bowl®.
Secret Ingredient! the flavor button! throw one in.
like magic!
4 Put the whole thing into the computer.
5 Let it do its thing. Calculating.
6 When it is done calculating, take it out!
Put some straws in there and it's ready to serve!
thompson
Watch as everyone freaks out!

MUSCLEMAN'S ULTIMATE WORKOUT

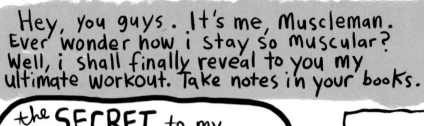

Hey, you guys. It's me, Muscleman. Ever wonder how i stay so muscular? Well, i shall finally reveal to you my ultimate workout. Take notes in your books.

the **SECRET** to my workout is you already have to be crazy strong.

1,002 lbs

① i like to warm up with a small lift. usually a concrete or marble block.

21,085 lb.

② i follow that up with some squats using some combo of head weights.

it's important to label your weights so you know exactly how much they weigh!

114 lb

③ Rowing. i like to use an iron ball.

8,249 lb.

④ Push-ups are pretty important. i like to put ancient dinosaur fossils on top as added weight.

⑤ Legs aren't important at all, so i usually put a ten pounder on my toes as i read one of my novels.

⑥ For a quick cardio, lift an exercise bike or running machine a few times. or BOTH!

⑦ Ah, yeah. time for the cool down. I usually reward myself with a steam box after a successful workout. (which is always.)

Beginner Level:
Most of you won't be able to do the ULTIMATE WORKOUT®, so here is a suggestion for a workout more your speed.

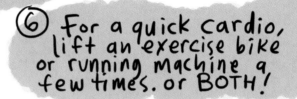

tunes: i don't usually listen to tunes, but you probably need to.

Poppy seed weights. about .024 lbs

comfortable shoes.

sit down pose so you don't get too exhausted too fast.

pillow. i'll bet you slouch, so put a little pillow back there.

put a little baby mat down.

Knight's Sculpture Garden

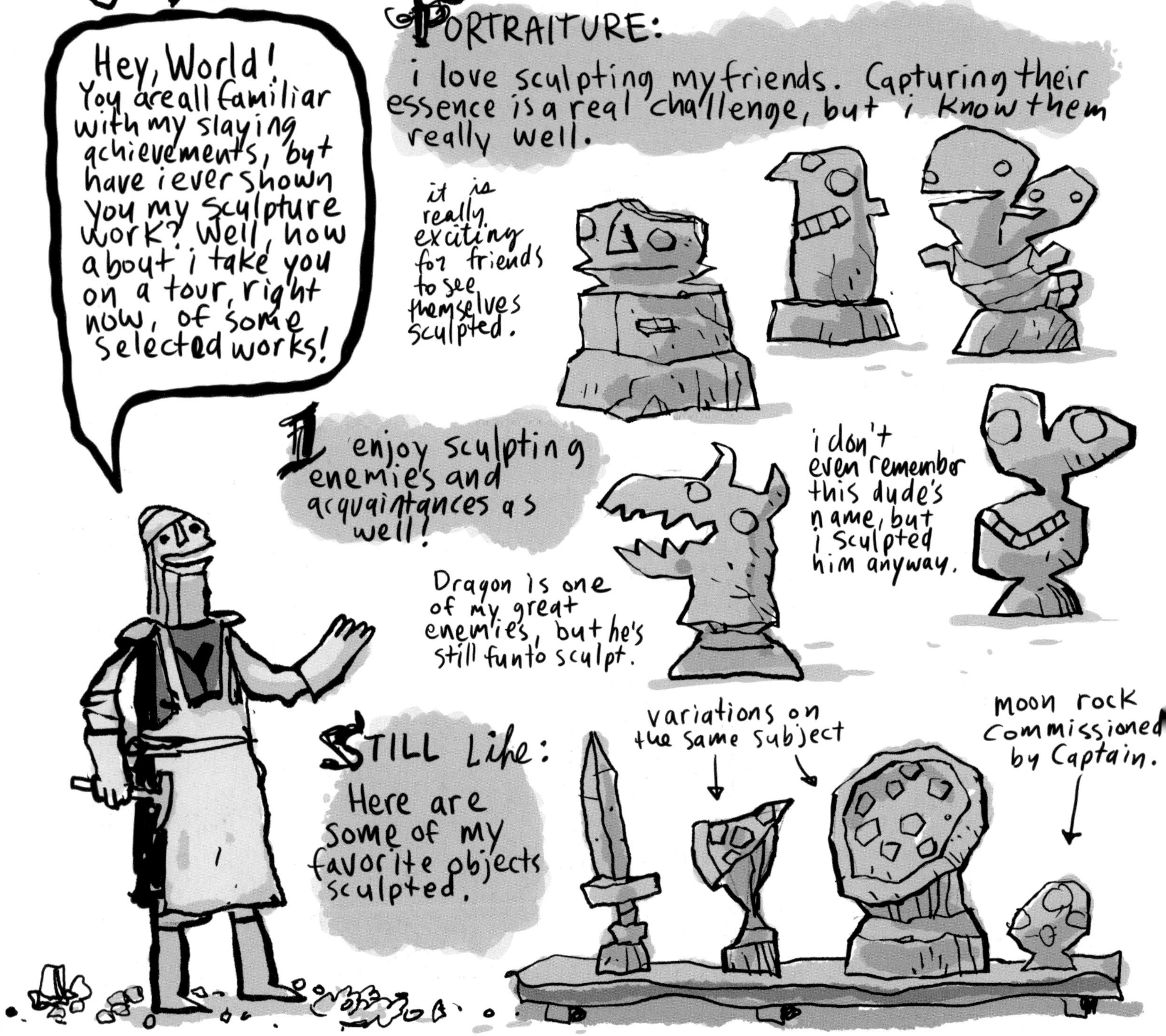
Hey, World! You are all familiar with my slaying achievements, but have i ever shown you my sculpture work? Well, how about i take you on a tour, right now, of some selected works!
PORTRAITURE:
i love sculpting my friends. Capturing their essence is a real challenge, but i know them really well.
it is really exciting for friends to see themselves sculpted.
I enjoy sculpting enemies and acquaintances as well!
Dragon is one of my great enemies, but he's still fun to sculpt.
i don't even remember this dude's name, but i sculpted him anyway.
STILL Life:
Here are some of my favorite objects sculpted.
variations on the same subject
moon rock commissioned by Captain.

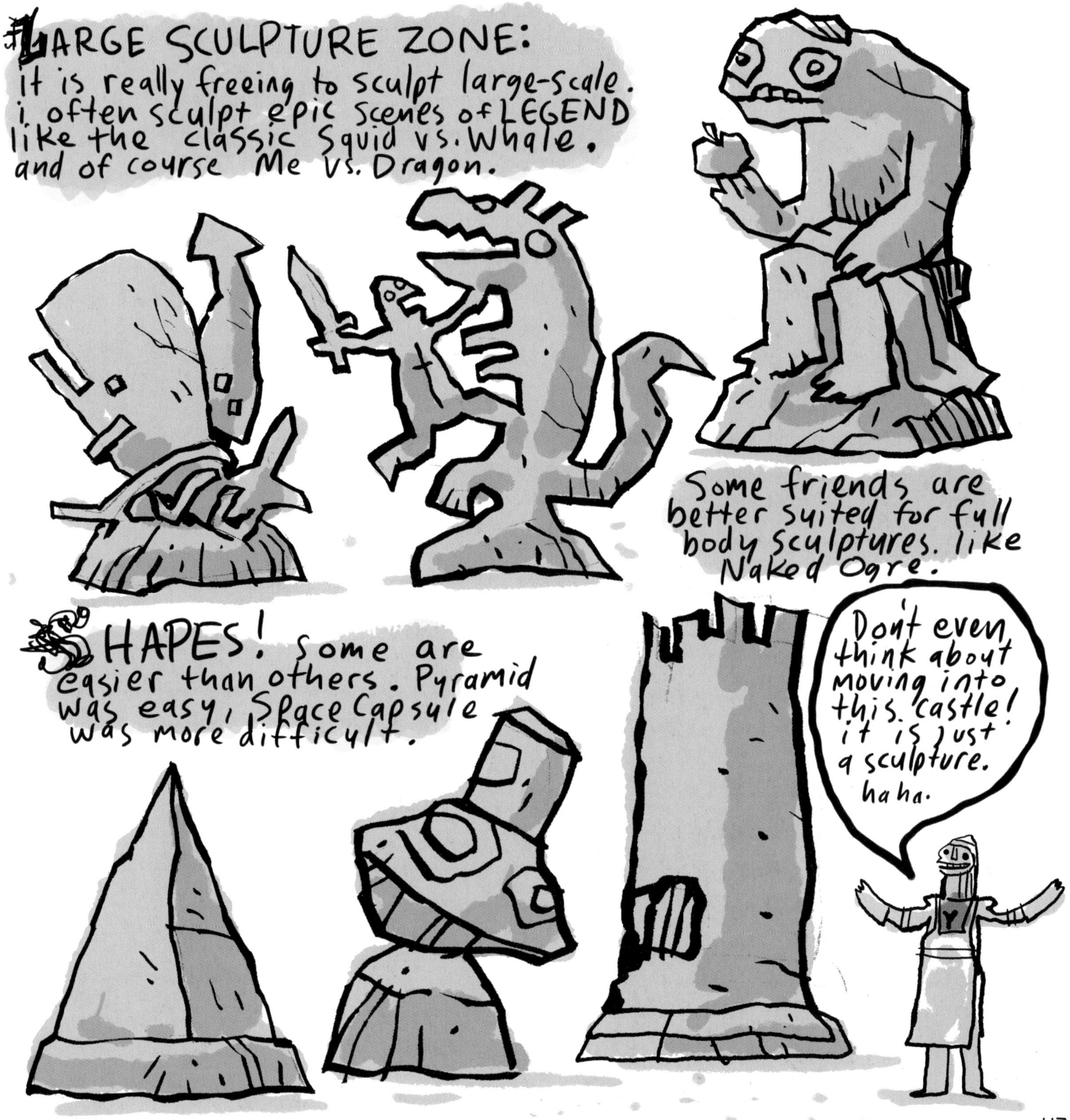
LARGE SCULPTURE ZONE:
it is really freeing to sculpt large-scale. i often sculpt epic scenes of LEGEND like the classic Squid vs. Whale. and of course Me vs. Dragon.
Some friends are better suited for full body sculptures. like Naked Ogre.
SHAPES! some are easier than others. Pyramid was easy, Space Capsule was more difficult.
Don't even think about moving into this castle! it is just a sculpture. haha.

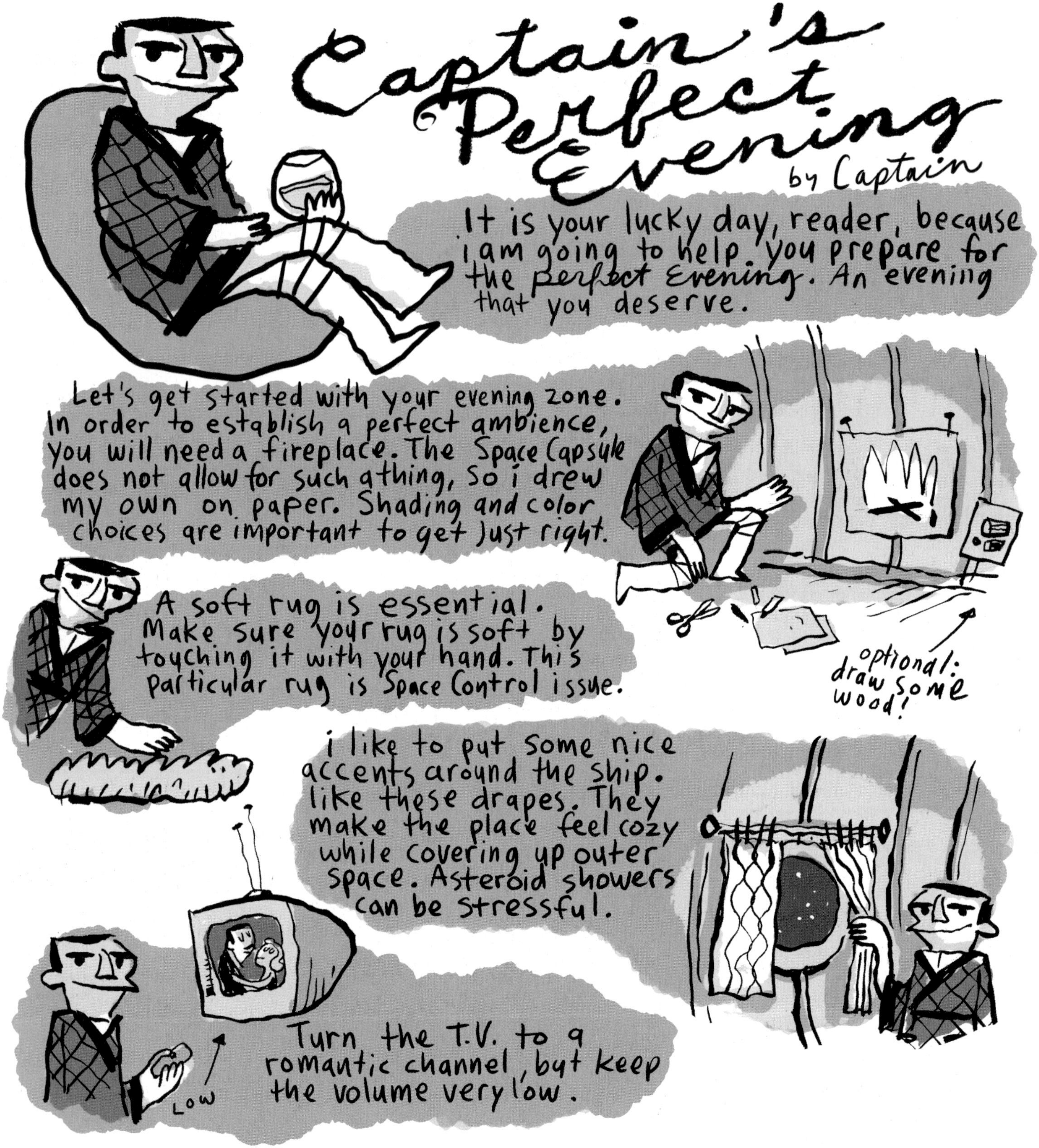
Captain's Perfect Evening
by Captain
It is your lucky day, reader, because i am going to help you prepare for the Perfect Evening. An evening that you deserve.
Let's get started with your evening zone. In order to establish a perfect ambience, you will need a fireplace. The Space Capsule does not allow for such a thing, so i drew my own on paper. Shading and color choices are important to get just right.
optional: draw some wood!
A soft rug is essential. Make sure your rug is soft by touching it with your hand. This particular rug is Space Control issue.
i like to put some nice accents around the ship. like these drapes. They make the place feel cozy while covering up outer space. Asteroid showers can be stressful.
Turn the T.V. to a romantic channel, but keep the volume very low.
LOW

Get some slippers. Space Control Catalog has tons of varieties.

MIX TAPE! It's always good to have a bunch of mix tapes ready to go depending on your mood. Mine are all quite solid.

For a *perfect* evening, I recommend some soft sounds.

Ah! a good old-fashioned pipe.

Some of my favorite pipe fuel:

 cherry maple butter tubular tooty

 chicken casserole moon rock bubbles

Pour yourself a tasty beverage. It doesn't matter what kind as long as it is in a sweet glass.

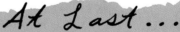

Lastly, you need a relaxing activity. I have chosen a 500 piece puzzle. Fairly challenging because most of it is space, but it is a relaxing challenge.

don't forget to have your favorite rock nearby!

At Last...

It is time to sit back, relax and enjoy this perfect evening that you have created for yourself.

Evening Variation: invite some friends.

OTHER BOOKS FROM ONI PRESS...

Vol. 1
DOUBLE FINE ACTION COMICS
by Scott C.
foreword by Tim Schafer

DOUBLE FINE ACTION COMICS
VOLUME 1
by Scott C.

120 pages, 9"x9"

ISBN: 978-1-62010-085-1

SCOTT PILGRIM 1
SCOTT PILGRIM'S PRECIOUS LITTLE LIFE
BY BRYAN LEE O'MALLEY
COLOR EDITION

SCOTT PILGRIM: SPECIAL EDITION VOLUME 1, HARD COVER
Bryan Lee O'Malley
184 pages, hardcover, color
ISBN 978-1-62010-000-4

THE SIXTH GUN
CULLEN BUNN
BRIAN HURTT
COLD DEAD FINGERS

THE SIXTH GUN, VOLUME 1: COLD DEAD FINGERS
Cullen Bunn, Brian Hurtt, Bill Crabtree
176 pages, trade paperback, color
ISBN 978-1-934964-60-6

RICK SPEARS
CHUCK BB
BLACK METAL
BOOK ONE

BLACK METAL, VOLUME 1: THE GRIM RETURN
Rick Spears & Chuck BB
160 pages, digest, b&w
ISBN 978-1-932664-72-0

Super Pro K.O.! 1
by Jarrett Williams

SUPER PRO, K.O.! VOLUME 1
JARRETT WILLIAMS
256 pages, digest, b&w
ISBN 978-1-934964-41-5

For more information on these and other fine Oni Press comic books and graphic novels visit onipress.com. To find a comic specialty store in your area visit comicshops.us.

ONI PRESS
REVOLUTIONIZE COMICS
www.onipress.com